PENGUI

A SHORT HISTORY OF THE 20TH CENTURY

Geoffrey Blainey is one of Australia's most significant and popular historians. He has written more than thirty books including *The Tyranny of Distance*, *Triumph of the Nomads*, *A Short History of Australia*, *Black Kettle and Full Moon*, and the best-selling *A Short History of the World*. Professor Blainey held chairs in economic history and then in plain history at the University of Melbourne for many years, and for some of those years he chaired the Australia Council. He has served on many Commonwealth and Victorian government agencies, including the Australian War Memorial, the Australian Heritage Commission and the National Council for the Centenary of Federation. In 2000 Professor Blainey was the recipient of Australia's highest honour, Companion in the Order of Australia (AC).

GEOFFREY BLAINEY

A SHORT HISTORY OF THE 20TH CENTURY

PENGUIN BOOKS

PENGUIN BOOKS

Published by the Penguin Group
Penguin Group (Australia)
250 Camberwell Road, Camberwell, Victoria 3124, Australia
(a division of Pearson Australia Group Pty Ltd)
Penguin Group (USA) Inc.
375 Hudson Street, New York, New York 10014, USA
Penguin Group (Canada)
90 Eglinton Avenue East, Suite 700, Toronto, Canada ON M4P 2Y3
(a division of Pearson Penguin Canada Inc.)
Penguin Books Ltd
80 Strand, London WC2R 0RL England
Penguin Ireland
25 St Stephen's Green, Dublin 2, Ireland
(a division of Penguin Books Ltd)
Penguin Books India Pvt Ltd
11 Community Centre, Panchsheel Park, New Delhi – 110 017, India
Penguin Group (NZ)
67 Apollo Drive, Rosedale, North Shore 0632, New Zealand
(a division of Pearson New Zealand Ltd)
Penguin Books (South Africa) (Pty) Ltd
24 Sturdee Avenue, Rosebank, Johannesburg 2196, South Africa

Penguin Books Ltd, Registered Offices: 80 Strand, London, WC2R 0RL, England

First published by Penguin Group (Australia), 2005
This edition published by Penguin Group (Australia), 2007

1 3 5 7 9 10 8 6 4 2

Cover design by Jo Hunt, Pigs Might Fly © Penguin Group (Australia)
Text design by Tony Palmer © Penguin Group (Australia)
Maps drawn by Alan Laver
Cover images: Chrysler building: Mitchell Funk/Getty Images, Globe: Photolibrary
Typeset in Fairfield by Midland Typesetters, Maryborough, Victoria
Printed and bound in Australia by McPherson's Printing Group, Maryborough, Victoria

National Library of Australia
Cataloguing-in-Publication data:

Blainey, Geoffrey, 1930–.
A short history of the 20th century.
Bibliography.
Includes index.
ISBN 978 0 14 300614 5.
1. History, Modern – 20th century. 2. Twentieth century. I. Title.

909.82

www.penguin.com.au

CONTENTS

LIST OF MAPS

PREFACE

A few years ago I wrote a history of the world in one volume. Deliberately I wrote more frugally about the 20th century, for the earlier centuries provided far more of the significant events that shaped our present way of life. This book tries to remedy the omission by tracing the history of the tempestuous century, just ended. It is written in narrative style, so that some of the excitement of the times as well as the power of the unforeseen can be felt.

The theme that dominates much of this book is war and peace: two massive wars and a nervous peace. Many of the peacetime events in the second half of the century, from the Iron Curtain and space race to the rise of the computer, were influenced by those two earlier wars. But war is far from the book's only theme. It also traces a wonderful series of medical discoveries, the impact of car and wireless and aircraft, the rising role of women and also the green movement, the liberation of the Third World, the mania for sport, the changing paths of Christianity and Islam, and such little-noticed but momentous episodes as the shrinking of the household kitchen.

Strictly speaking the new century began on 1 January 1901 but a century later we were perhaps less numerate about chronology: the whole world insisted on celebrating the birth of the next century in the year 2000. I have not worried about the choice of whether 1900 or 1901 was the birth of the century, and so the start of the book reflects the untidiness that characterises the course of history. The first part of the book depicts the condition of the world at about the start of the century. The second part embraces two world wars and much else besides. The third part of the book carries the story, on many fronts, from the late 1940s to two dramatic and symbolic events in 2001.

In this kind of narrative history, the question of why a particular event occurred can be allocated only a few sentences. Much of the causation has to be inferred from the story itself. My own view of why events take place has been set out in two earlier books. One, *The Causes of War*, examines peace and war, and the other, *The Great Seesaw*, tries to outline the way in which certain ideas sit on a seesaw that occasionally tilts, taking all the sitters with it.

My preference is pithier terms and words: Russia instead of the Soviet Union, and America instead of the United States. I use the phrase 'the west' from time to time, knowing it is not a perfect phrase and becoming less so. But in describing much of the century 'the west' is a useful way of referring to nations and peoples largely of European descent with their mix of Christianity and secularism, their increasing emphasis on freedom, and their preference for democracy and for regulated capitalism. Russians partly divorced themselves from the west in two successive episodes, in 1917 and 1945, and so 'the west' ceased to embrace all Europe. At the same time India and Japan and several other parts of Asia became more like the west in their institutions and social attitudes. The book uses both miles and kilometres, depending on the context. To select just one, and convert to it all measurements, can be distorting.

I express my gratitude to people who have helped me to elucidate the narrative and the assumptions used in this book. I especially thank SEK Hulme QC, John Day and Dr Tom Hurley, all of Melbourne, and Professor Claudio Veliz, formerly of Boston University. When I had almost completed the book, they were willing at short notice to comment on chapters, or discuss particular topics, and I am deeply in debt to them. For other help I thank Richard Hagen of Brisbane, Raymond Flower of Sarnano in Italy, and my wife Ann and daughter Anna. To my editor Miriam Cannell and her alert eyes and her astonishment at the slightest ambiguity I am especially grateful. Bob Sessions and Clare Forster of Penguin discussed the outline of the book at the very start and at later stages. It was their belief that the narrative should not exceed 500 printed pages, and I have almost complied. In expressing my debts I must make this clear: for all the faults in the book I alone am responsible.

I thank staff of libraries and museums in which I sometimes gathered information, and especially the University of Melbourne, the Deutsches Museum in Munich, the Smithsonian museums in Washington, the Science Museum and the Victoria & Albert in London, the Australian War Memorial in Canberra, and the newspaper room in the State Library of Victoria.

GEOFFREY BLAINEY

MELBOURNE

PART ONE

ICELAND

Novaya Zemlya

RUSSIA

FINLAND

NORWAY
St Petersburg
SWEDEN

North
Sea
Sheffield ● Kiel
Liverpool ● Berlin ● ● Moscow   Lake
London ● GERMANY   Baikal
Portsmouth ● Paris ●   Vienna   KAZAKHSTAN
Geneva ● AUSTRIA-HUNGARY
Bordeaux ● Lyons ● Trieste ● Belgrade   Harbin ● Vladivostok ●
Milan ● ● Sarajevo Crimea   Tashkent   Beijing ●   KOREA
Rome ● Sardinia BULGARIA Black Sea   ● ● Samarkand   Sea of   Tok
SPAIN   Messina ● Taranto ● Salonica   Bukhara   CHINA   Japan
         Sicily   GREECE   TURKEY   ● Shanghai
         Mediterranean Sea
                              IRAQ   PERSIA   TIBET
         FRENCH   EGYPT   Suez Canal   Calcutta ● Mandalay ● ● Hong Kong
         AFRICA   ARABIA   INDIA   ● Macao
                  CHAD   SUDAN   Red   Bombay ●   SIAM   FRENCH   Philippine Sea
         NIGERIA   Sea   Arabian Sea   INDO-CHINA
                  ABYSSINIA   NEW GUIN
                  KENYA   CEYLON   ● Singapore
         PORTUGUESE   Jakarta ●   NEW GUIN
         ANGOLA   ● Zanzibar   INDIAN OCEAN   ● Cocos   DUTCH EAST INDIES
         GERMAN   Islands   Timor Sea
         S.W. AFRICA   MADAGASCAR   AUSTRALIA
                  ● Johannesburg
         ORANGE FREE STATE ● Durban   ● Kalgoorlie
         SOUTH AFRICA
         Cape Town ●   Melbo

1 WORLD OF 1901

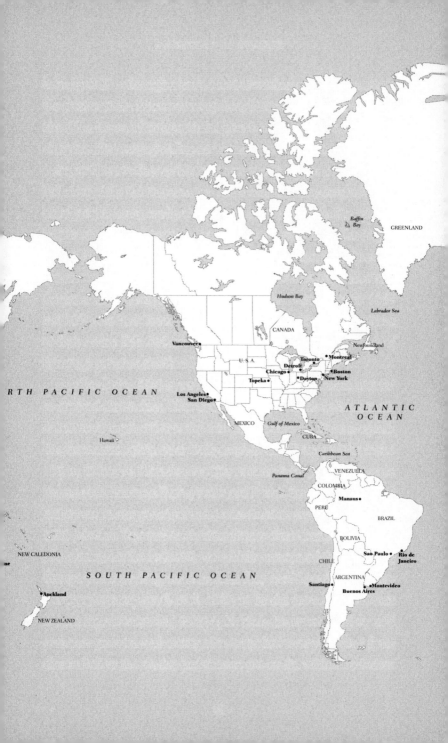

1

A FLAMING SUNRISE

The birth of the 20th century was like a flaming sunrise. More was expected of the century than any other. So much had been achieved in the previous one that it seemed sensible to expect that henceforth the world's triumphs would far outweigh the disasters.

This infant century promised most to the European peoples, whether they lived at home or in the far-off lands they had colonised. Their children had higher hopes of an education than ever before, and the day-long labour of 10-year-olds in farms and workshops was no longer normal. The standard of living was improving, famines were becoming fewer and people were living longer. Warfare between the major European nations seemed to be on the wane, though very large armies and navies were paraded at national celebrations. Democracy was spreading, and liberty too. But most of these advantages belonged to only one quarter of the world's people, and did not yet seem likely to spread to Africa, Asia, and the remote Pacific islands.

There was peril as well as promise in the approaching century. The sunrise of 1901 was dazzling, but a bank of dark, slowly shifting clouds hovered above the light.

EUROPE'S HIGH NOON: THE FAR-FLUNG EMPIRES

Europe ruled much of the world. Most of the ocean liners and large warships flew British, German or French flags. Most of the big cities, and their famous palaces, museums, art galleries and universities, were in Europe. Most of the world's railways and telegraph lines were built or financed by Europeans. Most of the major islands of the world were the provinces and colonies of Britain, Holland, France, Portugal, Spain or Germany. Nearly all of Africa and nearly all of the Pacific islands were ruled from Europe. In Asia the only major countries that stood outside the European empires were China and Japan.

Britain's empire, the widest the world had known, was not yet at its widest. It guarded a notable part of every inhabited continent and a chain of islands in every ocean. In 1900 it dominated the seas: its coal-carrying ships in the North Sea, its ocean liners speeding to remote ports, and its tramp steamers with 'their salt-caked smoke-stacks'. The British Empire and China each held about 400 million people, together holding half of the world's population.

Evolving and therefore untidy, Britain's was like no previous empire. In some colonies a residing British governor wielded sweeping powers but in others he was no more than an imposing ceremonial figure. In Egypt the highest British officials made the decisions but were content for dignified local pashas smoking their long cigarettes in lavish offices to retain the prestige. On the other hand Canada, Australia and New Zealand were largely self-governing, and their parliaments were more representative of the people than was the British parliament. Foreign policy, however, was one domain where they were not independent. Nonetheless the mother of parliaments on the banks of the Thames had digested the lesson of why the American colonies had broken loose in the 18th century, and so it permitted Canada, Australia and New Zealand sometimes to ignore or defy Britain's foreign policy on a topic vital to them. They increasingly paid for their own armies and navies, though in times of war they would accept Britain's leadership. At the other end of the scale of obedience were African and Asian colonies which had no parliament, no local judges or high officials and depended heavily on Britain for revenue.

Russia's empire had grown so rapidly that it was difficult for map-readers to disentangle what was old Russia from what was new empire. The Russian Empire swept all the way from the Baltic Sea to the Pacific Ocean. It was so vast that at one end it adjoined Turkey and Persia and at the other end it shared a border with Korea. In size it was second only to the British Empire.

A sign of the newness of this part of colonial Russia was that as late as 1860 the Russian flag had not yet flown over harbours as dispersed as Vladivostok on the Pacific Ocean and Batumi on the Black Sea, nor flown from the towers of such ancient Islamic strongholds as Tashkent and Samarkand. The largest block of new Russian territory was in central Asia, a rectangle about 1400 miles long and 700 miles wide, a vast area of mountains, plains and rushing rivers, extending from the Caspian Sea to the Mongolian desert and approaching so close to British India that it provoked international incidents. To travel from one end of the Russian Empire to the other was a slow journey demanding many weeks, and the crossing of countless rivers. Slowly the elongated Trans-Siberian Railway was pushed to the east, reaching Lake Baikal in Siberia at the start of the century and soon to reach the Pacific Ocean. The opening up of this vast area gave to some observers the intuition that the coming century would be the Russian century.

Germany's was a younger empire. Only a few spots on the map in 1880, it was now an eye-catching jigsaw. German soldiers and administrators, missionaries and merchants, had recently occupied parts of the west and east coasts of Africa, and New Guinea and nearby strings of islands. Across the Pacific Ocean, not far from the equator, lay German Samoa, German Nauru and other outposts. Most of the German colonies were so far apart that a Berlin inspector, making an annual inspection of colonial post offices and using only the regular mail steamers, might have taken eight months simply to reach them all. Once Germany became a colonial power, a navy had to follow. The existence of that powerful navy was an unstable force in Europe in the first years of the infant century.

France's was an older empire, the outcome of more than 300 years of colonising. Next to Britain's it was the most dispersed empire. Embracing tropical Indo-China and remnants of small colonies in North and South America, the French empire held much of Africa, including a row of provinces on the southern shore of the Mediterranean. Its Pacific islands extended from New Caledonia, which was one of the world's main miners of nickel, all the way to exotic Tahiti.

In area the French was only half of the Russian Empire but it embraced every major ocean in the world. Perhaps no more than 20 citizens of France had ever visited all their inhabited colonies. That statement can be made with some safety, for the whalers' island of Kerguelen lay in stark isolation in the stormy seas of the southern Indian Ocean.

A large empire widely believed to be on its last legs was the Ottoman. Ruled from Constantinople, it fronted the shores of the Mediterranean, the Black Sea, the Red Sea and the Persian Gulf. It had been stumbling for several centuries without actually falling over. Its perceived weakness, its limping and stumbling, were to shape the outbreak of the First World War.

China, rich in resources, dozed while European diplomats and traders smacked their lips. The most populous nation in the world, it was in grave peril of being treated as real estate and subdivided by foreign nations. Defeated by the resurrected Japan in the war of 1894–95, China remained intact partly because of its good luck. In short, ambitious European nations along with the United States could not reconcile their conflicting ambitions to annex or control Chinese territory. Already such Chinese ports as Shanghai, Macao and Hong Kong were controlled from Europe while Taiwan had recently been annexed by Japan.

Those European empires seemed mighty in 1900, and were still eager to expand. All would be broken up in the course of the century.

THE RISE OF THE STAR-SPANGLED BANNER

That the United States would eventually throw shadow and light over Europe, politically and militarily, was foreseen by perceptive

Europeans, but most were not perceptive. By 1900 the United States held close to 80 million people, easily 20 million more than Germany. In the making of steel – the economic barometer of the era – it led the world. In many commodities, ranging from tobacco to minerals galore, it was the largest or the second-largest producer. On the eve of the First World War its manufacturing output was to be as large as that of Britain, Germany and France added together.

It was the home of inventiveness, whether a new religion like Christian Science, founded by Mary Baker Eddy, or a new music like jazz, the creation of Afro-Americans. New York was the capital city of novelty. Edith Wharton's novel *The House of Mirth*, published in 1905, opens by describing a fashionable woman abandoning the afternoon rush at Grand Central Station – one of the world's fascinating sights – and walking towards elaborate houses of brick and limestone with flower boxes and shade-giving awnings, all 'fantastically varied in obedience to the American craving for novelty'.

Here too was a birthplace of ingenious phrases and words. Many visitors from the British Isles, on turning the pages of an American newspaper, found entire sentences a puzzle. By 1900, however, such American slang words as 'vamoose', 'skedaddle' and 'scallywag' were widely used in England. Likewise 'gerrymander' (named after Gerry Elbridge, Governor of Massachusetts) was soon to be employed throughout the English-speaking world to describe the altering of electoral boundaries so that they suited one's own political party. Even democracy could not escape wily inventiveness.

Here were the tallest office buildings in the world, the longest network of railways, and deep collieries that were about to surpass Britain in output of coal. America led in electrical engineering, and its skills and equipment were hired to build underground railways in the city of London in the early 1900s. A higher proportion of American than European children could read and write, and a proud nucleus of universities was taking shape. While the United States did not possess a long tradition in the visual arts, it was buying that tradition with dollars. Celebrated paintings were quietly passing from European castles and palaces to London auction rooms, finally to emerge in the private galleries of the Carnegies, the Fricks and other American steel and railway magnates.

The United States had recently become an imperial power though most of its citizens did not see themselves as acquirers of an empire. It owned Alaska, purchased from the Russians as recently as 1867. It owned Hawaii. It had recently defeated Spain in a brief war and taken control temporarily of Cuba and the Philippines. It was now enlarging its navy to match its territorial sweep, and one of the dramatic events of 1908 was the voyage of its great white fleet to the far shores of the Pacific where American sailors marched in a casual, un-European way through foreign streets, to the cheers of huge crowds. This elegant fleet, of a size not before seen in the Pacific Ocean, was relished by some observers as a warning to Japan. By 1914 it was the third-largest navy in the world, a strange contrast to the small American army.

While the United States had long preferred to live in isolation – even its favourite games such as baseball and football were its own inventions – it now glanced outwards. It was beginning to plan the Panama Canal, which would place North America astride a global trade route. In 1900 it sent its own troops to northern China to join the army of many nations that imposed order after the Boxer

Rebellion; and five years later on its own soil it steered the delicate discussions that ended the Russo-Japanese war.

MONARCHS AND ANARCHISTS

The monarchy, long abandoned in the United States, was found almost everywhere except in the Americas. The Czar of Russia was nearly all-powerful, while the emperors of Germany and Austria-Hungary were often more powerful than their parliaments in foreign policy. The King of Italy respected parliament but believed he had the right sometimes to step over it. The Queen of England, who ruled over one quarter of the world's peoples, was almost the least powerful of Europe's monarchs. She advised – rarely did she decide.

A high point in the prestige of the monarchy was her own funeral. She died on the Isle of Wight, in one of her palaces, on the afternoon of Tuesday 22 January 1901. Her wish was that she should have a military funeral, for she was the head of the armies and navies of the British Empire. Her coffin, covered with white satin, was carried in the royal yacht from the island to the nearby naval base of Portsmouth, passing for the whole 8 miles through a stately avenue of vessels – the British battleships and cruisers moored on one side and gunboats, ocean liners, and vessels from sympathetic foreign navies on the other. Eight destroyers, specially painted black, escorted the royal yacht, and those aboard could hear, rolling across the sea, the shipboard bands playing Chopin's 'Funeral March'. 'Over all the scene of mournful and stately symbolism there shone the glow of a winter's sunset of singular beauty', wrote one correspondent.

On the following day the royal coffin, carried by the funeral train to London, passed through stations crowded with mourners while in the fields the farm labourers could be seen standing in pouring rain, bareheaded as a mark of respect. Nearly all the bystanders had lived their whole life in her reign. In the city of London the hour-long funeral procession, moving slowly towards the Paddington railway station, was watched silently by an immense concourse of people. One journalist admired 'their patience, their self-restraint, the gravity of their bearing through the long hours of waiting, and the wondrously intense hush of concentrated emotion which fell upon them everywhere as the coffin passed before their eyes'. Prominent in the funeral procession, on horseback, were the King of Portugal who would soon lose his throne, the Archduke Franz Ferdinand who would be assassinated on the eve of the First World War, and the German emperor who would lose his throne at the end of that war.

Throughout the year royal trivia were eagerly reported everywhere, for no pop stars or film stars yet existed to vie with kings and queens. In 1905, newspapers scattered across the world described in overflowing detail how King Carlos of Portugal was visiting the English country house of Chatsworth, where he was so eager to hunt down pheasants, hares and wood pigeons that three servants accompanied him as 'loaders', enabling him to have a loaded gun always at the ready. That he enjoyed a snowball fight outside the luncheon tent heightened the reading-public's pleasure. At about the same time, the Czar of Russia, disappointed by the poor showing of his troops against the Japanese, was delighted to receive from his Siberian militiamen a petition of loyalty expressing their personal willingness 'to fight and die, for the Fatherland'. According to Reuter's news agency, the czar absent-mindedly wrote on the side of the sacrificial petition: 'I thank you sincerely, and hope that your wishes may be fully realized.'

The royal families of England, Germany and Russia, and even the French royal family living in exile, were loosely linked by marriages, past and present, and were sufficiently bilingual to converse, usually without the aid of interpreters. In generous moments they showered one another with national honours. The German emperor, on a visit to England, was given the honorary rank of field marshal in an army whose soldiers, 13 years later, would be firing at his own. Like all families, the dynasties could quarrel. In a secluded park in Paris in 1897, Prince Henri d'Orléans of the dethroned French royal family fought a duel with the nephew of the King of Italy. Each suffered a wound. Royal prestige was not often wounded seriously in what was a heyday for European monarchies.

In Africa the ranks of the kings were thinning. The royal family of Madagascar had been exiled by the French in 1897, and the Sultan of Zanzibar bowed to the British throne. The few independent lands remaining in Asia were ruled by monarchs, China and Japan, Korea and Thailand were monarchies, and even India had its absentee monarch, for the Queen of England was titled the Empress of India, and Indian princes, nizams, rajahs and other royal potentates gathered around with clipped wings. Here and there in the Pacific Islands were monarchies, of which Tonga's still flourishes.

In Europe the monarchs had one terrifying enemy – the anarchists. Conspicuous in Italy, France and Spain, at one time an ally of socialists, they saw strong rulers as the problem, not the solution. Most anarchists did not believe in parliaments, despised private property, and resented the leaders of nations. In their view all people were equally entitled to share in power and wealth. Their foremost weapon was, literally, anarchy.

The general strike that dislocated the nation was one anarchists' weapon while the assassination of the nation's leaders was another. Their more extremist members – already they were called 'terrorists' – were as willing to suffer death as were the militant Islamic terrorists of a century later. Thus in 1894, President Carnot of France was travelling in a horse-drawn carriage in Lyons when a well-known Italian anarchist, working in France, leaned forward and stabbed him. Soon after Carnot was buried, the Italian government passed a law suppressing anarchists and socialists – they were spoken of legislatively in the same breath – but many anarchists were not deterred. In 1897 the Spanish premier Canovas del Castillo was on holiday at the baths of Santa Aguada when in full light of summer he was assassinated by the revolver of an Italian anarchist. The assassin was arrested, tried and executed in the space of 12 days, so urgent was the need for order in Spain. In Uruguay in the same month President Borda was assassinated while leaving the national cathedral. In 1898 the Empress of Austria was walking incognito in the streets of Geneva – an incredible action for the empress of one of the world's five great powers – when she was stabbed to death by an Italian anarchist.

The popular King Humbert of Italy was almost assassinated in Rome in 1897. Three years later, at Monza near Milan, the anarchists killed him. In that same year in Paris, the visiting Shah of Persia was attacked, while in Belgium the heir to the British throne was assaulted by a young anarchist. There was almost no Edward VII – a title he assumed after the death of Queen Victoria a year later. In 1901 President McKinley of the United States was assassinated by an anarchist. Two years later the King and Queen of Serbia were murdered, though not by an anarchist. King Carlos of Portugal and the Crown Prince were assassinated in 1908 by an anarchist. As assassins had to be within close range they had virtually no chance of escaping: death was their penalty. They were the equivalent of suicide bombers.

Terrorism is an old activity, rising and falling, and then rising to strike again. When a new wave of terrorism hit Europe and the Middle East in the second half of the century the anarchists, with their revolvers and knives, had slipped from public memory.

WILL THE TEMPLE BELLS BE MUFFLED?

Churches, mosques, temples, pagodas and synagogues were vital to daily life, though were occasionally under siege. At almost every tick of the clock, somewhere in the world, incense was burned, candles lit or bells rung. The church bell sounding at midday or before divine service was one of the pervasive melodies of Europe – more pervasive than it is today. Westerners who went east decided that the temple bells, quieter than their own and leisurely in tempo, made the atmosphere distinctive. One of the best known poems of the time, Rudyard Kipling's *Mandalay*, echoed the sound of the old Burmese pagoda: 'For the wind is in the palm-trees, an' the temple-bells they say.' Even the more austere Protestants, who shunned bell and candle with devout intensity, followed their own rituals, including the saying of a grace before every meal.

In nearly all western countries, infants were baptised or christened in a church and adults were married in a church. The overwhelming majority of children had a Christian first name, for the time was unimaginable when a television soap opera would compete with the Bible as the fountain of names for newborn babies. It was almost universal for a burial – cremation was a rarity in Europe – to be accompanied by a reading from the Bible or a book of prayer; and it was general for people to be buried in a section of the cemetery devoted to their own sect. In death the members of the same sect lay side by side.

On Sunday in many western countries all kind of entertainments and sports were banned, and even trams and trains restricted. In big cities the most eloquent preachers were household names, and many leading scholars were clergymen. The talent that flowed into the church as a calling and career was impressive. A daily newspaper in a big city would employ journalists whose task was to report on the sermons given in fashionable churches, rather in the manner in which they now report on the menu in fashionable restaurants.

Buddhism and Christianity, the global religions with the largest followings, continued to preach that life on earth would remain imperfect and – in the Buddhists' eyes – even miserable. Many Christians, though a minority, wondered whether the 20th century might be the last.

On 1 January 1901 at Topeka in Kansas the theological students in the Bethel Bible College wondered on this the first day of the century whether they might witness the long-awaited return of the Lord. During their prayers one student, Agnes N. Ozman, began fervently to speak a language unfamiliar to her, though some, speculating after the event, thought it might be Chinese. Those who knew their New Testament pointed out that the early Christians had spoken in strange tongues and suggested that perhaps the Lord was empowering this young student to pray and preach in a language that she did not know. The students, conscious that they might be witnessing the birth of a mighty revivalist movement, were mesmerised. From this town they set out to spread the word. One hundred years later their Pentecostal churches and 'Assemblies of God' could be found in the thousands all the way from Moscow to the highlands of New Guinea and the crowded streets of Brazil.

The majority of people in the world believed, deeply or casually, that death was not the end of their own life and that the afterlife for many would be infinitely more rewarding. 'The belief in human immortality in some form is almost universal', wrote a British scholar of religion, Alfred Garvie, who was entrusted with the article on 'immortality' in a leading encyclopaedia. He added that the most learned minds had come to the conclusion on ethical, materialist, social and philosophical grounds that the human soul was immortal. At that time a belief in heaven and hell – though the belief in hell was declining – was seen as the anchor of western civilisation. It was believed that without divine rewards and punishments, civilisation might collapse.

At the start of the century, Christianity was more eager than Islam to spread its message. Islam was politically weak. Christians ruled most of the Islamic lands. The Dutch controlled Java and Sumatra, the British controlled the Muslim parts of India and the Malay states, and Russian Christians ruled the Islamic regions on the plains and mountains of central Asia, with the exception of Afghanistan. In North Africa most of the Islamic lands were colonies of France, Britain or Spain. The more ardent Muslims felt some sense of humiliation that in their homelands Christianity held the sword, that Sunday was the official day of worship, and that alcohol was freely available. The Ottoman Empire, centred on Constantinople, remained Islam's only powerful defender, ruling much of Asia Minor, the Arabian peninsula and a shrinking remnant of North Africa and the Balkans. The First World War would shatter that empire.

Thousands of Christian congregations in North America, Europe, New Zealand and elsewhere financed platoons of missionaries, women as well as men, who went to foreign lands to create – under the blessing of a colonial government – their churches, and perhaps next door a hospital and school. Sometimes an island was totally converted, sometimes a whole region, but in populous China and India the converts, while numerous, formed only a fraction of the local population. Missionaries themselves made sacrifices. Albert Schweitzer, a world authority on the organ music of J. S. Bach, left much behind when he travelled from Alsace to Gabon in 1913 to be a medical missionary amongst the west Africans. While most missionaries were not political radicals, many of those Asians and Africans whom they converted were eventually to lead their own countries to independence.

The major religions faced two main enemies, both of which were growing in influence. One enemy was science which was almost a competing religion, capable of performing its own miracles. Some theologians, using the latest linguistic and archaeological and scientific skills, questioned the literal correctness of the Bible, including the story of the creation of the globe in the space of a week. Many educated Christians felt a loss of faith. They wanted to believe but their intellect said 'no'. William Ewart Gladstone, a scholar of the Bible as well as longtime Prime Minister of Britain, said this loss of religious faith, amongst people who once believed, was 'the most inexpressible calamity which can fall either upon a man or upon a nation'. The sense of that calamity, sometimes called 'The Death of God', was becoming more frequent in educated circles.

The other enemy was atheism and secularism. Socialists, anarchists and other radical reformers tended to see the major religions as their enemy. Religion comforted people but perhaps the time had come, said the critics, for people to be aroused and not comforted by the sight of the injustices encircling them. Against these critics the Christian churches fought rearguard actions. When Charles Bradlaugh, an English 'freethinker', won a seat in the House of Commons and refused to take the normal Bible-affirming oath, he was ejected. The voters of Northampton elected him again and again until 1886 when he was finally permitted to take his seat. Christians won most of the religious battles that came before parliaments; but in France, Italy and several countries in Latin America the Catholic church was losing its traditional dominance over schools and what they taught.

The popes made fewer concessions to the new banners proclaiming the virtues of science, socialism and free theological debate. They usually stood their ground. In international relations they remained influential. Pope Leo XIII was probably the most influential person in the world, in months of peace. One sign of his prestige, and the lack of other grand arbitrators, was that he adjudicated a dispute between Germany and Spain over their rights to the Caroline Islands. But when a major war involved the great powers, he was no more influential than the biggest field gun. In such a war the pope's influence was limited by the fact that Catholic countries were no longer dominant. Three great economic powers, the United States, Britain and Germany, were more Protestant than Catholic. Of the eight great military nations in 1901, only France, Austria-Hungary and Italy were Catholic countries, and even France was a secular republic.

WHILE THE CRADLES ROCKED

So many of those who would shape the first half of the century were, in 1900, babies wrapped in blankets or shawls, or children under the age of 10. They included two boys who were to become leaders of Nazi Germany, Hermann Goering and Joachim von Ribbentrop. Adolf Hitler, slightly older, was aged 11, a quiet boy. In France, Charles de Gaulle celebrated his tenth birthday, probably with toy soldiers at his feet, as did a Kansas schoolboy named Dwight Eisenhower, who as a wartime general was to do much to liberate France. The Russian leader Nikita Khrushchev, who was to hold power in a perilous phase of the Cold War, was a peasant boy aged six.

Of a similar age was 'Bertie', a child who was forced to wear splints on his legs to reshape his knock-knees and was told that he must not write English with his left hand. He later became, as George the VI, the head of one of the few monarchies that survived in tempestuous Europe. And there was the baby Ruhollah Khomeini who would preside over Iran 80 years later as the feared 'ayatollah' – an Islamic title virtually unknown to the western world in 1900, the year of his birth. A few other children lived a long way from the lands where they would make their name: Golda Meir, a toddler in the Ukraine, was to be Prime Minister of Israel, a nation that did not exist when she was born.

Cuddled in their parents' arms or at play in the streets could be seen the future leaders of other nations not yet created: Tito of Yugoslavia and Kenyatta of Kenya. Three music makers – Oscar Hammerstein II in New York City, Paul Hindemith in Germany and Kirsten Flagstad in Norway – were soon to go to school, while Mary Pickford, who became an early film star, was already a Canadian child prodigy in the opinion of her dewy-eyed parents. In China, the seven-year-old Mao Zedong was the son of a farmer, but he was to become so powerful as a communist leader that he put an end to the very idea of private farms. Others who would be prominent as Asian leaders – Emperor Hirohito of Japan and President Sukarno of Indonesia – were born in 1901 which, in an intellectual climate that was perhaps more numerate than ours, was generally decreed to be the first year of the new century.

None of these children could sense where the collision of world events or the perils of war and peace would lead them. The statistical chances were that most of the world's young children of 1900 would not travel far in the course of their life. It was common knowledge that most people died in the small district or village, even the same house, where they were born.

The family was the main teacher, and no myriad of schools could match its influence. From Fiji to Japan, from Peru to Sweden the young were shaped by the family's hands but the ways of raising and guiding children varied widely. The contrasts inside Europe were slight compared to the contrasts inside tropical New Guinea where 600 different languages were spoken by people of many cultures. In Catholic lands a child was usually baptised soon after birth but in parts of New Guinea the children were not even named until they survived the perils of their first days. If they died in their first week, rarely were they mourned: it was not that parents lacked affection but rather that they accepted that another baby would soon be on the way. Muslims in North Africa honoured the child's seventh day of life, most families in Europe honoured its first birthday, but some New Guineans might celebrate the day when the child's hair was first cut. In some regions, attempts were made to elongate the head of a newborn baby by binding it with bark cloth.

Breastfeeding of babies was almost universal in 1900. In some lands the child was weaned before the age of one, while in others it might occasionally be sucking mother's breast at the age of four. If the mother died when the child was young, a wet nurse – in essence a substitute pair of breasts – would usually be found; but in New Guinea such alien milk was often rejected as poison.

In 1900 most children of school-going age did not attend school even for a week. Their labour was needed in the fields, forests, homes or even underground mines. Without their labour the standard of living in Africa and Asia would have been even lower. Japan was perhaps the only Asian land where child labour was unusual, but in India and China the mass of boys and girls worked during the day, and indeed the Indian census of 1911 reported that only 1 per cent of its females could read and write. Significantly, from India's small middle class a surprisingly high proportion of boys went to school and even to university.

The countries with a higher standard of living were generally the first to enforce attendance at school. Compulsory schooling, after all, was a ban on the custom of children working all day and every day. In Britain in the 1830s, children as young as nine had been working in factories, coalmines and mills, and were unfamiliar with a school book, but at the end of the century the attendance at school was enforced. The two main offences before the English magistrates' courts were drunkenness and the failure of children to attend school regularly.

Many children skipped a large part of their childhood. Visiting Bukhara in central Asia in 1909, a Russian bureaucrat was saddened to see the innocent faces of 'the nine-year-old mothers, tiny and sickly-looking, holding their puny babies in emaciated little hands with henna-stained nails'. In the hope of resembling grown women they overprinted their eyebrows with a black line.

A portent for the future was a novel attitude towards children within certain circles in the British Isles, Scandinavia, Germany and New England. Children in these circles were often viewed not as miniature adults but as persons in their own right who were more imaginative and lively than adults. In contrast, the traditional European and Asian manner had been to decree that children be seen and not heard; and if on formal occasions they spoke in the company of an adult, it was only after their opinion was specifically sought. In the tongue-in-cheek advice of the Scottish writer Robert Louis Stevenson:

A child should always say what's true,
And speak when he is spoken to,
And behave mannerly at table;
At least as far as he is able.

Children became the heroes in a new wave of children's literature. The tale of the mischievous puppet Pinocchio first appeared in

1880 in the Italian children's magazine, *Giornale dei Bambini*. Other striking stories appeared in the weekly or fortnightly newspapers specially written for children, including *The Boy's Own Paper* in England and *The Youth's Companion* in the United States. Some of the finest young British authors – including Robert Louis Stevenson and Rudyard Kipling – now wrote for children as well as for adults, and in the bookshops their new works vied with such rising favourites as *The Wonderful Wizard of Oz* and *The Tale of Peter Rabbit*. The creator of the rabbit was Beatrix Potter and her story opened with arresting simplicity: 'Once upon a time there were four little Rabbits'. In conferring on 'Rabbits' a capital letter, she proclaimed that they, like the children she wrote for, were creatures of some importance.

Meanwhile in Germany an older German author Karl May, who had been arrested several times for fraud and petty theft, entranced a widening circle of teenagers with his adventurous, far-fetched books set in the Arabian desert or in America's Wild West. The German sales of his 60 or more books were to exceed 7 million copies. Gripping books written for young readers in a variety of countries came with a rush during the years 1880 to 1910.

Many readers, long after they ceased to be children, remained under the spell of these books. When Adolf Hitler became chancellor of Germany, the bookshelves in his retreat in the mountains near Salzburg were observed by a 12-year-old visitor: 'I especially looked', he wrote, 'to see what kind of literature the Führer had chosen for relaxation.' Quite a few books, he discovered, were written by Karl May. Almost a decade later in wartime Chicago, when physicists were secretly preparing to trigger the first nuclear fission and so move a step towards the atomic bomb, they devised a distinctive name for each part of the fission process. The names came from A.A. Milne's popular children's book, *Winnie the Pooh*. And when Aung San Suu Kyi, later to be an heroic leader of Burma, sought a name for her newborn son she called him Kim partly because she recalled with affection the boy of that name in Kipling's story.

2

RYE-BEER AND PERFUME

The big city seemed to typify the age. Half a dozen European cities each held more than one million people whereas a century earlier there was only one such city, London. The largest city the world had known, it now held 6 million. Second, in 1900, was Paris, now approaching 3 million, and third was Berlin – the fastest growing of the trio – with nearly 2 million. They were followed by Vienna and the two Russian cities, St Petersburg and Moscow. It was not that Russia was highly urbanised but rather that its sweeping spaces held more people than any American or other European nation.

MAGIC AND MISERY IN THE BIG CITY

The huge cities were like conglomerations of specialist villages, each linked by railways and trams and horse buses and horse-cabs. In London in the early 1900s the newspapers were edited and printed

in Fleet Street, not far from St Paul's Cathedral, the diamond deal-
ers and jewellers gathered at Hatton Garden, the clockmakers
clustered around Finsbury, and salesrooms and garages for the new
motor car favoured Long Acre. All cities had suburbs for rich or
poor, and for those who were proud to be neither. Even then some
suburbs were changing face. Whereas in 1800 the London neigh-
bourhood close to the Bank of England held 128 000 inhabitants, a
century later the banks and business offices had reduced the residents to one-fifth of the old number. Numerous spired churches
remained, but their congregations had gone.

Many European cities were speckled with similar transforma-
tions, and old customs lived on precariously. In the city of Munich
in 1895 the Butchers' Festival was held on Carnival Monday in every
third year and the Coopers' Dance every seventh year. Everyone
knew what a cooper did – he made the wooden barrels in which butter, apples, biscuits, beer, wine, and dozens of other commodities
were stored in the era before cheap plastic, steel and cardboard containers took their place.

Cities grew rapidly by absorbing the surplus people of nearby
towns and countryside. In 1900 only half of Vienna's inhabitants
had been born there. The most expensive city in Europe, it was full
of cramped apartments, and so most residents used the neighbouring coffee house as a substitute for the living space they lacked at
home. Vienna was the home of whipped cream and iced cakes and
coffee – the drinking of tea was largely a British and Russian taste. It
was also a home of classical music – Mahler conducted one of the
orchestras – and the virtual birthplace of the new psychology shaped
by Sigmund Freud. It was also to be a birthplace of Nazism, for in

1907 the young Adolf Hitler, arriving from the provinces, began to imbibe the anti-semitism that was a growing strand of politics in a city where Jews formed one-tenth of the population.

Fine music and theatre centred on the large city. Live music was the only music, for the gramophone sat in few homes, and the radio set was unknown. Orchestras, operas and oratorios, piano recitals and military bands could be heard in scores of cities, and one of the joys for music lovers who moved from small towns to Leipzig or Prague was that for the first time in their lives they could hear a symphony orchestra or massed brass band. The English steel-and-cutlery city of Sheffield was one that rejoiced in choral music, and there during the Christmas of 1897 the oratorio *Messiah* was performed at least 15 times. Reflecting the ambitious amateurism of that era, each member of a choir practising a Bach mass for the Sheffield Festival received from the conductor Sir Henry Wood a massive set of notes on how to interpret and sing the music. The notes ran to 168 pages!

Most day-tourists in a large city stayed away from the tenements where residents crowded into tiny apartments, with the only tap and toilet at the end of the communal corridor. It was easy to avoid the slums, as they rarely lay near the famous sites – the palaces, art galleries, cathedrals, parks, boulevards, band rotundas and government offices. Most exciting were the railway stations – Gare St Lazare in Paris was the the world's busiest – and the streets jammed with horse-drawn vehicles, the street trams clanging their bells, and the bands of musicians playing on the pavement for the sake of copper and silver coins gathered from passers-by.

The faces passed in the streets of large towns were a mirror of daily work. Most residents went home with their day's work discernible on their clothes and hands – the ink from the printing works, the flour from the mill, the whiff of chaff and manure from the stables, the scent of leather from the boot factory, and the smell of coal smoke from factories and railways. Drinking and washing water was not always accessible. In 1897 a traveller on the night train speeding from Rome to France noticed a lace-veiled Italian woman of 50 or 60, licking repeatedly a corner of her handkerchief until she had cleaned every part of her face: 'It was exactly a pussy-cat's toilet.' Scent often compensated for the scarcity of water, and the corridor of such trains contained a clanking machine which in return for a penny dispensed a little eau de Cologne.

Clerks and white-collar workers were multiplying – a foretaste of the era when people working in clean clothes would be in the majority. A host of people worked at desks in offices, some standing up, some sitting down. The big office depended on inventions speeding the flow of information: the penny postage stamp and the three-times-a-day postal deliveries in big cities, and the steel writing nib that replaced the quill plucked from a goose. As recently as the year 1852, England had imported a total of 10 286 000 goose quills and 61 000 swan quills, mostly from those ports on the Baltic where the flocks of geese multiplied. Half a century later the steel pen was dominant.

City offices were now employing the Remington typewriter, the telephone and the adding machine – innovations of the 1870s. The senior clerks saved time with the new fountain pen that, unlike the steel nib, did not have to be dipped into the pot of ink once every half-minute. The typewriter profited from the sheet of carbon paper which, placed below the white sheet of typing paper, produced a neat copy of what had been typed. By 1910 a few express trains provided a typewriting room in which stenographers could take a message from businessmen and type it out while the train rushed along: the Wolverhampton to London express had such a room. Typewriting increasingly became a job for young women who poured into the big city offices each weekday, making their office a place not only for work but also for courting.

Capping these innovations was cheap paper. Hitherto, waste rags, old linen and second-hand clothes were the materials from which paper was manufactured, but by the 1870s cheaper paper was being made from wood pulp. As the forest supplanted the second-hand clothes shop and the rag merchant as the main source of paper, the volume of paper circulating on a typical day at the start of the 20th century was probably 100 times as great as that used on a typical day one century previously. Nonetheless paper was not wasted. Most of the primary schools of Europe used very little paper, preferring that their students learn to write on an oblong of flat dark-coloured slate which could be cleaned with a damp rag and used again and again.

The big department store, like the big office, went in for experiments. Frank W. Woolworth, reared on an American farm, went to work in those small stores that sold almost everything. Eventually, setting up shops of his own, he specialised in selling cheap items at the bargain prices of five or 10 cents. Whereas merchandise had traditionally been publicly displayed behind a window and a counter, thus preventing customers from soiling it with grimy hands or stealing it, his goods were arranged on a long table so that every customer could inspect them. His first successful 'five and ten' store was opened in Lancaster, Philadelphia in 1879: a quarter of a century later his chain extended as far west as Colorado. On the eve of the First World War, his firm owned more than 600 stores as well as the startling Woolworth building in New York, the tallest in the world. Its style, the Gothic Revival, seemed appropriate, for it was higher than a cathedral.

LANDS OF RICE, WHEAT AND HARD LABOUR

For much of human history the traditional ways had gripped the present with sharp teeth. These teeth were still sharp in 1900. The need to grow food and to look after livestock was the duty filling the days of nine of every 10 people in the world. Daily life was dominated by rice and wheat fields, the pastures for sheep and cattle, plantations of coconuts and bananas and rubber, and orchards, vineyards and olive groves. In Europe, daily life was still close to that of Africa. Each morning, from Norway to Mozambique, early risers watched the sky for a sign that rain would fall, or drying winds appear, or some other climatic happening that might help or harm their crops.

The harvest was the crucial event. If it failed, tens of millions of people were exposed to hunger, malnutrition or serious illness. Most harvests were gathered by hand, with a small army of female and male labourers – children too – working from sunrise to twilight. In western Europe, horse-drawn machines increasingly cut the stalks of wheat, rye and oats: further east men and women reaped the crop with sharp scythes. Following behind were workers who shaped the fallen stalks into bunches, or sheaves, and tied them with light rope. The sheaves, having been left to dry in the warm sun, were carried in a cart or wagon to a threshing ground where barefoot people thrashed them with wooden flails to release the grain.

Harvesting the grain was a team effort. The urgency of completing the harvest during the fine weather is glimpsed in a vivid but slightly overstated passage in Tolstoy's novel, *Anna Karenina*: '. . . everyone, from the oldest to the youngest, for those three or four weeks must toil incessantly, three times as hard as usual, living on rye-beer, onions and black bread, threshing and carting the sheaves at night, and not giving more than two or three hours in the twenty-four to sleep.' Tolstoy added, 'every year this is done all over Russia'.

In most parts of the world, heavy loads were lifted by sheer strength. Human carriers, bent down by the weight they shouldered, were a common sight wherever the steep mountains were not yet crossed by roads or railways. On the border of India and Kashmir one mountain pass used by load-carrying porters significantly bore the name *Banihāl*, which means 'blizzard'. In the interior of southern China nearly all the salt was imported by human carriers who arranged the heavy saltcake on a wooden frame that was fixed on their shoulders. The load was so heavy that on the mountain road the carriers could not sit down – otherwise they would not be capable of rising to their feet again. In snow and frost, the track was so slippery that carriers fell and, being heavily loaded, were unable to lift themselves up and stand upright. 'We had not gone a mile', wrote one traveller in 1931, 'before we found one corpse after another.' At busy ports, extending from the Red Sea to the Yellow Sea, a crocodile-line of men carried the coal in sacks and baskets from shore to steam ship, for the conveyor belt was rare. The coaling of the mail steamers was a hazard to their well-dressed passengers, and women who wore light-coloured hats and white gloves when going ashore for the day were perturbed to see how quickly they became speckled with coal dust.

In wealthier countries, for many tasks, the horse superseded the sweating men and women. The huge horse used for ploughing and harvesting had to be fitted with new iron horseshoes perhaps once every three months but the town horse, plodding on cobblestones and hard surfaces, had to be fitted every few weeks. Blacksmiths had to be strong, for they lifted up the horse's leg and hammered the iron shoe on its hoof; and sometimes the horse, weighing maybe a tonne, would lean against the blacksmith as he worked. A celebrated poem in the English-speaking world honoured *The Village Blacksmith* – that mighty man with muscular arms and 'large and sinewy hands'.

As armies relied on horses, they were accompanied by teams of farriers and blacksmiths. The British army, fighting the Boers in South Africa in 1901, possessed 248 000 horses and mules – more draught animals than soldiers. Even the United States, whose army was limited to 100 000 enlisted men, was recruiting more horsemen. The nation, about to fall in love with the motor car, was still enamoured of the horse. The new president Theodore Roosevelt insisted that the American cavalryman, capable of fighting on horseback or foot, was the soldier to be feared.

Most people kept animals and other pets for their utility rather than their companionship. The cat was a hunter of mice in the granary and kitchen. The dog assisted in hunting and shepherding, and a large species such as the Bernese mountain dog could be harnessed to draw along a light cart, while the huskies and Manchurian ponies were to be used in the exciting phase of Antarctic exploration just about to begin. The falcon was a fine hunter in the sky, and kept as such in Arabian lands, while a pigeon was valued because it could be stewed in the pot or, if it were a homing pigeon, could be sent aloft to carry messages over long distances. The songbird was perhaps the luckiest, being kept in a cage for the sake of its music and bright plumage, but if it twittered or squawked when a stranger approached it thereby served as a domestic watch-bird. Canaries had another use, being sent down coalmines to indicate whether dangerous gases were present.

A typical European rural family moving for the first time to a city had less need for animals and little space in which to keep them. As the cities grew and people became more prosperous and lived longer, a pet became more affordable and desirable. English cities were probably the first to house pets in large numbers – England organised the first dog show or dog fair, at Newcastle in 1859 – and then the custom spread to continental Europe where pet dogs often came to be known by English names such as Blacky and Red: it did not matter if 'Blacky' was not black. In the United States the popularity of domestic pets was visible in the first era of the cinema cartoon, *Felix the Cat* appearing in 1917 and *Mickey Mouse* a little later. Americans originally owned more pet dogs than cats, but in the last decade of the 20th century the cats would number 62 million. Meanwhile in 1900, Britons ruled their wide empire but the pets quietly showed their sense of status each evening when the rulers arrived home, only to find the cat occupying the comfortable chair and the dog lying in front of the fire.

In rural homes around much of the globe the daily tasks were similar. Water was fetched in a bucket from a well or stream; wood was carried some distance to the fireplace where all meals were cooked; and the fatty candles were lit in the main room of the house at night. The typical Italian family did not live the idyllic rural life now imagined by those who holiday in the old, refurbished, stone farmhouses in Tuscany and Umbria. Large families were crammed on the upper floor, animals on the ground floor, and moulding heaps of manure and straw – the fertiliser for the next crop – lying not far away. Barefoot children, not regular in attending school, followed the slow bullock cart into the nearby woods and filled it with firewood and bundles of twigs. Firewood was never squandered, even in baking bread. As the special bread-oven used precious firewood, the dough for the brown loaves was not kneaded, prepared, and baked every day. Bread, baked in big batches, was often served when stale. In lean years the gnawing question was often asked, or was too painful to ask: will there be enough bread to go around?

On rainy days, other tasks were pursued by the women. Fibres from the crops of hemp, perhaps grown on the farm, were woven into cloth and shaped into a coarse bed sheet or a yellow-coloured cloth for the dinner table. At night on Tuscan farms the older girls sat near the wood fire while diligently 'embroidering their wedding linen', a job that goes on for years, as does the 'engagement period'. Some couples might be engaged for as long as eight or 10 years. A bumper harvest, bringing short-term prosperity, would lead to a sudden surge of weddings in the village. In its dependence on rural life and the weather, Italy was like most other lands.

On the mountainous island of Sardinia, many of the farmhouses, made of sunbaked brick, had no chimney, and so smoke from the fire hovered unhealthily in the main room. The farms, once a granary of the Roman Empire, grazed pitifully small species of cattle, donkeys and other animals. The small flocks of sheep, whose milk gave rise to the cheese called pecorino, were guarded by the huge total of 35000 shepherds. For the benefit of farmers a kind of commodity-bank lent seed at the start of the sowing season, the loan to be repaid later from the resultant harvest. Soldiers from Sardinia on their way to fight in the First World War were astonished, knowing only the rural way of life, to find prosperous, teeming cities such as Genoa and Milan. It was as if the 18th century was being granted a peephole into the 20th century.

A few rural regions of Africa and Asia enjoyed a standard of living possibly higher than various parts of rural Europe. In the valleys of Tibet in 1904, the standard of comfort of the average peasant surprised Captain W.F. O'Connor, a member of a visiting British expedition. He noticed that the Tibetans were rarely happier than when sitting down and drinking 'buttered tea' made from the coarsest tea leaves. He added that the typical Tibetan was 'absurdly like the Irish', being fond of singing and yarning. In contrast with such cheerful places were the scattered parts of Asia and Africa where slavery was still practised.

To be a slave was a plight worse than that faced by any ethnic minority in Europe. Though slavery was abolished in Brazil and in the sugar island of Cuba in the 1880s, it persisted in Africa and the Arabian peninsula. At North African ports the slave ships were seen creeping out at night. Turkey employed domestic slaves in huge numbers, and continued to keep smaller numbers even after the Ottoman Empire banned slavery in 1889.

In the following year Britain transferred to Germany the tiny strategic island of Heligoland – a rocky knob in the North Sea – in return for Zanzibar and nearby African islands. Thereby Britain, having taken the lead in abolishing slavery in its own homeland and colonies, acquired territory where slavery persisted. Under the revised laws, Zanzibar's slaves at last could appear before the local courts and gain their freedom, but first they had to prove that they were capable of earning their own living. Many were content to keep their servile status, for they were entitled to a hut, a garden, and free days on which they could till their soil. When one slave heard that he was free, he complained: 'I will not leave my master; he treats me like a son, he gives me food and clothes, and everything.'

On the lush island of Pemba – the Arabic word for *green* – slaves still worked the clove plantations. A kind of cure-all, cloves were useful for preserving foods, flavouring the breath, and easing toothache. When the reddening buds were ripe, a regiment of Africans was needed to climb the trees, pick the buds from the cloves, place them in handmade baskets, and dry them in the sun before finally they were ready to be carried by other slaves to Indian traders at the nearest port. In 1895 a rough count of the people living on the islands of Pemba and Zanzibar came to a total of 209 000, of whom two of every three were slaves. Two years later the Sultan formally abolished the legal status of slavery, but people were still being captured on the African mainland and sent in tiny fishing boats to Pemba where they were landed in darkness, unseen by the British patrol boats.

Slavery persisted in Africa. In the Dita Valley of the Ethiopian highlands in the 1920s, many families had to work four days a week for their owner, tilling the ground, carrying firewood and fresh water, and looking after the large household including the babies. It is estimated that in the 1920s, 2 million slaves lived in Ethiopia. Three decades later, perhaps half a million slaves were at work in Saudi Arabia, mostly as domestic servants.

From tropical regions, men were recruited to work for low wages in faraway lands. In India, China and a few islands of the south-west Pacific some of these indentured servants were pirated from their home. Most were recruited on the understanding that after three or six or more years they would be returned to their homeland. Gold-mines in South Africa, tea plantations in Ceylon and Assam, the guano mines in Peru, and sugar plantations extending from the West Indies to British Fiji were the main workplaces for these indentured labourers. It is now common to refer to them as slaves but the label is misleading. Real slavery was like a terminal illness: there was no way out.

Few events did more to flavour the optimistic mood of 1900 than the fact that so many ancient ills were slowly being eradicated. Slavery was the foremost of those ills.

THE LADDER OF POPULATION

Europe held almost one-quarter of the world's population – a far larger share than it holds today. Its population in the last 250 years had grown more rapidly than that of Asia and far more rapidly than that of Africa. Europe's place on the population ladder would have been even higher but for the vast waves of its people who had emigrated, especially in the preceding 50 years. Indeed this procession across the seas to Boston and New York helped to make the USA a world power, and parallel outflows built up much of Latin America, Canada, Australia, New Zealand, South Africa, a few regions of North Africa, and many towns in the vastness of Siberia.

Despite this outflow, Europe displayed a congestion of people rarely found in Asia. Even Switzerland with its blend of bleak mountains and densely populated lowlands was more densely settled than China. The long period when Europe's population increased rapidly was one of the secrets of its rise to power across the globe but new evidence even before 1900 suggested that Europe's population might cease to grow so rapidly. One indicator was Ireland which, after the potato famine of the 1840s, steadily lost people decade after decade. A host of young Irish people sailed away in the migrant ships to the United States, and those who stayed behind married later. Numerous Irish women did not marry at all, or married at an age where their remaining child-bearing years were few.

France was a puzzle. Its population grew slowly by the standards of the era. As the French were not eager emigrants, the Irish explanation could not be applied to France. For a time the alcoholic drink, absinthe, was blamed for France's falling birthrate. Said to be a semitropical medicine favoured by the French soldiers when they fought in Algeria in the war of 1832–47, a glass of the vivid green elixir remained a favourite drink when they returned home. Said to induce 'horrible dreams and hallucinations', it was also denounced as a cause of infertility in men and of moral decay. As France had lost with lightning speed the war begun against Germany in 1870, its national vigour and virility were the subjects of a permanent post mortem. The green absinthe was part of that post mortem, and in the Great War it was to be banned in France.

The cause of the falling birthrate was in France's bedrooms rather than its bars. By the second half of the 19th century, most French couples were reluctant to have a large family. Marriages tended to be later than in neighbouring lands, and various means of birth control were used. France's declining birthrate was a foretaste of what was happening in 1900 in England and Wales (but not yet in Ireland), and in Norway and Sweden. In the north and west of Europe, the typical family had fewer children than families in the south and east. Today, nearly every European nation records a rate of population increase much lower than that experienced by France at the time of the absinthe debate.

Outside these few charmed nations of western Europe, and those overseas lands dominated by European peoples, human life remained precarious. The death rate both for infants and those of middle age was high. Natural calamities were frequent. In Africa and Asia severe famines ran their course. Plagues knocked at the gateways of Asian cities; and the bubonic plague, appearing in Bombay in 1896, killed a million Indians in the following decade. Malaria exacted its toll in the tropics, though even southern Italy was a haven for malarial mosquitoes: the word 'malaria' entered the English language from Italy, where more than 12 000 people died annually from malaria in the early 1900s. Italy too experienced Europe's greatest natural disaster of the first half of the century, the terrible earthquake that wrecked the city of Messina in 1908, killing more than 77 000 Sicilians.

Maybe half of the people living in the world in 1900 had not once spoken to a doctor, nor entered a hospital. If they fell seriously ill they sought a cure in folklore or ancient herbal cures. In many European villages the man who shoed the horses and pondered over their maladies was consulted occasionally about illness in human beings. In Africa a soothsayer, an astrologer or a necromancer might be summoned, as a last hope, when death knocked at the door. In many countries the first medical schools were founded only in the 20th century.

PART TWO

3

A TEMPEST OF CHANGE

Practical inventors were shaping the future. In the early industrial revolution, the age of steam, the notable inventor was usually a Scot or Englishman. In the second inventive era, running from about 1850 to the First World War, he was more likely to be an American. From the United States, after 1850, came the powerhouse and electrical transmission wires, the gramophone, the telephone, the cheap camera and celluloid film, the steel-frame skyscraper, the elevator, the techniques for drilling for oil and refining it, the aeroplane, and that sensational lightweight metal, aluminium. From continental Europe in the same period came radio transmission, the X-ray, explosives for the blasting of rock, the internal-combustion engine, various rifles and machine guns, and in addition to these far-reaching inventions came a host of improvements to existing machines, gadgets and formulae.

Most of these advances are usually attributed to a single inventor, an obsessive person working alone. In fact most depended on other inventors and theoreticians, often in foreign lands. The great inventor usually knelt on the shoulders of earlier inventors. As historians, we tend to remove the shoulders from our memories.

A thousand activities were influenced by new machines and processes. The counting and pinpointing of stars was transformed by the sensitive plates of new cameras and the latest spectrograph and telescope. A French catalogue in 1801 had listed the approximate position of 47 390 stars, but after the grand photographic congress in Paris in 1887 a string of observatories both north and south of the equator, dividing the heavens between them, defined the exact position of more than 2 million stars. The latest camera was also carried by astronomers; and when William Shackleton observed an eclipse of the sun in the regions of northern ice at Novaya Zemlya on 9 August 1896, his photograph caught the rare and evanescent quality of the eclipse. That the sun and stars were alike was one of the fascinating discoveries confirmed by the latest instruments.

Alert observers of the world marvelled at this tempest of change, one gust succeeding another. That tempest was really the 20th century. The change tended to be faster in material things – in weapons that crushed life and in medicines that prolonged life, in transport and energy and labour-saving devices. In the dispersing and spread of new ideologies the change was less predictable. The novelist Victor Hugo, writing in French – the language that had expressed so many of the novel ideas – proclaimed the relentless force of the dynamic idea whose time had arrived. 'You can resist the invasion by an army, but you can't resist the invasion of ideas', he wrote. In fact some of the new ideas in the fields of religion, economics, politics and philosophy advanced and then retreated, in disarray.

Waves of new ideas were crashing against the existing ramparts at the opening of the new century. Increasingly Europeans heard the slogans of socialists and anarchists, the demands of women for equal rights, and the protests and murmuring of ethnic minorities, while western ideas were shaking long-subdued Asia. Atheists were proclaiming that God is dead, or soon would be, or that He had never been alive. All these hopes and fears would be affected profoundly by the Great War. Indeed some formed the background to that war.

AN ERA OF HANDSHAKING

The first years of the 20th century formed a remarkable era of international handshaking. The world seemed to shrink. The electric telegraph, on land and under the sea, brought together nearly every city and large town in every corner of the world. From London or Liverpool it was possible to board fortnightly or monthly mail steamers bound for most major ports in the world. Long-distance railways united the remote corners of Europe, though not Athens. North America was crossed by railways from coast to coast. The Trans-Siberian Railway linked Moscow and Siberia and was almost at the shores of Lake Baikal which, at first, locomotives and passenger cars would cross with the aid of ferries. By 1900 even Africa and South America had long railways that eventually might meet and so form a transcontinental line.

Summaries of daily news raced across the world: a summary was vital for the telegraph was expensive. The steam printing press and the penny newspaper enabled newly literate people to know far more than their grandparents had known about events throughout the world. Here indeed was an information revolution, though that phrase had not yet been coined.

In every habitable continent, far from the sea, new cities were arising. Most were reflections of the extending arms of European commerce and the new means of travelling. Far up the Amazon, some 1600 kilometres by ocean steamer from the Atlantic Ocean, lay the little city of Manaus, perched on a low hill. It was the seat of the bishop of Amazonas who ministered to a Catholic flock scattered across a vast area of jungle and cleared land. Native canoes were often paddled into the town, and the arrival of a ship from the distant ocean ceased to be unusual. By 1902 the jungle port was transformed. Electric trams ran along a few of its streets, and the population was approaching 40 000. On a hot evening when the windows of the opera house were flung open to let in air, strollers in the street could hear voices of a sweetness or mellowness rivalling those heard in European cities. The opera house was even grander when rebuilt in the 1920s.

As the seasonal rise and fall of the river could vary by as much as 10 metres – the variation is now higher – it was hard to equip the port with suitable wharves; but by ingenuity the floating wharves next to long, riverbank walls of stone were taking shape. By 1907 large steamers from North American and European ports were loading cargoes of hides and horns, Brazil nuts, cacao, and especially rubber. Here was one of the busy rubber ports of the globe, at a time when the wheels of a myriad of bicycles and the first motor cars were demanding rubber.

Other remote cities were rising in response to signals from the global economy. On a high plateau in South Africa the grandest mining city the world had known, Johannesburg, began to yield much of the gold demanded, then more than now, by the world's banks and treasuries. In arid Western Australia arose the goldfield of Kalgoorlie, to which fresh water was sent a distance of 500 kilometres by a line of steam-pumping stations. Nowhere in the world, it was later proclaimed, had 'so much water been pumped so far'. In Manchuria the city of Harbin and its onion-dome churches began to rise. Holding more than 3 million people today, it had been founded to serve the new railway running all the way from Russia.

Travelling to other lands, for business or pleasure, was now an industry. As criminals also crossed foreign borders or arrived at foreign ports, there was an argument for inspecting passports and other travel papers at the borders but in this era of global goodwill the passport was usually viewed as superfluous. So many countries abolished the passport that on the eve of the First World War it was a rarity – the war was to alter that. The new passports were travellers' cheques – first issued by American Express in 1891 – and tourists thought it a miracle that one ornate slip of paper, when countersigned, could pay their hotel bill. The first all-purpose credit cards were not available until 1950.

There was a calendar of international conferences, whether of postal officials, peace workers, statisticians, scientists, meteorologists, soldiers, socialists, linguists or missionaries. International agreements, even on armaments, were reached. In 1899 at The Hague, the Czar of Russia convened a conference on war and peace, and one of its triumphs was to ban the firing of weapons from balloons in the sky. Other unusual signs of harmony between nations and creeds were discerned. In 1910 the new mayor of Rome was

Ernesto Nathan, who was born in England. He was a freemason: certainly not a Catholic.

The latest communications technology is often hailed as the prince of peace; but the electric telegraph, at first hailed as a messenger of brotherly and sisterly love, could also convey declarations of war. The railway, which carried bands of peaceful tourists, could also carry regiments of armed soldiers. That the world was becoming smaller did not mean that it was necessarily becoming friendlier. More nations imposed tariffs on foreign goods, and the ideology of free trade was fading. Armies and navies were receiving more of a nation's budget. Nonetheless the forces of international peace seemed so vigorous, in the eyes of some observers, that an optimistic article entitled 'Peace' appeared in the edition of *Encyclopaedia Britannica* published in Cambridge in 1911. It foresaw 'the reign of reason' steadily superseding militarism. No such article could be found in the next edition of the encyclopaedia.

And yet in the first years of the century the belief was widespread that the global web of commerce and ideas was prolonging the period of peace between the big powers. Many statesmen in Europe consoled themselves with the prediction that the whole way of life of Europe now relied on a continuing flow of imports from overseas, whether oil for the new battleships, wheat and chilled foods for civilians and soldiers, gold to reinforce the banking system, and a host of other vital items. Accordingly they predicted that a major war would utterly dislocate commerce and finance and would spur inflation. Economic collapse would then bring the war to a sudden end.

Most Europeans who thought about the state of the world in 1900 considered that they were fortunate. They had lived – even if they were aged 80 – through a period that was relatively peaceful inside the great nations. Moreover most thought that the peace would persist. The hopes of international peace, however, stood uneasily alongside the heavy spending on battleships and armies.

Somewhere in the world a war was nearly always being fought, but most of the fighting was on a low scale, and the casualties were usually light, being confined to those actually fighting. Europe had had its share of international wars in the 90 years after the Napoleonic Wars. Russia and Turkey fought each other once in every generation, like a sporting fixture. In turn, Germany, France and Austria-Hungary engaged in a series of short wars between 1859 and 1871, the Red Cross organisation being an indirect effect of one of those wars. The Balkans too had its brief wars, with a rush of fighting just before the First World War.

Amidst all this fighting and flag-waving, Europeans were entitled to applaud themselves. Between 1815 and 1914 they had experienced not one general war; and it is the general wars that are usually the more devastating wars. Only once, in the Crimean War in the 1850s, did more than three major nations take part. They were France and Britain on Turkey's side and Russia fighting alone. Not a major war, it was over in three years. Another reason for hope in 1900 was that Europe's international wars were shorter than those of a century earlier. Indeed it was widely anticipated that when big European nations fought one another, they would not fight for long. Germany was expected, as in 1870, to be the master of the short war, using railways and telegraphs and the latest artillery and machine guns in such a way that it applied overwhelming force almost before the enemy had time to put on its uniform. Modern technology, it seemed, was mercifully tending to shorten wars, especially those fought between industrial nations.

The most significant war between 1900 and 1914 was fought by Russia and Japan who were both determined to expand into the cold corner of north-east Asia. When their war began in Manchuria on 8 February 1904, the Japanese held an advantage because, fighting close to home, they could easily send troops and supplies. In contrast the Russians had to send their armies overland on the world's longest railway. In addition the Russians, in order to augment their depleted navy, had to send their warships more than halfway around the world. From the Baltic Sea, the Russian war fleet eventually set out, crossing the North Sea where they mistakenly fired on British fishing boats near the Dogger Bank in October 1904, passing the tip of South Africa and then the narrow strait near Singapore, and so steaming slowly across the South China Sea towards Japanese waters. Every few days the world's newspapers printed the whereabouts of the Russian fleet as it slowly proceeded on the longest attacking voyage in the history of naval warfare.

At last, in May 1905, the two navies met in misty weather. At the end of the second day most of the Russian warships could not be seen. They lay, mangled and holed, at the bottom of the sea.

The Russo-Japanese war was a prelude to profound political changes. Almost spurring a popular left-wing revolution in Russia, it also declared that the era of eastern Asia, long in eclipse, might be dawning again. Moreover, this war hinted at another momentous possibility. If a short war fought far from Europe could reshape so much, what might a great war in the heart of Europe do and undo?

THE SURGE OF SOCIALISM

Socialism resembled a widening river to which many side streams contributed. Christianity itself had a socialist as well as an individualist stream, for Christ said it was 'easier for a camel to go through the eye of a needle, than for a rich man to enter into the kingdom of God'. A century ago, the romantic poets of Germany and England had viewed peasant, ploughman and milkmaid as no less worthy than duke and duchess, and their verses influenced millions of readers. Radical ideas were spread through the continuing exodus from country to city – socialism in its various versions was more a city crusade. Capitalism itself, in its ability to produce an increase of wealth decade after decade, unintentionally raised the question: why can't more people share in that growing wealth? The revolutionists, inspired by Marx and others, announced that they had a formula for expropriating that wealth, their main plan being to nationalise the farms and factories, railways and ships, shops and banks and insurance offices. A large number of sympathisers wanted a pragmatic form of socialism, a bit here and there. Whether they should be called socialists was a matter of debate but often they were.

Socialism gained from a rising sense of injustice and envy too. George Bernard Shaw, Irish-born critic and wit, pointed out that in New York a lady could order a luxurious coffin lined with pink satin for her dead dog while 'a live child is prowling barefooted and hunger-stunted in the frozen gutter outside'. He labelled this as the 'grotesquely hideous march of civilization from bad to worse'. Whether the contrast between the extremely rich and the extremely poor was actually increasing is uncertain, but more critics pointed to it. In lands such as Russia, India and China the contrast between the grand palaces and the tiny, chill, rural hovels was breathtaking.

In many workplaces, discontent was expressed by strikes. Some were violent, and the armies and police responded with force. Early in 1902 a strike of workmen demanding an eight-hour working day in the Austro-Hungarian port of Trieste led to 12 deaths. The United States experienced fatal clashes outside steelworks and mines. A strike by goldminers on the Lena River in Siberia in 1912 was put down by the firearms of the secret police, and 170 lives were lost. A new tactic, the general strike, dislocated whole cities and countries for several days.

Karl Marx, the prophet and economic historian, labelled religion *das Opium des Volkes* – the opium of the people. But socialism itself now resembled a powerful and, to many, a persuasive religion, with its own theology and sacred texts, and its own diagnosis of evil and sin – capitalism was its name – and its own belief in the triumphant destination of the human race. And yet many leaders of the rising labour movements combined their version of socialism with Christianity. Methodists were prominent in founding the Labour Party in Britain.

While intellectuals in the United States did not follow the collectivist path with a European-like ardour, they began to harry the mightiest capitalists. Journalists known as muck-rakers attacked big business and scored decisive hits. Washington enacted anti-trust laws in an attempt to curb the private monopolies so visible in oil, steel, and railways. A labour party was never to become one of the big two parties in the United States, but who could have predicted that in 1900? In emphasising equality, the Americans were early, not late. Their pursuit of economic opportunity and individualism, and their dispensing with kings and baronets in the revolution of the 1770s, had been their own route towards equality long before the European socialists could be heard marching.

At this stage, socialism or half-socialism did not have a majority of supporters in any country. It was strong enough in France in 1899 for one of its adherents, Alexandre Millerand, to be invited to join the French Cabinet, and became strong enough in Australia for a 'moderately radical' Labor Party to hold office briefly in 1904 and frequently after 1908. In Finland, a half-independent part of the Russian Empire, the socialists won 80 of the 200 seats, while at the German elections of 1912 one in every three voters opted for a socialist party. The clamour for social reform was like a vast army with many regiments, some marching on the extreme left, and some wheeling to the right in order to defend the status of private property so long as it was held in small lots.

The view was common that socialism could win office only by peaceful means, not by armed revolution. Even in 1848, the year of revolutions, the rioters and protesters who briefly occupied city streets in regions as far apart as Sicily and north Germany mostly failed. There was a bloody revolution in Paris in 1871 – it collapsed. Russians attempted a revolution in 1905 – it failed.

If political observers had been asked which of the world's nations would be the first to make a distinctive socialist experiment, a frequent answer in 1910 would have been New Zealand. There the government ran many industries and nearly all the railways, and provided old-age pensions and free schooling. In some industries the government stipulated a minimum wage, short working hours, and the compulsory arbitration of work disputes. Large landed estates were prohibited, and the trade in alcohol was severely regulated. Such laws excited visiting socialists. 'New Zealand is better suited for the experiment of a closed socialistic state than perhaps any other country in the known world', wrote a Canadian authority on socialism. He thought Russia was less likely to experiment. There, 'in the absence of democratic government, the prospects of socialism are doubtful', he decreed.

WHO IS WORTHY OF THE VOTE?

Democracy, though bawling lustily, was an infant. Most people in the world had no right to vote. Nine of every 10 adults in the world had never voted at an election. While democracy was making headway in Europe and more or less flourishing in such lands as France and Britain, Scandinavia and Switzerland, it would not be called a thorough democracy by today's standards. In Europe, which seemed likely to rival North America as a home of democracy, most men over the age of 21 and all women still lacked the right to vote.

Russia, the most populous land in Europe, had no parliament until the Duma was created following the thwarted revolution of 1905 and it was more a house for speech-making than for governing. In Germany, the second most populous nation, some important decisions were outside the control of the elected parliament, the Reichstag. The Ottoman Empire was dabbling in a limited form of democracy, with only one toe in the water. In most of the democracies the very poor usually had no right to vote. In Brazil, which had recently become one of the few genuine democracies in South America, beggars could not vote, members of monastic orders could not vote, and the rank and file of the army and navy could not vote. For long the United States was almost the purest democracy in an imperfect world; but its blemish was that it positively discouraged or debarred its substantial minority of poor, Afro-American people from voting.

Some democrats feared that their system of government was liable to be corrupted if it spread too quickly to nations where illiteracy was high and experience of self-government sparse. Lord Bryce, a British politician who became ambassador to the United States in 1907, was perhaps the best informed assessor of the world's democracies. He feared the power of newspapers and politicians to disseminate misleading propaganda. He regretted the democratic tendency to bribe voters, electorates and interest groups with money or other benefits that they would never receive if the government had the whole national interest in mind. He declared emphatically: 'The two best-administered democracies in the modern world have been the two poorest, The Orange Free State before 1899 and the Swiss Confederation.' They apparently did not bribe the voters.

The signs that democracy would expand were unusually favourable, even in China. When its commanding figure, the empress dowager, died in 1908, the boy prince who succeeded her was unable to preserve the crumbling Manchu dynasty, and abdicated after four years. Here was an opportunity for those young Chinese nationalists who, mostly educated in the west or Japan, admired the United States and its democratic institutions. Their leader was Dr Sun Yat-sen, a Christian Cantonese who was educated in American Hawaii and British Hong Kong. The young doctor and his colleagues, after helping to overthrow the Manchus, tried to set up a democracy; but to be effective a democracy requires a tradition of debate, the introduction of civil liberties, and some sense of civic duty. China's first national election, held in 1913, was won by the young reformers, but it also proved to be China's last. An ambitious general, Yuan Shih-k'ai, soon dissolved the parliament. Abandoning the old divine emperors, China accepted a succession of military rulers.

It was not only in China that the right of free speech, essential in a democracy, was seen as dangerous. For three out of every four of the world's peoples, civil liberties were weak or precarious in the early years of the century. Even in Europe several of the largest empires showed a persistent reluctance to grant personal liberties. The Russian novelist Leo Tolstoy, so famous that he could criticise his government, reminded the czar in 1901 that the peasants – they had been upgraded from mere serfs 40 years previously – were still a lower order of creation. They required a passport to move within their own country. They had an obligation to lodge and feed visiting soldiers and to supply carts in order to carry military supplies even when the cart was needed for their own rural work.

Russia imprisoned vigorous political and religious dissenters, and the special political police held wide powers of arrest and detention. In the 1890s the Russian dramatist Anton Chekhov, visiting Vienna, wrote to his mother to explain his sense of liberation: 'It is strange that here one is free to read anything and to say what one likes.' In his homeland, detectives working in pairs watched political dissenters and noted when they left a house, the addresses on the letters they posted, the newspapers they read, and the names of visitors who called on them. Often a detective, disguising himself as the driver of a horse-cab, waited patiently outside the house of a political agitator. The cab could easily follow him after he walked from his apartment.

In Russian universities, when students wished to discuss their grievances, their meeting had to be presided over by a professor. The millions of Russian Jews – almost a nation within a nation – could practise their religion only so long as they lived within the cramped zones prescribed for them. The other choice – to emigrate to the United States – was increasingly preferred. Russia outwardly was highly civilised, a beacon in literature, music, ballet and other creative arts, but those who had the right to be civilised were few.

THE WOMEN'S WING

Amongst European peoples the crusade for equality had its women's wing. Its leaders wanted equal right to obtain a divorce, the right to property on the same terms as men, the right to vote and the right to enter a university and especially a medical school whose dissecting room, with all that raw flesh on display, was seen as indelicate for young women. By 1900 most of these rights were being won, especially in Protestant countries. Nowhere in Europe, however, was there even one female judge, one female politician, one female general, or a female leader of big business. Curiously it was one of the most ancient of institutions, the monarchy, that sometimes allowed a woman to be ranked above all men. The most famous woman in the world in 1900 was Queen Victoria, who was celebrating her sixty-third year on the British throne.

Few women in the world had ever voted at an election. New Zealand in 1893 had been the first country to allow women to vote in a national election, at which time women in three small American states already held the right to vote on state rather than national issues. The ballot box remained out of reach of European women. Bands of women lobbied diligently, as did men, to obtain the vote for women, partly in the belief that thereby they would purify national life by attacking prostitution, the culture of hard drinking and other social ills.

The first national election in which women could vote and also stand for parliament was held in Australia in 1903. Of the handful who stood, Vida Goldstein was the one with a prospect of winning a seat. Aged 34, unmarried, strong-willed, and capable of replying forthrightly when interjectors interrupted her speech in a public hall, she craved to be the first woman in the world to sit in a parliament. In central Melbourne on Wednesday 16 December 1903 she walked along the wet street to a polling booth and waited impatiently for some 40 minutes before finally the doors were opened – precisely as the clock in the post-office tower chimed 8 a.m. One of the four senate vacancies was her goal, and to win it she required about 100 000 votes. She was defeated but her tally of 51 000 votes was regarded as a triumph. It seemed probable that sooner or later she would win a seat, but 40 years passed before the first woman was elected to Australia's national parliament.

Female novelists could be read in every bookshop – it was occasionally predicted that in the English language they would soon dominate the novel – and female actors and singers could be heard in the fine opera houses and theatres from Vienna to Buenos Aires; but female conductors and composers were the rarest of musical birds. Ethel Smyth, daughter of an English artillery officer who fought against the Indian Mutiny, made her own mutiny in England by resolving to be a musician. This stormy petrel, as her mother called her, studied in Leipzig within the Brahms' circle, and was acclaimed by some critics as the first woman in the world to compose operas, oratorios, a large-scale symphony and a mass. Her acclaim came more readily in Germany where her first opera was staged in 1898. Back in England she joined the crusade to secure votes for women, and as a suffragette in search of publicity she served a short sentence in Holloway Prison where she gained further publicity by standing at the window of her cell and conducting her own protest music with a toothbrush. In 1914, after a decade of strong agitating, women had the right to vote in only two European nations, Sweden and Norway.

In Russia the young women, having few opportunities for higher education, went abroad if their parents would both allow them and finance them. Their mecca was radical Zurich where they sometimes sat in coffee shops and listened to radical talk. Treated with more intellectual respect than in their homeland, they tended to become critics of the czar and the Russian Orthodox Church. In 1894 the chief of police in Russia reported with astonishing precision that 42 per cent of the young Russian women studying medicine in Swiss universities were likely to absorb 'pernicious' views. Eventually a medical course for women was set up in Russia.

In China and India the rights of women, with few exceptions, were almost invisible. The practice was for the parents and perhaps other relatives to choose the bride or bridegroom. A widow did not remarry, the social pressures forcing her to remain loyal to her dead husband. Not until 1950 were these practices, already in decline in China, prohibited by the new communist government. While these

Asian marriage practices now seem antediluvian, those who obeyed them would probably scorn some of the later western attitudes to marriage, divorce and child-rearing.

In east Asia in 1900 three generations typically lived in the same household. In Korea at least nine of every 10 women lived out their married life with a man selected by the parents. As late as 1960 South Korean laws stipulated that a woman under the age of 23 and a man under the age of 27 required their parents' permission to marry. A parallel custom persisted in Japan where most newlyweds lived in the house of parents, usually the husband's. Taking the world as a whole, it was the new European attitudes to women's property, to marriage and to children that were abnormal in 1900.

ETHNIC FLASHPOINTS

Tensions and flashpoints often occurred at those places where the traditional European powers faced ethnic minorities either in their midst or just across the border. If the ethnic minority worshipped in a different church, the tensions were likely to be higher. Amongst these flashpoints were British Ireland, the Balkans and the Black Sea from which the Turks were in slow retreat, central Europe where Slavs faced Germans, and the Alps where Italians faced Austrians. Both world wars were to begin where strong European powers defended their sovereignty and prestige against that of distinctive but weaker ethnic groups.

The Poles, who had no nation of their own, could recite a long list of grievances against German as well as Russian rule. They resented German attempts – initiated by Otto von Bismarck – to persuade or compel them to abandon their Polish language and the strong emotions it expressed. At the town of Wreschen in 1901, about 20 Polish school children, presumably inspired by their parents, refused to recite their religious catechism in the German language. The school inspector had them flogged. When some of the parents protested with strong language, they were punished with prison. Several parents were additionally incensed because they had always understood that the tongue in which Christ spoke to his disciples was the one which was now banned – the Polish language!

Austro-Hungarian territory was the most densely settled of the great empires, and the most diverse with 11 main ethnic groups. It bordered four powerful states, in three of which lived ethnic groups that also inhabited the Austro-Hungarian empire. The position did not always make for harmony. Ethnic tensions quickly flowed from one state to another, and such tensions formed the background to the coming Great War.

In the Balkans three different ethnic groups and religions competed. Though the Turks' control had ended, large Muslim populations remained behind. Thus in the small city of Sarajevo, which was the capital of Bosnia and Herzegovina, half of the people were Muslims, and they worshipped in about a hundred mosques, including the most handsome in Europe. As Sarajevo was part of the large Austro-Hungarian empire, its Muslims were ruled by Catholic Austrians based in Vienna. In the same city and province lived a large Serbian population, Orthodox in religion. Its loyalties were towards the new kingdom of Serbia, just across the border.

In Bosnia and Herzegovina many young Serbs felt that they belonged to a special Slav brotherhood and that they must recapture the place usurped by the Austro-Hungarians. Gavrilo Princip, one of these patriotic Slavs, was brought up in a Bosnian house with an earthen floor, no windows, and a roof-hole rather than a chimney to let out the wood-smoke. He tried in 1912 to enlist in the Serbian forces fighting against the Turks but was rejected because of his short stature and his physical frailties. When that short war was over, he was just as eager, being a member of a secret Slavonic society called Black Hand, to play his part in pushing out the Austro-Hungarians who occupied his homeland. A faction of the Serbian Army gave him and his comrades the six bombs and the four Browning revolvers they needed to carry out their bold plot, and they were smuggled into Sarajevo without detection.

On 28 June 1914, a day of Serbian national celebration, an official military inspection of Sarajevo was to be conducted by the Archduke Franz Ferdinand, heir to the Austro-Hungarian throne. Accompanied by his wife Sophie, he was an easy target, because his exact timetable was announced publicly. Moreover the collapsible hood of his royal Viennese limousine was lowered on this summer day, further exposing the couple to attack.

The visitors were being driven to the town hall for an official lunch when Princip and comrades, waiting along the road, prepared to explode their first bomb. The comrades, inexperienced with weapons, missed their easy target but injured a soldier. After lunch the archduke decided generously to make a detour and visit the hospital – the call was not on his official program – and to console the wounded soldier. On the way his chauffeur made a wrong turning and had to reverse the car slowly – a second opportunity for an assassin. From a few paces away, Gavrilo Princip fired his revolver several times, killing the archduke and his wife.

As the Emperor of Austria and King of Hungary, Franz Josef was the most experienced monarch in Europe and the ruler of diverse territories, and therefore his ordained heir was a prince of importance. On hearing of the death of the heir, most Austrians were incensed. Kaiser Wilhelm of Germany supported them with equal indignation. The Serbian government, while not initiating or sanctioning the plot, was vulnerable since its laxity had allowed explosives and revolvers to reach the conspirators. The Serbs, finally given an ultimatum, made apologies, though not quickly enough. Belgrade, the capital city of their landlocked nation, lay just across the river from Austrian soil. On 29 July 1914, one month after the assassination, the first Austrian shell was fired on Belgrade.

Meanwhile Princip and the other conspirators were caught. Several were executed, but Princip, being a teenager, was spared. He was to die of tuberculosis in a Bohemian prison in 1918, near the very end of the war that his revolver had helped to ignite.

4

THE WAR OF WARS

The First World War was the momentous event of the century. It was not only traumatic to live through but profound in its effects. It helped to spur the Russian Revolution and to mould the trade depression of the 1930s, which proved to be the worst economic slump the world had known. That war, directly and indirectly, spurred the rise of Hitler and Nazi Germany, and helped to provoke the Second World War. It ended the heyday of western Europe and its global dominance and also accelerated the reign of the United States and that of the Soviet Union. During that same war a British statesman made a plan for Palestine that still maintains tensions in the Middle East.

Much of the century's inventiveness, including the long-distance aircraft, atomic energy, the exploration of outer space, major innovations in medicine, and even the first computer, was driven by the needs of the two world wars. The century would have been momentous without the war of 1914–18, and some of the inventions and political ups and downs would have happened without it, but that war shaped a multitude of events, speeding or retarding or redirecting them.

Even if war had been averted in 1914, there would have been later wars, some of which might have produced a different set of winners, so altering today's political map of the world. But the sheer scale of the First World War had profound effects. The way in which the war was prolonged and widened, contrary to expectations, and the anger and hatred it provoked, and the specific victors it produced – all left deep scars on its generation and the next.

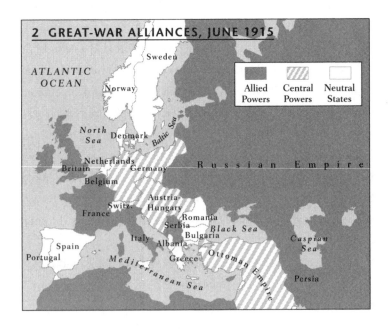

2 GREAT-WAR ALLIANCES, JUNE 1915

THE TIMETABLE OF WAR

The war commenced in 1914 with a strange mixture of optimism and pessimism. It was anticipated that the loss of lives might be heavy but, as compensation, the war would be short. The widely held prediction of a short war arose partly from the fact that most of the recent wars in Europe had been short. The last European war involving at least two major powers – the war between France and Prussia that began in 1870 – was virtually won within a few months with the aid of railways, the telegraph and modern weapons. The faith that this latest war might be over by Christmas, or soon after, was accentuated by the feeling – a feeling more than knowledge – that the sophisticated banking and financial system could not sustain a long war, that people would not tolerate a long war, and that increasing scarcities of food and war materials would summon the national leaders to the peace table.

As the war was expected to be determined by the opening battles, the various allies had to be ready to assist each other at short notice. The tight timetable by which nations declared war and rushed their armies to the border and sent their navies out to sea is sometimes said to have been a subsidiary cause of the war itself. On the contrary the tight timetable was the result of the belief that the war was almost inevitable, and that it would be short: the laggards and the latecomers would pay a high price, being overwhelmed or shocked before they were ready. So the war began on 28 July 1914 simply as a war between Austria and Serbia – the purportedly guilty party at Sarajevo. In the next seven days the two were joined by allies, Germany fighting on Austria's side, and France, Russia and Britain forming their own alliance. Within a week, five major powers and several minor powers were fighting or about to fight over a spacious European zone extending from the North Sea eastwards to the plains of Poland and the mountains of Hungary, while naval battles were in the offing as far away as the China Sea, the cold tip of South America and harbours of tropical Pacific islands.

Nations that at first were onlookers chose their time cautiously. Should they enter what already was called the Great War or should they remain neutral? In the first month after the outbreak, Japan entered the war against Germany, employing its fine navy but refusing the request to send an army to fight in Europe. In November 1914 the Turks joined on the side of Germany, and in the following May the Italians – to the surprise of many – joined the opposing side. Other nations in ones and twos declared war, a few leaving their decision until 1918. The more nations that joined in the fighting, the harder the task of bringing all to the negotiating table. Even by the end of 1914 a calmly negotiated treaty of peace was impossible.

In the first week, nationalist passions and patriotism bubbled over, exceeding expectations. Loyalist meetings were held in hundreds of village and suburban halls. On the first Sunday, church bells were rung countless times, and patriotic sermons were preached from pulpits. The outbreak of war was hailed by a German historian as a moment of 'profoundest joy', while the young English poet Rupert Brooke wrote:

Now, God be thanked
Who has matched us with His hour.

Brooke, a naval officer, was to be buried on a Mediterranean island in the first year of war.

Trade unions and labour parties in some of the warring countries had been expected to stand up and oppose the war. Instead most of their younger members stood and enlisted or calmly accepted the call-up. Patriotism became aggressive. Birmingham holiday-makers stranded in Germany after war began, or Viennese merchants marooned in British ports, found themselves without friends. Royal families vied with each other in shoring up their national credentials. The Russian royal family which had strong German connections vigorously displayed its Russian patriotism by changing the German-sounding name of its capital city, St Petersburg, to the more Slavonic Petrograd. Likewise a senior member of Britain's royal family, carrying the German surname of Battenberg, was forced by a surge of anti-German emotion to resign from the supreme naval position of First Sea Lord in 1914. Three years later his family adopted the English-sounding surname of Mountbatten.

Ethnic minorities expecting to stand aloof from the war actually bathed in the public cascade of patriotism. Ireland, on the verge of civil war and divided in its loyalties to Britain, reasserted its loyalty temporarily and provided regiments of recruits for the British army. In Russia, leaders of the downtrodden minorities pledged allegiance. Poles and Estonians, Latvians and Lithuanians promised to stand shoulder to shoulder with the Russians. A Jewish spokesman pithily expressed what others said in grand language: 'We have lived and we live in particularly oppressive conditions. Nevertheless, we have always felt ourselves citizens of Russia and faithful sons of the fatherland.'

National unity blossomed in politically divided France. When, at the outbreak of war, all members of parliament stood and listened to the president's outline of the thwarted negotiations made in the hope of preserving the peace, they broke their silence to applaud his sentence, 'We are no longer partisans here, we are all Frenchmen.' Even the French press, like the press in most free nations, accepted censorship of the truth for the sake of national unity and the need to repel the invading Germans.

In France the truth was not palatable. The army was short of shells for the big guns to fire. Medical help for the wounded was slow. Bleeding or bandaged French troops lay around, waiting for a motor ambulance. When none arrived they were lifted on stretchers to railway trucks that had previously been used for carting cattle and horses. So swiftly did the German army advance through Belgium and the north of France that there was a likelihood that Paris would be captured.

The French commander-in-chief General Joffre advised the government to retreat to the distant port of Bordeaux. On the night of 2 September 1914 the president of the republic and the ministers secretly left from a Paris railway station, followed by another special train – much delayed along the line – carrying foreign ambassadors and lesser diplomats. Bordeaux was in confusion, not a bed to be found. Two of its music halls, Apollo and Alhambra, were fitted out so that they might stage the next meeting of the two chambers of parliament. Printing presses were requisitioned to serve those daily newspapers that were hurriedly moving their offices from Paris. At last on the battlefield in northern France the French soldiers, aided by British troops, stood firm. Paris was safe, and its people welcomed home the government in December.

The rival armies on the western or French front now stood

opposite one another and neither could be repelled. The swift German advance in the first weeks of the fighting had slowed to a walk and then to a crawl and finally a halt. The opposing armies dug trenches and made the earth their shield. Ground gained – a few hundred metres or even fewer – was won at enormous cost in dead and wounded, for the opposing enemy could pour massive firepower at the advancing troops. Replacements for the wounded arrived quickly and it seemed that an army could hold its lines of trenches almost indefinitely. This was one reason for the prolonging of the whole war long beyond its expected end.

Armies, large when the war began, became larger. By 1914 most European nations compelled nearly all young men and even middle-aged men to undergo military training. As early as 1880, Germany and Austria, France and Russia, Italy and Japan had set up compulsory training. In earlier wars it had been impossible to field very large armies because the task of growing and buying the food and carting it to the army camps was beyond the carrying capacity of most nations. But by 1914 the more productive economies enabled vast numbers of men to be diverted to armies, and large numbers of women to be diverted from other work to munitions factories. Whereas in Napoleon's wars a fighting country could manage to spend just over 12 per cent of its total 'national product' on the war, now the main fighting nations could afford to spend almost 50 per cent on the war. In effect, the energy-harnessing and labour-saving changes of the previous hundred years released, in the opening months of the war, vast numbers of people for the making and firing of guns.

Casualties in the first four months of the war were far higher than expected. On the western front, 8000 Belgian soldiers and 17 000

British had been killed along with a total of 85 000 Germans. These deaths were dwarfed by the French death toll of 300 000. For every foreign soldier killed on French soil, four French soldiers were killed. To this sombre list had to be added the army of the wounded as well as the deaths on the Russian or eastern front.

Day after day there was consternation in thousands of homes as relatives of a soldier heard the knock at the door and learned the news of his sudden death from a telegraph messenger, postman, pastor or priest. This was no consolation for the next-door family whose sons were fighting at the front. Soldiers whose lives were spared in 1914 were in higher danger in 1915, because the barrage of artillery and the chatter of machine guns had become deadlier.

While civilians in many lands, all the way from New Zealand to Poland, from French Senegal to Newfoundland, began to dread the posting of the lists of the dead in the newspapers or on church doors, many observers found a heightened interest in simple things and relished the renewing cycle of the seasons. French women who kept diaries relished the day of the new spring when they heard the season's first nightingale and cuckoo sing, Austrians noticed the first crocus appearing in the wet grass, and Italians saw the flowering red of the hawksbeard in the high pastures. The novelist D.H. Lawrence noted in his *Journals* for 7 February 1916 the strong wind and the waves thundering on the English coast and the new scents in the fresh air – 'as if new blood were rising'. He asked himself: 'What does it matter about that seething scrimmage of mankind in Europe?'

GALLIPOLI – A VANISHED PRIZE

The war was laced with turning points, with opportunities lost or seized. Gallipoli was such a turning point. A Turkish peninsula, it commanded the entrance to that short and narrow seaway, the Dardanelles, which connected the Mediterranean Sea and the Black Sea. Less than 27 miles long, the seaway was almost like a bottle-neck, and at one point near Chanak it was barely a mile in width.

Before the war the Germans, realising the seaway's importance, tried to control it by wooing Turkey as an ally. They reorganised the Turkish army which, though courageous, had suffered defeats in recent wars. They gave naval support by stationing one of the world's finest battle cruisers, *Goeben*, within the harbour of Constantinople, in sight of the magnificent German embassy. Brilliantly lit at night, her powerful guns admired by passengers sitting in passing ferries, the warship was like a floating cheque promising everything that poor Turkey needed. Germany's cheque was successful. Less than a week before the war, Germany and Turkey secretly signed their military alliance. Since the Turkish empire ran far south, and almost overlooked the northern bank of the Suez Canal, this was another crucial seaway that Germany might seize in the event of war.

The Dardanelles was vital for Russia too. It could not use the Baltic Sea because its outlet was commanded by German ships and submarines. The Black Sea was therefore vital for Russia's navy and for the Russian grain ships which could supply some of the western allies with food. Increasingly, as the war went on, Russia needed arms and munitions from its western allies but how could they be shipped? As the map suggested, supply ships from England could sail past northern Norway to the Arctic port of Murmansk,

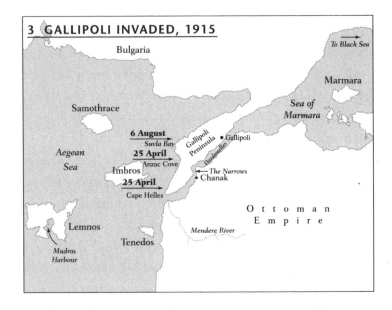

3 GALLIPOLI INVADED, 1915

Bulgaria

To Black Sea

Marmara

Sea of
Marmara

Samothrace

6 August
Suvla Bay

Gallipoli
Peninsula
• Gallipoli

Aegean
Sea

25 April
Anzac Cove

Imbros

Dardanelles

← *The Narrows*
• Chanak

25 April
Cape Helles

O t t o m a n
E m p i r e

Lemnos

Mendere River

Tenedos

*Mudros
Harbour*

and indeed whole convoys were to sail that bleak route in the next world war. But in 1915 Russia had not yet built a railway out of Murmansk, not even a road fit for wagons, and so Murmansk was useless. Admittedly the heartland of Russia could be reached from the faraway Pacific coast but that link was the longest railway in the world. It was a single track most of the way, and even 120 locomotives working day and night along its entire length could deliver only a trickle of war supplies to Moscow. The terminus of the railway, the Pacific port of Vladivostok, began to amass imported stocks of barbed wire, ammunition and other essential materials, all waiting for locomotives to carry them away to the distant Russian frontline where soldiers were already short of ammunition.

Russia was half strangled by its own unique geography and by the German navy's ability to control the mouth of the Baltic and, with

Turkish help, the Black Sea. Even St Petersburg and its high chimney stacks was hurt by the sea blockade. Once the war began, its factories and foundries were short of coal, which hitherto had been imported in Baltic ships. The leaders of the Russian Revolution, three years later, were to be aided by the economic dislocation stemming from the long, wartime blockade.

Early in 1915 the Dardanelles became crucial. Britain and France urgently needed a way of sending arms and munitions to Russia which was rich in soldiers but desperately short of booming heavy guns, light machine-guns, rifles and ammunition, and even winter uniforms. The huge Russian army had been likened to a giant steamroller, not easily set in motion, but decisive when at last it rolled. But in the first year of the war the steamroller began to roll and then began to halt.

It was pointless enlisting more Russians unless each could be handed a rifle or, even better, a machine-gun. If only more arms and munitions could be procured, the Russians would field a huge and effective army and so force the Germans, in self-defence, to divert hundreds of train-loads of troops from the western front to the eastern front. Then the outcome of the war could be changed on both fronts.

Britain, with all its naval strength, began to toy with the idea of capturing the Dardanelles. It might then conquer Constantinople, the capital of Turkey and the heart of its armaments industry, and so reopen the sea route to Russia. Such an attack seemed easy. Only three years previously, Italian torpedo boats, during a short war against Turkey, had actually entered the straits of the Dardanelles. Over-confidently the British navy made its own ambitious plans, first bombarding the Turkish forts near the mouth of the Dardanelles. The attack was a costly failure.

The Turks took fright. The naval attack seemed so likely to be followed by a land invasion, that they initially resolved to transfer their capital city from Constantinople to the railway terminus of Ankara, far inland. In January 1915 only two Turkish divisions guarded the Dardanelles, but by April six divisions were on guard, and moreover the forts themselves had been strengthened.

The Turks accomplished this partly because the British and French, somewhat complacent, did not hide their own massive preparations slowly going ahead not far from the Turkish coast. From 11 April, a fortnight before the invasion, the immense harbour of Mudros on the Greek island of Lemnos was – according to the official British war history – 'now so crowded with vessels of every imaginable description, from the majestic *Queen Elizabeth* to the humble North Sea trawler, and from the proud Atlantic liner to the dirtiest of Thames tugs' that another harbour on another island had to be found for the next convoys of arriving troopships. And all this activity was reported on daily by a Turkish army aircraft which, quite unopposed, flew over the harbour and then hurried back to Turkey with the latest news. An Anglo-French invasion, if one happened, could no longer be a surprise.

Finally, on Sunday 25 April 1915, the British, French, Australian and New Zealand forces landed at beaches on the Gallipoli peninsula and gained a perilous foothold near the Dardanelles. Casualties were heavy. The fighting was soon deadlocked. Later the British and French sent reinforcements which, if landed earlier, might have helped conquer the high ground. Meanwhile a Russian army had been assembled at the Black Sea port of Odessa in readiness for a separate attack on Constantinople. Eventually this army was diverted elsewhere.

The Turks were under acute pressure. Attacked by the British–French forces near the Dardanelles they were also threatened by a large Russian army near the Caucasus mountains. On 27 May 1915, just one month after the invasion of Gallipoli, the Turkish government concluded that its country also harboured a dangerous internal enemy. It resolved to deport the Christian Armenians, with the exception of those living in the port-cities of Constantinople and Izmir where surveillance was easy. Slowly the Armenians carrying their few portable possessions were driven from eastern Anatolia towards the Syrian desert. Along the roads men, women and children were killed by Turkish soldiers and civilians, while even more died of sickness and hunger. The death toll of Turkish Armenians is usually estimated as 600 000 but some historians, raising the estimate to 1 million, enlist the name of genocide. Adolf Hitler in 1939 was to chew over this terrible expulsion and to express the vague wish that it should be repeated against his chosen enemies.

After fighting the Turks on a shallow strip of coastal hills and beaches for eight months, the British and French concluded that victory in the Dardanelles was impossible. Near the end of the year, night after night, their soldiers were silently evacuated and shipped away. At last Gallipoli was deserted, except for the Turkish fortifications and all the graves.

If the Allies had succeeded in capturing the Dardanelles and Constantinople, they could have sent weekly convoys of military supplies to the ill-armed Russians. The outcome of the war, for Russia, might have been different. But this potential turning point in the war did not eventuate.

A BLOOD-TINTED RIVER

Close to the border of France and Belgium flowed the River Somme, a quiet stream that touring cyclists, on the eve of the war, barely glanced at when they rode across. Close to the Somme, two years later, a vast army of British and French soldiers was quietly assembling in trenches and dugouts, in tent cities behind the lines, and inside shelled, half-ruined villages, in readiness to fight one of the fiercest battles in the history of the world. Here the Allied soldiers, many of whom had come from abandoned Gallipoli, hoped to break through the lines of German trenches and artillery posts, and open up a war which had become static and deadlocked. Quantities of heavy guns and howitzers, machine guns and rifles were ready. A week before the planned battle, the Germans guessed what was about to happen. Their lines were now bombarded incessantly. Against their narrow stretch of the western front were fired about 1.5 million shells.

Soon after sunrise on the morning of 1 July 1916, the British attack began. Tens of thousands of soldiers, hidden in trenches, began to climb short ladders to the top and advance towards the German lines. Behind the British trenches were reserves of trained soldiers, and in their turn they came forward. Overloaded like backpackers, carrying their own food and ammunition and water, they walked, ran and stumbled over earth that was scarred with craters and blocked by barbed wire. Here and there the defending Germans were driven back or killed, enabling a whole line of trenches to be captured. Ahead lay other trenches, fortified posts, and all those heavy German guns that were landing shells on the advancing soldiers.

The British generals had little idea of how the attack was proceeding, so fragile and intermittent were the messages they received. Their hope was that armaments and sheer manpower would win out and that, some time on that opening day or even the next, the Germans would be routed. But the next day came, and the next week too. In most places the Germans held firm. Meanwhile, out in no-man's-land were thousands of dead bodies or fragments of bodies, and occasionally freshly wounded soldiers bleeding to death, for the hope of rescue was small during that hour when their life could be saved if they were carried to waiting field-doctors and nurses.

The Battle of the Somme went on for more than four months. Waves of soldiers emerged from the trenches to renew the attack, the guns roared, and casualties mounted. The battle formally ended on 18 November 1916. The British casualties were counted at 419654; and when the French and the Germans were added, the tally of dead and wounded in that one long battle was close to 1 million. The total would have been higher but for the fact that ammunition was virtually exhausted on certain days. Distant steelworks, copper refineries and munitions factories just could not keep up the supply needed by both sides for such thunderous days of firing.

The outcome of the war depended partly on what the rival munitions factories could provide. Germany at the outbreak of war was Europe's leading maker of chemicals, vital machine tools, and a range of items from ball bearings to spark plugs and optical munitions. Britain and France, unable to match Germany's industrial might, had to import heavily from the United States. Without American supplies, Britain and France might have lost the war during the first year. More than any previous war, the First World War would be won in factories, steelworks, coalmines, munitions shops, and shipbuilding yards.

Germany set out to intercept cargo ships carrying American war materials to Europe. It built more and more of the big cigar-shaped submarines equipped with diesel engines and capable of making quiet undersea voyages at night. The submarine had the advantage of concealment and surprise: it could fire deadly torpedoes at nearby ships which had no time to change their course. In September 1914, on the sea between England and Holland, three British cruisers steaming in line just three miles apart were surprised by the German submarine *U9*. The three cruisers were sunk by torpedoes, with a loss of life almost equalling that of the giant passenger liner *Titanic* when it had collided with an iceberg just two years previously.

As the German shipyards increased their tempo, brand-new submarines appeared in the east Atlantic, North Sea and even the Mediterranean. Passenger liners and cargo ships, more than British warships, were their target. One sensational attack was on the ocean liner *Lusitania* which, nearing the end of her voyage from the United States, was close to the south coast of Ireland, her decks crowded with women and children, on the afternoon of 7 May 1915. A German submarine suddenly fired two torpedoes at the *Lusitania*. The German commander, from his submarine, watched the great ocean liner slowly disappear. That evening, 1198 women, men and children were missing.

The world outcry was loud, and thereafter the Germans resolved to spare passenger liners and neutral ships. Nonetheless, neutral vessels were sometimes sunk. Nothing did more to propel the United States from a neutral nation to a fighting nation than the German submarines and their intermittent attacks on American ships, especially in the first months of 1917.

On land, diseases increased the casualties. On the western front the battles were fought on heavily manured farm fields. Microbes infected the soldiers' wounds and many died from tetanus – also known as lockjaw – until a new serum was developed. To the camps housing war-prisoners, especially in eastern Europe, came epidemics of typhus. For perhaps the first time in a war, nervous disorders – widely known as 'shellshock' – were widespread but were not easily treated. Fifty years later, living in asylums and hospitals as far apart as Auckland, Salzburg and San Francisco, were men whose memory had been snuffed by shellshock. After gas was used as a weapon, fired in shells, yet another illness affected hundreds of thousands of men on both sides.

Amoebic dysentery, though common in North Africa, did not rage in Europe until the summer of 1915 when it swept through trenches in Gallipoli. There most of the British soldiers suffered, for dysentery was spread by the swarms of flies, and only after the flies vanished in cold weather did the disease diminish. Indeed 'dysentery was one of the deciding factors in the failure of the Gallipoli campaign', wrote Lieutenant-Colonel Arthur F. Hurst, a medical specialist. Bacillary dysentery – spread by flies from the latrines – was common in summer in east Prussia and the wide eastern front, and in the later battles fought in the warmth of Salonika, Mesopotamia and Palestine. In

Macedonia in the summer of 1916 nearly every soldier suffered from the swarms of malarial mosquitoes. In Mesopotamia many soldiers suffered from heat stroke 'which was very nearly always fatal' until special heat-stroke stations were set up. In the four years of the First World War, one soldier died from disease to every four soldiers killed by bullets, shrapnel and high explosives. Such a low death rate from disease was almost a miracle, by the standards of most wars.

While war killed on a frightening scale, it also saved lives – long after the killing was over. The war promoted the art and technique of blood transfusion which had been boldly tried in at least four operations during the American Civil War in the 1860s. In the following half-century, a few North American surgeons became skilled in transfusing blood, usually using the blood from a member of the same family. In 1916 on the western front a Canadian surgeon taught this lifesaving skill, and a year later the arrival of American surgeons with their troops increased the practice. On both sides of the trenches, the lives of tens of thousands of wounded soldiers were saved by new anaesthetics, blood transfusions and surgical techniques.

THE DILEMMA OF NEUTRAL NATIONS

The title of world war now conveys the impression that every nation of substance took part, but at Christmas 1914 – nearly five months after the war commenced – people in at least 10 European nations could thank themselves that they were not part of the war. The three Scandinavian nations did not fight. Holland remained neutral while Belgium, next door, was engulfed. It is easy to forget that a nation can be neutral only if its neighbours give their consent. Belgium wished to be neutral in 1914 but the Germans had other plans and gobbled it up, using it as their main military gateway into France.

Spain remained neutral while Portugal performed the juggler's act of being half neutral and half a British ally until 1916 when it finally received a declaration of war from Germany. Italy remained neutral for a time, and there the war memorials of white marble in thousands of village squares proclaim a chronology that at first sight seems strange: they mourn the Italian soldiers who died in the Great War of 1915–18. Bulgaria, Romania and Greece were even later in joining the fighting. Of the few big nations outside Europe, two of the greatest – the United States and China – were not to join the war until 1917, and China's role remained small. Latin America, too, had many neutral nations until the war approached its end. But the scattered British dominions, commonwealths and colonies were in the war from the start, some suffering massive casualties in relation to their small populations.

In a war fought with blockades as well as weapons, even neutral nations felt the pinch. Tourism, more important to the Swiss than to any other European peoples, was dislocated. In the Alps the keepers of hotels and boarding houses, and the housemaids too, were dismayed to see the empty beds and dining rooms. The Swiss village of Zermatt, nestling at the foot of the Matterhorn, employed 170 mountain guides to attend to the tourists who arrived for the last peacetime summer, but now no mountain guides were needed. Switzerland in peacetime had imported part of its grain: in wartime it tried to reduce the consumption of grain and flour by decreeing that shops could sell only stale bread.

As an army of Swiss had to guard the frontiers – an invasion was feasible – the scarcity of rural labour was partly met by teenagers.

As vegetables became scarce, boys dug up the once-pretty public gardens and planted potatoes and parsnips. As Switzerland mined no coal, travel on trains had to be restricted. The paddle-steamers and their trail of black smoke vanished from some lakes. The postman was seen less often.

The war gave social reformers the chance for which they had been waiting. The temperance movement, strong amongst women, won millions of allies, and persuaded the United States and Australia to limit the sale of alcohol. Several of the royal families now drank their patriotic toasts in lemonade. Russia banned the sale of vodka.

In the western world the campaign for votes for women gained strength from the war. Women pointed out that they were manning munitions and chemical factories and that their sons, brothers and boyfriends or husbands were dying at the front; and yet they themselves did not possess the right to vote for peace or war. Parry's now-famous tune *Jerusalem* was first sung in the Albert Hall in London in 1916, at a huge rally in support of women's suffrage. In 1919 the vote was granted to the women of Germany, Sweden and Poland, and in the following year American women were allowed to vote at a presidential election for the first time. For most or all of the women of Britain, France and several other longstanding democracies the right to vote was still to be won, but the war had boosted their campaign. In New Zealand, which was the first country in the world to grant a vote to women, the right to stand for parliament at last arrived.

Meanwhile the fighting went on. When would it end? The rumbles of discontent suggested that it might end on the home front rather than the battle front.

5

REVOLT IN PETROGRAD:

PEACE IN PARIS

By the end of 1916, many of the fighting forces were experiencing grave discontent, almost to the point of mutiny. Casualties were soaring, the trenches in winter were abominable, the food was monotonous, and the goal of decisive victory no longer seemed possible for either side. Weak morale in the armed forces infected the civilian population: and the letters written by the soldiers – even when censored – injected further doubts at home. The army that was the first to disintegrate might determine the outcome of the war.

THE REVOLUTIONS

Russian forces were the first to wilt. Their loss of officers in the first months of war had been high. They were unable to receive, because of the blockade in the Baltic and the Dardanelles, adequate war supplies from their overseas allies. Many Russian soldiers did not possess a rifle or boots. The shortage of rifles was matched by a want of light and heavy ammunition. At various points on the long front-line extending from the Baltic to the Black Sea, Russians were being slowly driven back by the Germans and Austro-Hungarians, each of whom controlled a long part of the eastern front. Warsaw was lost; vast areas of farmland near the Baltic and in the Ukraine fell into German hands; and the horde of Russian peasants that fled east and had to be fed was a drain on a disorganised bureaucracy. The press in Paris and London rarely reported the disturbing news that the soldiers of their ally were content to become prisoners of war, and that the Russian armies had already lost close to a million men simply through desertion.

The weaknesses in the army aggravated the mood of rumbling fear and discontent at home. The Russian people on the whole were intensely patriotic but their nation now faced the prospect of losing a third major war in succession. Having lost the Crimean War in the 1850s, and the war against Japan in 1905, it now faced a more ominous defeat. No major nation, in the last few hundred years, had experienced such a triple defeat.

The royal family, the traditional focus of loyalty, disappointed the loyalists. Czar Nicholas II, now commander-in-chief of the armed forces, was shedding his popularity with speed. His wife Alexandra, increasingly unpopular, was the willing captive of the mesmerising monk Rasputin, for her sickly son seemed to respond to Rasputin's healing powers. In the cities supplies of food and fuel were erratic. Late in 1916 the industrial upheavals in Russian cities became frequent. Initially expressing grievances in the workplace, many strikes now expressed a wider political discontent. While it was risky for groups to voice hostile political opinions, it was legal for them to express their political discontent by striking.

The disruption of daily economic tasks, with so many men at the front, became acute. Inflation galloped ahead of wages. Between 1913 and 1917 the price of flour multiplied by three, salt by five, and butter by more than eight. Many families were hungrier than in peacetime, partly because the railways could not handle the carriage of food as well as war supplies. The secret police – the ears of the government – reported privately that demoralisation amongst working people resembled the turbulent mood they had noted during the failed revolution of 1904–05.

Many Russians sought solutions for their nation's crises. In St Petersburg in December 1916, after the monk Rasputin was assassinated by royalists, it was hoped that sanity would return to the royal palaces. The czar, however, could be almost deaf to sane advice. The czarina herself was still praying at the grave of Rasputin.

In that bleak winter a victory seemed far away. Riots broke out in Petrograd, and even women – not often seen in street protests – staged a long march on International Women's Day in March 1917. A common sight was the long queues of housewives and servants and children, patiently waiting in sleet and snow outside the bakehouses in the hope of buying bread. Admittedly food was scarce in Britain and Germany too, but they had wisely devised rationing systems embracing every citizen. Russia was different. Skilled in rationing freedom, it was unable to cope with the simpler task of rationing flour and sugar so that nearly all people might have their share. Administrative ineptitude, in many corners of national life, was driving the discontent.

The czar tried to suppress the signs of revolution by summoning loyal officers and soldiers from the front. The railwaymen refused to carry them. In March 1917 he was forced to abdicate. A coalition of citizens, including one of Russia's richest men, formed a new ministry in the hope of winning the war and rejuvenating the nation. Reformers rather than revolutionaries, they offered hope. Their main opponents, members of the tightly organised Bolshevik party, resolved that hope should not be on offer except from their own hands.

The Bolsheviks' leader, the intellectual known as Lenin – a pseudonym he adopted in 1901 – had been in exile, living for varying periods in England, France, Austria and Switzerland. Stocky and fit, slightly smaller than average height, with a large forehead, determined jaw, and a gift for forceful prose, he devised cunning tactics for his party and took advantage of the few windfalls that fell. It so happened that his Bolsheviks had long been viewed by the secret police as more predictable and tameable than other radicals, while Lenin himself was viewed as a quarreller, a leader unlikely to unite the socialists. Seen as a loser, he and his party could be quietly helped. At a crucial conference held in the Austro-Hungarian city of Prague in 1912, Lenin was present and prominent, whereas his Russian radical opponents were actually prevented by the political police from leaving Russia and so could not attend.

In such odd ways was the flame of Lenin kept burning, though he himself did not yet dare to venture back to Russia. By 1917 the Bolsheviks were strong in the army and the factories, where they controlled hundreds of the workers' councils known as 'soviets'. It was time for Lenin to come home.

In April 1917, with Germany's money and official blessing, he and a few colleagues travelled in a guarded railway carriage from their exile in Switzerland through wartime Germany, across the Baltic by ferry, so to Russian Finland and then by train to St Petersburg. The German intelligence service hoped that Lenin, back on his home soil, would stir up revolution and so force Russia to retire from the war. Lenin was happy to play his allotted role.

His return to St Petersburg, and his wisdom and strategy, were welcomed by the jubilant Bolsheviks. Guiding the political manoeuvres, he worked diligently to set up what he called 'a revolutionary-democratic dictatorship of the proletariat and peasantry'. His hope was to achieve a revolution at home and then stir up revolutions abroad. To continue the war was of no interest to him: indeed the war was a dangerous diversion. For this reason the German government had secretly given him money and sent him home. His success was in its interests.

Kerensky, the minister for war in the new government, hoped that one last effort, one last appeal to Russian patriotism, would produce victories on the eastern front. He went with General Brusiloff by automobile along the frontlines in the hope of rousing the Russian soldiers to repel the enemy in one last triumphant offensive. From an improvised platform they would speak, while thousands of soldiers – what Kerensky called 'the discontented, hesitating mass of armed human beings in gray' – crowded around. At this stage huge numbers of Russia's rank and file soldiers were still willing to die for their country and even to join special 'Battalions of Death', while an opposing band of their colleagues, now 'dominated by Bolshevik agitators' wished to lay down arms and begin to build a communist society.

The Russian counterattack failed. The Germans continued to advance, capturing the Baltic city of Riga and meeting less and less resistance. Many Russian soldiers simply threw away their rifles. Many had no rifle to throw away.

In France and Britain there was alarm that the Bolsheviks might take control of Russia and withdraw its forces from the war. But perhaps the scales could be tipped if the big numbers of Russian Jews, some of whom were powerful in the new political movements, were persuaded to continue fighting the war against Germany. A persuasive offer was made. On 2 November 1917, just before the Bolsheviks seized power, the British foreign secretary, Arthur Balfour, announced that at the end of the war his country would look favourably on fostering a new Jewish national homeland in Palestine. Jewish delegates were sent to St Petersburg to spread the good news of what would later be called the Balfour Declaration. The Middle East would never be the same again, for Balfour kept his promise.

The commander of the Russian forces tried to put down the Bolsheviks and other disrupters who, on their more effective days, virtually controlled the streets of the capital city. He called on his shock troops to restore order, but the army was no longer under control.

Lenin, who in the turmoil had retreated to a hiding place in Finland, prepared to exploit the chaos that he had helped to create. He returned in disguise to St Petersburg, his beard shorn and a wig cloaking his bald head. He knew that he was in danger of being arrested, or even shot, on the eve of the Bolshevik coup that could be his day of triumph. On the evening of 6 November – it was still

24 October in the Russian calendar – he wrote an urgent message to senior comrades: 'We must at all costs, this very evening, this very night, arrest the government.'

Overnight his men – prepared by the skilled Leon Trotsky – took over railway stations, post offices, the telephone exchange, banks, electrical powerhouses, crucial bridges crossing the canals and rivers, and all the nerve centres of the capital city. In Moscow the Kremlin was captured. In control of many cities Lenin formally became the head of the first Council of People's Commissars.

Though Lenin had won, the danger of counterattack by his enemies was high. The peasants – and they formed the great majority of the Russian people – were likely to oppose his communist government. Lenin was a step ahead. He had already promised free farmland to the peasants though he did not believe in private ownership of property. By granting them land and at the same time paying no compensation to the big landlords whose estates were confiscated, he delighted the peasants and also the city radicals. So the communists, as they now called themselves, became the promoters of rural capitalism.

Lenin was determined to extract Russia from the war. He wanted peace so that he could build a revolutionary society that would inspire socialists throughout Europe. Even so, his signing of the peace treaty with Germany and Turkey at the town of Brest-Litovsk in western Russia in March 1918 was a humiliating blow to Russian patriots. Parts of Russian territory passed into the hands of Germany, Romania and Turkey. For a time even the Ukraine and Georgia were lost though they were eventually recaptured. Soon Russian Poland, Russian Finland and the three Baltic provinces of Latvia, Estonia and Lithuania became independent nations. A vast expanse of grain land, now outside Lenin's control, aggravated the scarcity of food in the new land of experiments.

THE AMERICANS TILT THE SCALES

The revolution in Russia delighted Germany. That one of its three major opponents had put down its arms was the most heartening news heard in Berlin since 1914. The peace in the east would permit a huge number of German soldiers to be diverted to the western front where at last they might win the war against France.

In France the first enthusiasm for war had been draining away. By the middle of 1917 close to half of the French divisions felt reluctant to fight unless their grievances were remedied, and unless their food and leave-allowances were improved. Soldiers reaching Paris on leave carried copies of radical newspapers and talked of mutiny. In November 1917 the Italian army, with the onset of another icy winter in the foothills of the alps, almost rebelled. Sections of almost every other allied army were, at times, low in morale. On both sides, the soldiers were risking their lives in a hail of shrapnel and bullets, with no visible effect on the outcome of the war.

In these months of turmoil in Russia, another uncertainty was the United States. Its president, Woodrow Wilson, was unpredictable. Would he quickly pour soldiers across the Atlantic to fight the Germans or move cautiously, like a half-spectator, preparing painstakingly for war before selecting a major role?

Of high talent, Wilson was the son of a Presbyterian clergyman and an adoring mother whose slightly fussing ways were supplemented by those of her two daughters who were older than the juvenile president-to-be. He grew up in the southern states during and after the American Civil War, but his talent was not immediately visible because of childhood illnesses. At Princeton University he showed signs of originality, a quality that some university examiners do not always recognise, but no definite signs of brilliance. Almost becoming a lawyer in Atlanta, Georgia, he eventually went back as a teacher to his old university where in 1902 he was chosen as its president. A secular preacher, almost in his father's footsteps, Wilson showed fluency, sincerity, empathy and a slight outward nervousness that, disguising the supreme confidence of his own opinions, attracted his listeners. As a Democrat he became the Governor of New Jersey in 1910. Less than two years later he won the race for the presidency of the United States. In politics he had risen like a rocket – a rocket that, he sometimes hinted, was guided by God.

Standing again for the presidency in 1916 he won. He tried to keep his country neutral in the war, in the face of provocation from German submarines, but Germany provoked him too often. In April 1917 Congress agreed to declare war against Germany. America's army was small – it had been no larger than the Serbian army just four years previously – and so much recruiting and training was needed before the first American division could reach the frontline in France six months after Wilson's declaration of war. At the start of 1918, which would prove to be the final year of war, a mere 175 000 American soldiers had reached France.

Germany still had an opportunity to win the war. After the Russians sued for peace, Germany was able to transfer soldiers from the eastern to the western front where it launched a fierce offensive that advanced within 70 kilometres of Paris before coming to a halt.

Thereafter its chance of victory slowly slipped away. In August 1918 an Anglo-French offensive drove the Germans back, and that victory was heightened by the assurance that nearby were more and more American soldiers, either fighting or soon to fight. Perhaps no single fact did more to convince the Germans that the war was lost than the presence of an American army now totalling 1 500 000 and capable, if the war went on, of tipping the scales in the fighting. The US army was a decisive factor in the defeat of Germany – decisive for what it might do rather than for what it had done.

By September 1918 Germany's partners decided that they'd had enough. Bulgaria signed a separate armistice. The Austro-Hungarian monarchy was in splinters, and the Yugoslavs and Czechs and Hungarians were breaking away to form their own nations. At the end of October, the Turks signed an armistice. A few days later the Austro-Hungarian offer to surrender was accepted. As Germany's own allies disappeared, enterprising nations especially from South America became Germany's latest opponents, perhaps hoping to secure bargains at the peace table.

Germany was now alone. Its soldiers were still fighting bravely on the western front, but in the first 10 days of November 1918 civilian life in Germany was fracturing under the tensions, privations and loss of hope. At the harbour of Kiel, German sailors were mutinying; in several cities the strikes were crippling munitions factories and shipyards; in Bavaria a socialist revolution succeeded; and in Berlin the Kaiser Wilhelm II abdicated. On 11 November, a day of ignominy for Germany but long prayed for elsewhere, an armistice was signed, and at 11 a.m. the war ceased in Europe. Three days later it ceased in German East Africa where the fighting against the British had been intense for four years. During the following days the news of the armistice slowly reached those cargo ships that either carried no wireless or were too far from land to pick up a transmitted message.

THE BATTLE AROUND THE PEACE TABLE

Peace had arrived, but what did it mean? Every nation wanted peace, but on its own terms. More than a year before the end of the war, the peace plans had been sprouting. In August 1917 Pope Benedict XV hoped that the coming peace would be based on the national boundaries that existed before the war. In December 1917 Britain's Labour Party, still a minority party, argued that the war was no longer justified unless it guided the world toward democracy and a peace based so firmly 'that there should be henceforth on earth no more war'.

On 8 January 1918 in Washington, President Wilson put forward his 'Fourteen Points': one wit said that only a professor would require as many as fourteen points. Wilson wanted a permanent global parliament, a League of Nations, to act as the future peacemaker and the healer: he did not originate this idea but he gave it momentum. He wanted a soft peace on the loser, not a harsh peace. He hoped that the Germans, if they were promised a fair and lenient peace, might promptly summon home their submarines. Wilson wished to break up empires, where possible, and liberate the minorities who lived in the Austro-Hungarian and Ottoman empires. As for the victorious nations, he silently hoped to clip the wings of their colonial empires.

Eight months later, at the opera house in New York, with thousands of eager faces in front of him, and the end of the war almost in sight, he elaborated a viewpoint that clearly would not impress the French. Implying that France especially should forgive and forget, he called for a lenient peace treaty. He called on the big winning nations, once the war was ended, to dispense 'impartial justice' and disown economic selfishness. For a few months, in the eyes of hundreds of millions of people, he seemed to speak for most of the peoples of the world and even for many of the soldiers who lay silent in their graves.

One month after the end of the war, the president set out for Europe where he stepped ashore on 13 December 1918. Hailed as the statesman unfolding his remedy for the sick world, he was welcomed in France and then England, even by those who did not quite understand that his message conflicted with their own attitudes. T.S. Eliot, the young American poet living in London, watched Wilson approaching Buckingham Palace through a corridor of rising applause and waving flags – an 'extraordinary and inspiring' spectacle – and explained to his mother by letter that all the nations 'trust us as they trust no other'. When Wilson reached Rome and Milan, he saw banners proclaim, 'Welcome to the God of Peace'. When at last the mighty one reached the peace conference in Paris, with almost a halo shining around his dignified head, only one thing was missing. His halo was not visible to the other major statesmen. The 77-year-old Clemenceau, the voice of France, while courteous and even warm to the visitor, thought his message had nothing for the bruised people of France.

Leaders of the victorious nations, assembled in Paris for the long negotiations, were less interested than Wilson in the idea of a fair and just peace. Having carried the burden and endured the heartbreaks of a long war they wanted massive compensation from Germany and Austria. Their peoples, perhaps even more than their leaders, wanted revenge. They agreed with the British politician Sir Eric Geddes who, likening the German nation to a lemon, insisted that it must be squeezed 'until the pips squeak'. In Paris the winners wished to slice territory from the heartland of Germany which eventually they did; they wanted to take away all her colonies and eventually they did. Confiscating her navy and disbanding her army, they imposed on Germany a huge fine, called 'reparations', to defray part of the cost of the war. As Germany in 1871 had imposed a harsh peace on defeated France, this new peace treaty, signed at Versailles in 1919, echoed the same punitive spirit. The punishment of 1919, however, was more severe.

The peace treaty insisted – not very logically and not very fairly – that Germany and Kaiser Wilhelm II were solely to blame for the war. Many Germans were entitled to feel a little cheated. They vividly remembered that before they signed the armistice Wilson himself had promised them a fair peace, and that he had firmly announced that the United States felt no 'jealousy of German greatness'. In essence, President Wilson's eloquent tongue had made a series of sincere but irresponsible promises that his tied hands proved powerless to deliver.

Fairness perhaps was not to be expected in the peace treaty. The war had been long and terrible; sacrifices of human life had been immense; and the financial cost of the war was incalculable. If Germany had won the war it would have been equally vindictive, sternly blaming France and Russia and Britain for causing the war and therefore demanding the highest of penalties.

Meanwhile Europe rejoiced in peace, but it was not like the old peace of 1914. War had disrupted the trade links, ruined thousands of rural villages, devastated vast areas of pasture and farmland, killed millions of cattle, shaken hundreds of railways and road bridges, and sunk more cargo ships than had existed in the whole world in 1900. Dislocation kicked its way into every facet of daily life, especially in eastern Europe. In 1919 milk was so scarce in cities that little children were dying, and the diet of most people contained no fat. In many districts no crops were sown. In east Poland, out towards Pinsk, people were 'living upon roots, grass, acorns and heather'. Much of their bread was baked from acorns and a pinch of rye flour. In the first postwar winter many people owned no boots or shoes and could buy no fuel to burn in their stoves because the war-damaged railways carried little coal from the mines to Polish or Czech cities. Prisoners of war returned with typhus which spread amongst the malnourished people. These were the observations penned at length by the British director of humanitarian relief, Sir William Goode, who worked in eastern Europe in 1919. He sensed the contrast between 'the nervous rich and the starving poor', especially in Vienna.

At the same time the whole world suffered from something more devastating. A new strain of influenza, reportedly spread at first by the mingling of European, American and African soldiers on the congested battlefields of France in 1918, swept around the globe. It surfaced in Aboriginal camps in remote parts of Australia and in jungle settlements on Africa and South America. It killed millions in India. It appeared on ships at sea. Called the Spanish flu, it killed more people than had the First World War.

In all the discussions and table-thumping at the prolonged peace conference in Paris, Woodrow Wilson was not as successful as in his earlier speeches. He liked abstract principles rather than chiselled compromises. Furthermore he was only one forceful voice amongst many, though at times his voice had its way. That the charter or constitution of the proposed League of Nations was called the Covenant, in the Presbyterian style, was one sign of his influence. Meanwhile his health began to fail under the strain. He could not sleep, he began to suspect his own staff of trickery. When his temperature rose high he was advised – advice not released to the press – that he had caught the Spanish influenza. Possibly he had experienced a stroke.

A peace treaty drawn up by many hands – and fists too – is inevitably a maze of compromises and a clash of principles. And once the peace treaty had been signed at Versailles, Wilson had to sell it to his own people. He had to persuade them that the League of Nations, about to be constituted, would help the United States as much as it would help Europe and the rest of the world. To a nation with a strong tradition of isolationism as well as interventionism, to a proud nation that had achieved much by its own efforts and wished to remain its own master, Wilson's League of Nations seemed a threat as much as a blessing.

Wilson returned home, confident that his own nation would wield the most influence in the League of Nations. Public opinion largely smiled on him, and 33 state governors supported him, but the doubters multiplied. He no longer was king in his own land, having lost control of both the senate and the congress. Touring the nation by train, shaking outstretched hands all the way across the country from the Atlantic cities to the harbour of San Diego on the Pacific, ardently addressing open-air audiences that were numbered in many thousands, he wore himself out. His cheek muscles began to twitch spasmodically. On 2 October 1919, back in Washington, he suffered a stroke and his left side was paralysed. His second wife Edith quietly accepted many of his civic responsibilities until, more than a year later, his four-year term of office was over. His legacy was a League of Nations that his own nation refused to join.

Meeting for the first time in 1920, the League of Nations seemed to be the lighthouse of the world. Its aim was to shine on a path ahead. It was to prevent wars and impose social justice, though on a humble scale. It was to protect the native peoples who lived under European rule, to wipe out the remnants of slavery, and to ease the lot of those who laboured hard day after day. It was like a parliament with two houses, a small powerful upper house or council that met more frequently, and a general assembly of all the member-nations meeting just once a year.

The inaugural council consisted of four regular members – Britain, France, Italy and Japan – supplemented by representatives elected from the assembly itself. The absence of the United States, China, the Soviet Union and Germany was a damaging blow to the prestige and influence of the council. Two of these four were absent simply because losers in the war had no right to join the new League of Nations. Moreover, in the assembly, the members were not representative of the wide world, being mainly European nations and their former colonies from across the seas. The British Empire was especially prominent, for the 29 initial members included Britain, Canada, Australia, New Zealand, South Africa and British India.

To solve disputes that might otherwise erupt into war was the goal by which the League was judged. At first that goal seemed attainable. The Finns and Swedes, at loggerheads over some Baltic islands, agreed that the League of Nations should adjudicate, and in due course they accepted the verdict awarding the islands to Finland. The border of Poland and Lithuania and the border of Albania were amongst other disputes. Not all were resolved satisfactorily. The more tantalising question was whether one of the big powers, finding itself at the heart of a dispute, would actually accept a verdict delivered by the League of Nations. Mussolini's Italy was to provide a sobering answer. In a dispute on the Greek island of Corfu in 1923, Italy initially thumbed its nose at the League of Nations. A decade later Japan, having invaded a corner of east Asia, poked out its tongue at the League of Nations. Mussolini, when warned by the League to end his war against Abyssinia, did not hear.

A BALANCE SHEET OF A GREAT WAR

The lists of war casualties were almost endless. Serbians, who perhaps triggered rather than caused the first outbreak of war, suffered the most. Of its males between the ages of 15 and 49, one in every four was killed during the war. For years to come the shortage of Serbian bridegrooms was heartbreaking to the young women. Turkey and France, Romania and Germany were the next of the heavy sufferers, losing 13 to 15 per cent of all their men, whether soldiers or civilians, who belonged to that same vulnerable age-group. Of the other fighting nations, Austria-Hungary lost 9 per cent, Italy lost 7 per cent, and Britain as a whole was closer to 6 per cent, though the death rate in Scotland was much higher. Russia's percentage of war deaths, at 5 per cent, was lower than might have been expected, falling just below New Zealand's and just ahead of Australia's, but then Russia withdrew early from the war. Canada, where most young French-Canadians refused to enlist, and the United States, which was late in entering the war, stood further down the table of death. Nobody could ever measure the talent lost to the world – the poets, statesmen, engineers, priests, union leaders, teachers, painters, architects, pilots on sea and air, surgeons, hospital matrons, and the silent statesmen of the next generation.

The war weakened Europe. The economic and political giant of the world had cut several of its own arteries. Its warring nations had incurred huge debts and had to meet them by selling off many of their outside investments. Even the winners were financial losers. Britain, which was the world's largest lender in 1914, surrendered much of its financial supremacy to the United States which hitherto had been in debt to Europe. France, a great financial power, lost wealth, and Germany lost even more. Meir, a Jewish prophet living in Asia Minor one century after the time of Christ, glimpsed a simple truth when he wrote: 'The tree itself supplies the handle of the axe which cuts it down.' Europe had been mutilated by its own axe, held in its own hands.

The large financial gainer was the United States, which had played a lesser role in the war and had built up its own industries while its European competitors were absorbed in the fighting. Japan was another gainer: for the first time in many centuries an east Asian nation was honoured as a world leader, and at the Paris peace conference Japan took its seat as one of the great five. Its territorial rewards for taking part on the winning side were few, and it also struggled to achieve its ambition of inserting in the Covenant of the

League of Nations a clause that promised fair and just treatment to all 'alien' citizens who resided in nations that were actually members of the League.

The ostensible aim of the delicate clause was not primarily to permit unfettered immigration by Japanese and Chinese and others to a variety of more spacious and prosperous nations, but rather to help those Japanese who, living in California, were prevented by a recent state law from owning land. But Japan also had in mind a possible flow of Japanese immigrants to other lands. When invited to disown such a wish, its delegates refused. A clause affirming a version of racial equality was not added to the Covenant.

Nonetheless Japan was accepted in the ranks of the mightiest nations, and two years later displayed its curiosity about them by allowing for the first time an heir to its throne to travel outside Japan. In March 1921, with some trepidation, the Japanese people farewelled Crown Prince Hirohito as he sailed away in a battleship to Portsmouth, calling at Hong Kong and five other British Empire ports on the way. At the end of three weeks in Britain, when he was about to depart to France, Belgium, Holland and Italy, he announced: 'It has been my happiness to see something of almost every side of the national life and institutions.'

While rewarding for Japan, the war was sobering for the west. It proved to be a severe blow to the west's long era of material and spiritual optimism and its belief in human progress, a belief so ardently held in many quarters and circles in 1900. But the war was not a crushing blow. In some ways it extended the faith in progress because the infant, socialist Russia became a fountain of hope to hundreds of millions of people in many countries. Here was one of the most unusual experiments in human history, conducted inside a vast nation.

For socialists, the war seemed even more a turning point then, and for the following half-century, than it seems today. Across Africa, South America and Asia, many young radicals marvelled at the post-war experiments in Russia. Nehru, a young Indian – and later prime minister – was inspired by the new Soviet Union: 'I had no doubt that the Soviet revolution had advanced human society by a great leap and had lit a bright flame which could not be smothered, and that it had laid the foundation for the "new civilization" towards which the world would advance.'

6

UTOPIA AND NIGHTMARE

All over the literate world, people opened their morning and evening newspapers and looked eagerly or apprehensively to see what was happening in Russia. One of the most extraordinary creations in human history, communism was viewed by millions as a foretaste of their future. Perhaps the whole globe, it was thought, would eventually become communist. Even if Russia remained a lonely experiment it was bound to influence the outside world. It was not only the world's largest nation in area but also the third most populous, holding even more people than sleeping Africa.

The new Bolshevik leaders, controlling a divided nation, were soon challenged. Civil war broke out, with the armies of the White Russians fighting the Red Russians here and there. In August 1918 British and Japanese troops advanced into Siberia from the east. In the cold north of Russia, the ports of Murmansk and Archangel were attacked by the British. In the warmer south, on the Black Sea, an anti-Bolshevik republic was set up near the Don River. In the new year the French sent a military expedition to the port of Odessa to help the White Russians. For a time it seemed possible that advancing prongs of Allied soldiers, though not large in number, would tip the scales against Lenin and his communists.

Once the world war was ended, the Allies did not throw their weight against communist Russia. Most of the soldiers and sailors of the Allies had had enough of fighting. Their governments could no longer raise the massive sums required to keep ships and regiments in action. War exhaustion had set in – the same exhaustion that had prompted the Russian government to sue for peace in 1917. The attempt to win back Russia was half-hearted.

SCARECROWS AND COMMISSARS

While the civil war was raging, Russian citizens poured out of the vulnerable cities. There was food for them in the countryside, and safety too. Epidemics of typhus hastened the flight from the cities. Between 1918 and 1920 the population of St Petersburg – renamed Petrograd and soon to be named Leningrad – was almost halved, while in the new capital city of Moscow many streets were strangely silent and houses empty. Supporters of the old czarist regime, when they had the opportunity to leave Russia, slipped away. It was often easier to evade arrest by making the long journey towards China, travelling on the Trans-Siberian Railway, than the short escape route to France; and soon the Chinese cities of Harbin and Shanghai gained suburbs of Russian emigrants.

Monetary confusion set in. The rise of prices, breathtaking during the Great War, was worse in the civil war. The nation endured its bout of hyperinflation – the kind of inflation that was statistically astronomical – before Germany experienced its own bout. One Russian rouble in 1913 bought a parcel of sugar, but at the start of 1921 a housewife needed about 17000 roubles to buy the same amount. The official index of inflation is usually an unintended test of whether a government is financially competent. By this test Lenin's Russia was initially a dunce.

The official aim was to build a new society, but at first various parts of the old society, torn to pieces by war, had to be put together again. The railways were in ruin. At one point in the civil war the White Russian forces held four-fifths of all the railway tracks in the nation, and in the course of their capture and recapture a total of 3762 railway bridges had been destroyed. Before the war Russia had possessed 17000 steam locomotives; but in January 1920 only 4000 remained. Perhaps no major railway in the world had ever been so devastated. And yet steam trains were essential for a thousand tasks, including carrying the harvested grain from the countryside to hungry cities and conveying coal to shivering towns.

Horses – not motor trucks – provided the transport around the cities, but there was scant fodder for them in wintertime. Probably hundreds of thousands of horses were eaten – that was the only remaining use for them. The horse-drawn sledges either disappeared or were each pulled by a couple of men. As fuel could not be carted into the big cities unless the railway was working, many offices and factories worked in the intense winter without the benefit of heating. In the theatres the audiences shivered, while the actors rubbed their hands and wiggled their toes in the chill air.

Fear was a growing weapon of the government, brandished night and day with a mixture of brutality, clumsiness and ruthless skill. Many people became frightened to express their thoughts, even to close friends. Citizens suspected by the government of wrongful thinking on such topics as politics, religion, economics, literature or the visual arts, were taken forcefully from work or home, and not heard of again or not seen for years. Neighbour turned against neighbour. Some were rewarded for spying on acquaintances and friends. Others were interrogated and imprisoned on the grounds that they were themselves enemies of the people.

The Bolshevik regime, now taking the name of Communist, declared war on the old middle classes, the bourgeoisie. In November 1918 in the newspaper *Red Terror* a chief of the secret police argued that no evidence was needed to justify an allegation that a member of that class had 'acted in word or deed against Soviet power'. Even goodwill towards the new regime could not save a former banker or factory-owner. 'We are exterminating the bourgeoisie as a class', he announced. In organising forced-labour camps for their enemies, the communists learned from the czars. They even hired their old guards and warders.

Bertrand Russell, a British philosopher who was sympathetic to new political ideas, visited Russia in 1920 in a privileged position as a member of a somewhat radical delegation. In Petrograd the daily scenes of poverty – alongside the luxurious life lived by many of the new officials – shocked him, though he shared in the official luxury. One day he met four of the leading poets, each resembling a scarecrow, dressed in rags, their fingernails dirty and faces unshaven. More alarming to Russell than these hungry poets was the atmosphere of fear. He said that the time he spent in Russia was one of 'continually increasing nightmare'.

Many excuses were made for the new Russia, and some were legitimate. The country had been half destroyed by war. Any government – communist or liberal or conservative – would have had trouble in resuscitating such a devastated land. Even the communist rule of terror could be temporarily excused by sympathisers because the czar, now dead, had operated his own secret police. For the blood-soaked events in Russia there was another excuse that many liberals and radicals in the west initially accepted – that communism was an experiment and still in its awkward phase. They felt entitled to plead with the critics: 'Please, give the communists the time to complete their experiment.'

The civil war was won by the communists mainly in the year 1920. In March, Anton Denikin's White Russian army virtually collapsed. In August, the Red Russians were defeated by the Polish army near Warsaw, and sensibly made concessions, enabling the satisfied Poles to withdraw from the war. In November the Red Army captured the southern port of Sebastopol. It was not until 1922, however, that the far eastern province, centred on the Pacific port of Vladivostok, rejoined mother Russia.

WITH A FEW STROKES OF THE RED PEN

At times the experiment halted, then it suddenly ran ahead, only to halt again. From the start most industries in the cities were nationalised. Banks, private railways, shipyards and big factories were taken over and run by the government. The smaller factories were exempted, and those with only 10 workers and no power-driven machinery were allowed to remain in private hands. The regulations were punctuated by exceptions, and a factory employing a machine but only five workers could also remain under private management.

The large estates were nationalised. With a few strokes of the pen the largest confiscation of property in recorded history was accomplished. The shockwaves circled the globe. In the view of most conservatives and those travelling in the centre of the political road in that era, private property was the bulwark of civil order and freedom. Since then the world has become more accustomed to acts of confiscation and redistribution.

From the Baltic Sea to the faraway Pacific Ocean, in ten thousand villages and the encircling terrain, most of the fences were removed or rearranged. The tiny family farm of an acre or two – entirely tilled by the family – prevailed. The rich farmers were losers in the revolution and the millions of poorer peasants were at first the winners.

Huge numbers of Russians, remembering the old miseries, welcomed or accepted the new regime. Millions living in the outside world read about the rebuilding of Russia and rejoiced. If it succeeded, surely their own nations would follow the same path. Enthusiastic socialists could not wait for that happy day and set out for the new holy land. Some were Americans who set up farming communes with names such as Red Banner and Proletarian Life. From Canada 2500 Dukhorbors returned to set up their commune, and Austrian, Jewish, Czech, and Finnish socialists arrived and set to work. From faraway Queensland came Australians eager to set up their collective farm in the Ukraine. A band of Jewish enthusiasts arrived with their own tractors – a luxury in this land of the draught horse. Some of these communes lasted only as long as the initial enthusiasm.

A wave of social reforms rolled across Russia. The western calendar was introduced. New people's courts were set up. The state took over all education. The publishing of books and newspapers became a government monopoly, and anti-communist ideas ceased to circulate. The army was reformed, most of the old generals and colonels vanished or emigrated, and the new officers did not display gold stars and ornate badges on their caps and stripes on their sleeves. A quarter of a century after the revolution, when Moscow was imperilled by the advancing Nazi army, the standing collar and other insignia of the old czarist army uniforms would return.

Marriage was turned upside down. Divorce was easily granted on demand from either husband or wife, for women were equal partners in the marriage. Women undoubtedly gained from the new order: their status was higher than before, unless they were the minority that had possessed money and servants during the czarist regime. Initially the private inheriting of land and money was banned, but in 1922 the rule was altered to allow small sums to be inherited. Travel on trains and trams was free – until the government could no longer afford it.

Religious freedom accompanied the revolution but was soon under attack. Christianity was officially scorned, and many churches were turned into museums of atheism. Marriage ceased to be a religious ceremony. The Russian Orthodox church lost its status, lands and revenue, and had no money to pay the salaries of bishops and priests. When the new patriarch in February 1918 threatened to excommunicate the opponents of his church, he was ignored. Many of the Orthodox bishops and priests were shot or imprisoned for real or imagined offences against a government they could not support. They were enemies of the revolution: that was irrefutable.

Forced to shoulder one of the tumultuous episodes of modern history, the economy stumbled. In the growing of food, the Soviet Union lagged. Previously one of the world's leading grain exporters – Odessa was a bustling cereal port before the First World War – it could no longer feed its own people. All incentives had been taken from the peasants, and now their surplus food had to be sold to the government in return for paper money of little worth. Why then should they produce a surplus of food? Lenin, admitting that farmers were caught by an 'extraordinarily acute crisis', relented. In March 1921 he temporarily turned the clock back. Peasants were given incentives to grow more grain and to sell part on the open market. Trading in grain was previously a crime but now was seen as a public benefit. Peasants were even allowed to hire labour. It was called the New Economic Policy, but it was really the old policy, temporarily restored in order to prevent famine and curb unrest.

A fierce drought in the summer of 1921 impeded the revival of economic life. The grass in the Volga region dried. Farmers had pitiful crops and no money with which to buy food. It was said that on the side of one road, women fought for the possession of scraps of fresh horse dung containing undigested grains and other fodder, which could be cooked. Typhus wiped out tens of thousands of weak people. Aid – it was called 'relief' – came belatedly from the United States government, the American Red Cross, the YMCA and YWCA, and a host of American churches ranging from Quakers to Lutherans.

Organised by Herbert Hoover, who later became the US president, these foreign supplies of food, seed grain, and medicines would save millions of lives. The Soviet Union swallowed its pride and accepted the help. In all, eight million Russians in the areas of the epidemics were inoculated or vaccinated with American medicine. And then the rains came, the green shoots of the crops brought delight, and by 1923 Russia was actually exporting grain.

The New Economic Policy helped the towns. Private shops were reopened in 1921, and suddenly a private restaurant or bookshop reappeared here and there, while further down the street an old trader who had hoarded his stock of toys or woman's hats opened his shop again. In the temporary outburst of freedom, travelling vendors walked openly in the streets – no longer frightened that the militia would arrest them on the charge of trading for profit. The pleasant pastime of window-shopping had been frowned upon in the first years of communist Russia but now Arthur Ransome, writing his book *Six Weeks in Russia*, marvelled at the crowds suddenly reappearing in the shopping streets.

Many of Russia's finest musicians, writers and painters did not think that liberty would creep back. Their departure was a snub to the prestige of the communist government. Feeling ambivalent or hostile towards the revolution, they did not cease loving their native land and its forests and grasslands, or its people's manners and ways. Sergei Rachmaninov, who left Russia after the revolution, found that his spirit was so impoverished by the absence of his native country-side and the distinctive cultural climate that for years, living in France and the United States, he was unable to compose his symphonies. The music forming in his mind was suffocated. 'I felt like a ghost wandering in a world grown alien', he said in 1939, but he refused to return. Marc Chagall, who lived permanently outside Russia, realised that during the six decades of his exile all of his paintings were tinted with 'nostalgia for my native land'.

The composer Igor Stravinsky, already living abroad in 1917, had jumped in delight when he heard that the Russian monarchy had been erased. To his mother in St Petersburg he wrote: 'All my thoughts are with you in these unforgettable days of happiness.' Slowly from afar he saw the happiness watered down, even poisoned. Invited in 1955 to visit nearby Finland he refused, explaining that it was 'too near a certain city that I have no desire to see again'. In 1962 he relented and revisited Russia. In his feelings and personal loyalties he remained intensely Russian, and whenever he composed music he dated the finished score according to the old Russian rather than the western calendar.

Maxim Gorki was celebrated as a realist novelist long before the revolutionary era. As a rebel who had fought for change he applauded Lenin's Russia and continued to watch its perilous infancy from his writing desk. After retreating to the Isle of Capri, partly to safeguard his health, Gorki returned to the Soviet Union, now ruled by Stalin, to spend what would be the last five years of his life. Feted by the government he was pleased that many hundreds of streets, kindergartens, and writers' clubs – and even a city – were named after him. The returning hero, however, began to see that Stalin's intense interest in writers, filmmakers and artists was a form of manipulation and that their role was simply to be malleable servants of the ruling party. Gorki rebelled. He privately likened Stalin to 'a monstrous flea', biting the flesh of the people around him. Rumour said that his death was the result of a secret order given by Stalin.

Meanwhile Lenin was enthroned as the hero of the revolution. When he died of a stroke in 1924, at the age of 54, his body was embalmed and placed in a mausoleum, originally of wood, in Red Square in Moscow. A few of the tourists who saw him 40 or more years later, having been escorted (as was the custom) to the very front of the queues patiently waiting to pay tribute, thought this ginger-bearded man resting in his neat grey suit was rather like a polite bank manager from a thrifty czarist suburb. His brain long ago had been removed and dissected by faithful Soviet scientists who pronounced it to be a special brain befitting the first leader of a nation reborn.

ENTER THE MAN OF STEEL

Lenin had triumphed through pragmatic actions as much as ideological correctness. His successor, Joseph Stalin, thought that it was time to rekindle the fire of communism. Whereas Lenin made Russia into a communist land, Stalin converted it again into a world power.

He came from an outlying province in the Caucasus mountains, the son of a cobbler and a washerwoman. Russian was not his native tongue and when he became fluent in speaking it his Georgian accent was still noticeable. His real name was Dzhugashvili but much later he converted it to Stalin, meaning 'a man of steel'. The dense moustache and the smallpox scars on his face – like battle scars in the eyes of many who first met him – strengthened his commanding presence, the scars hinting that he had once

4 RUSSIA AND TURKEY, 1925

Murmansk

Archangel

Finland

Ural Mountains

Helsinki

St Petersburg
(renamed Petrograd)

*Baltic
Sea* Estonia

Latvia Riga

Russia

Lithuania

Moscow

East Prussia

Warsaw Brest-Litovsk

Don River

Volga River

Ukraine

Carpathian Mtns

Hungary Odessa

Romania Sebastopol

*Caspian
Sea*

*Aral
Sea*

Yugoslavia *Black
Sea*

Bulgaria Georgia

Caucasus Mtns

Armenia

Azerbaijan

Greece Ankara **Turkey**

Syria

Cyprus

*Mediterranean
Sea* Lebanon

Palestine Iraq **Persia**

Trans-Jordan

Kuwait *Persian
Gulf*

Egypt

fought dangerous battles for his Bolshevik party. Later he was to be portrayed frequently as a physical giant, for tall statues of him arose in his heyday. In fact he was stocky rather than tall.

After a time in a theological seminary – rarely did the Orthodox church nurture a more bitter enemy – he turned to politics. With Karl Marx's writings as his guide, he plotted throughout his twenties and for much of his thirties to overthrow the czar. As a punishment for his zeal he spent periods in Siberia. His first wife Ekaterina, a devout Christian, died before the longest period of exile.

In 1917, with ferment in the air, Stalin hurried back to St Petersburg and served as editor of the main Bolshevik newspaper. The press was a powerful platform for an intelligent and manipulative person who was rising rapidly but was not yet at the top. After Lenin's death in January 1924, Stalin, already close to supreme power, grasped it. Leon Trotsky, who had seemed the more likely to succeed Lenin, was elbowed into the long corridors, and was expelled from Russia five years later. He could not flee far enough. In Mexico City in 1940 he was to be assassinated, on Stalin's orders.

Under Stalin the peasant domain was slowly broken up. The poor country folk who in 1917 had supported the revolution because they were each promised a small parcel of land were, a dozen years later, slowly deprived of their reward. Some 25 million tiny family-farms were taken over in the name of the people. The collective farm, with its numerous employees, ruled the plains. It was one of the most dramatic changes in the global history of farming, for the populous Soviet Union was essentially rural, and most of its people worked the soil. The advantage of the collective or state farm was that it was easily mechanised and produced more food with less labour.

Without doubt a host of the poor peasants eventually preferred the more gregarious life on the big farm and the opportunity to work machines or become specialists.

Most of the individualist farmers, the kulaks, whose efficiency had contributed much to the new Soviet Union in its time of famine, were singled out for punishment in 1929. Even when they owned only a couple of cattle, but leased a few additional handkerchiefs of land, they were accused of being capitalists. What crime could be more serious? They were sent to remote places or even killed. Meanwhile those who briefly remained on the land were slaughtering their animals and eating or smoking the meat rather than see it confiscated by the government. Russia's flocks of sheep – even its goats – declined by half. Through a blend of poor weather and rural disorder in the early 1930s, famine set in. As many as 10 million people died.

Stalin strengthened the defence forces of the nation. Just as outside nations viewed the Soviet Union as potentially hostile, so the Soviet Union viewed most of the outside world as hostile. Large sums were devoted to army and navy and an infant air force. A vast effort was devoted to industrialising the country so that it could fight a war without depending heavily – as had czarist Russia – on the importing of war materials. The Gallipoli campaign in the First World War had been designed to open a seaway along which munitions could flow to poorly armed Russia. Understandably Stalin had no wish to rely on precarious outside help in the event of another war.

He launched a campaign to produce more electricity, heavy machinery, iron, steel and coal. Inaugurated in 1928, and called the Five Year Plan, it achieved its goals in less than five years and was followed by another Five Year Plan. Peasants who visited new and old cities were astonished at the noise of mechanical hammers, machine-saws, jackhammers, steamrollers, cranes and novel new engines. Grain fields they had known disappeared under the roofs of factories, warehouses and new housing apartments. At first the local sky was striped with chimney smoke, until the first electricity arrived on long power lines.

Between 1928 and 1940 the country's annual output of steel, cement and coal quadrupled. Truck and car manufacture increased from 800 to 145 000 annually, though the resultant fleet was puny by American standards. The shipyards, locomotive workshops and tractor factories expanded with a speed that was the envy of many engineers in the west. The coal-burning power stations and hydro-electric schemes received high priority, and were depicted adoringly on coloured posters. One of the most rapid phases of industrial advance ever recorded, it was paid for by many Russians who ate less bread than before and whose weekly ration of butter was reduced. Since the Soviet Union could not easily borrow overseas – it was not likely to repay a loan – it had to make sacrifices to pay for its own industrial success. The people's smaller serve of thin stew helped to pay for the new electricity grid. The smaller rations of beer and tobacco paid for the new schools.

By 1939 the Soviet Union ranked third amongst the industrial powers of the world. It was an astonishing achievement. The state and its citizens were entitled to exult in many of the material advantages they had acquired. In education and some aspects of culture the gains were remarkable. Levels of literacy, so poor when the last czar came to office, became almost equal to those in most countries of western Europe. Higher and technical education were free, attracting large numbers of young women as well as men. Health services were much superior to those provided a quarter of a century previously. In a variety of the performing arts, especially the ballet and opera and the symphony orchestras, the standards were high; and the proportion of people who attended cultural performances in the big Russian cities was higher than in most western nations.

The latest foreign ideas in science and technology were eagerly scrutinised. The newest foreign machines were taken to pieces and imitated. The engineers and technicians, and they ranked high in the Soviet Union, were quick to inspect or adopt new technology. Even the special police force known as Cheka tried the new aids. Many of the policing innovations so useful to dictators of the 20th century were borrowed from the democracies. Motor cars had been used for the first time by the police in Akron, Ohio, in 1899. One year later police dogs were used – probably for the first time – in Ghent in Belgium. The English technique of classifying fingerprints was easily applied by dictators to political protesters. Radio and the microphone were vital aids to a totalitarian society, as means of propaganda and ways of spying and eavesdropping.

THE CULT OF STALIN

Eventually the supreme committee that governed the country fell away. Joseph Stalin, the general secretary, virtually became the committee. So the Bolshevik party, which originally had paid more than lip service to democratic discussion, produced a dictatorship.

Stalin was entitled to high praise because his country had been rebuilt and modernised at such a fast pace, but he was not satisfied that his prestige, already enormous in his homeland, was being accorded due respect. He began to enlarge his place in the history books, especially the history of those years when he was not important. It so happened that Lenin had praised the book written by an American communist who witnessed the Russian revolutions, John Reed's *Ten Days That Shook The World*, but the book did not please Stalin because his own name was not listed amongst the heroes of 1917. He removed the book from Russian libraries. As one of the operas composed by the celebrated Shostakovich did not impress Stalin, it was silenced. Biologists and botanists, economists and soldiers who displeased him were demoted, sent to the far-off provinces and to camps in Siberia, or shot.

Loyal servants of the October Revolution of 1917 were not safe. Groups of them fell, about 20 years later, to the firing squad or the bullet in the back of the head. Foreign communists who, when their life was in danger, had sought refuge in Moscow and been welcomed, now heard the sudden knock at the door, and were seen by their family no more. Whereas Hitler, now ruling Germany, usually showed a sense of loyalty to old party comrades, Stalin began to fear loyal comrades, especially if they were in high posts. Between 1936 and 1939, platoons of his perceived enemies were arrested and placed on trial, or shot without trial. Military commanders who fought for their country against the Japanese in a little-known war in Mongolia in 1938 were arrested. Marshal Bliukher, who had helped to safeguard communist Russia during the civil war, but apparently did not lead his troops effectively against the Japanese at Lake Khasan, was summoned to Moscow and shot.

All the time an exaggerated campaign of publicity extolled Stalin as the benevolent father of the Russian people. This one-time trainee monk, now an atheist, was viewed by millions as a god, capable of answering prayers or transforming lives. In Moscow the newspaper *Pravda* advised its readers: 'If you meet with difficulties in your work, or suddenly doubt your abilities, think of him, of Stalin, and you will find the confidence you need.' While a myriad of citizens learned to fear him, countless others respected him because he had rebuilt the nation and renewed their self-respect. The patriotism that persisted inside the proud Soviet Union was one of Stalin's enduring assets.

Meanwhile the successes, both apparent and real, of communism in the Soviet Union affected politics in other lands. Though communist parties in France, Italy, Germany and several other democratic nations did not win power, they each commanded large followings. Certainly they would snatch national power by force, if the opportunity arose. Their emphasis on force shaped several rival political parties and made them equally determined to employ force. The rise of the Fascists in Italy and the Nazis in Germany – political parties with their own street armies – was partly a reaction to the rise of communism and the powerful appeal it exercised on tens of millions of European minds.

7

OLD SULTAN AND YOUNG TURK

Russia and Turkey had long been bitter enemies, but after the First World War they followed new paths with a similar determination. Employing defeat and adversity to reshape themselves, they tried to wipe out much of their past. While the early Soviet Union was an eye-catching experiment, Turkey also made one of the boldest experiments in the history of an Islamic land. Its new soldier-leader tried to take away the Islamic veil from a wide cross-section of Turkish life.

Of these two experiments, the Russian was, for some time, the most influential. Pointing to collectivism and materialism as the way of the future it won a host of admirers around the globe. But in the very long term perhaps the events in Turkey were the more significant. There Islam was tamed but not defeated. By the end of the century it was Islam and not communism that displayed the crusading vigour.

AN EMPIRE'S LAST GASP

The Ottoman Empire in 1900 was vast, intruding into three continents. Though it had lost most of its grip on North Africa and the Balkans, it remained the major power in Asia Minor, governing most of the cities recorded in the Old and New Testaments. It was ruled by the Sultan, and he had the added prestige that he was the caliph, the representative of the prophet Mohammed. The holy city of Mecca was in his empire; and to expedite the annual pilgrimage a long railway was being laid from the Mediterranean Sea to Medina with the aid of coins and banknotes collected from the faithful in many lands.

In its religions and races the empire of 1900 was diverse. Constantinople with its skyline of mosques, minarets and domes held a million inhabitants, but only half were Muslims. The commerce of the busy port of Smyrna, now called Izmir and standing near the ruins of the biblical city of Ephesus, was dominated by Greeks. Salonika, the big Ottoman port on the other side of the Aegean, was the only important city in Europe where the Jews were the largest ethnic group. Another large minority within the empire consisted of Armenians who were Christians and commercially adept. But the largest groups of outsiders in this compact empire were Arabs. Numbering 6 million they lived far from Constantinople and the Anatolian high country and certainly did not see themselves as Turks.

The Turkish people dominated the empire, providing the officers for the army and clerks for the civil service. From time to time Turkish nationalists tried to introduce democracy to an empire long ruled by the Sultan and the upholders of tradition. With the aid of army officers they gained power in 1908. It was this regime that helped shape the military alliance with Germany. It was a young army officer who, after Turkey's defeat in the First World War, began to build a nation on the ruins of the Ottoman Empire.

RISE OF THE YOUNG TURK

Mustafa Kemal was born in the port of Salonika, on what is now Greek soil, the son of a minor Ottoman official who did not see himself as minor. The mother was 20 years younger than the father and exercised the keener influence on the boy. He had fair hair and blue eyes, determination, a sense of duty, and a shy kind of pride. 'We all noticed how he spoke, head raised, hands in pockets', observed the mother. Though Mustafa was reared in Islam – one of his grandfathers knew the Koran by heart – he had a hankering for the western ways that were edging their way into that cosmopolitan port. How pleased he was when he could abandon the baggy, ballooning Turkish trousers worn by schoolboys and put on the western-style uniform of his military college!

By the time Major Mustafa Kemal was in his twenties the Ottoman Empire was fighting for survival. He went with the troops to Libya where, outside the tiny port of Tobruk, he tried to prevent the Italians from advancing inland. A few years later, during the First World War he distinguished himself, more than any other Turkish officer, as a tactician and brave defender on the heights of Gallipoli. He recognised the power of myth and propaganda, and harnessed them for his ends. Though the Germans under General Liman von Sanders mainly organised that successful defence, Mustafa Kemal later claimed that he was the chief strategist of Gallipoli. His colleagues increasingly observed his ability to organise. They also noted his restless ambition.

He nurtured the hope that some day he might modernise Turkey, an ambition that grew when he met the man who was to become the ruling Sultan. About to set out in 1917 on a wartime delegation to Germany, Mustafa Kemal noticed the arrival of a courteous delegate unfamiliar to him: 'He came in, bowed slightly in our direction, and sat on the right side of the sofa.' Where people sat was important in the Ottoman Empire, and the strange, aloof visitor was clearly an official of importance: 'He shut his eyes and appeared lost in deep thought.' Next year this lost and silent one became Sultan Mehmed VI. When the new Sultan failed to provide the leadership that a defeated empire required, and allowed the victorious Allies to occupy Constantinople and other key parts of his country, Mustafa Kemal came to the fore.

As leader of the Turkish Nationalist Movement, formed in 1919, Kemal tried to regain control of the country. He drove back the Greek forces which – with the backing of Britain, France and the United States – had occupied the busy port of Smyrna and large areas of the interior. He was again the nation's hero. So swift and ruthless was his campaign that 180000 Greek and Armenian refugees fled from Asia Minor to mainland Greece. So clever were his tactics that his army in September 1922 seemed even likely to recapture the Dardanelles and even invade the Gallipoli peninsula. His army far outnumbered the troops of victorious Allies – the British and French and Italians who, under the terms of the postwar treaty, occupied both shores of the narrow straits.

The Allies, astonished at the turn of the events, were faced with the decision whether to refight the war they had recently won. In London at an urgent meeting of the British Cabinet, the prime minister Lloyd George confided that it was inconceivable that we should 'allow the Turks to gain possession of the Gallipoli peninsula, and we should fight to prevent their doing so'. At his request New Zealand promised to send troops, and Newfoundland too. Serbia and Greece and Romania were invited to send armies. British reinforcements were soon on their way – battleships, cruisers, a squadron of submarines and a flotilla of destroyers, troopships from Gibraltar and Malta and Egypt and even Britain, and aircraft from Egypt. At a long meeting of the British Cabinet on 15 September the implications of a possible Kemal victory were debated, and set down in a secret cable sent to the British dominions: 'A defeat or a humiliating exodus of the Allies from Constantinople might produce very grave consequences in India and among other Mohammedan populations for which we are responsible.' That the war graves at Gallipoli might 'fall into the ruthless hands of Kemalists' was another fear. For a few weeks, war seemed likely.

The Allies, who had been victorious in the long war against Turkey, faced the prospect that their military superiority was now erased by the presence of Kemal and some 70 000 Turkish soldiers. They were now divided in their opinions and in their sense of urgency or calm. France definitely refused to fight and Britain hesitated too. Negotiations commenced, and the determined Mustafa Kemal won most of what he demanded. Gallipoli again became Turkish territory, and the Allies withdrew their occupying army from Constantinople.

A triumphant time for Turkey, it was an ominous time for Britain and France. The defeated Germany would eventually do what the defeated Turkey had done: employ determination, patriotism and armed force to erase the penalties imposed on them after the First World War.

In Turkey in this month of triumph two governments still presided, one formally led by the timid Sultan Mehmed VI in the occupied port-city of Constantinople, and the other led by the aggressive Mustafa Kemal in the free inland town of Ankara. Kemal again took the initiative. He called on the Sultan to dismiss the ministers he had appointed in Istanbul. When the Sultan refused, the national assembly met in Ankara on 1 November and resolved with only one dissenter that Turkey should become a republic. Indeed, the assembly went further, decreeing that the Sultan had ceased to rule since 16 March 1920, to be precise. That was the day when he had permitted the victorious Allies to occupy the noble city in which he presided.

The news of the dismissal was conveyed to the Sultan. His hope that public opinion in the city would, miraculously, rally behind him was mistaken. For his own safety he and his young son were conveyed secretly from their palace to the waterfront on 17 November 1922. The first of the Sultans to live in Istanbul had entered in triumph nearly five centuries ago. Now the last Sultan departed unseen for the harbour in a British ambulance. A few wits were heard to remark that this was a symbolic end for the regime that was long called 'the sick man of Europe'.

The last Sultan sailed from his homeland in a British warship HMS *Malaya* which, by chance, bore the name of an Islamic land. For a time he lived in Mecca, the holy city that no previous Sultan had deigned to visit, before spending his remaining days with three of his wives in the Italian sea resort of San Remo. He died there in May 1926, of apoplexy.

The Sultan had gone, and with him the caliph too. The Sultan of the Ottoman Empire had long served as the caliph – the living representative of the prophet Mohammed and the titular head of Muslims throughout the world. In a quiet way, and exercising rather less authority, the caliph was the pope of Islam. His potential prestige was considerable; and in the First World War he had formally called for the tens of millions of Muslims living in the British Empire to rise and carry out a jihad against their Christian oppressors. The Indian brigades fighting in Gallipoli had actually been rained with leaflets from little Turkish aeroplanes calling on them to desert the British army and join their fellow Muslims in the Turkish trenches 'or have your heads cut off'. That the jihad summoned by the caliph did not eventuate suggests that his authority, far from Turkey, was faint. In the view of Mustafa Kemal the caliph's influence even in Turkey was no longer needed. The post of caliph, following the expulsion of the Sultan, was not only vacant but redundant.

Kemal accomplished the taming of Islam with slow and muffled steps, like those in a funeral march. He conferred the title of caliph on the Sultan's cousin, Abdül mecid. Almost a nationalist, and somewhat sympathetic to Mustafa Kemal, the new caliph learned that he had to make concessions. He had first appeared at Friday's public prayers in the robes and turban favoured by earlier sultans, but strict orders arrived from Kemal that he must wear western dress and even a formal frock coat.

Shorn of his peacock feathers, the new caliph appeared in public each Friday but not for long. The Grand National Assembly resolved at the quiet bidding of Mustafa Kemal that a caliph was no longer needed. A simple substitute was found. A new government department could supervise the mosques and their schools and even sideline the Islamic courts, while some Arabian potentate would surely feel honoured if invited to assume the title of caliph. In March 1924 the national assembly resolved to dismiss Turkey's own caliph. At his palace in Istanbul the telephone line was cut, preventing him from seeking outside advice. With two of his four wives he was escorted early one morning to a suburban railway station and kept waiting until midnight, when at last the Orient Express arrived with a special carriage for his entourage. His transition from the Islamic to the western world met with a mishap or two along the way. Temporarily he was refused entry to Switzerland, which did not permit polygamous marriages.

The remote town of Ankara was confirmed as the capital of the new republic of Turkey. Known in the west as Angora – the Angora goat and its mohair fleece came from this upland region – the town had been chosen by Kemal as the temporary capital in 1920 partly because it was so far from the sea that it could not readily be attacked by the Greeks or any other invaders. It proved to be a windswept retreat in winter, while on summer evenings the malarial mosquitoes rose like a dark cloud from the swamp near the railway station. In 1925 it was becoming more presentable: the swamp was being drained, a comfortable hotel was open, a public park beckoned those who wished to discuss politics in the evening, and an electric power station lit the street-lamps when they strolled home. There was eager talk of erecting a telephone exchange and radio station that could serve nearly 50 000 inhabitants as well as the few embassies which, reluctantly, were transferring their staff from the lovable old capital by the sea.

THE CRUSADE AGAINST FEZ AND VEIL

Kemal's ambition as president was to set up a version of the secular French republic. The mosques, at first, remained exempt, and the people could worship in the old ways. In the dusty villages there was no apparent change in the religious observances of the mass of people who ploughed the ground, picked the fruit, tended the flocks in the pastures, and rode donkeys or led camels along the roads.

One by one some of the traditional Ottoman bans and prohibitions were removed. Kemal, frowning on the female custom of wearing veils, announced in 1924: 'Let them show their faces to the world.' Women were not compelled to accept his advice but in the cities they increasingly discarded the veil.

For men his instructions on the appropriate headgear were more emphatic. The fez was almost the sign of the respectable Turkish man, and even Kemal himself had worn this red, soft and tall cap for much of his adult life. So tightly was the fez identified with Islam that those publicly wearing a hat with a brim virtually defined themselves as western infidels. Probably Moroccan in origin, and possessing no peak and no brim, the fez could be conveniently worn throughout the religious service in the mosque, because it allowed the worshipper seated on the floor to bow deeply so that the flat of his forehead actually touched the ground. In a dramatic and even provocative step the wearing of the fez was banned in 1924.

As most men preferred still to cover their head while inside the mosque, there arose in place of the fez a vogue for berets, peaked cloth caps and baseball-like caps, the peak being worn at the back so that the devout forehead could easily humble itself by touching the floor. Other rules of dress were disseminated; and civil servants had to wear European hats, and girls and boys at school had to wear black pinafores in the French manner.

The leader himself did not enter the mosques and rearrange their rituals and prayers, but he virtually stood at the doors. At his decree, the Muslim call to prayer delivered from the high minarets was spoken in the Turkish tongue instead of the Arabic. The priests ceased to wear their traditional dress while walking in the street. Even the ban on drinking alcohol – a ban that permeated Islamic life – was challenged by Kemal in private and then in public. Long before alcohol was permitted in public, one visitor noticed him welcoming the arrival of a large brass tray on which neat whiskies were arranged and busily beginning to swallow them like a thirsty man who had come straight from the desert.

In the 10 years after the expulsion of the caliph, Turkey was progressively spring-cleaned. The clock was altered, and the solar calendar of the Muslims, in which time was counted from sunrise, was discarded in favour of a new day beginning at midnight. International numerals were adopted, the Latin alphabet arrived, and surnames became compulsory. Constantinople, a Greek name, became Istanbul, and Angora was officially confirmed as Ankara.

The status of women rose, though more rapidly in the cities than on the farms and more in public than in private. The right of a man to divorce his wife, or one of his wives, gave way to a Swiss-style law on divorce. Daughters received the same right as sons to inherit a share of a family estate; women won the right to vote in parliamentary elections; and 18 women took their seats in the reformed assembly in 1935, by which time the first women were sitting as judges. The first Turkish beauty contests were conducted, and a beauty queen was crowned amidst the clicks of disapproval from the dark-veiled, older women. In the eyes of some moderate critics the status of women had fallen just at the moment when it appeared to rise.

Having almost transformed social life, Kemal attempted to invigorate economic life. He boasted that his country now owned more than a thousand petrol-driven tractors. But in 1925 that was a humble tally compared to the hundreds of thousands of horses, donkeys, mules, oxen and even men and women who were pulling the ploughs and farm-carts. Rural life changed less than the new industrial zones. Even the cities and their shops and bazaars were as leisurely as they were in the last Ottoman years; and some visitors vowed that commerce was actually less vigorous because so many of the Greeks, Jews, Armenians and other astute businessmen in the cities of the old empire were no longer present. As for new opportunities, they were curtailed when the oil potential of the Middle East, little known at the end of the First World War, passed into the hands of westerners following the dissolution of the Ottoman Empire.

Dynamic in his thinking, Kemal was dictatorial in a wide range of topics and situations. An Englishman, who was his guest at dinner in 1923, made a conversational comment that was not acceptable to his host, whereupon Kemal gave a 'frown that brought the whole of his forehead down, like a thundercloud, upon his brows'. This frown increasingly ruled the nation. Numerous citizens, with talents to offer, were forced into exile. Formidable enemies were not allowed to leave the country, and some were tried and executed. Political parties that seemed likely to be a thorn were pulled up by the roots and eradicated. The father of the nation admired the western idea of parliaments and national assemblies, only so long as he could select who spoke in them. He was more than a president. Near the end, seeing himself as *the* nation, he adopted the name of Atatürk (Father Turk).

This strong man died on 10 November 1938, 20 years – almost exactly – after the armistice ended the First World War. While he received little respect from the Armenian, Kurdish and Greek minorities who had mostly fled Turkey during his regime, he was revered or respected by most of the Turkish people. Few other leaders had done more to transform their nation.

The merits of Atatürk' s whirlwind – described as an overdue reform by many and a disgrace by many others – were eagerly and angrily debated in nearby Islamic lands. King Amanullah of Afghanistan began, with some caution, to copy Atatürk. He even talked of educating women – a proposal that evoked thunderous protests from the ridges and ravines of Afghanistan. In 1929, after an outcry by Muslim leaders, he was driven into exile. Iran went even further in 1935 and largely discarded the custom of wearing veils. There the outcry against the new secular ways rose and fell, reaching a crescendo nearly half a century later when strict religious rule returned to Iran.

It was widely expected that more of the Muslim nations would begin to follow the new Turkish ways by tasting democracy, championing the rights of women, and loosening the grip of the mosque on political and social as distinct from religious life. But half a century later, in most Muslim lands, the mosque towered over daily life, the sheikhs and the generals prevailed, and the ballot box was viewed more as a little coffin than as the home of freedom.

8

FASTER AND FASTER

A few inventors, working in complicated fields, succeed in solving a perplexing question when they are very young. Guglielmo Marconi, an Italian in his early twenties, half-invented the radio. At a time when messages, by phone or telegraph, could only be transmitted along wires, Marconi perfected a way of sending them without the aid of connecting wires. The first name given to his astonishing process was 'wire-less', which in retrospect is rather a negative way of expressing it. And yet for a generation the name 'wireless' was pure magic.

THE MIRACULOUS MESSAGE

Marconi's invention of the radio relied on the work of earlier theoreticians: he made their theory work. His early wireless equipment had showed its promise in 1899 when a British naval cruiser sent a message to a nearby ship. To signal a ship within eyesight and earshot was not a momentous event, but to send it far along the coast was a miracle. The miracle happened in June 1901 when a message was transmitted from the Isle of Wight to Cornwall without the aid of wires. The innovation was dismissed by many scientists as of limited use because, they argued, the curvature of the earth would prevent the message from crossing a wide ocean or continent. On 12 December 1901 this idea was largely disproved when a wireless message was sent from England across the Atlantic Ocean to Newfoundland. By the end of 1907 the press messages sent by wireless signals across the Atlantic were cheaper than those sent along the old underwater cable.

While the radio was not yet capable of transmitting the sound of a human voice, it could quickly transmit the familiar dots and dashes of the morse code – the same signals as the telegraph sent on. These coded signals were heard more clearly by night than by day, and that was to be true of the voice messages sent by the radio stations a generation later.

Could the human voice be clearly transmitted by radio? This possibility was exciting because the telephone, now old as an invention, could be used only for communicating over relatively short distances. Nearly all phone calls were made within cities, and even then a call was costly. In 1910 a wealthy person in London could reach a phone subscriber in Paris but not Rome and not New York. When in 1914 the First World War was about to begin, and the statesmen's anxious messages passed from one European city to another, they were not carried by telephone. Most of their urgent messages went as printed telegrams.

Between continents the swift communication was by the under-water telegraph cable; and in the wide Indian and Pacific Oceans the repeater stations on remote islands were easy targets in times of war. A cable could be cut, the isolated telegraph station could be destroyed, and silence would set in. All kinds of fears and rumours would circulate to explain the absence of messages – until at last, maybe a fortnight later, a naval vessel carrying a well-equipped team would arrive from a remote naval port to restore the cable. In 1914, out in the Indian ocean, a German armed cruiser shelled Cocos Island, one of the important cable stations of the oceanic world. It was therefore fortunate that radio or wireless – with no cable wait-ing to be cut – was becoming an alternative link.

The war boosted research into radio waves. When the United States army entered the war and needed safe and quick communi-cation between Washington and France, it built near Bordeaux a radio station equipped with Poulen arc generators. From afar it resembled a provincial railway station, surrounded by lofty pyramid-shaped masts. Though this station did not transmit the human voice, because the Atlantic was too wide, it sent coded signals in imitation of the telegraph line. By 1920 the world held perhaps a dozen of these long-distance radio stations. Their signals could reach every land, though it was occasionally complained that at sunset and sun-rise some signals were blurred.

As the radio could not carry the voice very far, each town had to build its own radio station to serve its local audience: Pittsburgh was the first, founded by amateurs and experimenters in 1920. After Dame Nellie Melba gave a recital in a radio studio near London, there was a sensation in the following days when reports from arriving ships revealed that several hundred kilometres out to sea the captain, radio operator and a few passengers had huddled into a room and managed to hear her faint but thrilling voice. The radio stations multiplied, much of their time being given to transmitting music from a gramophone or from live artists performing in their own studio. By 1930 a radio station in London or Auckland could broadcast, at some expense, a local race meeting on a Saturday and a local church service on a Sunday, but such events required technical staff, the presence of outside vans, and a scattered thicket of microphones.

In wealthier nations most households owned a wireless set by the mid-1930s. A large instrument with very big valves, all hidden in a box made of ornate wood such as walnut or oak, it stood on four legs and was too heavy to move regularly from one room to another. On the front of the set was a handsome dial, sometimes made of the novel brown plastic called bakelite, and showing each radio station within potential hearing. The more costly sets could also pick up, though mostly in the darkness of night, a few of the foreign radio stations that used powerful transmitters. These foreign radio stations were specifically marked on the dial – Oslo, Warsaw, Paris, Rome, Trieste, Vienna – and could be heard only if a high aerial was erected outside the house. There was in 1939 a sobering guide to the swift impact of radio on daily life. Whereas most people had learned of the outbreak of the First World War from newspapers – or by word of mouth – millions of Europeans were to hear the momentous news of the Second World War in 1939 while listening to their own elaborate radio in the living room of their home.

The radio spurred an interest in recorded music, boosting the gramophone. Invented by Edison as far back as 1877, the cumbersome gramophone had to reinvent itself several times before it was really practicable. Even in the 1920s one side of a gramophone disc carried only about four minutes of music, and had to be turned on its other side, by hand, thus releasing another four minutes of music. Nonetheless the sales of gramophone records, especially those playing jazz, boomed in the 1920s. The long-playing record, made of vinyl, did not challenge its short-playing parent until after the Second World War.

Entertainment was in turmoil in the first quarter of the 20th century. Of the powerful new ideas the cinema at first did not seem so dramatic. It had no airs and graces. Being silent it was not seen as an art form compared to the live theatre. Without the aid of words an actor had to overact, gesturing with hands, eyes and mouth, or falling flat on his face at an appropriate time. Many of the early films were made by promoters who owned a city arcade into which pleasure seekers poured, each paying a penny for the right to look through a peephole at a simple motion picture.

A film could be made for a very small sum, and so filmmakers could be found in many countries, especially in France. The makers of films did not worry about lighting techniques, and most actors appeared on the filming set without the help of a costume maker or make-up artist: those professional helpers belonged more to live theatre than film. Every film was made quickly. David Wark Griffith, a pioneer maker of films in New York, completed 142 films, mostly short, in the year 1909 alone. When Hollywood on the distant sunny coast became the centre of the industry, the making of a film became a slower and more expensive process.

The best films from Europe and the United States went around the world. As they were 'movies' without sound, they usually faced no language barrier when shown in a hall or theatre in a foreign land. When subtitles were placed at the foot of some of the scenes they consisted of only two or three printed words. So an interpreter would stand on the platform beside the screen and in a loud voice give his own translation to the audience. If the film was high in drama, a hired pianist or violinist might play suitable music – tense or relaxed according to the needs of the film's story. As most films were short, 10 or more might be screened in one evening.

In the South American or South African countryside, if the weather was fine, the imported film would be shown in the open air at night – a large white sheet serving as the screen. The film operator drove his own truck from town to town, and he operated by hand the reel holding the film. Most films, made for the masses, were seen in aggregate by large crowds in the course of their first years in global circulation. The pleasure they gave – especially a comedy featuring the American, Fatty Arbuckle – was intense for those who attended a cinema for the first time.

Mary Pickford was the first person to be called 'America's sweetheart'. Her real surname was Smith, her birthplace was Canada, and in 1909 she appeared for David Griffith in what was then called 'a motion picture', *The Violinmaker of Cremona*. The actors in Griffith's films were anonymous but Mary insisted on her name appearing on the billboard, just like an actor in the live theatre on Broadway, or a great singer in the opera house. Eventually hers became the first female face to be known right across the globe, for even the face of Queen Victoria, who presided over one-quarter of the world, had been known only through the tiny colonial and home postage stamps crowned by her face. Mary Pickford was married three times, as befitted the new film star, but she was really the whole world's sweetheart. Europeans, however, were not so sure, many favouring the Danish star Asta Nielsen.

Big cities in the 1920s built expensive picture theatres with seats for 2500 or more people, hiring an orchestra of many players to provide the music and a bevy of discreet dancing girls to perform at the intervals. Saturday night at the pictures became a social institution, even for many of those couples who when younger had spent that evening mentally preparing for worship on the Sunday. When the silent movie was replaced by the 'talkie', and colour film began to replace black and white, the film star enjoyed a fame that no live actor performing on the stage had ever achieved.

Another innovation, the microphone, quickly changed the political message as well as the popular song. A politician without a strong voice could now address an outdoor gathering totalling thousands of people. A new breed of popular entertainers, untutored in the skill of projecting or throwing their voices, was just as eager to clutch the microphone. For the first time the traditional ingredients of the successful voice began to diverge for popular compared to classical singing. Singers such as Bing Crosby and Perry Como rejoiced in the new technique, and could sing softly into the microphone, even whisper or murmur, and reach audiences of a size that no traditional well-trained singer had ever reached. The low-pitched voice and the husky voice came into favour, for the microphone smiled on them.

The radio and gramophone-record multiplied the audiences of the new breed of singer; and when Bing Crosby sang 'White

Christmas' in the wartime year of 1942 he reached a global audience. At the same time a few of the new singers were beginning to shun the lessons in taste, morality, diction and grammar that compulsory schooling had once emphasised. The ubiquitous schoolroom, expected in the 19th century to be the saviour of civilisation, was being confronted by a persuasive and sometimes ignorant opponent.

The long-distance wireless message, the radio station, the gramophone, the microphone and the movie had their main impact on home life, politics and entertainment from the 1920s. A parallel invention, the motor car, was a little quicker in transforming daily life, but was not yet a household item except in the United States.

THE TERROR AND JOY OF THE CAR

In 1900 some countries possessed not one car. Most of the roads linking big cities were unsuited for a vehicle travelling at 30 kilometres an hour, and engines of the early cars were imperfect. Many of the cars actually consumed more water than petrol, and frequently the motorists driving up a steep hill saw, just in front of them, steam jetting from the boiling water in the radiator. Cars were not yet designed to be driven at night, except in brightly lit cities, and even the headlights, burning kerosene, were not bright.

Women rarely drove a car, for it was still a machine for the physically strong and the mechanically dextrous. The frail tyres of cars were often punctured on country roads; perhaps by a sharp thorn, or the nails in a discarded horseshoe, or a sharp piece of road metal or broken glass. To fit the spare wheel and tyre on the car was a dirty and heavy job. Even to start the engine, a crank-handle had to be turned arduously by hand. If the engine backfired, the crank went berserk, and an arm could easily be broken.

A few of the luxury cars could be started electrically. In 1908 the Czar of Russia owned a French car that could be started with a flick of the switch and then driven briskly away. For a monarch living in constant danger of assassination, such fast and reliable cars were vital. In 1912 America produced an expensive Cadillac car with an electric self-starter, and in France seven years later the new Citroën tourer – not an expensive car – had its own electric starter and impressive electric headlights. That France contributed much to the early car is visible in the French descriptive names which have long survived: chassis, carburettor, garage, limousine and automobile itself.

More women thought of driving a car. For each adventure they carefully dressed in a protective hat, gloves and top coat. They knew that at the end of a journey they must brush their hair afresh and rearrange their clothes, for wind and dust found their way into most cars. The idea of driving to a friend's house for a formal afternoon tea and walking straight to the front door was unthinkable.

The early car and noisy motorbike made enemies. In New York in 1902 a medical journal denounced the 'evil-smelling' automobiles that frayed the nerves of people strolling along the streets as 'terror alike to pedestrian and horse'. Woodrow Wilson, not yet President of the USA, was appalled by the arrogance of wealthy motorists: 'Nothing has spread socialistic feelings in this country more than the use of the automobile', he said. In his country, it should be added, socialistic feelings had not spread far.

America's vast spaces and soaring prosperity were tailor-made for the car. By 1914 more cars were manufactured in the United States than in any other nation. The heart of the world's automobile industry was the city of Detroit, and one of its advantages was that small-time makers and assemblers of cars could contract out tasks to the hundreds of little engineering plants and foundries at work nearby. Here, at Highland Park, Henry Ford, a farm boy who became a gifted mechanic, made his cars. Perfecting the assembly line, an innovation almost as important as the automobile itself, he manufactured cheap but reliable cars. Every person in his employ did a narrow and specialised task: turning a screw, tightening a bolt, adding an extra part, or inspecting and checking the finished work. Carrying out the same work for hour after hour, the typical employees had rather less need of initiative and versatility than their predecessor who made railway carriages or horse-drawn carts. Meanwhile bottlenecks in the production of cars were removed. Vast sheds had been needed in which to park the new cars while the fresh paint was slowly drying, but in 1923 came the bright idea of spraying the new cars with a nitro-cellulose paint that dried quickly.

Henry Ford's rise to riches was marvelled at. He was one of the most talked-about people on earth. His life story, published in 1923, reportedly went through 30 editions in Germany, where one of its avid readers was Adolf Hitler, then in prison. Even in the new Soviet Union, which did not approve of rags-to-riches stories, Ford's method of producing cars was studied intensely by engineers. Far outselling such major rivals as Citroën in France, Austin and Morris in England, and Fiat in Italy, he was almost too successful. Year after year he refused to alter the basic design of his Model T Ford, and eventually a grand total of 15 million of these Fords travelled the world's roads: a record only passed by the long-lasting Volkswagen more than a generation later.

Cars became steadily cheaper, more comfortable and more reliable. By 1930 the typical new car had a watertight roof, steel doors and glass windows, thus protecting passengers from the weather. Most of the new cars used the safer hydraulic brakes, their tyres were stronger, and with the addition of lead to the petrol their engine was quieter. Engines, however, were not yet powerful, and when small cars had to climb a very steep hill they became slower and slower after each manual change of the gears. Some had to halt and pause for breath – while the hot water in their radiator bubbled over – before they resumed their noisy climb to the top of the hill.

Most families in Europe did not yet own a car or motorbike and thought they would never afford one, but in the United States a new or second-hand car was within the average family's reach. Sometimes the busy intersections in big cities were jammed at peak hours, and the slow-moving horse vehicles, though in decline, aggravated the confusion. Outside peak hours the traffic was light, and most motorists could find a parking place by the kerb.

The trams, which dominated the main streets of nearly all big American cities, were suddenly in danger. Cars wanted the space. The long-distance railways held their own, but not for long. In the late 1920s the American railways still employed 1 700 000 people including more than 300 000 clerks, but soon they were closing the minor branch lines, a precedent that was copied by railway chiefs from Yorkshire to Tasmania and wherever cars and trucks were multiplying. The deserted railway station and the silent railway tunnel were common sights in the second half of the 20th century.

The way of life in spacious countries was being reshaped by cars. In cities the streets were cleaner and the flies fewer in summer as the piles of horse manure became less frequent. In suburbs people could build houses away from the railway stations, and so cities extended over a wider area. Holiday resorts by the sea or in the mountains hitherto needed a railway or steamship to bring in their tourists but now the new resorts could rely solely on the car. Small wayside towns, however, were in peril, for car-owners went to bigger towns for their shopping and services. In many countries Sunday had been a day of quiet, during which trams and trains provided few services before midday, but the car-owner broke this traditional restraint on Sunday travel.

Cars were liberators. They conferred freedom, dispensing with the timetables that dominated all other forms of transport, and enabling their drivers to throw aside old drudgeries and routines. A car affected courting and marriage, where people shopped, where they picnicked and holidayed, how they formed funeral processions, where they went to church and cinema. Car-owners demanded facilities that Americans were quick to devise. In the 1920s the world's first motel appeared in California, the first drive-in cinema was opened in New Jersey in 1933, and two years later in Oklahoma the first parking meters were set up. The drive-in cinema and the drive-in bank were not far away. On the other hand Britain designed the world's first pedestrian crossing. It gave the right of way to pedestrians brave enough to exercise it, for cars were killers, and their toll in the United States alone would reach millions by the century's end. War as well as peace was to be moulded by motor vehicles, and Hitler's tanks, armoured cars and other vehicles in 1940 were to win quick victories that were impossible in the previous world war.

FLIGHT: 'ON A STRANGE MACHINE'

The Wright brothers were making and repairing bicycles at Dayton in Ohio when they became absorbed in the puzzle of how to build a flying machine. Beginning with glider planes they began to ponder how to build and fly a plane driven by an engine, and though their formal schooling was scant they made numerous calculations and experiments of high sophistication before they built a four-cylinder engine in their bicycle workshop. On 17 December 1903 Orville Wright flew his plane and for 12 seconds it was airborne. Later that morning another flight by his brother Wilbur was aloft for almost exactly one minute: the distance covered from start to finish was 260 metres. While Orville thought their achievement was remarkable, having made it in a strongish wind, the press did not really believe their story. This was fortunate for they had not yet secured a patent for their flying machine.

Their ingenuity – and they flew longer and longer distances – was not quickly emulated. But in July 1909 a Frenchman who saw the promise of these simple aircraft made a flight that fired the imagination. On a summer's day, in the time of less than 40 minutes, Louis Blériot flew from Calais right across the English Channel to Dover. A year later the first attempt to fly across the Alps from Switzerland to Italy, using the Simplon Pass, ended in death: that was the destination for many early flights.

Within 20 years of the Wrights' experiment, aircraft were flying with ease at speeds far exceeding those of the fastest ocean liner.

There was one big difference. An ocean liner could carry a thousand passengers in spacious luxury whereas one of the larger aircraft could carry only a pilot and a couple of passengers and a little of their luggage; and even then the pilot had to land frequently to take on more fuel. The plane with its two wings, one large wooden propellor and cramped cabin was like a big ungainly bird without even the power to ride safely through a heavy tropical storm.

In 1926 Alan Cobham, an experienced British pilot, decided to fly across the Middle East to Singapore and Australia, deliberately following the Asian coast during the monsoonal season. As the huge banks of black clouds were a danger, he selected a plane that, equipped with a pair of skis or floats, could land in an emergency on the sea. His powerful Siddeley-Jaguar engine gave him confidence, and he flew all the way from London to Naples in one long summer day, arriving after dark. Much later, when he had to pass through the walls of tropical clouds, he felt helpless. He was able to dodge around a few of the storms but the rain blinded him even in daylight.

Cobham carried no wireless, was guided by no weather forecasts along much of the way, and yet he felt that a mail route could be operated in the monsoon season – so long as a pilot was prepared to wait a day or two for a break in the clouds. A year later Charles A. Lindbergh showed what could be achieved in fair weather by flying alone from New York to Paris. Making no stops, he was 33 hours in the air. If he had carried two passengers or if he had not been favoured by the prevailing winds the long journey would probably have been impossible.

For long-distance travel the huge gas-filled balloons or airships pointed to the future. In May 1926 a big airship was even ready to cross the North Pole. Captain Roald Amundsen, the Norwegian who had been the first to reach the South Pole, planned the expedition, while General Umberto Nobile piloted the airship in what Mussolini called a remarkable alliance: 'indomitable Italian courage combined with inflexible Norwegian will'. After many attempts to forecast the weather, the airship rose majestically above the Norwegian island of Spitzbergen; and General Nobile looked down on the white sea, and listened carefully to the throb of his petrol engine. Ice formed on the rigging, and tiny parts of the airship broke away, pricking holes in the vast fabric holding the gas. The airmen were so busy making repair patches that they had no time for sleep.

On the third day an Italian crew member parachuted to find a landing place; and the airship floated down to flat ground near a remote Alaskan settlement after a flight of 3400 miles. Some time later in Rome's streets the afternoon newspapers excitedly predicted that this new route over the North Pole would eventually link Europe and East Asia.

The large airships, though they travelled at little more than twice the speed of an ocean liner, had a carrying capacity that none of the existing winged aircraft could match. But they were costly and in their early years seemed prone to accidents. In 1922 the US army's grand zeppelin Roma crashed into high-tension wires, and 34 people were killed. In the following year the great French zeppelin Dixmude plunged into the sea and all aboard were lost. Britain's most famous airship, the huge R-101, shaped like a massive whale, set out for India in 1931 but crashed during a storm over France, and 46 people died. The Akron, built in Ohio for the US navy and capable of carrying five small aircraft in its hold and a host of passengers, was flying near the coast of New Jersey in stormy weather in 1933. It hit the sea and 73 lives were lost.

Germany's finest commercial airship, the Hindenburg, powered by four Mercedes-Benz diesel engines, was more massive than the jumbo jet of a later era. In 1937 it was running a regular passenger service across the Atlantic, its fastest crossings – with a tail wind – averaging just over two days and nights. While landing near New York it burst into flames, and 36 lives were lost. Meanwhile General Nobile himself led a charmed life in the clouds. During another expedition to the North Pole his Italian airship crashed with the loss of seven lives. He was then hired as a designer by the Russians, and their new airship, after creating a world record by staying aloft for 130 hours, met its end in 1938 while trying to save Soviet scientists marooned on polar ice; 13 lives were lost.

The smaller winged aircraft began to triumph, and no plane was more effective than Donald Douglas's fast, practical all-metal, DC 3. A few aero companies began to organise a weekly flight across the Atlantic and even the Pacific Ocean, mostly using flying boats, but few passengers could afford the fare and many who could afford it refused to run the risk. Most politicians of importance continued to make long journeys to diplomatic conferences by ocean liner or long-distance train, meanwhile keeping in touch with their colleagues through occasional radio-telegrams and even a phone call.

The advances in aircraft, whether in speed or carrying capacity, were accelerated in the 1930s by the likelihood of war. Victory at many of the decisive junctures of the Second World War would be determined by skill in the air. It was France, which in 1911 had possessed more certified air pilots than all the other nations of Europe combined, that failed to create an adequate air force in the 1930s. It was Germany that, in the five years before the outbreak of the Second World War, boldly built the world's mightiest fleet of combat and trainer aircraft – some 30 000 in all.

THE NEW PETROLEUM KINGS

At the start of the century the most important mineral was black coal. No nation could become industrially great without its own large seams of black coal; and Europe's early ascendancy in the age of steam had owed much to its dominance in coal. The murky skyline of whole regions was pierced by the poppet heads and mullock dumps of the coalmines. No year passed without one mining disaster, and the aggregate of accidents could kill 1000 coalminers a year in Britain alone. By 1920, however, coal was being challenged by a fuel that was found less easily, and seemed to be lacking in most of Europe.

The challenger was petroleum – a name stemming from two Latin words for rock and oil. It was first sought systematically by Americans who drilled into the rocks of Pennsylvania in 1859. Russia too became a big producer of oil. The religious group known as the Parsees worshipped fire, and some of its members had long visited Baku – a town on the west shores of the Caspian Sea – to pray at the fires which burned oil that flowed to the surface. Baku was an ideal place for the Russian oil drillers. In the 1870s they found rich oil, and eventually pumped it via a pipeline – 560 miles in length and easily the longest in the world – across the mountains to the Black Sea. There in 1892 the pioneer oil tankers loaded it, carrying it through the Dardanelles and the Suez Canal to East Asian ports. The ascendancy of Russia as the main oil producer was brief.

From these early oilfields a useful product was the kerosene that provided the evening light in millions of houses where candles had once burned. The rise of the motor car and aircraft, and the additional demand for oil and diesel fuel by ships and power stations, created an even greater demand for oil, much of which came from the United States and its new oil wells in Oklahoma, Kansas and California. By 1925 half of the world's monthly output of oil came from the United States, while another large flow came from nearby Venezuela and Mexico. Such was the glut of oil that some magnates hoped that no fresh fields would be discovered for a decade or more.

In the Middle East the deep reservoirs of oil lay hidden by layers of sand and dry rocks. The first oil was discovered in Persia in 1908 by a syndicate initiated by a Queensland lawyer and entrepreneur, William K. D'Arcy, who had made his fortune from the goldmine at Mount Morgan, right on the Tropic of Capricorn. Two decades later the first oil in neighbouring Iraq was found at a depth of 1500 feet. The oil, when struck, spouted above the derrick and, splashing down to earth, quickly formed a flammable swamp.

The Arabian peninsula, with its deserts and mountains and long beaches, was seen as potentially rich in oil by a New Zealand mining expert, Major Frank Holmes. He arrived in 1922 at the island port of Bahrain, distinctive with his white umbrella, sola topee, and his veil to fend off the flies. Bahrain's promising sources of wealth were the date plantations and especially the pearl fishery along its sandy coastline – until the Japanese cultured pearls began to compete with the real pearls. A new source of wealth was therefore needed. Gratifyingly, the oil that Holmes predicted was found by the drills of

Standard Oil of California in 1932. Six years later, further oil was discovered in Kuwait and in Saudi Arabia. For a little longer the camel, horse and ass remained the busy carriers of people and goods in Arabia; and these worthy animals required hay, shrubs and other fodder rather than petrol.

As the world possessed plenty of oil, the Middle East was not yet required to be a large producer. In the second half of the century, however, it would be the dominant producer in the world, and capable of making the great powers dance to its tune and come running when the music stopped.

THE BRILLIANT EINSTEIN AND HIS BLIND EYE

Those who practised pure science were mysterious and out of sight, and their work was not easily explained by those newspapers that were dedicated to carrying scientific milestones to their readers. But their research was pointing to another potential but unexpected source of energy, at the very time when more and more oil was being located in the Middle East.

In Germany at Christmas 1895, Professor Wilhelm Röntgen reported his discovery of the X-ray. One of his first memorable photographs showed the wedding ring on the finger and the bones of the hand of Mrs Röntgen. From the discovery of the X-ray flowed, directly and indirectly, a brilliant line of more abstract research in a variety of European universities, laboratories and studies. In France, Henri Becquerel found that uranium had the capacity to emit rays, and Pierre and Marie Curie discovered radium and also showed that its radioactivity was in the realm of physics rather than chemistry. In England, J. J. Thomson discovered that the atom was divisible; and

Ernest Rutherford, a migrant scholar from New Zealand, shaped nuclear theory and grasped some of the implications of the incredible amount of energy 'latent in the atom'. In Germany, Max Planck developed his quantum theory and revolutionised knowledge about the flow of energy: the flow was not continuous, as once thought. The young Dane, Niels Bohr, working in England, carried this bold thinking a step further in 1913 with his paper, 'On the constitution of atoms and molecules'. Year by year the previously accepted truths in physics, or 'natural philosophy' as it was widely called, were being swept up and tossed about by a whirlwind. Many of the new theories were erroneous. Naturally, it is the winners that are remembered.

In every intellectual invasion of new territory a few scholars arrive too early, and their discoveries find few sympathetic listeners. Ludwig Boltzmann, an Austrian, developed a controversial theory on energy and atoms at a time when some chemists and philosophers doubted whether atoms even existed. He committed suicide in Italy in 1906, when the climate at last was turning in his favour.

Albert Einstein joined in creating this whirlwind as well as making sense of it. To most scientists capable of comprehending what was occurring in other realms, Einstein was the finest scientist of the 20th century. He came to be viewed as the senior member of the royal family of science. Whether he will stand so high a century later is not certain because each century rearranges past heroes.

A German Jew, Einstein spent his early childhood in Munich where his father experienced ups and downs in the electrical industry. At first Albert was not so successful at school – the violin was his love. His real education began in Zurich, where he blossomed as a mathematician, and then in Berne where he was a young official in the patent office. He was cheerful, generous and mentally brilliant without parading it. In appearance he was shortish, with a small mouth, plump cheeks and nose, and rather frizzy black hair. His woolly moustache was to be his hallmark when his photo began to appear in the world's newspapers.

The saying that the Swiss invented nothing except the cuckoo clock is mocked by Einstein's work, much of which was carried on in Swiss cities. In 1905 at about the age of 26 he transformed thinking about light, space and time with his special theory of relativity. His second notable advance, the general theory of relativity, was finally announced in 1916, by which time he was a professor in wartime Berlin. Resting on the deflection of starlight, the general theory could be precisely tested only when a total eclipse of the sun took place. On 29 May 1919 such an eclipse – meticulously observed by a British expedition on an island in the Gulf of Guinea and by a series of painstaking calculations – proved that Einstein's general theory was correct. No person had contributed more to understanding the simplicities and the complexities of the universe.

How did Einstein tunnel his way to these hidden truths? Since science is the epitome of what is logical and rational, it is believed that great scientists arrive at their truths through logical thinking and, above all, through verbal processes. Einstein was one of those who reached bold and dislocating conclusions not by systematically plotting his course. Nor were words and statistics his vital stepping stones. His progress towards new knowledge was by mental leaps of breathtaking brilliance.

It was assumed that he was a genius who could enter any field and throw a dazzling light on it. His views on peace and war were seen as products of the same genius. While he more than anybody appreciated the complexity of physical nature, he saw no complexity in human nature and in international relations. For a time he believed that war could be easily abolished. Unwittingly, by preaching a version of pacifism at an inappropriate time, his influential voice helped to weaken some of the barriers standing against the rise of Hitler. Wisely, Einstein left Germany for the last time, moving to the United States at the end of 1932, just before Hitler became chancellor.

The first third of the century had experienced a remarkable seedtime in fundamental research into matter, time, space and energy, the practical consequences of which could not be foreseen. One avenue of research, not necessarily viewed as important, centred on the atom and the explosive energy locked inside it. That avenue of research was to lead to a precipice in 1945.

9

AN ITALIAN DRUMMER

Italy blended the sophisticated and the primitive. In Rome were the enchanting choirs, adept surgeons, dedicated theologians, and the noble architecture from many ages; in Milan were the skilled engineers and craftsmen and the acclaimed opera house; but in the countryside most people were impoverished. On the eve of the First World War the typical Italian family was rural, and their standard of living was closer to a North African than to a German family. In the cities in 1910 the law still allowed nine-year-olds to work in factories.

THE EMERGENCE OF MUSSOLINI

For long a divided land, with many regions and many dialects, Italy was not easily united in spirit. In the south illiteracy was widespread. Of every 10 people in Calabria only three could read and write, though in the far north the readers were more numerous.

A relatively new democracy, Italy's voters were few until 1912 when the vote, in a leap of faith, was conferred on literate men over the age of 21, on illiterate men over the age of 30, and on former soldiers.

Italy's heavy industry was not strong enough to compensate for the inadequacies of agriculture. Alone amongst the more populous countries of Europe, it possessed no rich coalfields and no large iron-ore fields and no smoke-shrouded steelworks to match those of the Ruhr and England. Of people, however, it was well endowed. Its population jumped from 21 million in 1861 to more than 37 million on the eve of the war, and the total would have been higher but for the flood of emigrants leaving to make their fortune across the seas. The personal remittances posted to Italy from the Americas were a Christmas present to the whole economy as well as to the families remaining at home.

Temporarily neutral in the opening months of the First World War, Italy was wooed by both sides. Unexpectedly it joined the side of Britain, France and their allies. For more than three years it fought against the Austrians and Hungarians in the foothills and middle heights of the Alps with bravery but no resounding military success. Eager to become a great power, Italy hoped for – indeed was virtually promised – rewards from the winning side, but was so disappointed by negotiations at the Paris peace table in 1919 that on one occasion its delegates walked out. Britain and France, already with huge empires, secured the richest colonial prizes, especially in the Middle East and Africa, and did not appease Italy with the promise of Togoland in west Africa and a possible colony in the high Caucasus. Rejecting such offers, and accepting only a few skerricks of African territory and a prized piece of the Austrian Tyrol, many Italians felt disillusioned that their heavy human sacrifices in the war had been so meagrely rewarded.

Here was a strong nationalist drum, waiting to be beaten by a rising politician capable of catching the ear of the former soldiers. Even civilians were eager to catch the sound of a nationalist drummer. They had suffered during the war through a periodic shortage of bread, partly because the flour and grain ships from the Black Sea ports could no longer arrive. In August 1917 a bread riot in the industrial city of Turin had caused the death of some 50 people.

After the war the economic distress was heightened by political unrest. In 1920 the country was on the brink of a revolution. In the Adriatic port of Ancona a battalion of the army mutinied. That was a signal, both north and south, for peasants to seize rural estates and for workers to take over factories. Strikes dislocated the railways, city tramways, and electric power stations. The troubles were deepened by the severe but brief postwar depression which hit nearly every country in Europe. The time was ripe for the rise of Mussolini.

THE BLACKSHIRTS REACH ROME

Most Italians first saw Benito Mussolini in black and white photographs which, aided by a judicious angle of the camera, made his face and especially his jaw appear strong and authoritative. He persuaded Italians that he could do something for their troubled nation. For a time he succeeded.

His father was a blacksmith and a revolutionary; and so the son received the Christian name of another revolutionary, Benito

Juarez, the liberator of Mexico. His mother Rosa was the village teacher, a devoted Catholic who wished for no revolution. Young Benito, taking something from each parent, wished to be a radical and a schoolteacher. After his requests in the early 1900s for a teaching post were refused in town after town, he went to live in Switzerland.

Gifted with words, both on the printed page and on the speaking platform, Mussolini returned to edit radical newspapers: in his home town of Forli where his paper was called the *Class Struggle* and in Trento just across the border in Austria. For his outspoken views he spent time in prison. Eventually he was invited to become editor of the official socialist paper *Avanti*. When the First World War broke out he defied the socialists' position – they favoured neutrality – and advocated that Italy join in the war against the German-speaking peoples whom he viewed as the natural enemy, for they occupied part of north-eastern Italy. As his nationalism supplanted his socialism, he produced in November 1914 the first issue of his paper, *Popolo d'Italia*. After Italy entered the war he served as a soldier in the cold mountains of the north, close to the Austrian border. In 1917 he was wounded by a grenade. His war service was to prove a political asset. Many war veterans thought that when he spoke in public he spoke for them.

Pugnacious and ambitious, Mussolini founded his party of Fascists in Milan in March 1919, four months after the end of the war. A small player on the violent political stage and active mainly in the north of Italy, his party called for order in place of civil chaos, while itself adding to the chaos. It denounced the high level of unemployment; it believed in helping working men but not through trade unions; and it promised to curb the individualism of capitalism. In the place of strong corporations, strong unions, strong universities, and a strong parliament, it asserted the power of the state as enforcer, arbitrator and inspirer. It also believed in the nation rather than internationalism.

A believer in the power of words, Mussolini trusted also in the power of the fist. Indeed fasces, the origin of the name of his party, were the rods that symbolised authority in the Roman era. He was eager, like several other leaders of rival political groups, to create his own armed force which grew and grew. In Italy firearms were easily bought in shops; and in a short period in 1921 – a year of civil disorder – the government issued permits to nearly 900 000 Italians to buy firearms. By 1921 his fascists in their black shirts were bruising opponents, taking over public offices, and breaking up rival political rallies. In some cities the Blackshirts fought armed socialists, in others they fought the police. Retaliation was frequent. In Florence in 1921 a bomb was thrown by a communist at a procession of schoolboys displaying patriotic fervour. In another episode in the same city the small son of a factory owner was killed. Violent episodes occurred almost weekly – even a funeral procession was not safe.

At first a party of the cities, Mussolini's fascists won recruits in the countryside where they showed sympathy for struggling farm labourers. As the eventual confiscation of private property by communists and socialists was often feared in the countryside, many farmers preferred the fascists. In addition many war veterans favoured Mussolini. And yet in total his electoral support was only enough to sustain a minor, not a major party. At the 1921 elections the Fascists won 35 seats but the two major parties each won more than 100 seats.

By October 1922 his Fascist Party held enough supporters to make plans for a mass rally and a threatening show of force. At the Rome railway stations over a period of just a few days there arrived a succession of trains conveying some 30 000 fascists, soon to grow close to 50 000. Nearly all were distinguished by black shirts made of a variety of cloth of varying shades of darkness. The weapons of this motley army were rifles, pistols, sticks, clubs and whips. In any clash with the national army they would surely lose. But in the event of a confrontation in the streets of Rome it was possible that the soldiers might refuse to fire on their fellow countrymen, many of them being ex-servicemen.

In the face of the crowds of assembled Blackshirts in Rome, King Victor Emmanuel III and the prime minister agreed that they must proclaim a state of emergency. The army would then have the authority to impose order in the streets. Next morning the king, changing his mind, refused to sign the proclamation declaring a state of emergency. While the king himself was not a supporter of Mussolini, he believed the time had come for a strong leader to form a coalition and guide temporarily the drifting, faction-torn nation. Mussolini was his private choice. It was an astonishing decision because in the large parliament, Mussolini's party was far outnumbered by liberals, Catholics, conservatives and even by the combined tally of socialists and communists. Moreover Mussolini was a republican and might eventually overthrow the monarchy.

Mussolini was in Milan when he received the royal telegram summoning him to Rome. On that memorable Sunday evening in

October 1922, he was escorted to the railway station by his mistress, Margherita Sarfatti, a wealthy Jewess who was well known as an art critic. Even then Mussolini was supremely confident that, if the chance arose, he could impose order and efficiency on Italy. Just before 8.30 p.m., when the express train for Rome was due to depart, he said to the saluting stationmaster that it had to leave on time: 'From now on everything must work perfectly.' It was easier said than done in a nation where morale was low and industrial discontent, especially in the railways, was high.

It was almost 11 o'clock the next morning before Mussolini finally reached Rome by the indirect train route of that era. After briefly visiting his hotel, he met the short, shy and strong-willed king who invited him to form a cabinet. In his team of 14, Mussolini selected three other fascists and two war heroes – the heads of the armed forces. His message to the public was implicit: the armed forces and not his ragged Blackshirt army were again in control. Six weeks later the parliament voted by a large majority (the dissenters being social-ists and communists) to grant Mussolini and his cabinet one year in which they could run the country by decree rather than by act of parliament. In Mussolini's first year of experimenting he provided enough order to please most Italians. His own plans were already ambitious. He hoped that the Roman Empire would be reborn.

At the national elections in 1924 the Fascists harnessed all the resources of the state to boost their vote whereas their opponents, hopelessly divided, did not even use the resource of common sense. The Fascists won 403 of the 599 seats. Eventually they dispensed with elections, Mussolini explaining that the country did not need them. In a land where democracy had put down young but seemingly virile roots, he pulled up those roots. But democracy – it could equally be said – had helped to destroy itself.

Italy was not alone. Most of Europe's democracies did not function effectively amid the tensions and economic distress of the first postwar years. A number of the new parliaments had been elected on a voting system – based on French and Belgian models – that encouraged a multitude of parties, none of which was capable of winning enough seats to rule in its own right. The injection of the voting method called proportional representation increased the splintering. Indecisive, unstable governments became normal. A version of Italy's strong-arm solution was to be copied by various other European nations.

ITALY'S SPOTLIGHTS AND SHADOWS

Italy became a talking point of Europe. A host of visitors passed judgment on what Mussolini had achieved in his opening years. While many were impressed, democrats were often appalled at what they saw or heard: the banning of rival political parties and the deporting of political dissenters to island prisons, without the benefit of a trial. Democrats regretted the ban on strikes, the interference in universities and the censoring of the media. Newspapers, books, radio and even signboards were censored. For those who held heretical political thoughts, the privacy of the home or the confessional box were about the only places where they could be safely expressed. One-party government went hand in hand with one official set of ideas.

Mussolini's noisy drums fascinated and then repelled Arturo Toscanini, one of the world's leading conductors and the head of La Scala opera house. After the war, like so many Italian patriots,

Toscanini had been sympathetic to Mussolini, so much so that in Milan in 1919 he stood for parliament on a fascist ticket. Slowly becoming disillusioned with fascism, he protested with his musical baton, refusing to conduct the playing of the fascist anthem at one of the most anticipated musical events of the 20th century, the premiere of *Turandot*. Many thought him courageous, many condemned him as disloyal. But in the eyes of the world he was perhaps the most famous living Italian – apart from Mussolini – and so his protests on the podium damaged Italy's reputation. Revenge was inevitable. In Bologna on 14 March 1931, entering a theatre where he was about to conduct, he and his wife were bashed by fascist thugs. Three months later he left his country.

Many tourists did not observe the bullying and the intimidation that permeated public and intellectual life. Others argued that it was preferable for fascists rather than communists to impose a straitjacket on Italian life. Moreover in the early years of Mussolini the country had regenerated itself. The change was not unique – a national blossoming was experienced in Finland and several other European countries – but it was impressive in Italy which had virtually emerged from chaos. Economic life grew in confidence. Unemployment was less menacing, strikes were rare, and the civil servants less susceptible to bribery. In the south the lawless Mafia was curbed. In the countryside, Mussolini gained prestige by draining marshes, once the home of the malarial mosquito, and by increasing the numbers of small landholders and share-farmers in a country where hitherto most rural workers owned no land.

He electrified many of the busier railways and began to excavate tunnels enabling a direct railway to pass under the mountains separating Bologna from Florence and Rome. Visitors were assured that for the first time the notorious Italian trains were running on time – a slight exaggeration but at least they were running. Mussolini built the first motorway – from Milan to the lakes – and some of the cars speeding along that road were stylish models such as Maserati, Lancia and Alfa-Romeo which proclaimed Italy's belated talent for engineering.

Italy displayed policies that many of the early Fascists would not have predicted. At the party's congress held in Florence in August 1919 some members wished to confiscate the property of religious orders. A decade later their tune was altered. Mussolini prepared to sign in 1929 a treaty that made the Vatican, the home of the pope, an independent nation. For decades the Papacy had been, in its eyes, a prisoner in its own land. In living memory the owner of territories extending from Rome across the spine of mountains to the Adriatic, an independent state distinguished by the plural name of the Papal States, it now owned no territory. Even the huge church of St Peter, the most influential church in the whole world, was on the soil of a secular state.

Now, in a series of negotiations between Mussolini and Pope Pius XI, it was agreed that there should be in one tiny quarter of ancient Rome a completely independent Vatican city-state, to which Italy would assign an ambassador and the Vatican would reciprocate. When he left his own state and entered Italian territory the supreme pontiff had the same legal protection from insult and physical injury as the Italian head of state. Just as important to Catholics, the bishops were accorded the legal right in all Italian state schools to appoint priests to give religious instruction to the children of

Catholic parents. The wearing of the crucifix became almost compulsory in schools. The state even recognised the Catholic feast days, on which, in return, prayer would be offered for the state. Nonetheless the new Vatican city-state had the right to pursue its own foreign policy, and in one phase of the Second World War it was to be a place of refuge for people fleeing Italy.

A robust quality, rarely witnessed in Italian life since the Renaissance, impressed numerous observers standing at the centre or to the right of the political compass. Italy enjoyed wide success in international events, especially in 1933 and 1934. The boxer Primo Carnera, from Udine, won the World Heavyweight boxing title; Italy won the World Cup in soccer; Italian flying boats – at that time the main means of fast long-distance travel – were the envy of most nations; and the Italian ocean liner *Rex* broke the record for the Atlantic crossing. Mussolini basked in the glow of these national feats.

Though Benito Mussolini is now diminished by the shadow of Hitler, he was immensely influential in the 1920s. Amongst his many admirers was the young Adolf Hitler who was still far from gaining office. Even those cultivated Germans who travelled to Italy to hear fine music or to see the classical sights were sometimes surprised to see how much this cheerfully chaotic country was being reshaped. If so much could be achieved in Italy with all its economic disadvantages, what could be achieved in Germany with all its advantages? To some degree, Mussolini's success paved the way for Hitler.

10

A WORLD DEPRESSION

The First World War so weakened Europe that its share of the world's population and economic output fell considerably. The hub of the world's finance moved to the United States which was already the dynamo of economic activity. For the first time the main European powers were partly dependent on New York which, as a financial leader, was naturally less experienced than London in facing crises. Unfortunately the financial crisis that bubbled up in New York in 1929 was more serious than any other crisis that London had ever been forced to face.

While the United States had its economic weaknesses in the 1920s, they were less acute than those crippling most European nations. Their war had to be paid for. The national debt of Britain and Germany was multiplied by 11, and that of France and Italy by six. Europe suffered from another financial infection soon after the war. In the uncertainty, all prices went up like leaves in the wind. By 1922 Austrian prices were up 14 000 times, Poland's 2.5 million times, and Russia's four billion times. A year later Germany broke even those astronomical records. Such inflation was difficult to comprehend even by those who lived through it. They did know, however, that the pay they carried home on Friday night bought far less if they spent it on Saturday night. While we call it inflation, it was really total chaos.

Britain, France and various other nations, while avoiding the worst inflation, could not avoid its consequences. The world economy was like a vast heating system, with the air circulating everywhere, and the blistering heat in some rooms affecting the atmosphere in others. Inflation was eventually curbed but left its legacy.

Another disruption of the 1920s can be easily understood by Europeans today because they are witnessing it in reverse. The creation of the European Union, simply by flattening national boundaries, has enabled commerce and investment to flow freely over much of Europe, thus increasing prosperity. The opposite process was at work after the war ended in 1918. Europe then had a cluster of new nations that erected national boundaries – an astonishing 12 500 miles of them – where none existed. New nations imposed tariffs and erected customs houses where none had existed. Ports were cut off from their old hinterland, railway lines were parted from their nearest port, and flour mills severed from their source of grain. In Europe there circulated 27 different national currencies instead of the 14 on the eve of the war.

PANIC ON WALL STREET

The United States boomed for much of the 1920s. Shining cars poured onto the roads, and suburbs of new houses financed by a myriad of banks, spread like a tide. The stock exchanges boiled and then simmered, for it was absurdly easy to borrow money for the purchase of shares. The clamour for shares could not be sustained. By October 1929 the steelworks and car factories were not quite so busy, and builders were laying off carpenters, bricklayers and electricians. But optimism persisted, and nowhere more than on sections of the stock exchange.

On Thursday 24 October 1929, the stock exchange in New York opened briskly with only faint signs of gloom. Then for some reason, valid or invalid, a gloomy hysteria set in, hour by hour. Nearly everyone wanted to sell; and as prices slumped, the bargain hunters jumped in, only to find an hour later that their bargain was no longer a bargain. Others jumped in to buy at the very low prices and were bemused at the end of the day to see their own bargain had also evaporated. As the news of the panic spread, spectators poured onto Wall Street to watch the scoreboard. It was remarked by the *New York Times* that many young women as well as men were nervously watching the prices creep down and down. That day the total number of sold shares exceeded, by more than 50 per cent, the number sold during any previous day in the exchange's history.

The money-losing transactions were so many, the demand for paperwork so unmanageable, that broking houses hired whole floors of hotel rooms so that their clerks could work late, sleep in the hotel, and start early at their offices. The gloom in the share market crossed to other markets. In sympathy the price of cotton, copper and most bulk commodities – cocoa was a curious exception – fell too.

In the following days most of the bankers and brokers announced in loud voices that the economy and the stock exchange were in sound health. The prince of millionaires J.D. Rockefeller, and his son too, openly bought shares as a sign of faith. Five days after the panic, sobering but reassuring assessments pervaded most of the newspapers. *The World* in New York announced that 'the country had not suffered a catastrophe', and reputable newspapers in Louisville and Chicago agreed that the slump, while overdue, would soon give rise to a recovery. Almost alone, a daily newspaper in Tulsa, Oklahoma, warned that the crazy speculators, with their booms and busts, could 'endanger the entire country'. The *New York Times* summed up the nation's mood with its headline of 30 October, 'Basic Condition is Sound', and still displayed large advertisements for such luxurious items as a chauffeur's 'dressy' uniform made of off-wool whipcord, and expensive women's shoes in blue-fox suede. Such fashionable advertisements would soon disappear.

The public was in no mood to accept such assurances from the wealthy. Their own shares had fallen markedly – why should they pretend all was well? In some weeks American shares rallied a little and then fell by more than they had rallied. Radio messages, disclosing the latest collapse of the American share market, shocked many passengers in the first-class lounges of the mail steamers speeding across the North Atlantic – it was still the era when the rich travelled by sea. A few of the travellers sent a private radio message requesting that many of their shares be sold. A few, waiting until their ship reached port, thought that there was plenty of time in which to sell. When ships did berth at New York's wharves there was a rush of passengers to the public phones on the wharf. It was too late.

As share prices fell, property values followed them down, though not so rapidly in London and Paris as in New York. In every country the price of virtually every major commodity except gold fell away. It was normal enough for an economic boom to be followed by a slump; but this slump had a frightening severity. Fear gave way to panic. Banks began to close, 9000 small banks closing in the United States alone, and major banks closing in Austria, Germany, Czechoslovakia and other wealthy nations. In France the monetary policy, intent on accumulating gold reserves, increased the international carnage.

Most people ceased to buy items they regarded as no longer essential. New cars could not easily be sold, and so Detroit and Turin car-works bought less steel and rubber. In turn their suppliers put off workers, their wives ceased to buy new clothes for the family, and the demand for wool, cotton, and leather fell in cities and farms thousands of miles away. When the season's holidays arrived, the resorts on beaches in South Africa and the Riviera, and mountains in Japan and Switzerland, were half empty.

This event, far more than the world war, conveyed the impression that the world was one and that no place – not even the slopes of the Andes and the bays of Rio – could escape the ripples of a gigantic event in the Northern Hemisphere.

THE ISOLATION OF LATIN AMERICA

In the early 1900s, Brazil was seen as the drowsy giant that one day would awake. It embraced coastal deserts – where a drought had helped to kill half a million people – vast rain forests and high tropical mountains. Possessing about half of the South American continent and nearly half of its people, it shared a border with every South American nation except Chile. With such long boundaries, Brazil participated in various border disputes. One prolonged scuffle with tiny British Guiana was settled by arbitration in 1904, after the King of Italy gravely announced his verdict. Possessing the world's largest belt of rubber trees – a vital commodity on the eve of the motor era – Brazil had also been the main supplier of diamonds until the rise of the Kimberley field in South Africa. Formally known as the United States of Brazil it was rich in resources but often poor in tapping them. It had almost become accustomed, like many of its neighbours, to financial shocks and political upheavals.

Brazil's main rival was Argentina. Back in 1800 Argentina had been the most sparsely peopled land in Latin America but a century later its population was growing at about the same rapid pace as that of the United States and even faster than Brazil. By 1910 it was a beacon of prosperity. Most travellers whose ship called at Rio and then at Buenos Aires tended to prefer the Argentinian capital in all except scenery. Buenos Aires, just a river estuary fringed by a flat plain, was a marvel. By far the largest city in South America and one of the top 15 cities of the world, its large railway stations despatched trains to the pampas, and its opera house and Catholic cathedral were stately. While the British owned and ran the railways, the Italian settlers lined the decks of most of the big passenger ships that sailed up the wide estuary. Only the USA outshone Argentina as the goal for Italian migrants at a time when they were becoming the main emigrants of Europe. Indeed so big was the Argentinian harvest – grain surpassed beef as the main export in 1904 – that many Italian and Spanish labourers came out just to earn high money at harvest time.

Chile, Bolivia, Peru, Paraguay and Uruguay were amongst the other South American nations that shunned Europe's military alliances. When the world war broke out in 1914, these independent states of South America did nothing. Most prospered during the war, and all escaped serious destruction. Only Brazil, vexed by the German submarines' attacks on several of its ships, joined in the war for the last 12 months, despatching a naval fleet to European waters, and aviators and doctors to the frontline in France. In contrast Chile, possessing strong links with both Germany and Britain, did not lift a finger. Other states, if they joined in the war, lifted a hand only in the final months.

Little harmed by the world war, South America could not escape the world depression, which was overwhelmingly a global event. Almost as devastating as a major war, the Depression shocked and impoverished its victims rather than killed or wounded them. The Depression's victims, however, were far more numerous than those of any war.

UNEMPLOYMENT – A GLOBAL INFECTION

Those countries that had received a fast stream of migrants in the 1920s ceased to receive them. Italians no longer emigrated to Brazil and Argentina. Australia, once a hub for immigrants, lost more migrants in the early 1930s – they returned home – than it gained. The United States received fewer than 100 000 immigrants in 1931 – the lowest total since 1862, when the American Civil War was being fought. In 1933 it received only 23 000 immigrants.

Thousands of people, being unemployed, were tempted to leave Europe until they learned that in the Americas the distress was just as severe as at home.

Some of the passenger ships that had carried the migrants paid off their engineers, chefs, waiters and cabin crew and rusted at anchor, a caretaker walking the wooden decks that had recently been crowded with promenaders. Of course the ships ceased to buy coal, and that put numerous coalminers out of work. They in turn could not afford to buy new shoes and clothes for their families, and that decision – multiplied 500 times – destroyed jobs in distant factories. The effect of losing five jobs here, and 500 there, rippled around the world, reaching tin miners in Bolivia, sawmillers in New Zealand and steel-makers in France. When they lost their jobs, or worked only three days a week, another ripple commenced. The world was engulfed in these economic ripples.

Unemployment spread swiftly, taking hold of Montevideo and Valparaiso in South America, Capetown and Algiers in Africa, and shunning not one city in the world. Nothing like it had been seen before. By 1932 a few countries had an official rate of unemployment that exceeded 30 per cent. As most nations did not offer more than a modicum of social security, the hardship and despair were on a monumental scale.

Heinrich Hauser, after driving along the Hamburg–Berlin highway, reported in 1932 that an 'almost unbroken chain of homeless men extends the whole length' of the road. Some were experienced craftsmen wearing the costumes of their craft guild – bricklayers wearing high felt hats, or milkmen wearing red-striped shirts. Many job-seekers carried their shoes, slung over their shoulder, and this saved the leather from wearing out. Here and there mother and children followed a pram or wheelbarrow piled with possessions and pushed along by the father. Thousands were approaching the very city that others, now passing them on the other side of the highway, had recently left. Occasionally they would see a crop almost ready for the digging, and in no time as many as 100 people would be stealing potatoes. The farmers could not easily interfere, being outnumbered. Such scenes were reported from every industrial nation except Russia.

In rural districts in the new world, lone men or families were on the roads, looking for work. At a free camping ground outside a town near nightfall arrive the first vehicles 'loaded high with tents, household gear, children and bedding', and a few dogs trotting behind. An old loaded truck appears, a hawker trying to sell his pots and pans, and cyclists carrying their food and clothes in second-hand sugar bags. The glow of campfires and the smell of cooking bring to an end the tiring day. In Australia there were hundreds of such staging posts for those who were on the move but with nowhere to go.

Hundreds of thousands of European families, their breadwinner lacking a job, shared their home with relatives to cut their living expenses. They limited their shopping list to potatoes, rice, onions, treacle, tea and sugar, and the cheapest loaves. They walked miles to attend bargain sales; they walked along railway lines and picked up lumps of coal that had fallen from locomotives; if they lived near a coalfield they climbed over the dumps of discarded rock and with the aid of a hammer gathered what coal they could. When no money remained they took their brooch, locket, watch, and other small, valuable possessions to a pawnbroker and borrowed money.

Many employers gave preference to the young because they were allowed to pay them less. So unemployment was often lower amongst teenagers than adults. This policy hurt the former soldiers. Millions who, at the age of 20, had escaped death on battlefields and at sea in the First World War found themselves some 15 years later economically abandoned in the nation they had patriotically served.

The Depression hit China early. The export market for silk, a luxury item, almost collapsed. Furthermore the demand for raw silk was hurt by the competition from Europe's new synthetic, rayon. The making of cotton textiles in Chinese cities was shaken by cheap exports dumped by Japan. China, so reliant on the weather, suffered additionally because the floods in the Yangtze were high in 1931, and three years later too much rain was followed by too little.

Japan had become competitive as a manufacturer in the 1920s and showed a foretaste of the energy and skill that it would display again from the 1950s onwards. Japan's special success was in textiles, and by 1932 its exports of cotton goods were larger than those of Britain. Manchester, the original home of the textiles revolution, now had empty mills, partly as a result of Japanese commercial vigour and India's expanding textile industry. But even Japan was finally pummelled by the world depression. Its answer, like that of nearly every nation, was to try to export more. The result was a glut of unsold goods in the world's warehouses and shops.

The slump sweeping across the globe did less damage in Africa, India and wherever small farmers grew food only for themselves and their neighbours. A central African tending a plot of maize for her family's use did not lose much, but the cousins growing coffee for the world market earned perhaps only one-half of their former income. Malays working in a rubber plantation suffered because the demand for rubber tyres slumped in all lands, but their neighbours growing rice, vegetables and a few chickens for their own use were much less affected.

Some economic statistics have an innate tendency to be gloomy. Statisticians always measure the people who have no work rather than the far larger number who do go to work. Even in the worst months of the Depression, more than two of every three British people of working age were at work, and they earned enough for their family, once in a while, to put money into the football pools, buy a packet of cheap confectionery, go to the cheapest seats in the cinema and buy a hot serve of fish and well-salted potato chips, eating them in the streets, while the steam arose from the paper they were wrapped in. Perhaps such simple and pleasing products, argued that astute observer, George Orwell, went some way towards preventing a revolution in Britain.

Why was the world's economic life almost frozen into inertia, and why did no leader or group step forward to revive it? This depression was worse than any previous one, partly because so many people now sold their products and services to each other. Five hundred years ago, when the main occupation of a village – and most Europeans lived in villages – was to produce food, fuel and clothes for its own needs, there was little outside trade; and so a dislocation to national or international trade could do little damage. By 1930, in contrast, more than half the people of the world depended directly or indirectly on trade, and so a slump in trade endangered their jobs and their standard of living. While there was a forum for political co-operation, called the League of Nations, no major forum aided economic co-operation.

Surely, argued politicians and preachers and economists, a solution for the Depression must exist. Economic theory, however, was suspicious of perhaps the wisest solution: for governments to pour money intelligently into the sick economy. That solution, while creating jobs, might also create some inflation. And inflation was now a snake, dreaded everywhere because of the severe inflation hurting all countries during the war and especially Germany in 1923. Actually, a cautious bout of job-creating and inflation by national governments proved to be a practical solution to unemployment. But understandably it was viewed, in the light of recent experience, as more a poison than a medicine. Curiously, Hitler's Germany was to try this medicine, and it worked.

THE KNIVES OF POLITICS

Politics was affected by the economic turmoil. In the year 1930 Prime Minister Hamaguchi of Japan was assassinated, Gandhi launched a campaign of civil disobedience in British India, Kurds rebelled along the borders of Persia and Turkey, Ethiopians staged a revolt against their emperor, and Jews and Arabs fought in Palestine. Everywhere, people appealed to force. In a speech delivered in Florence, Mussolini conceded that words had their own beauty but that 'rifles, machine-guns, ships, aeroplanes and cannon are still more beautiful'. That year he called for a revision of the Versailles treaty – the can of wriggling worms was opened wide. In Germany the same call for a revised treaty came from Hitler's Brownshirts who, still far from winning power, had enough freedom to kill Jews in the first of many attacks in German towns. Meanwhile in Finland the fascists attempted a coup, and in Poland radical leaders were sent to prison.

In Latin America, during 1930 and 1931, long strikes, street marches and violent protests were frequent, leading to the overthrow of the ruling party in 11 of its 20 nations. In 1931 Japan invaded and captured Manchuria, a prelude to its invasion of China six years later. In 1932, South America was facing armed turmoil. Bolivia and Paraguay went to war, and Peru was fighting Colombia – a dispute which the hapless League of Nations was invited to resolve. Even in relatively stable nations there were dramatic disputes. In 1933 Western Australians tried to secede from Australia – and voted to do so by a large majority.

Capitalism was in disarray. It was condemned in various circles as a moral and economic disgrace. John Maynard Keynes, the Cambridge genius who eventually did so much to strengthen and repackage capitalism, struck the warning bell in 1936: 'It is certain that the world will not much longer tolerate the unemployment' that, in his opinion, was part and parcel of 'present-day individualistic capitalism'. The economic system that had once worked miracles could no longer provide work for tens of millions of wage-earners, and as a result communism was now in high favour.

In the world depression the Soviet Union provided work, though at low pay and high risk, for all who wanted it and many who didn't. Many Russians finally returned home from their self-imposed exile: the famous composer Prokofiev arrived to a warm welcome and remained. Returning Russians quickly found work. While they acknowledged that Russia had no idleness, they did not fully realise how much work was performed, out of sight, by a host of political prisoners in the early 1930s. Thus the long White Sea–Baltic Canal was visited decades later by a western historian who admired the canal's avenues of frost-covered trees, stark in the pale sunlight, but was relieved that he could find few traces of the miserable camps of the canal-builders, of whom some 200 000 died at their work.

Basic political ideas rise and fall in prestige; when they are rising they often seem impregnable, and when they plunge they seem about to vanish forever. Communist Russia, not capitalist USA, was widely hailed as the formula for the future during the 1930s. George Bernard Shaw, in his brilliant and jesting way, spoke for millions of western reformers when he predicted that the collective farms and garden cities of the Soviet Union were such 'an immediate and enormous success' that they would be copied throughout the west. Shaw enthusiastically pointed to Stalin's 'flourishing slumless civilized cities' now dotting the Russian steppes and deserts. He barely needed to mention that in contrast most of the big cities of Europe held pockets of grimy slums as well as big numbers of the unemployed.

The world depression, following the devastating world war, lowered confidence in the concept of human progress. The loss of confidence, not visible in Russia, was notable in western Europe. Thomas Mann, the German novelist, deplored the decline of the west's faith in progress and the derailing of the once-strong crusade for liberalism, humanism and democracy that had promised so much in 1900. Where, he asked in 1937, had the crusade failed? His answer was that it had suffered from its own virtues – 'from its repugnance to fanaticism of every kind, from its tolerance, and from its leanings towards an indulgent skepticism: in a word, from its natural kindness'.

In the face of a dictator, all these virtues, unorganised and disputatious, were as feeble as a line of matchsticks. In Germany these matchsticks were about to be crushed.

11

THE RISE OF HITLER

Germany, more than almost any other nation of Europe, was bruised by the world depression. It was wide open to new political solutions. Did communism, socialism or capitalism offer the answer, or was there a home-brewed solution?

Germany had already experienced a period of chaos. After the end of the war the kaiser went into exile in Holland, the German colonies were shared amongst the victors, most of the navy was scuttled, and most of the merchant navy was confiscated. Under the Versailles peace treaty, slices and lumps of German territory were excised and transferred to France, Poland, Czechoslovakia, Denmark, Belgium and Danzig Free City. Huge sums of money and quantities of commodities had to be paid by Germany to the victors of the war, though not all were paid.

In the elegant little city of Weimar, which temporarily replaced

Berlin as the capital of Germany, the members of parliament could not feel completely in charge. In various cities the communists were strong and, taking heart from the Soviet Union, looked for ways of staging a coup. Their rivals were also alert and aggressive. In the new democracy the bullet competed with the ballot. An early victim was the German orator, Rosa Luxemburg, who was one of the first women – other than a member of a royal family – to become a national figure in the politics of any country. Kept in a German prison during a large part of the First World War, she became a founder of the communist group called the Spartacists and was a postwar politician of importance. In 1919 she was murdered. For months, political violence and revolution and counter-revolution were widespread in German cities.

Various leaders still hoped for a strife-free Germany. Walther Rathenau, the head of one of Germany's main industrial firms, a philosopher too and a leading member of the cabinet, hoped that the clash of rich and poor could be eased. In a speech made in Stuttgart in June 1922 he spread his belief that Germany could become a peacemaker so that Europeans would no longer live 'in a world poisoned by hatred and on a planet flaming with the passion of mutual revenge, in a world of destruction and dissension'. Two weeks later, bullets and hand grenades killed him as he was being driven from his home to the foreign office.

What were the failings of this patriot? In the eyes of a rowdy minority of Germans, he failed to stand up to the victorious French: he was also a Jew. The political loyalties and animosities in Germany had many cross-currents and complexities, of which anti-semitism was one. And yet the Jews were prominent in postwar politics out of all proportion to their numbers, and such success could have occurred only if they had an element of support from those who were not Jewish. The city of Munich at the end of 1918 was briefly the capital of the Bavarian Socialist Republic, most leaders of which were Jews. But Jews, like Germans, were divided. The head of the socialist republic was Kurt Eisner, a Jew, and he was assassinated by an army officer who himself was part Jewish.

By 1924 the season of assassinations and attempted coups had passed, and Germany seemed to possess a stable democracy. And yet large sections of Germany, including the bureaucracy, were not happy with it. To many Germans, democracy was an inefficient form of government imported from further west. There were numerous parties, none of which was strong enough to govern in its own right, and so a coalition of minor parties often ran the government. Even these coalitions did not have a majority. Thus in 1926 four single parties came together to form a new government, though between them they held only one-third of the seats in the Reichstag. This new government faced the thirteenth political crisis in seven years. The dispute was over the flag which had itself become a symbol of disunity.

The republic flew two flags, the major one being of black, red and gold – colours that celebrated the revolution of 1848 and also the postwar republic. Large numbers of more conservative Germans did not like it, preferring the prewar imperial flag of black, white and red. The lesser of the two flags, it was called the merchant flag and was used in ships in overseas ports but not in Germany. Hans Luther the chancellor – the equivalent of the prime minister – preferred the old imperial flag and wished it to be used more often. With the vital support of President Hindenburg, Luther altered the rules, rendering the old flag of Bismarck and the deposed kaiser almost equal to the official republican flag. The result was a political crisis in which he lost office.

Not enough talent went into national politics. That Hans Luther should be the chancellor was a reflection of the strength of regional as distinct from national politics. He had been the mayor of the big industrial city of Essen but was not an elected member of the parliament. When his successor in Weimar was sought, fingers at first pointed to Konrad Adenauer, who was presently the Catholic Mayor of Cologne and not a member of the parliament. Adenauer, not selected, would have his chance after the next war.

On and off in the 15 years after the end of the war a host of Germans wished for a strong leader, a fearless patriot, a man of action who could rise above the debate of politicians and if necessary silence it. Eventually that leader did arrive. A dozen years later most Germans had to conclude, as they surveyed their ruined fatherland, that he was not the miracle-maker they had wanted.

IN HITLER'S MIND

Adolf Hitler was originally an Austrian. His home town was Braunau where his father was an officer in the Austrian customs house. By the standards of the time Hitler had educational opportunities that were above the average, and his ambitions were fixed on the fine arts when he arrived in Vienna at the age of 16. After years of achieving little as a painter he moved to the German city of Munich where, at the outbreak of war, he enlisted in the army. Fighting on the western front he was disabled by gas and decorated for bravery: his was one of the more arduous tasks, running messages amidst bullets, exploding shells, din and smoke. Camaraderie in the trenches cheered his spirits; the final defeat of Germany dismayed him. Even more than most other soldiers he felt betrayed by the nation's leaders and also – he irrationally decided – by the Jews.

To those who insisted that Germany must find new leaders, this former corporal put forward his own name. Moving to the top of a little Bavarian group that soon called itself the National Socialist German Workers' Party, Hitler spoke urgently to street audiences about Germany's woes. Members of his party were only too happy to fight in the streets against the stronger communists. Hitler protected himself against would-be assassins. The driver of his car directed a glaring searchlight at the windscreen of any suspicious car that was following him.

Hitler had little experience of politics compared to the older Mussolini who had served a long apprenticeship in radical movements. Mussolini, about to capture power in Italy, had not even heard of Hitler. In the following two years a few Italian newspapers began to notice Hitler, partly because his storm-troopers, his street fighters, created news in Germany. After trying to overthrow the Bavarian government Hitler went to prison where he employed his time in the cell to elaborate his solutions to Germany's problems; and his consequent memoir and manifesto entitled *Mein Kampf* (My Struggle) was read by only a few thousand soon after it was published in 1925.

Hitler's Nazi Party still occupied a lowly place in virtually the second division of the German political league; and in successive elections for the Reichstag it won only a small share of the total votes, falling far behind socialists and communists. Hitler continued to be the unforgiving enemy of communism or what he preferred to call the 'Jewish-Bolshevik conspiracy'. His constant promise was that he would make Germany great again.

Except for his emphatic ideas and strident speeches he did not initially behave like most populist leaders. There was something spartan about his way of life. He did not smoke or drink, he shunned meat, he guarded his health, and nursed a special fear of cancer. A bachelor, he gave as much attention to his dogs as to pretty girls: he did not lack personal admirers. A nationalist, he rejoiced in the German forests and mountains and in the more passionate German composers, of whom his favourite was Wagner. As for foreign travel, he had no need for it. Germany was his globe.

His disciplined appearance, his black hair brushed flat across the forehead, and his homely conversation at private occasions seemed to mark him as a restrained individual – until he mounted a public platform and shouted into the microphone. Whereupon the lamb became the tiger. He could speak with fervour for an hour, even two hours, not a note in front of him. He spoke with such energy that sweat poured from him. The sweat he replaced with mineral water, pure German water, sometimes consumed at the rate of more than a dozen small bottles during one speech.

Guided by a voice coach he improved his gestures and his oratory, adding a rasping eloquence to a natural frenzy. On the platform he displayed magnetism as well as blind rage. He fired up his audiences, and in turn their alternations of reverent silence and enthusiastic applause inspired him. It was as if the mood of a pop concert – a phenomenon not yet known – was taking over the once dignified theatre of German political life.

Hitler's Nazi Party would have remained on the sensational fringe of politics but for the arrival of the world depression. Ever since 1918 the German economy had been vulnerable. The need to pay large reparations to the victorious enemies was a blow to long-term confidence, though the money actually paid under the modified terms of the peace treaty did not prove to be a crushing sum in the end. Moreover the economy was weakened by featherbedding on all sides, the big Prussian farmers winning protection against grain imports, the steel and coal industries keeping prices high, and the unions gaining high wages because of the recurring scarcity of labour caused partly by the war's massive death toll. Whatever was the exact mixture of dislocating causes, the new republican Germany, with its parliament meeting in the romantic town of Weimar, was never quite successful. Germany's miracle economy of the years 1850–1914, having strenuously climbed to the top of Europe's tower, began to sway in the strong wind.

In the early 1920s Germany was hit by hyperinflation. For months, economic chaos hovered above every main street, farmhouse and factory chimney. When the world depression set in, Germany was again hit harder – and hit itself harder – than any other large nation. Banks and factories closed, and the owners of small stores and workshops could no longer afford to employ so many staff. By 1932 the German industrial output was only 60 per cent of that recorded in the last prosperous year, 1929. In Berlin, Dresden and other big German cities, the sight of people dressed in rags, gathering stray sticks for firewood, or groping into rubbish bins was probably more widespread than at any time for a century. The nation registered the appalling unemployment rate of 30 per cent, where Britain's was 22 per cent.

From these humiliations and sufferings, Hitler's party gained. The rival ruling parties, whether the socialists or the centre or the coalition of the right, were seen to have failed. Germany's well-organised Communist Party at first sight should have gained more than the Nazis from the Depression – it offered solutions – but its radical wares were now on display in the Soviet Union. Fear of a communist takeover of Germany persuaded owners of small farms and businesses to think of supporting Hitler. While his party was called national socialist, it had won a dozen times as much support in the rural areas of Schleswig Holstein, near the Danish border, than in the industrial suburbs of the Ruhr and Berlin in the 1928 election.

Hitler offered patriotism and decisive action. People now flocked to join his party, and its membership jumped above 200 000, of whom half were willing to parade in their brown shirts. At the elections in 1932 – few countries held so many elections – Hitler won a surprising 18 per cent of the vote. At yet another election in that same year he won 37 per cent of the vote, thus making his Nazi party the largest of all the parties. In January 1933 he was invited to be chancellor or in effect prime minister in a coalition government. In August 1934, on the death of the aged president of the republic, Hitler was popularly elected to the combined post of chancellor and president with 88 per cent of the vote. During that election his harnessing of radio, loudspeakers, torchlight processions, slogans, banners and the full orchestra of propaganda was uncanny.

THE DEATH OF GERMAN DEMOCRACY

Having climbed the stepladder of democracy, Hitler threw the ladder away. Indeed he broke it and burned it. Nonetheless, if after three years in office he had agreed to stand for election and woo the German voters afresh, he would have won their support with ease. He responded to the German people's deep need for self-respect and security, following the humiliating defeat in the First World War, the perceived harshness of the peace treaty, and the privations of the ensuing Depression.

He mutilated the political life of Germany. The other political parties were abolished. Trade unions were trampled on. Nazi loyalists were added to the boards of many big companies. The senior officers of the army were forced to give him personal pledges of loyalty. The churches were controlled – the Catholics with the agreement of the Vatican, and the Protestants with the consent of five of every six Lutheran clergy. As an act of defiance Pastor Martin Niemöller, who had been a submarine hero in the war, formed a new Confessional Church; but he and hundreds of his fellow Lutherans were arrested. The fear of being beaten up, imprisoned, or publicly humiliated became part of the new way of life.

Led by Dr Joseph Goebbels, the Ministry for Popular Enlightenment and Propaganda seized control of press and radio, theatre, music and films, and – contrary to the title of this portfolio – made them definitely less enlightened. Propaganda doused the school rooms. The crucifix was replaced by a secular cross, the swastika. Such was the popularity of the Nazi regime at home that Goebbels did not need to jam or silence the radio broadcasts coming from foreign lands. Rather he encouraged all Germans to buy their own cheap radio in the sure knowledge that they would prefer their homeland's programs. The people's own radio set, a little fortress of propaganda, preceded the people's own car, the Volkswagen.

A new prosperity settled on those millions of German children and women and men who previously did not have enough to eat. Unemployment, falling dramatically, was probably the lowest in the industrial world at the start of 1935. It was less easy for Germans to protest against the rise of a ruthless dictatorship, when economic hope was sprouting, and smoke was again pouring out of factory chimneys.

The German government spent heavily while other nations were still saving public money. It created jobs by building a network of concrete highways, replanting forests, and building city apartments. And all the time it was rearming. Even before Hitler came to power the German armed forces, prevented by the treaty of Versailles from testing their weak muscles, secretly used Soviet territory to test weapons and practise tactics. Now Hitler openly rearmed, speedily rebuilding his navy, air force and army at a time when the democracies were prevented by their own voters from doing likewise.

After Hitler became more oppressive, his opponents struggled to define who he was. The communists and socialists saw him as a creature of capitalism, alleging that he was the front man for the industrialists who financed his party. But small rather than big business supported his party in its first 10 years. From time to time he attacked monopolies. Their profits were all controlled in Nazi Germany, sometimes in an arbitrary way.

From the other side came the allegation that Hitler was a masked socialist. Certainly the official name of his party was 'National Socialist', and he did declare that May Day, the left-wing day of rejoicing in Europe, would be a national holiday. But Hitler approved of private property. He was less than half socialist after the socialist wing of his party flew away in the late 1920s.

It is not easy to stereotype Hitler using the categories of left and right. He was revolutionary but it was his own kind of revolution. He was against democracy and the independence of the courts. He was against any organisation that did not submit to his will. He mixed his own ingredients, changing them as his people's hopes and fears fluctuated. He saw himself and his party as working for no single sector and pressure group but only for Germany. He was a nationalist of nationalists.

Hitler's Germany was not alone in moving towards authoritarian rule. The experiment of democracy failed again and again in central and eastern Europe and Mediterranean Europe. In 1919 Bulgaria went a long way towards setting up a dictator, and in 1923 Spain began to follow a zigzag course between military rule and uprisings against that rule. In 1926 Lithuania followed the fresh precedent of Poland whose army and its famous leader Pilsudski became powerful. Yugoslavia virtually abandoned democracy, adopting a royal version of dictatorship, and Portugal also became virtually a dictatorship, while Romania made its move in 1930, Hungary in 1932, and Germany and Austria in 1933. Latvia, perhaps the best educated nation in Europe, went the same way in 1934 when its prime minister became a dictator and interned many parliamentary colleagues. Estonia also wanted a strong leader, but after five years it flirted again with democracy. Assassinations, purges, and political imprisonments were common in the political life of many of these new nations. In this period in central and eastern Europe, perhaps the Czechs were the most effective in making democracy work for them.

These were not easy years for a government. Unemployment was high, and ethnic and class rifts increased tensions. There was virtually no experience of democracy in most of the nations that experimented with it. Moreover, at national elections, their favoured system of proportional representation led to parliaments with too many parties, none of which had sufficient members to enable it to govern alone.

Europe's political troubles and economic hardships gave Hitler his opportunity to dismantle the Versailles peace treaty of 1919. He dismantled it by threat and force. The major European nations, absorbed in the economic distress of their people, did not give sufficient attention to the threat he posed. The task of winning elections absorbed the leaders of the two big democracies of Britain and France, whereas Hitler himself could dispense with elections.

He acted, as always, decisively. On 16 March 1935 he simply announced that the Versailles treaty restricting the size of the German army no longer was relevant, and that he intended to conscript an army of nearly half a million Germans which would far outnumber the French soldiers stationed in France. Three months later, Hitler persuaded Britain to let him rebuild the German navy until it was one-third of the size of the British navy. Germany was also permitted to build the submarines that the treaty of 1919 had specifically banned. Britain made these concessions, without even consulting France.

Harmony between British and French politicians, and between public opinion in the two nations, was never more vital than in 1935 but rarely less apparent. If the two main European victors of the First World War had kept their heads and acted swiftly they could have threatened Hitler with instant invasion, while his army was still in recruiting mode. He would have had no choice but to back down. Next year, his confidence high, he took another step, sending his much-enlarged army to reoccupy the Rhineland. In 1938 it moved into Austria which, being German-speaking, was not likely to offer fierce resistance, and into Czechoslovakia. Like a boxer he timed his blows carefully.

After the Second World War many observers wondered how it could have happened: a weak Germany boldly reasserting itself and rearming in full sight of the victors of the previous war. After all, the victors of 1918 had rejoiced in their massive and overwhelming victory, the hardest-won victory in the history of warfare; but now, two decades later, they had literally thrown it away. They lost it unthinkingly. In the 1930s, weary of war, they took their victory for granted. That was disastrous.

The sad fact was that Britain and France, the main victors of the war, were not natural allies. For the past 600 years they had usually been enemies, and they did not easily cooperate as allies in the 1930s. The British, being islanders and endowed with the natural defence afforded by the sea, could sit back and hesitate while Hitler began to rearm. France, on the other hand, could not afford to hesitate. But it did not wish to confront Hitler without positive British military support, and that support was slow to appear. Inside both Britain and France were large but diverse sectors of public opinion that – for reasons that seemed valid at the time – hesitated to stand up to Hitler at this crucial moment of confrontation. Many people, mostly conservative, saw Stalin rather than Hitler as the more dangerous enemy. Even more people placed their trust in the League of Nations as a peacekeeper, not accepting that it had already failed. Hitler knew that the League was pitifully weak: his actions weakened it even further.

Britain especially had a powerful and popular peace movement, full of noble ideals, but also loaded with pragmatic passengers who really wished to pass the responsibility for maintaining the peace to somebody else: the League of Nations was that somebody. Like people in most democracies during the world depression, they wanted their own government to spend more money on social security and less on defence. Stanley Baldwin, Britain's trusted middle-of-the-road leader, did not dare defy this multitude of voices at election time: 'Supposing I had gone to the country and said that Germany was rearming and that we must rearm . . .?' He later admitted that, with such a policy, he would have lost rather than decisively won the general election of November 1935. Later, he confessed his error in bowing to the opinion of 'this pacific democracy'.

By opposing rearmament, public opinion in much of western Europe proved to be an unknowing ally of Hitler. Though eloquent in expressing its hostility to war, it did not quite understand the dubious effects of its actions. What was desperately needed in the mid-1930s, for the sake of international peace, was not a peace crusade in Britain and France but a peace crusade in Germany. There, unfortunately, such a crusade was out of the question. It would have been ruthlessly banned.

THE PLIGHT OF JEWS AND GYPSIES

In 1900 most Jews lived in central and eastern Europe, especially in Russia and the Austro-Hungarian empire, and even there they were a minority. Most dressed distinctively, and worshipped on Saturday rather than on Sunday. In an era of nationalism they were different and usually saw themselves as different.

There were synagogues in every big city in Europe, and hundreds of Jewish congregations flourished far from Europe. The United States had a fast-growing Jewish population, though it would have seemed inconceivable that in 1995 it would hold the world's largest population of Jews. In Australia and New Zealand small clusters of Jews in the larger cities provided leaders for many institutions, not least the government and the army. Wherever big commercial ports arose in the Orient, a Jewish cemetery could be found. In 1846 little Singapore held more Jewish trading firms than Chinese, and 60 years later it held two synagogues, including 'The Shield of our Father Synagogue' whose lofty pillars, balconies and whirring fans can still be seen in Waterloo Street.

Jews were blending into western society more than before because the ancient restrictions against them were being relaxed. In Europe as a whole no other small ethnic group was so successful in the universities, classical music, literature, science, medicine, the law and business. In Germany, to which they migrated from further east, they were especially successful. There the anti-semitism, whether rising or waning, was less noticeable. German Jews remained a very small minority – they were less than a million – and were active in national life. They served in the armed forces in the First World War, contributed to good causes, and mostly went out of their way to become assimilated.

Hitler attacked the Jews in his book *Mein Kampf*, but amongst its many sentences of hatred there was no precise call for their extermination. Indeed most Jews living in Germany probably felt, in the month when Hitler gained power, that their lives were not in danger. After all, they controlled or influenced many of the main institutions. Three major German newspapers were largely owned by Jews. The football club FC Bayern, the champion team of 1932, placed its trust in a Jewish trainer and president. But in the following six years, as the government's policies and speeches became more anti-semitic, most of the Jews left Germany, leaving their assets behind. Many Germans remained sympathetic to Jews, and indeed their sympathy was officially denounced in Nazi booklets printed as late as 1938. By then Hitler's edicts against the Jews were firmly in place.

Under those edicts the Jews were no longer classed as German citizens, and even their passport was stamped with the stigma, 'J'. They were not permitted to marry German citizens. On the eve of the war they could not own motor cars, could not practise in their professions, and could not visit cinemas or places of public entertainment. They could live only in designated Jewish areas.

Many Jews who hitherto had the opportunity to flee Germany – and flee Austria too, where Hitler also applied his anti-semitic policies – failed to seize the opportunity because they could not imagine in the years of mild oppression that Hitler's bite would become so venomous. In the same way most of the German Catholics and Lutherans were at first deceived by Hitler's self-restraint in his first months in power.

The Jews stood at the top of the list of peoples and groups whom Hitler increasingly despised, almost to the point of hysteria. Next to the Jews on the list of the unwanted were the Slavs, many of whom lived close to the postwar borders of Germany. The dislike between German and Slav tended to be reciprocal in many regions. Some Slavonic leaders had already shown what they thought of the Germans by penalising them when opportunities arose; and the new republic of Poland had tried to edge out Germans – including the German Jews – who continued to live in Polish Silesia after it was transferred from Germany. In that province in the mid-1930s half of the German 19-year-olds were reported never to have held a job of any kind. After Hitler conquered his half of Poland in 1939 he reversed and accentuated the flow of prejudice.

The ferocious attacks on Jews in Germany were imitated in Italy in milder form. There the Jews were few – numbering about 55 000 – but influential in the universities and a few professions. In November 1938, Mussolini placed a ban on them serving in the public service and armed forces, virtually prevented them from studying or teaching in universities, and prohibited their marriage to non-Jews. As a concession he did decree that if Jews had died while fighting for Italy, their wives and children should be exempt from the anti-semitic laws. Jews who were pioneers of the Fascist Party were also exempt. Though now designated as second-class citizens, Jews were not to be in peril until Italy was taken over by Hitler's forces.

Gypsies, like Jews, became targets for Hitler but not for Mussolini. Gypsies or Romanies were distinctive, their ancient homeland being India. Like Jews they had a strong sense of family and tradition, and in moving about Germany with their horses and little house-wagons, they refused to conform to the ways which a conforming society demanded. Whereas Jews were often feared because they were so hard-working and successful, Gypsies were scorned because they were rather less industrious, and were absorbed in their own ways and values. Their fate, compared to that of the Jews, is little discussed. A half-nomadic people is not adept at building memorials and museums and less capable of arousing public interest.

The Second World War – and not primarily the racial manifestos that preceded it – exposed Jews and Gypsies to acute danger. By 1939 their freedom and property had been imperilled. Three years later their very existence was to be in peril.

12

A SECOND WORLD WAR

The generals of Germany anticipated that they would be unable to fight a long war. While rich in coal, their nation possessed no oil-field; and lacking colonies, it could not produce rubber, tin and other wartime commodities which came largely from the tropics. Shrewdly it had stockpiled vital raw materials, but its hoard of some metals – copper and iron and magnesium and lead – would last for only nine months. In essence it was poorly equipped for fighting a prolonged war, because it might soon run out of munitions and oil and thereby be forced to negotiate a peace on unfavourable terms.

Such a precarious situation had actually been the wish of the victorious Allies who imposed the stern peace treaty on Germany in 1919. The peace treaty, however, backfired. It persuaded Germany, when planning its next war, to seek quick and decisive victories in the first phase, so that it could capture vital supplies from the enemy.

The peace treaty at the end of the First World War also backfired because it deprived Germany and Russia of what they continued to believe were their rightful possessions. In 1939 the two aggrieved nations were ready to snatch back those territories by force. Though their ideologies were far apart and their enmity profound, the two nations secretly agreed to invade Poland and carve it up for themselves. Their pact, when at last it became public knowledge, dumbfounded many European leaders. It was the equivalent, in our era, of Israel and its Muslim neighbours together signing a secret pact to wage war on an unsuspecting enemy and then carve up its territory.

THE PLIGHT OF POLAND

Poland, one of the larger nations of Europe, had been formed from large pieces carved from three separate nations – Germany, Russia and Austria-Hungary. That two of the three donors had been unwilling donors was not a happy omen. As Germany and Russia wanted to expand, Poland was the obvious target. In expanding they could simply argue that they were recapturing old lands taken from them unjustly.

Proud of its own distinctive language, literature and traditions, Poland for its part longed to return to the greatness it had once possessed. But as a nation it was not united. While its population of well over 30 million was largely Catholic, its variety of nationalities was not conducive to harmonious government. In the 1920s its second-largest city was the German-speaking Breslau, renamed Wroclaw, and many of its citizens wished their city, recently part of Germany, could have remained there. Likewise many Poles who had lived under German rule until 1918 remembered how poorly they had been treated and retaliated by making it hard for resident Germans to earn a living. Poland also held the largest Jewish population in Europe, and towards them there was often suspicion, or envy.

The Poles were further divided amongst themselves. In 1926 the popular Polish soldier Marshal Pilsudski and his army entered Warsaw, and choked democracy. Opposing politicians had to be on their best behaviour: some were imprisoned. After Pilsudski died of cancer in 1935, other army officers took up the reins. At first their firm ally was France which was becoming less capable of defending itself, let alone others. A united and well-armed Poland, possessing alert allies, might have made Hitler think twice about launching an attack. But he did not have to think twice.

Hitler and Stalin could attack Poland with confidence. Between them they could devour Poland before its allies living far to the west could lift a finger. And so it came to pass. On 1 September 1939, Hitler invaded Poland and a fortnight later Russian troops marched in to complete the conquest. Russia went a step further and tried to reconquer that part of Finland that had been part of Russian territory before the revolutions of 1917. The Finns fought courageously in ice and snow but ultimately resolved to concede defeat, gaining terms that were far from disastrous. Britain and France, Canada and Australia and New Zealand were opponents of Hitler from the very start but had no influence on these early events of the war. They waited: Hitler acted.

THE FALL OF FRANCE

Once the trees in western Europe were in leaf in the spring of 1940, the conditions were ripe for Hitler's fast-moving army and skilled air force to extend the conquests. Relying on surprise and superiority in the air, Hitler began to eat up much of Europe, a mouthful at a time. Denmark and Norway fell in April, Holland and Belgium in May. Now it was France's turn. For the first time Hitler had to fight a major nation which, on paper at least, was almost as well-armed as Germany. If the military strength of France's ally, Britain, was added to the balancing scales, the balance was tipped in favour of France.

In high places in Paris the optimistic view was that Hitler's army might not even succeed in breaking more than a few miles into French terrain. Most of the French leaders anticipated that the war would be a replay of the First World War, defensive and deadlocked. In 1940 the French placed their faith in a long fort facing Germany. Called the Maginot Line it was a wall of concrete, with underground stores and arsenals, linking railway lines, and galleries where whole armies could shelter. It was the longest and most expensive line of forts in the history of warfare.

The Germans did not butt their heads against the concrete pill boxes of the Maginot Line. They simply made a wide detour with tanks and armoured cars, entering France through a side door that was left ajar: the poorly defended forest of Ardennes. The mighty Maginot Line was soon useless: a deserted museum of the history of warfare.

As Britain was slow to send help, the French initially defended all alone. On their home ground they should have been a match for the invading Germans but at every turn they were outgeneralled. In the space of a week or two Hitler's motorised armies crossed the French farmlands where, during the four years of the previous war, the fighting had been concentrated in a deadly stalemate. The

Germans virtually leaped over the old 'western front' and approached Paris.

Ahead of them, often blocking the roads, moved a vast column of French refugees hastening south with their hastily packed possessions in farm wagons, trucks, cars, and even bicycles, prams and hand-pushed carts. Soon they were joined by Parisians deserting their city. Paris normally held 5 million people, and maybe 2 million were preparing to leave their houses and apartments, shops, offices and factories and flee south, some taking their pet cats and dogs.

CHURCHILL'S 'GREAT DAYS'

Rarely in the history of western Europe did so much now rest on one man's shoulders. Winston Churchill had become Prime Minister of Britain just when Paris seemed likely to fall. If London was the next city to fall, personal freedom and civil liberty in most of Europe would die.

Churchill was born in 1874 with a silver spoon in his mouth and some iron in his soul. His father was a lord and his grandfather a duke, though his mother, a New Yorker, possessed no title until her marriage. From an early age he showed determination though he was a plodder as a schoolboy. Ravenous for excitement, action and fame, as a young man he watched or fought in wars in Cuba, the Indian frontier, the dry Sudan where he rode with the British cavalry in the Battle of Omdurman, and South Africa where the Boer War unexpectedly tested Britain's strength against an army of fighting farmers. By the age of 26 he had fought in wars in three continents, and had written about each war. His gift with words he demonstrated on the printed page, on the political platform and at banquet speeches.

By the age of 30 he was a rising member of the House of Commons, with a trace of the bulldog in his jaw and shoulders, a touch of ginger in his hair, and as much energy as two politicians. Though he spoke with a slight lisp he could make an entire audience lean forward and listen. Unpredictable, he crossed from the conservative party to the liberals and later would cross in the other direction. A social reformer in his early political career he sought to improve life in British prisons and coalmines. Later, as the political head of the world's largest navy, he diligently prepared it for the war that came in 1914. Not content to be ashore he spent a total of six months at sea in a variety of ships, thus provoking the public comment that he was trying to be an admiral rather than a cabinet minister. When war broke out, the British navy was prepared.

There will always be debate about Churchill's role in planning the invasion of Turkish Gallipoli which began with an attack by the British navy. Debate has not ceased about his role in 1925 when, as chancellor of the exchequer, in effect the treasurer, he restored Britain to financial dependence on gold: a decision that in the opinion of some was to intensify the world depression in the early 1930s. But few critics question his foresight in insisting, once Hitler gained high office, that he would launch a new European war. For years his warnings were strong but lonely. His call for the British to rearm, at heavy expense, did not win him friends.

His whole political life was a succession of tumbles followed by triumphant ascents. At the start of 1939 his career, except as a historian, seemed finished. Then the outbreak of war vindicated his warnings. At the age of 64 he was escorted, like an old battle cruiser, from his quiet anchorage and placed at the head of the home fleet.

Curiously it was the Labour Party, even more than his own Conservative Party, that wished him to lead the nation; and all the major parties were to take part in his coalition government. In May 1940, one month before the collapse of France, he became Britain's prime minister.

If there had been in the French political circles a Winston Churchill, and he had been given supreme power earlier, France might have been saved. But at the time when Churchill was recalled to office, probably nothing could save France. There was a slight prospect that if Britain poured all its own forces across the Channel, the German advance might be halted. Making quick visits to Paris to listen, speak, observe and negotiate, Churchill was not altogether impressed by morale at the top and the sharp divisions of opinion almost everywhere. In the end Britain refused to send additional aircraft to France: it would need them for its own defence. The refusal to help, while justifiably unpopular in France, was crucial to Britain's own defences against Hitler later that year. The decision not to give further help to France in the middle of 1940 was to prove vital, four years later, in assisting in the ultimate rescue of France from her harsh conqueror.

By the end of May the British army in France, endangered by the speed of the German conquest, had to be rescued. Nearly 900 British ships, large and small, were assembled under British air cover to evacuate troops from the beaches near Dunkirk: the harbour itself had been bombed into uselessness by German aircraft. More than 340 000 British and French and Belgian soldiers were saved near Dunkirk and another 220 000 Allied troops were rescued by British ships from Cherbourg and French ports further east. If all these had been taken away as prisoners, the blow to Britain's morale, let alone its ability to defend its coast, could have been crushing.

To sustain morale was Churchill's task. Defeatism was now creeping into his parliament. Should Britain try to negotiate a truce with Hitler? Though some powerful voices whispered 'yes', Churchill made no concessions to the pragmatic or the timid. Even the advice that the most valuable paintings in the National Gallery should, for their own safety, be shipped from London to Canada was shunned. 'None must go', he said. They will be safe in Britain, he thundered, because ultimately the Germans will be defeated.

In this tense month so much of the news that reached Churchill was intimidating because of the fears it aroused. Would Spain enter the war on Hitler's side and snatch Gibraltar? Would Japan seize the chance to enter the war and snatch weakly defended British colonies and bases in East Asia? Would Italy at the last minute invade the south of France? Would the French admirals surrender their great navy to the Germans rather than sail to the safety of British ports? Most of these fears, during that tormenting time, seemed justified.

On 14 June 1940, just 10 days after the final evacuations from Dunkirk, the first German soldiers prepared to enter Paris. Now a ghostly city it had farewelled its citizens as they set out for the south, just ahead of the rumbling German forces. As for the leaders of the French government they were already in mental retreat before they retreated from Paris by car. They could see that their armed forces, after massive defeats, were gravely outnumbered in armaments and in manpower. The German supremacy in the air was formidable. And yet perhaps the French could still fight back. Utilising their knowledge of their own terrain, exploiting the increasing length and vulnerability of the German supply lines, and mustering patriotism in a nation that had never lacked patriots, surely they could regroup in the rugged mountains and continue the fight. Defeatism, however, set in. On 17 June an American correspondent, arriving in the German-occupied capital, summed up the mood: 'I have a feeling that what we're seeing here is the complete breakdown of French society.' The dramatic chain of events, he added, is 'almost too tremendous to believe'. Five days later, the French were ready to sign their formal surrender.

The French defeat and the manner of the defeat make one of the momentous events in the history of Europe. After the First World War, France had rightly been viewed as the leading nation in continental Europe. It had won the war – or was foremost on the winning side – and had hosted the peace negotiations in which the map of Europe was torn up and redrawn. Thanks to the provisions of the peace treaty it became a military giant while Germany was shrunk to the size of a military midget. France became larger than defeated Germany in territory, while as a colonial power it was second only to Britain. France was entitled to see itself as a leader in international diplomacy and the convenor of great conferences. The new League of Nations had its home in Geneva, a French-speaking city. Various parts of the world were willing to accept or tolerate the French idea that its cultural and intellectual life was the most influential of all. In the view of many scholars, admittedly a minority, France *was* culture.

One of the world's oldest democracies, France showcased the principle that democracy was innately superior to other kinds of government. On the eve of France's collapse, however, there was valid

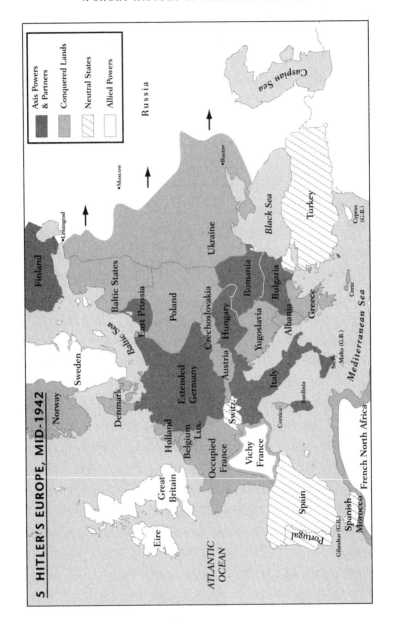

5 HITLER'S EUROPE, MID-1942

Axis Powers & Partners
Conquered Lands
Neutral States
Allied Powers

Russia

Caspian Sea

Leningrad
Moscow
Rostov

Finland

Baltic States

Sweden

Baltic Sea

East Prussia

Poland

Ukraine

Black Sea

Turkey

Cyprus (G.B.)

Norway

Denmark

Czechoslovakia

Hungary

Romania

Bulgaria

Albania

Greece

Crete

Holland

Extended Germany

Austria

Switz.

Yugoslavia

Italy

Sardinia

Malta (G.B.)

Sicily

Mediterranean Sea

Great Britain

Belgium
Lux.

Occupied France

Vichy France

Corsica

Eire

ATLANTIC OCEAN

Spain

Portugal

Gibraltar (G.B.)

Spanish Morocco

French North Africa

reason to argue that democracy was one of the causes of its failure. The French voters, and those who guided them, had refused to make the heavy sacrifices needed to give to their nation stronger defences. In French politics the divisions between those sympathetic to an alliance with Hitler's Germany and those sympathetic to an alliance with communist Russia were wide, as were the divisions between those who wanted rearmament and those who were pacifists. The nation was too divided. Its premiers changed too often. France was the first major democracy to collapse in the course of a war.

A remarkable characteristic of France's leaders, in a dire crisis, was to seek salvation in an esteemed, retired politician in his seventies or eighties: a time of life that was then achieved by few people. In the military crises of 1871 and 1917 and 1940, when the Germans were threatening France, an elderly statesman was summoned to the pedestal and invested with authority. In June 1940 it was the turn of Marshal Petain. The 84-year-old soldier, who had been the hero of Verdun in the previous Great War, was called upon to form a French ministry and negotiate a peace treaty with Hitler's emissaries. Petain, though his navy was intact, thought that the war was lost, and that Britain itself would have to surrender within a few weeks. He even ordered his troops to cease fighting before he had learned the nature of the peace terms imposed by Germany. He thought the terms were harsh but, in the circumstances, relatively favourable. He himself was permitted to rule much of France, now a disarmed country, from a new capital in the spa-resort of Vichy, leaving the Germans to control a wide military zone along the west coast and northern borders. More than a million French soldiers were to remain as prisoners of war, in effect as hostages, so that Petain would obey Hitler's orders.

The armistice was signed by a French representative late in the afternoon of 22 June in a French forest, the place for the signing having been selected by the Germans with symbolic care. The signatures were affixed in the same wooden railway carriage where the Germans had been forced to sign their surrender in November 1918. Hitler was present for the first part of the ceremony: Petain was not. For a few days Hitler went on tour, marvelling at the elegance of Paris, paying a kind of homage at the tomb of Napoleon, inspecting closely the Opera which he called 'the most beautiful theatre in the world', and touring his old battlefields of the First World War before returning to Germany. He felt elated. France had fallen so easily that Britain would probably sue for peace.

THE BATTLE FOR BRITAIN

Churchill deplored the French surrender. Moreover he feared that Hitler, using French ports, would invade the British Isles. As Hitler's forces occupied the whole European coastline facing England and Scotland, they could employ any of a hundred captured ports and airfields to launch their invasion of Britain. Moreover German submarines could slip out to sea from new-won bases close to the Cliffs of Dover. Thereby Hitler's prospects of either blockading or invading Britain were increased. His position in western Europe was more commanding than Napoleon's had ever been.

The Germans, in preparing their massive air raids on Britain, were thwarted by one early obstacle – a far-reaching effect of Marconi's radio waves. In the 1930s a few physicists had observed that an aircraft gave rise to an echo as it hit the pulsations of the radio waves. 'Radio detection' – or radar, as it was named – picked up echoes and so could detect the approach of enemy planes and their exact forma-tion even when they were 80 kilometres away. On the eve of the Battle of Britain, new radar stations as well as thousands of human sky-watchers gave London a fighting chance, often enabling fighter planes to be in the air in time to intercept the approaching German aircraft. There was one catch. Many of the single-seater fighter planes were too cramped to allow room for a portable radar.

With a reserve of 3000 attacking aircraft the Germans still had the advantage. On 8 August 1940 they began their campaign to defeat Britain with scattered raids on ports and ships, airfields, radar stations and the vital aircraft factories in the south of England. The smokestack cities in the midlands were bombed at night. The peo-ple of London wondered when it would be their turn. It came in September. On the first day more than 400 German aircraft attacked, and nearly 100 were shot down. The following daylight raids were also costly for the Germans.

Perhaps the night was the effective time for attack. A full moon on late-summer nights, with the serpentine River Thames shining in the light, helped the German bombers to find their way to many of their chosen targets. The size of the German raids, the number of planes taking part, was frightening for bystanders. In London the air-raid sirens and the noise of bombers overhead, and the crashing of bricks and mortar, the unroofing of offices and houses, became familiar to householders on almost every night. Throughout recorded history, hundreds of cities had been besieged, and in recent centuries they had been heavily damaged by artillery, but this was the first war in which the heart of a large city could be bombed thoroughly from the air. By Christmas much of the old city – the churches, banks, monuments and ancient buildings – had been destroyed or wrecked. The crucial question was whether civilian morale would cope with the nightly devastation and danger. The collapse of morale on the home front, as Russia demonstrated in 1917 and Germany demonstrated in 1918, could be as destructive as a collapse on a battlefield.

In these dark days of 1940, an eccentric but strangely reassuring picture of Churchill came from those who observed him at work. Late to rise in the morning he sat in his bed, smoking a cigar, a red dressing gown wrapped around him, gleaning the latest war news and military messages from a box resting on the bed or dictating responses to a secretary who tapped the keys of a manual typewriter on a table nearby. At the foot of the bed peacefully rested Churchill's black cat Nelson, named after Britain's naval hero in the previous century. The mixture of stern duty and cheerful relaxation was confirmed by those who saw Churchill, at lunch and dinner, drinking his champagne, whiskies and brandies.

At his most creative and most argumentative after 10 p.m., he would conduct strategic discussions that ran past midnight, by which time many of his listeners were close to exhaustion. Some of his conversation came from the mass of war documents he had skimmed that day. The documents that bored him he passed on to others. His knowledge of past wars, and sometimes his intuition about people, guided him in warding off those colleagues who tried to persuade him to think as they thought. He would, according to his personal secretary, reach conclusions that were at first sight contrary 'to logic and contrary to the normal mental workings of everybody else'. While Churchill's mind was complicated and elusive, his sense of purpose and determination were awesomely simple.

Here was an eccentric but determined statesman, defending a civilisation in unprecedented peril. Amidst the gloom he spread sunshine and a feeling of inner strength: 'These are not dark days: these are great days – the greatest days our country has ever lived.' Here was a great man in what was later seen to be his greatest year.

His wife Clementine, equally formidable, could not conceive of defeat even when offers or feelers of peace were expected to arrive from Hitler's headquarters. In London in 1940 she went to St Martin-in-the-Fields, where she heard a sermon of such ardent pacifism that in disgust she walked from the church. During the war she was prepared to carry her own private burdens. Her sister's son, a prisoner of war of the Germans, was designated by them as a special hostage; and Clementine knew that the young man, simply because he was her nephew, might be threatened with death if Germany were in danger of losing the war.

Churchill thought that Hitler so far was favoured by luck as well as a highly professional army and air force. Nearly all of western Europe was in his hands – except for those few countries such as Spain, Portugal, Ireland, Switzerland and Sweden which were more or less neutral. They could remain neutral only with Hitler's consent, and their leaders understood that simple truth. Cautious and alert, they tried not to antagonise him. Sweden's neutrality was especially tainted because it allowed German troops to cross over the country to their destinations and it continued to be a busy shipper of iron ore to Hitler's Germany.

The wide shores and the islands of the Mediterranean were the next target for Hitler. The Germans invaded Greece, and in April 1941 they took the city of Athens. By the end of May the Greek island of Crete was mainly occupied, after German paratroopers had made daring descents. Large Italian and German forces were already amassing in north Africa, and it was feared by Churchill that Egypt would fall into their hands. If it fell, the Suez Canal, providing a vital shortcut between Europe and Asia, would also be in Germany's control. And if the Suez Canal was lost, then the British could send out the reinforcements – urgently needed in India, Singapore, Burma, Hong Kong and other colonies – only by the long sea route past the foot of South Africa and so into the Indian Ocean.

Hitler's lightning assault on Europe gave him the ability to prolong the war for years to come. His direct or indirect control of Poland, Norway, Holland, France, Romania and other nations ended his desperate shortage of some of the raw materials for war. He could now tap a flow of foreign materials including bauxite and aluminium from France, copper from Yugoslavia, iron ore from Sweden and oil from Romania – the largest oil producer in Europe – as well as stocks of oil in the occupied lands. German ingenuity solved other problems. It made synthetic rubber on a large scale, it converted German coal into synthetic oil and aviation gasoline, and it produced synthetic nitrates – vital for explosives – by using the process invented by its chemists in the First World War. Germany and its occupied lands became a self-sufficient fortress, capable of fighting a long war on many fronts.

THE WAR OVERFLOWS INTO RUSSIA

Meanwhile Hitler gave Stalin a free hand on the plains to the east. Just after Paris had fallen to Hitler's forces, Stalin took the opportunity to annex the three Baltic nations of Lithuania, Estonia and

Latvia. Russian provinces before the dramatic events of 1917, and then independent for the best part of a quarter century, they were again in Russian control. Further south the kingdom of Romania, faced with a Russian ultimatum, yielded territory that was demanded. Its vital oilfields, however, did not pass to Stalin, for German troops intervened and took over most of Romania. Nonetheless Russia in the space of a year had regained most of the land she had lost when she accepted defeat during the First World War.

That ribbon of weak and mostly new nations near Russia's western border – nations stretching from Finland and the Baltic in the north to Romania and the Black Sea in the south – had resembled a long, frayed bandage. Stalin had ripped it apart, with Hitler's acquiescence. But the friendship of the two dictators was opportunist. They had rarely trusted each other, their ideologies were far apart, and their territorial ambitions clashed. The fact that Hitler had signed a pact of friendship with Stalin did not perturb his conscience in the least. The existence of the pact actually made it easier for Hitler to catch Stalin when he was not fully alert.

Hitler alone made the decision to invade Russia in 1941. He hated the communists, whether German or Russian. He had already conquered the German communists, long before the start of the Second World War. Now he vowed that his assembled army of 3 200 000 men, and the heavy reinforcements at hand, would conquer Russia itself in the space of less than six months. He had adequate reasons for his confidence. His armed forces had speedily trounced all their enemies in western Europe, had been superior in the air and on the ground, and had shown again and again the value of surprise in their choice of timing and weapons. Hitler also gained confidence from his belief that Stalin had wrecked the Soviet Union with his purges and his collectivisation, even crippling his own army by shooting many of its best generals. Hitler hoped that the Soviet armed forces would perform as poorly as they had in their brief war against tiny Finland in the cold winter of 1939–40.

Justified in being confident, he ran high risks whenever he became overconfident. Increasingly imagining that he was a military genius, a new Napoleon, he made some decisions on the basis of intuition. Few German officers dared to argue with him, and as many flattered or humoured him, his overconfidence grew. In some discussions he mouthed nonsense. Would the United States eventually become a powerful fighting nation? Of course not, argued Hitler, because its much-vaunted industrial might was 'the biggest fraud in the world'. As for the typical British soldier he was lazy, in Hitler's view, and 'would almost rather die of cold than build himself a shelter'. On the other hand, in scrutinising the Russians he was about to attack, Hitler was entitled to gain assurance from the fact that their aircraft, and their artillery (drawn by farm tractors or even horses) were inadequate. In his view the Ukrainians and other ethnic minorities would rise up against Stalin soon after the war began. With such arguments Hitler reassured himself.

He forgot that the Soviet Union could easily assemble an army much larger than Germany's. And he did not comprehend fully the size of the Soviet territory. It provided enough space for endless Russian retreats, as Napoleon discovered more than a century previously when pursuing his enemy across the plains, marshes and wide rivers – until he himself was the exhausted one. The same vastness of Soviet territory would also enable Stalin to build new industrial cities on the far side of the Urals, where they were almost immune from German attack.

The evidence suggests that Stalin was warned by his own intelligence services about the possibility of a German invasion but he personally doubted whether the invasion would soon eventuate. His view was that Hitler would wait until he had defeated Britain before turning his forces towards the east. At this stage Britain, though bombed heavily, was far from defeated.

For many months Stalin slowly was preparing his own plans of attack. Late in March 1941 he secretly called up 20-year-old men for military training. That the 20-year-olds totalled 394 000 was a sign of the massive manpower at Stalin's disposal. It was his belief that attack was the real form of defence, and that the French had lost the war against Hitler because their Maginot Line was a mirror of their defensive spirit. He hoped that the Soviet Union would have the time to prepare not for defence but for an all-out offensive. But Hitler's invasion came when he did not expect it.

With high confidence Hitler's forces, on 22 June 1941, launched their invasion of the Soviet Union. In the north the Finns were strong allies and in the south were armies from Hungary and Romania, later to be joined by Italians who, advancing on Russian soil, became the last European soldiers ever to fight on horseback. The names of the bravest of these Italians are inscribed on the honour roll, still visible in the gateway of the old Italian cavalry school at Modena.

For the first few months Hitler seemed likely to succeed, for his army found few obstacles. The port of Leningrad was the toughest, having prepared for a long siege by erecting outer embankments that could block the oncoming enemy tanks and keep at bay the German and Finnish armies. The besieged Leningrad, month after month, survived on the leanest rations of food. In one year it lost 650 000 lives through epidemics, starvation and the shells fired by the German artillery. And yet during the siege such losses almost became a public benefit because they reduced the number of mouths to be fed.

Occasionally the enemy's blockade was weakened, allowing temporary supplies to reach the city, and enabling the evacuation of hundreds of thousands of the sick, young and old. Then the enemy, tightening its grip, waited for the city to be slowly starved, thereby forcing it to surrender. But there was no such word in the Leningrad vocabulary. Civilians and soldiers held firm. By the summer of 1943 the open spaces, courtyards and public gardens of the besieged city were a mosaic of potato and cabbage gardens, enabling the daily ration of food to be increased.

In the first months of the invasion of Russia, Hitler was triumphant. The German soldiers had won a vast tract of enemy land by the time the terrible winter set in. What did the siege of Leningrad matter when German forces were close to the city that counted – Moscow and its outer suburbs?

Astonishingly, Germany as a nation did not fully exploit its military advantages. While the army fought and suffered on foreign soil, a host of civilians sat back on the home soil and enjoyed almost the comfortable well-fed life of peacetime. Hitler was slow to divert workers from less essential occupations. Housemaids, kitchen maids and domestic cooks continued to serve the nation in large numbers at a time when they could have been diverted into the expanding munitions plants. Britain, though slower to prepare for war, at last was manufacturing more aircraft, tanks and self-propelled guns than the Germans.

One sign of Hitler's overconfidence was his refusal to use all the skilled and captive labour in his new empire. He had at his command maybe 6 million Jews, all across Europe, but during the first phase of the war he used them only as menial or manual labourers and then on a limited scale. By the beginning of 1942 he had firmly resolved to try to exterminate the Jews not only in Germany but in all the European lands his forces occupied. From many parts of Europe, especially from Poland, Jews were sent in freight trains to the concentration camps where most were killed with cold and systematic efficiency. In western Russia and the Ukraine, hundreds of thousands of Jews were killed by the advancing and even the retreating German troops. Likewise Gypsies were sent to labour camps, more for punishment than usefully to harness their labour. In 1942 they too, including those part-Gypsies who formed the great majority, were marked down for destruction or humiliation. It is estimated that at least 250 000 and perhaps as many as 500 000 Gypsies, men and women and children, died in German camps.

These events, perhaps the most barbaric in modern history, were named by the German leaders as 'The Final Solution'. Only later, in the wider world, did the phrase The Holocaust come into use.

TOKYO'S DILEMMA

There was a supreme confidence in German military circles, and until the end of 1941 that mood was understandable. Hitler's armies, having conquered far more of Europe than Napoleon's had ever conquered, seemed likely to capture Moscow and maybe Leningrad in the coming spring. It was now conceivable that the Japanese would suddenly attack the Soviet Union from the east, while the Germans continued their attack from the west, thus squeezing the Russian Bear to death. Japanese decisions, unpredictable from afar, would partly determine the outcome of this war, now in its third year.

In Tokyo the Japanese leaders knew they had a remarkable opportunity to defeat their old enemy. They had fought Russia in a victorious war in 1904–05 and very briefly in an indecisive armed clash that began in Mongolia in May 1939. Here was the opportunity to strike decisively. For the Russians were sending whole train loads of tanks from their defences in eastern Siberia to reinforce their defences near Moscow. On the other hand the Japanese now had an equal opportunity to launch a southern attack against the weakened European colonies extending from British Hong Kong and Burma to the oil-rich Dutch East Indies.

This dilemma was weighed again and again at secret conferences of army and navy in Tokyo where the advantages of attacking south became more enticing. The approaching northern winter, when the icy Siberian terrain would be harsh, was now militating against an attack on the Soviet Union. On the other hand the Dutch East Indies held vast reserves of oil, and the Malay peninsula held tin and rubber too, all of which were vital military materials that Japan itself lacked. The decision to invade this region near the equator was virtually confirmed by the increasing American and British hostility towards Japan, its longstanding war against China, and its recent, unopposed military occupation of French Indo-China. The United

States, once the main shipper of oil to Japan, abruptly terminated the trade in July 1941. Japan's response was to fight for its supply of oil. Late in the year it was in full readiness to make a coordinated series of attacks that had no equal in the long history of invasions.

13

FROM PEARL HARBOR TO THE
FALL OF BERLIN

Pearl Harbor, on the isolated island of Hawaii, was one of the world's larger naval bases; and on the morning of 8 December 1941 – Tokyo time – it sheltered about 70 fighting ships of all sizes. Its commanders thought that a Japanese naval attack, while conceivable, was not very likely. The United States was still technically a neutral nation, and that increased the sense of security felt at Pearl Harbor. The nearest Japanese naval base was far across the ocean, increasing further the feeling of safety.

The Japanese secretly sent across the Pacific six aircraft carriers to launch the planes that were to deliver the main attack on Pearl Harbor. Their triumph was remarkable. A long list of American ships and 188 planes were destroyed or damaged. The Japanese pilots and submarine commanders experienced, however, one acute disappointment, for the three American aircraft carriers were at sea on the morning of the attack, and escaped detection.

On the same morning, the Japanese prepared to launch a surprise attack on the islands of the Philippines, a young nation that was halfway to independence but still relying heavily on America for defence. Lying far from the naval bases in California and Pearl Harbor, it could be attacked more easily from Japan than defended from the United States. And yet the resident American general, Douglas MacArthur, thought that he could adequately defend the Philippines, for his army was supported by some 250 military aircraft and a naval force that included 29 submarines. Furthermore he possessed seven new radar sets with which he could gain an early warning of an air raid by the Japanese, though only two of the radars were so far working. He also possessed anti-aircraft guns that could defend the new airfields, though the guns were not first class. His consoling hope was that if the Japanese did attack, their bombers and fighters and especially the pilots would quickly prove to be inferior. As for the possibility of the Japanese making a simultaneous attack on a wide range of American, British, Dutch and French tropical bases, the idea did not enter his head. Such a wide and coordinated attack was virtually unknown in naval history.

Two hours after the devastating raid on Pearl Harbor, the momentous news reached the Philippines where it was gravely reported on the public radio stations. The US navy in Manila independently learned the news. The Japanese, it seemed, now had no chance of raiding the Philippines by surprise. Moreover, General MacArthur made decisive steps to thwart any attack on his main air base at Clark Field, near Manila. As a precaution, his fleet of bombers – without their bombs – took off from Clark Field and remained aloft for some hours, thus averting the danger that they would be standing on the tarmac, a ready target, if attacking Japanese aircraft arrived.

Meanwhile, in Taiwan, the Japanese were quietly preparing to carry out their secret attack on the American base at Clark Field. At 10.15 their aircraft took to the sky. A powerful force of 108 twin-engine bombers and 84 Zero fighter aircraft flew steadily south. At various towns on the Philippines coast and even in the interior the oncoming Japanese aircraft could be seen high above, and various postmasters sent telegrams or made phone calls to Manila, warning of the danger. Such messages reached the radio station at Clark Field. Somehow they were not heard. It was said that the Japanese had jammed the local air frequencies. It was also said that the chief American radio operator had gone to lunch. For years excuses, plausible explanations and alibis were to be tossed to and fro.

The danger facing the American defences was heightened by another piece of misfortune or misjudgment. Their bombers had just returned to the tarmac at Clark Field, the risk of a Japanese attack having been estimated as low. Many were being filled with gasoline and loaded with bombs so that, at short notice, they could set out to attack the distant Japanese bases. Attack more than defence was General MacArthur's priority.

Suddenly the Japanese aircraft could be heard buzzing almost overhead. They attacked Clark Field in waves. To their pilots' delight the American aircraft were neatly arranged on the ground, as if set out for the target practice. More than 100 were destroyed and many others damaged during these initial raids; and in the space of one week the American air force in the Philippines was reduced to a few fighters. There was briefly the hope that additional aircraft would arrive any day from the United States but the hope was ended by the quick Japanese capture of Guam and Wake – vital islands on the sea and air route to the Philippines. The American navy was almost helpless. It had to abandon the Philippines because it had no protection from the air.

On the day that the war broke out in the Pacific, an American convoy was steaming westwards to the Philippines. Escorted by a heavy cruiser, the seven cargo ships carried artillery, ammunition and fighter aircraft. The Japanese advance was so swift and the superiority in the air was so pronounced that the convoy, warned that it had no chance of reaching its goal in safety, changed course to Brisbane in Australia. Its vital cargo never reached the Philippines.

HALF-ALERT IN SINGAPORE

On the first day of the new war, the British naval and air base at Singapore was almost as vulnerable as the American bases in the Philippines, 1500 miles away. The British leaders in Singapore anticipated a Japanese attack but were as confident as General MacArthur and were reassured for additional reasons. They were led to believe that Japanese pilots could not see at night, that their aircraft were slow, and that their army in the preceding four years had shown itself incapable of conquering the Chinese and their disordered defences. What was not realised was the extent of the Japanese drive to rearm themselves during the preceding decade.

In London, Churchill himself had valid reason to be wary of Japan. It possessed a powerful navy, originally trained by British officers. It had defeated a Russian fleet in 1905, and nine years later had held its own against German warships in the Pacific. It could certainly be expected to outnumber the British ships if and when war broke out in South-East Asia. Moreover the fall of France in the previous year had fractured Britain's plans for their naval defence of Singapore. Originally it had been agreed that if Singapore were in danger the French fleet could patrol the Mediterranean, thus allowing the British to divert warships to Singapore. Now the French fleet, however, was either under German control or out of action, and could not help.

Britain had no naval fleet or fast aircraft that could be spared for this new war zone. They were all urgently needed to defend the British Isles and her nearby sea lanes, to patrol the convoy routes in the Atlantic, to prevent the Germans from capturing Egypt and the Suez Canal, and to conduct air raids on Germany. With the crisis approaching in South-East Asia, Britain could divert only two first-class ships, the new battleship *Prince of Wales* and the old battle cruiser *Repulse*, which reached Singapore just before the Japanese attacked Pearl Harbor. These two mighty ships were to have been accompanied by an aircraft carrier, the *Indomitable*; but she ran aground in the West Indies, and a replacement could not be found.

The commander of the arriving British fleet, Admiral Sir Tom Phillips, believed that he could probably survive without the aircraft carriers which, in Japanese eyes and experience, were now essential in naval warfare. He argued that his two heavily armoured ships, both carrying anti-aircraft guns, could fend off most Japanese aircraft. While he conceded that smaller British warships had actually been crippled by German air attacks near Crete and near Norway, his larger British warships would be safe – in his considered view. Admittedly he knew that one year ago his own navy had proved the value of despatching aircraft against a small fleet of enemy ships, for British torpedo planes, flying from the decks of aircraft carriers, boldly attacked the Italian fleet. Phillips, however, pointed out that these powerful Italian warships were trapped in their own harbour at Taranto and therefore a sitting target for enemy aircraft. He was satisfied that his two warships, large and fast, would defend Singapore against the Japanese.

The fall of France had struck another blow to the security of Singapore. The neighbouring French colony of Indo-China, exposed to diplomatic pressure and strong threats, had permitted a Japanese army of 200 000 men and a fleet of Japanese ships and planes to assemble in its territory and ports, from which they could easily attack British Malaya and Singapore, just across the water. Hours before the Japanese attacked Pearl Harbor, their forces in French Indo-China set out to invade Thailand and the northern end of British Malaya. On 8 December 1941 the first alarming reports of their invasions reached Singapore. That evening, just before sunset, the two big British warships, accompanied by four destroyers, left Singapore harbour. Throughout the night they sailed along the east coast of Malaya, hoping to intercept or frighten away a Japanese naval fleet escorting one of their invasion forces.

The two British ships needed fighter planes to protect them in the event of a Japanese air attack, but such fighters were not readily available. The hope was that British and Australian planes could fly from nearby airfields if needed. It was also hoped with undue optimism that the Japanese in the area would possess few fighter aircraft: surprisingly little was known about their planes, flying speed and location. So these mighty ships and their four escorting ships, with officers and crew totalling more than 3000, sailed in the dark tropical seas towards the enemy. No such fleet, in the open ocean, had ever been destroyed from the air. Admiral Phillips at first was entitled to feel relatively secure.

On the first night at sea, a Japanese submarine fired torpedoes at the British fleet. All five missed their mark. But now the Japanese knew the position of the *Prince of Wales* and *Repulse*. At Saigon the Japanese aircraft were loaded with torpedoes, and at dusk on the 9th they set out to find the blacked-out, fast-moving British ships. Unable to locate them in the dark they returned to Saigon at midnight. At dawn next morning the Japanese sent a dozen reconnaissance planes to search for the British ships, which had changed direction and so were easily missed. The planes, having flown all the way to Singapore without sighting the ships, found them on the way back. Far below, at 10.20 a.m., the British warships could be seen moving at rapid speed, about 150 miles from Singapore. Guided by the new information, some 85 Japanese bombers and torpedo bombers converged.

The Japanese were the world's masters of the technique of using torpedoes in aerial attacks. At 11.45 a.m. on 10 December 1941 a low-flying Japanese plane fired a torpedo that crippled the *Prince of Wales*. Three quarters of an hour later, torpedoes coming from many directions hit the *Repulse*, which began to sink. The captain, standing on the bridge and speaking through the loudspeaker, praised the surviving members of the crew before they went overboard. 'I never saw the slightest sign of panic or ill discipline', he said. Soon the mighty battleships, and their admiral, were no more. British destroyers, not far away, plucked the survivors from the sea.

The attack aircraft – except the three lost in the course of the fight – returned to Saigon, 400 air miles to the north, carrying their astonishing news. In the history of warfare this was the first notable aerial victory over a major naval force. Churchill, on hearing the news, declared that it was one of the blackest days in the history of Britain.

Almost everywhere in this zone of war, Japan seized control of air and sea. On Christmas Day her troops finally captured Hong Kong. On New Year's Day 1942, Manila was about to fall, and on the following day the Japanese flags were raised up the city's flagpoles in triumph.

Japanese soldiers, aided by a victorious air force, increased their grip on the northern half of the long Malay peninsula. They encircled port after port, crossed fast and wide rivers, and riding bicycles where possible they pushed through the jungles and rice paddies. As they advanced towards Singapore they were outnumbered by the British, Indian and Australian defenders but their momentum did not diminish. Their officers were superior, their gathering of intelligence was skilled, their soldiers adapted themselves to jungle warfare, and their morale and determination were rarely shaken.

Lieutenant-General Arthur Percival, the leader of the British land forces, had been decorated for bravery in the First World War but was indecisive during this campaign that was swiftly drawing to its close. When the Japanese forces approached the island of Singapore he refused to build fortifications along the narrow strait facing the invaders. To be seen to build such defences, he explained, would be 'bad for morale, for both troops and civilians'. Still outnumbered, the Japanese easily crossed the narrow channel and moved into Singapore. The port and its magnificent naval base fell on 15 February

1942. In no part of the world had so many troops under British command been captured in the one day. Tens of thousands of those captured by the Japanese in South-East Asia were to die in prisoner-of-war camps, railway works and makeshift prisons in the following three and a half years.

Almost every plan of the British and the Americans was torn up or thwarted by the unexpected events in the Pacific War. After the fall of Singapore, the Dutch East Indies was in peril. The Japanese, landing troops with ease, captured the island of Java in March. Even before Sumatra and its valuable oilfields were captured, the advance forces of the Japanese were in New Guinea and its nearby islands.

In March 1942 the American forces in the Philippines were doomed. It was at least hoped to rescue General MacArthur who, on the president's orders, had secretly made a long voyage by patrol boat from Manila Bay to an isolated landing field on the island of Mindanao. Three precious B-17 bombers landed there and took aboard MacArthur, his wife and young son and Chinese nurse, along with a few American officials. The night flight to safety across Japanese-controlled islands was hazardous. Soon after reaching Australia, which was to become his attacking base for the remainder of the war, he made the prophecy: 'I came through, and I shall return.'

There was now a galloping fear, a terrible sense of foreboding: would the Japanese attack India? On the first day of the war it was not conceivable that the Japanese forces could approach within a distant glimpse of the Indian border. But the southern half of British Burma, an exporter of rice and producer of precious oil, was now in danger, and it was a potential gateway to India. In March 1942 its capital city Rangoon was captured, and on 1 May the inland city of

Mandalay surrendered. If the whole of Burma fell, would eastern India be the next target of the always-advancing Japanese armies? Indian leaders who had been clamouring for their country's independence from Britain now possessed an opportunity, if they so desired, to disrupt Britain's war effort and even to invite Japan to enter as liberator. In the end they shunned the opportunity.

The Japanese now commanded every port on the coastline of East Asia, the Indonesian archipelago and Philippines, stretching from Japan and Korea southwards past Shanghai, Hong Kong, Saigon and Penang to Singapore, and so on through Jakarta and Ambon to Rabaul in Australian New Guinea. This long corridor of land and intersecting sea extended from Japan almost to the coastal waters of northern Australia. Japanese planes, rising from the same aircraft carriers that had attacked Pearl Harbor, bombed the Australian port of Darwin for the first time. Japanese soldiers, climbing over the high Owen Stanley Mountains, quickly moved down until they almost reached the harbour of Port Moresby, near the south-east corner of New Guinea.

Port Moresby commands the entrance to Torres Strait, the narrow sea separating New Guinea from northern Australia. In the first week of May 1942 a Japanese invading force of troopships, aircraft carriers and other warships attempted to capture Port Moresby by approaching it on a long, roundabout route. The naval force, spotted from the air, was intercepted by the Americans. For several days the Battle of the Coral Sea was fought, the first major naval battle ever to be conducted without the rival fleets sighting one another. The aircraft launched by the opposing fleets made most of the devastating attacks, while other aircraft flew from the Australian mainland in

6 JAPAN'S EMPIRE IN 1942

Soviet Union

Mongolia

Peking·

China

Shanghai·

Korea

Japan

PACIFIC OCEAN

·Tokyo
·Hiroshima
Nagasaki

× Midway Island
Battle of Midway

Burma

Hong Kong

Taiwan

Thailand

Vietnam

·Manila
Philippines

Mariana Islands

·Guam

Caroline Islands

Marshall Islands

Malaya

Singapore

Sumatra Borneo

Jakarta

Java

Dutch East Indies

Darwin·

New Guinea

Solomon Islands

Nauru

×
Battle of Coral Sea New Hebrides

New Caledonia

INDIAN OCEAN

Australia

·Brisbane

New Zealand

Perth·

·Sydney
Canberra

search of the Japanese fleet. The Japanese won a technical victory – they destroyed the most ships though they lost the most planes. But they had to deliver a knockout blow if they were to be capable of continuing on their planned course of invasion. In the end their fleet voluntarily turned back. The tide for the first time was running against them.

A month later at the Battle of Midway – near a lonely island lying between Tokyo and Pearl Harbor – the American and the Japanese navies prepared to fight again. One of the world's most important naval battles had just been fought in the Southern Hemisphere, and now a replay in the Northern Hemisphere was to be fought by the same navies and some of the same aircraft carriers. The Americans, having broken the Japanese navy's secret code, knew about its forthcoming plans and tactics. In effect they had pilfered Japan's deadly weapon – the weapon of surprise.

In a sea battle extending over several days the Japanese invading force of 5 aircraft carriers, 2 seaplane carriers, 11 cruisers, 9 battleships, 39 destroyers, and numerous submarines and minesweepers at first held the ascendancy. A huge force, it seemed almost invincible. At a crucial moment, just before 10.30 a.m. on 5 June 1942, Japanese planes were refuelling and rearming on the crowded decks of the four aircraft carriers when unexpectedly they were attacked with devastating force by American dive bombers. It was almost a replay of what had happened at Pearl Harbor and Manila exactly six months previously. This time the Japanese were surprised.

Japan lost her most valuable aircraft carriers – the key to success in a war being fought over a huge ocean. In contrast the United States lost only one aircraft carrier, the *Yorktown*, which had been damaged in the Battle of the Coral Sea only a month before and then had been miraculously repaired. Now Japan's chance of ultimate victory was slipping away, though such an outcome could not yet be confidently foreseen.

Japan exploited its huge empire, won in the space of a few months. British, French, Dutch and Portuguese colonies and American defence bases were available, along with several hundred million Asians who lived in those lands, and all the vital materials of war – rubber, petroleum, tin and quinine – that the lands produced. More than three years of fighting were needed by the American, British, Australian, and other armed forces to recover just part of the territory won by the Japanese in their triumphant months of 1941–42.

THE WAR TURNS AGAINST HITLER

The year of the invasion of Russia, 1941, was Hitler's last year of triumph. In the following spring and summer, at the very time when Japan was reaching the limits of its conquest, Hitler's forces were making little headway. They captured the prized city of Stalingrad but lost it again. They now held the northern shores of the Black Sea and the southern shores of the Baltic Sea and a huge expanse of Russia west of the Urals, but the land of Russia was vast. New munitions and aircraft factories were arising far beyond the reach of the German invaders. Moreover, convoys were bringing supplies from Britain through chill and perilous seas, past the northern headlands of Norway, to ports in northern Russia.

Germany began to taste its own medicine – the massive bombing raid. In the middle of 1942, 1000 British aircraft bombed the cathedral city of Cologne, on the Rhine. America, now at war with

Germany as well as Japan, began to use British air bases in preparation for its raids on German soil. Appearing on the horizon like flocks of birds, the American bombers attacked Berlin and other cities that had been relatively immune. In Berlin in 1943 a well-connected woman who kept a diary wrote less and less about coffee and cake and embassy parties and more and more about the bombing of her city. She recorded that civilians hiding in basements and kitchens heard the sound of glass breaking and the rumble of falling masonry, and when they emerged with protective wet towels covering their heads they saw the red haze of suburbs aflame; and when they tried to make a cup of coffee they found no water in the tap, no electricity and no gas. On Tuesday 23 November 1943 the diary noted that 'the sky on three sides was blood red'.

In North Africa and the Middle East, the German and Italian forces, after capturing nearly all the coastline of the Mediterranean, and scenting the prospect that they might even capture the Suez Canal, lost the initiative in 1942. They were driven out of North Africa, and that became the planned springboard for the American and British invasion of Sicily and Italy. In the summer of 1943 Sicily was invaded, and within four weeks was captured. The far south of Italy was attacked from the sea. The Germans, having deposed Mussolini and taken control of much of his territory, defended it by exploiting the mountain barriers above the narrow coastal plains, and retreating slowly when retreat seemed an advantage. After they lost the city of Naples in September 1943, they managed to hold on to nearby Rome for another nine months. In Italy the fighting went on for 600 days. A heavily fortified part of the north was still held by Germany when the war ended.

In the middle of 1944 Hitler still reigned. He held the entire coast of western Europe running from Norwegian bays near the Arctic Circle, along the eastern edge of the North Sea and English Channel, and so to the Bay of Biscay where met the borders of occupied France and neutral Spain. But D-day, the long-promised Allied invasion of France, was about to begin.

On 6 June 1944 the invaders went ashore in French Normandy, a point of attack that Hitler had not anticipated. The largest sea expedition in the history of warfare, consisting of some 7000 ships ranging from battleships to torpedo boats and trawlers and merchant ships, and supported by thousands of aircraft, it approached the French coast under the protection of darkness. By the end of the first day 133 000 Allied soldiers had landed and another 23 000 had come down by parachutes. By the end of the month the force that had crossed the sea from England numbered more than 800 000 Americans, British and others. The Germans were driven back. Paris was captured late in August, and Brussels less than a fortnight later.

When winter set in – the sixth winter of the war – victory was almost in sight on the western front. But the German borders had not been reached. German soldiers were amongst the hardiest, most determined in the world. They would not easily give in.

Meanwhile the battles in the air were crushing Germany's spirit and muscle. Its factories, mines and steelworks continued to produce busily until 1944, after which the sheer weight and accuracy of the raids by British and American bombers cut Germany's industrial output. Essential war materials, ranging from ball bearings to synthetic rubber, became scarce. German commanders in the field pleaded in vain for more munitions and tanks and for more aircraft overhead.

THREE LEADERS SHAPE THE PEACE

Decisions, vital to the postwar world, were made not only by events at the fighting fronts but by the likes and dislikes of the leaders of the three nations whose efforts were largely winning the war. Never before had so many strands of the world's future been held in the palms of just three pairs of hands. At the end of 1944 the future of Europe was being decided not only on the battlefields but by the willpower, personalities and clashing ambitions of the three Allied leaders – Stalin, Roosevelt and Churchill, who occasionally conferred in person and frequently by messages. Each leader pursued different national and global interests, had a different ideology, and possessed varying naval, military and aerial strengths. While each wanted victory, they disagreed on how it could be achieved. Within any alliance, held together by a common enemy, fierce internal rivalries often flourish.

The present viewpoint is that Stalin proved to be the most resolute leader, that the Soviet Union exerted undue influence in reshaping the map of postwar Europe, and that a war purportedly begun to defend the independence of small European nations ended up by sacrificing them. The question – did Stalin outwit and outjostle Roosevelt and Churchill – will remain one of the enigmas of the 20th century.

In some ways Franklin D. Roosevelt was the stranger amongst the three leaders. His nation was the last to enter the war, just as it had been late to enter the First World War. Moreover he was less vigorous physically than the other leaders. He had contracted poliomyelitis in his late thirties and met the demands of public office only with the aid of crutches and a wheelchair. Coming from a wealthy patrician family, an east-coast dynasty that was partly of Dutch ancestry – New York was originally called New Amsterdam – his politics were less conservative than his background. Seated on a public platform, in his expensive business suit, he rather resembled the benign and eloquent president of a successful university or the pastor of a huge congregation.

Roosevelt was not easily moulded by others. Strong and independent he knew the pulse of America and its regional and ethnic peculiarities. After a term as governor of his home state of New York he was elected president of the United States by a massive majority late in 1932, when he was on the verge of his fiftieth birthday. In trying to cope with the world depression he virtually introduced social welfare to his nation; and in guiding his wary people during the first two years of the Second World War he increasingly applied his own meaning to the concept of neutrality. His nation, in helping to arm Britain, was only half neutral.

In those days an American president, even in full vigour, was like an old-time pope: he rarely travelled far from home. It was not until August 1941 that Roosevelt and Churchill held their first formal meeting in a British battleship in a bay off Newfoundland. There they agreed to do everything possible to overthrow 'the Nazi tyranny', including offering military aid to the Soviet Union in its struggle against German invaders. By the end of the year Roosevelt was in the fighting team. Following the sudden Japanese attack on Pearl Harbor, he was commanding a nation at war, while the *Prince of Wales*, the battleship in which he and Churchill had conversed off Newfoundland, was lying on the seabed near Singapore.

A meeting between the two democratic leaders of the alliance and the communist leader was not easily arranged because Stalin was even more reluctant than Roosevelt to step outside his own domain. But at last, one year after the conference in Newfoundland, it was Churchill who set out on a roundabout route to Moscow. Flying in a Liberator bomber from Cairo, and stopping for the night at Teheran, he reached Moscow with a feeling of deep weariness. Meeting Stalin at the Kremlin that evening, for the first time, he was surprised to find the meeting passing pleasantly. His unwelcome news, that he and Roosevelt were postponing the promised Anglo-American invasion of Hitler's Europe, was almost forgotten during the vodka toasts and mutual expressions of concord.

On the second evening the harmony was shattered when Stalin criticised the performance of the British army and insisted that Churchill had broken his promise to open at an early stage a second fighting front in France or some other part of western Europe. At the end of the third evening, prolonged by a banquet in the Kremlin, Churchill felt so dejected that on reaching his apartment he flopped into an armchair and confided: 'Stalin didn't want to talk to me. I closed the proceedings down. I had had enough. The food was filthy. I ought not to have come.' It was 3.45 a.m. when Churchill put on his eccentric black eyeshade and tucked himself into bed. On the final evening they discussed grave topics for hours before Churchill, again in a cheerful spirit, commenced the long roundabout flight to Teheran and Cairo and so to London.

The assessment of Stalin, the decision whether to trust him and accept his vague promises or to pin him down as firmly as possible, was not easy for the two English-speaking leaders. Churchill partly trusted Stalin at first but later stiffened his view. On the other hand

Roosevelt felt some sympathy for Stalin and his courageous armies long before they held their first meeting. Early in 1942 he expressed his private view that all that Stalin really sought was security for his nation. As Russia, so Roosevelt argued with perhaps some validity, had been treated shabbily by her allies at the end of the First World War, perhaps a helping hand would soothe Stalin's feelings. If Stalin were treated fairly, wrote Roosevelt, 'he won't try to annex anything and will work with me for a world of democracy and peace'.

Roosevelt felt that in international negotiations he himself was more skilled than his own advisers and more skilled than Britain's diplomats. On 18 March 1942 he confided to Churchill: 'I know you will not mind my being brutally frank when I tell you I can personally handle Stalin better.' As he had not yet met Stalin, his opinion was unusually confident. Probably he was trying to prepare himself for the postwar world which, he correctly foresaw, would be largely controlled by the two great powers, the USA and the Soviet Union. If rapport were patiently established now, and Stalin proved willing to cooperate with Roosevelt, the atmosphere of trust between the two leaders might persuade the American people to accept what they had not accepted in 1918 – that they were partly responsible for the peace of the world. In retrospect Roosevelt was somewhat like a noble horse eagerly meeting a lion and trusting that the lion would prove to be a vegetarian.

A strong strand of opinion within the United States was sympathetic, at this time rather than before or after, to the Russian people. Their defence of their homeland had been heroic, their losses huge. Significantly, after the Leningrad symphony had been composed by Dmitry Shostakovich, partly while living in that besieged city, it received a hero's welcome in the United States where Toscanini conducted it for the first time to a huge radio audience in 1942. During the following concert season 'the Leningrad' was heard in concert halls throughout the country. In academic circles the name of the Soviet Union had never stood so high. Through some American spectacles the Soviet Union was for a time seen as an exotic version of the United States, a land of fresh vision where the wide open plains promised individual opportunity.

Amongst many soldiers in the western armies, the Soviet Union was viewed as the land of promise. In 1943 a bright New Zealand sergeant was occasionally invited to speak to 'large groups of soldiers on current world affairs', and he recorded how strongly pro-Russian they were. At the same time most Britons felt sympathy towards the Soviet Union and its ideal of full employment and social equality, for the trauma of the world depression was fresh in British memory. Thus Churchill and Roosevelt could count upon a high level of silent public support when occasionally they nodded their approval to ambitious Soviet demands.

In some negotiations, Stalin gained because of Roosevelt's empathy. When the three leaders met for the last time, in an old czarist palace at the Black Sea port of Yalta in February 1945, Stalin and Roosevelt had formed something of a personal rapport, even exchanging in private their opinions, sometimes disparaging, of Churchill. Furthermore, Roosevelt shared Stalin's suspicion of western Europe's long control of the world, a control that it had exercised partly through its overseas colonies. Both leaders, unlike Churchill, believed that the time would come when those colonies would be liberated; and they were determined to accelerate their liberation.

The future of Poland was the most vexatious topic discussed at Yalta. Even Churchill trusted Stalin's promise that there would be an independent Poland, free to conduct elections and decide its own future. In London at the end of February 1945 he did not fully persuade the House of Commons that Stalin could be trusted on this matter. Nor it seems did he fully persuade himself, because he gave a promise to Poles living in exile in Britain, and too frightened to return home, that they could remain with the solace of British citizenship.

Stalin's negotiating ability stemmed from his long experience as a dominator. Moreover he, and his publicists in the west, made the most of his belief that he had been poorly treated by his allies. In fact he had received heavy military aid from the United States and Britain. Without that aid, wisely offered him, his forces might have been driven even further back by the Germans in the dark months of 1942. Admittedly, Stalin had also pleaded for his allies to open a western front and so ease the German pressure on his own struggling forces; and it was an intense disappointment to him that the western front was not opened until the American–British invasion of Italy in 1943 and the invasion of France in 1944. His resentment about the second front, often voiced, can be partly discounted. The war against Japan could equally be called a second front. Britain and the United States had to fight Japan – without any Soviet help – until the very last fortnight of the Pacific war. Stalin, however, had one indisputable argument on his side. His soldiers and civilians made massive sacrifices. In the loss of their own blood and in the destruction of German soldiers, the Russians were the mighty contributors to victory; and that had a profound effect on the negotiating table as the war approached its end.

THE COLLAPSE OF BERLIN

No matter what agreements were reached by the three leaders, especially at Tehran in 1943 and Yalta in 1945, each knew the old saying that possession was nine-tenths of the law. And if Stalin proved to be the first to reconquer a region then he had the real opportunity to control it after the war. In the vital race towards Berlin, the Soviet forces were already outpacing their American and British rivals. After liberating Leningrad from its 900-day siege, they again controlled ports on the Baltic Sea. By July they were close to Warsaw but stood back. With encouragement from Moscow radio, the Polish underground forces had begun to fight the occupying German army in Warsaw, but the Soviet army did nothing to help the Poles. A British request to land supplies for the Polish underground was shunned by Moscow. In the end the Polish 'home army' was defeated. This cynical behaviour by the Russians helped to eliminate the fervent Polish nationalists who would oppose attempts to set up communism in their homeland.

Soon after the Allies had landed on the French beaches on D-day in June 1944, the Russian advance forces were moving close to the eastern borders of Hungary and Romania and moving closer to the Danube River. In the hinterland of the Black Sea the gates here and there were unlocked to welcome the Russian soldiers. Romania, under the rule of the dictator General Ion Antonescu, had been an ally of Hitler; and now as the Russians came nearer he was deposed and his armies were turned against the retreating Germans. On the other side of the Danube River, most Bulgarians welcomed their fellow Slavs from Russia, and some Bulgarian regiments joined in the Soviet advance. Early in October the Soviet forces were ready to penetrate far into Yugoslavia where the Tito partisans were preparing the way. Belgrade fell on 19 October. Having moved west, in slow fighting stages all the way from the far-off Ural mountains, the Soviet forces advanced not far from the Adriatic Sea.

Early in 1945 the Russians captured the Polish capital, Warsaw, and the Hungarian capital, Budapest. Therefore at the very time when the three leaders met at Yalta in order to shape the future of Europe, Russian troops had outflanked the slower-arriving American and British troops. By first occupying a nation or territory, and by protecting the bands of local communists and imprisoning or shooting their rivals, the Soviet troops, and their bureaucrats and secret police, prepared the way for the new order.

By April the war in Europe was almost over. Vienna fell to the Russians and Berlin was in their sights. The Germans, while desperately defending, were squeezed into a narrow home space by the armies coming from both west and east. Even in Italy where about one-fifth of the entire German army had been effectively engaged, the end was in sight. A symbolic event was the capture of Mussolini and his mistress by Italian partisans near the shores of Lake Como where on 28 April they were shot in what is now a sedate suburban street. The next day the Germans abandoned Venice. That stately city and its treasures had been preserved. A day later Hitler, besieged in half-ruined Berlin, resolved to commit suicide: he refused to face his accusers. Another two days passed, and the Russians were in command of Berlin.

On 7 May 1945, in the sixth year of the war, the German forces surrendered unconditionally. Much of their country was in ruins – bridges blown up, railways blocked, factory towns with walls and roofs missing, and the hearts of big cities reduced to piles of rubble in which stood the occasional stump of what had been a spire. These ruins, however, were not extensive compared to the sum total of devastation in the countries that the German armies had fought over and its aircraft had bombed, and in the seabeds where lay a huge fleet of corroding Allied cargo ships and warships – the victims of torpedoes.

Stalin, by dint of obstinate negotiating as well as the formidable fact that his armies kept on advancing, was winning most of what he wanted. In essence he wanted eastern Europe: a tract of land, languages and cultures stretching from the Black Sea to the Baltic. That vast area included most of prewar Poland, a nation on whose behalf France and Britain had formally declared war in 1939. It embraced Czechoslovakia, Hungary, Romania, Bulgaria, eastern Germany and the three Baltic states of Estonia, Latvia and Lithuania. For most of these peoples the hopes of independence were beginning to fade even before the war was formally over.

Churchill and Roosevelt, at their first formal meeting on the coast of Newfoundland in 1941, had drawn up an Atlantic Charter in which the rights of self-determination for small nations were proclaimed. Stalin in practice disagreed with the idea that small nations should be protected. Even Churchill disagreed if the rights were extended to colonies that hoped to become small nations. At the end of the war the smaller nations of eastern Europe were in peril.

14

A MOST SECRET WEAPON

The war was over in Europe in mid-1945 but not yet won in East Asia and on the shores of the Pacific. Japan still occupied more than half of the territory it had captured in the first phase of the war, its zone of occupations spreading from the Northern to the Southern Hemisphere, and from the far north of China to tropical islands near the coast of Australia. While the British had recaptured much of Burma, while American forces had recaptured most of the Philippines and crucial islands to the south of Japan, and while American aircraft could now use those stepping stones to stage massive raids on Tokyo, the Allies were not ready to invade Japan.

A successful invasion would require an American armada even larger than that which invaded France on D-day. An army large enough to invade the main Japanese island of Honshu, and supporting navy and transports and aircraft, could not be ready earlier than

1 March 1946. Such an invasion, it was predicted in Washington, might succeed only at the cost of almost a million American dead or wounded, for Japan would probably fight to the end. The morale in Japanese cities had not been broken even by the huge bombing raids that set alight inner Tokyo at the end of May 1945.

The Japanese army was determined to fight. Thousands of young kamikaze pilots, carefully trained, were ready to give their lives in the continuation of the suicidal attacks already made by small planes on American warships and bases. These Japanese attacks, in their audacity and technique, were a forerunner of those made by the terrorists on the World Trade Center in New York in 2001.

Could the Americans and the British – and perhaps the Russians too – mount an effective invasion of Japan? The debate was waged in Washington in high secrecy. An alternative plan of assault was to the fore. Unknown to Japan's leaders, and unknown to Stalin, the Americans held a weapon whose tortuous origins went back to the years of peace preceding the Second World War.

BENEATH THE STADIUM

Albert Einstein, the world's most celebrated scientist, influenced briefly the birth of this terrible weapon. In August 1939, at the request of friends, he sat down in his holiday house at Long Island, near the city of New York, and wrote to the president of the United States, his new homeland, pointing out that secret experiments on the 'nuclear chain reaction' might well produce an unusual bomb. The bomb, while not certain to succeed, was promising. Of its enormous destructive power, Einstein had little doubt: 'A single bomb of this type, carried by boat and exploded in a port, might very well destroy the whole port together with some of the surrounding terri-tory.' But why carry the bomb in a boat? On the advice of experts, Einstein concluded that the atomic bomb might be too heavy to be carried in an aircraft. If in fact it could be delivered only by a slow-moving ship, then its usefulness was in some doubt, because the ship might well be sunk by a torpedo or aerial bomb before it reached its destination.

Einstein's advice was a foretaste of the price eventually to be paid by Hitler and Mussolini for their treatment of the Jews. Here was a German Jew advising the United States how to defend itself against his old fatherland. The bomb itself gained from the research of another refugee, the brilliant Italian physicist Enrico Fermi, who had recently arrived in the United States with a Jewish wife and two children unable to feel safe in Italy.

Fermi was set to work on nuclear experiments at the University of Chicago. In 1942, after the United States entered the war, and the university's football fixtures were curtailed, he was able to use the grandstand as a secure shelter in which to create an atomic chain reaction. Under the unroofed concrete grandstand, in a large space used for racquets courts, Fermi and his team built their nuclear reactor from some 40 000 small graphite blocks, grey in colour. When approaching completion it resembled a building site with a pile of grey bricks, in some 50 layers, neatly resting one on top of the other. The pile was not enormous, being no more than twice the height of a grown man. Embedded in the 'bricks' were thousands of slugs of precious uranium, shipped all the way from the Katanga region of what was then the Belgian Congo but is now the nation of Zaire.

On 2 December 1942 this first nuclear reactor was completed, and numerous instruments were in readiness to measure the radio-activity and other effects. Playfully, Fermi and his team gave to each instrument a name chosen from the popular children's book, *Winnie the Pooh*. The delicate experiment was set in motion, the nuclear fission reaction took place, and plutonium – the core ingredient of a nuclear weapon – was produced. Fermi declared the experiment a success. Italian chianti was produced in its familiar globe-shaped bottle, and a little wine was handed around in paper cups, in celebration.

Another refugee from Hitler's Europe joined in the quest. In Copenhagen in the 1930s Niels Bohr ran perhaps the most advanced of all centres of research on theoretical physics. After Hitler's forces occupied Denmark he was possibly in some danger, his mother being Jewish. He added to the danger by expressing his hostility to the German occupation. In 1943 he and his family escaped in a fishing boat to Sweden where he was picked up by a small Mosquito bomber, quite unarmed, and flown to Britain. After a few months he travelled with a British team of nuclear researchers to New Mexico, the secret centre for research on the new bomb.

THE BLINDING LIGHT AT ALAMOS

There was a valid fear that Germany might be working on a similar weapon, for several of the innovations in atomic physics had been made by its scientists before the war began. The atomic bomb, however, was not yet viewed as a decisive weapon in wartime Germany, nor by several American leaders who privately doubted whether it could be relied upon to inflict damage. The president's chief of staff,

Admiral William Leahy, expressed his doubts: 'The bomb will never go off, and I speak as an expert in explosives.' General George C. Marshall, head of the army, expressed his caution, arguing that a trial under experimental conditions would not necessarily prove whether the weapon was valuable in open warfare. Even so, the project to develop an all-powerful bomb continued to receive high priority.

At last, nearly two and a half years after Fermi's first experiment succeeded, America's atomic bomb was ready for testing. Though a deep secret, it could not be prevented from announcing its own birth. On 16 July 1945, just before sunrise, Mrs H.E. Wieselman was driving through the darkness, having just crossed the border of Arizona and New Mexico, when suddenly the high mountains were bathed in orange-red for about three seconds. 'It was just like the sun had come up and suddenly gone down again', she recalled. On another road a blind woman being driven in a car thought, to her astonishment, that she 'saw' a bright light. Ten miles from the site of the explosion, Enrico Fermi, watching through dark protective glass, saw 'a conglomeration of flames' slowly rising, followed by a mushroom cloud which, he calculated, rose to a height of six miles before staying poised in the air. The wind then began to disperse the smoke. Less than a minute after the explosion he felt the hot blast of air brush past him.

This was one of the most momentous days in the history of the human race, but the experiment went almost unmentioned by the media. Miraculously the government managed to keep the story out of nearly all radio bulletins and newspaper headlines in the United States, the official alibi being that the dazzling light had come from an accidental explosion of an ammunition magazine. That America was actually testing an atomic bomb for use against Japan remained one of the few well-kept secrets of the war.

The news of the successful test was conveyed to President Harry Truman who had taken office when Roosevelt died three months previously. Even Truman had not heard of the bomb's existence until he became president: such was the secrecy. Meeting Stalin and the incoming British prime minister, Clement Attlee, in the German city of Potsdam, Truman at first said nothing to Stalin. Eventually Stalin learned the news, nine days after the test at Alamos in New Mexico. He was not completely surprised, for his spies had informed him that the weapon was well advanced.

The dilemma for Truman was whether he should now employ one of the two atomic bombs that he held in his arsenal. He had no wish to use it if the Japanese were likely to surrender, but they steadfastly refused.

To release the new bomb on a Japanese target, a heavy, long-range bomber had to be employed. The Americans possessed such a bomber, the superfortress, B-29. Driven by four deafening engines it could fly 3000 kilometres to its target and return to home base. A suitable new airfield was now available on the tropical island of Tinian, one of the Marianas group, lying 15 degrees north of the equator and captured from Japan one year previously. Here on 6 August 1945 a heavy atomic bomb carried by ship from California was loaded into the superfortress *Enola Gay*, named for its pilot's mother.

The target was the Japanese port of Hiroshima, sitting beside a delta. Now a global symbol of tragedy, the port city was not widely known outside East Asia. Japan's eighth-largest city, it was a naval base, an army headquarters, and a fine manufacturer of needles. That summer morning its people went to work, especially to their wartime factories, not knowing that they had been chosen at the last moment for this experiment in warfare. Three Japanese cities had been selected as possible targets but Hiroshima was belatedly chosen that morning because the sunny weather in its vicinity seemed most favourable to the pilots who had to take exact aim and release the bomb.

Enola Gay was preceded by two aircraft that surveyed the weather, and by two other aircraft carrying observers. The big bomber arrived over the bustling city at 8.15 a.m. and met no opposition. From a commanding height it dropped the bomb which exploded before reaching the ground. The man-made explosion, the largest in the history of the world, blew up the core of the city.

Out on the Japanese farmlands, people at work saw the tall cloud of smoke rising. The pilots themselves called it a 'mushroom' cloud – the same phrase had been used by observers at Alamos in the previous month. But the photographs they collected of this astonishing event give the impression that it was not so much a smooth gigantic mushroom standing on its stalk than a ragged cone, filled with ice cream that was frothy and dazzlingly white. As far away as 500 kilometres the white pall of smoke could be seen by spectators.

Eight of every 10 buildings in the centre of the city were pulverised by the bomb. Of the 298 doctors in the city, 270 were killed. Of the nurses numbering nearly 2000, some 1800 were killed. Therefore the medical help for the tens of thousands of people who were injured in the raid was slow and inadequate. The Japanese at first estimated – the estimate proved too cautious – that more than 71 000 people were killed in the raid, a total that was less than the death toll caused by conventional bombs dropped during a night raid on Tokyo in March. It was not yet understood that the long-term effects of the radiation would increase the death toll.

The casualties at Hiroshima on its day of death would have been far lower if the people had taken to their air-raid shelters; but they were becoming accustomed to the sound of air-raid sirens and ignored the warning messages that preceded the explosion. They were in factories, schools, offices, walking on the street or hanging out the washing, when suddenly they were hit by the blast and heat.

At first Japan's leaders showed no signs of surrendering. After all, why should they surrender? Their honour and their martial spirit were at stake.

On 9 August, three days after the bombing of Hiroshima, an American bomber could be heard approaching the city of Nagasaki. The air-raid sirens sounded their warning, giving civilians time to hurry to the network of hillside shelters. Many of those who preferred to remain at work, and many hurrying along the streets, suddenly saw a dazzling flash of light, almost white in colour. Their familiar world tumbled down. Fortunately for many inhabitants, the immense explosive force of the bomb was partly absorbed by the harbour, thus reducing the casualties.

Between the exploding of the first and second atomic bombs, the Soviet Union entered the war against Japan. Soldiers and armoured vehicles no longer needed in Europe invaded the Japanese-occupied Manchuria, moving across the summer-ripe countryside with speed. That invasion gave Japan an additional incentive to surrender. But fear of the the atomic bomb, and fear of an American invasion, were the main threats that persuaded the Emperor

Hirohito and his government that the nation should lay down its arms. On 14 August 1945, Japan unconditionally surrendered.

THE GOD OF SCIENCE

The atomic bombs were momentous not only because they ended the Second World War but also because their destructiveness almost expelled a god from the heavens. In the preceding century Science, and its more earthly partner, Technology, had increasingly been hailed as gods. Their creed, with its emphasis on the rational, and its constant questioning of old beliefs, had indirectly weakened the authority and prestige of the Christian church, thus leaving a gap that science itself half-filled. Slowly, and with some justification, the belief had spread that science was the guide to the future and indeed the guarantor of the future. Thousands of scientists, working with utter dedication, were almost viewed as the modern theologians and missionaries. They were hailed, in countless robed ceremonies, as the servants of a cause greater than themselves. Perhaps even more than the great painters and poets, scientists were praised as the powerful exemplars of creativity, partly because their creativity was visibly changing the world.

In the front row of this new religion stood the specialists in physics. At first their research had been seen by the public as so abstract, so visionary, that it was unlikely to change the way people lived. But on this dark morning their triumph – the cumulative result of research, faithfully performed in scores of universities and laboratories – damaged the spires on their own cathedral.

Were the scientists and politicians capable of handling the enormous increase of power entrusted to them? No question was so momentous and so tormenting in the last months of 1945. The most destructive human episode in history, a total of six years of war culminating in two mighty explosions, had just come to an end. Adolf Hitler, perhaps the most ruthless tyrant in modern history, had just died. Joseph Stalin, another tyrant whose actions were not yet fully exposed to the world, was still in power. Nobody could be sure whether this destructive era had yet ended.

Wise and observant people, century after century, had weighed the dangers and benefits of allowing huge power to be held in one pair of hands. The world's great religions in their own ways had dwelt on this dilemma and danger. In modern times the scholar who expressed the danger most memorably was Lord Acton, a historian who was born in Naples, spent most of his scholarly life in England, and died in Germany at the start of the 20th century. Owner of one of the largest private libraries in the world – a collection of 59 000 volumes, many thousands of which he had annotated in ink – John Acton immersed himself in the history of western nations, and especially the Catholic church as well as in contemporary English politics where he was a close friend and adviser of William Gladstone. As a devout Catholic who saw the evil as well as the good in human nature, he gave deep thought from the 1860s onwards to the moral harm that fell on the possessors of mighty power, and the physical and emotional harm inflicted on the hosts of people who were at the mercy of their power.

It was in a private letter to an Anglican clergyman and historian, Mandell Creighton, that Acton penned a few words of warning which were not made public until after his own death. His words became poignant when the careers of Stalin, Hitler and other leaders unfolded a generation later. 'Power tends to corrupt, and absolute power corrupts absolutely', wrote Acton. 'Great men are almost always bad men', he added with more gloom than is appropriate.

Acton's conclusion about power was perhaps unduly pessimistic. Many people, having lived through extraordinary times, proceeded to invest Acton's conclusion with an even deeper layer of pessimism. His quotation is often remembered, not as 'power tends to corrupt', but simply and emphatically as 'power corrupts'.

Acton died in 1902, when the world seemed more optimistic. He did not experience the two world wars. He lies buried near the peaceful lake of Tegernsee, not far from the streets of Munich where, two decades after his death, Hitler took his first steps towards absolute power.

PART THREE

15

A CURTAIN FALLS

It had been the most devastating war in the history of the world. The lists of dead and wounded soldiers and civilians, even when incomplete, exceeded those of the First World War. The destruction of houses, schools, churches and temples and synagogues, roads and bridges, railways and wharves, factories and offices, aircraft and warships and cargo ships and other military equipment in many nations rivalled, in total, the destruction inflicted by all the major natural disasters in the previous century. The ability of the world to feed itself in the short term was reduced because so much farmland had been scarred, livestock killed, and flour mills, breweries, bakeries, sugar refineries and food factories wrecked. Furthermore the capacity to carry food to places of need or famine was diminished by the heavy losses of ships and railways. In most of the once-prosperous lands, food remained scarce long after the war.

The map of the world, redrawn so extensively by the First World War, was not redrawn dramatically by the Second World War. Nearly all the European-owned colonies of 1939 were still colonies in 1945. But in the following few years the march of liberation had dramatic effects on India, Indonesia and many parts of the Third World. The three great nations of Europe proper – Britain, Germany and France – were permanently weakened by the war. Britain, financially and industrially, was exhausted in 1945. Never had a winner of a major war been so sapped by its long ordeal.

Now there were only two great powers, the Soviet Union and the United States. Each was a land-mass nation embracing a huge continental domain, whereas the western European nations owned a relatively small area at home and vast colonies lying across the seas. Curiously the 'superpowers' – a newish word in the political vocabulary – 'owned' almost nothing in the Southern Hemisphere – a sphere in which earlier giants such as Spain and Portugal, Britain and France, and even the Kaiser's Germany had been colonisers. There was one other novelty. The two superpowers were not neighbours. Washington and Moscow lay further apart than the capital cities of any previous pair of world rivals.

THE UNITED NATIONS – BRIEFLY UNITED

At first there was a widespread hope that these great powers would be kept in order by a new version of the League of Nations. The first league had failed: the second must not fail. The prime promoter of the new league was the United States of America which had helped to found and then had abandoned the original League of Nations. Stalin and Churchill were less enthusiastic but

Roosevelt was determined. He died just before the conference was called to set up the new United Nations.

Into the great meeting hall in San Francisco on 25 April 1945 crowded the 850 delegates, including five prime ministers and 37 foreign ministers. It was really a meeting of the victors of the war – the losers would join later – and the victors were themselves divided. The Soviet Union would not be happy with the new United Nations unless its satellite republics became members. France would not be happy unless it also sat in the special Security Council along with the other big four nations – the Soviet Union, the United States, Britain and China – and received comparable privileges. The small nations, led by Dr H.V. Evatt of Australia, criticised the right of veto claimed by those nations who were members of the Security Council. Why, on every matter of debate and decision, should a big nation have more power to block and to negate than the general assembly which consisted of all nations, large and small? Even amongst the smaller nations disputes arose. It was loudly complained that the Latin American nations who had done little to win the war now possessed a phalanx of votes.

In the cold of January 1946 the general assembly of the United Nations met for the first time in London, in a large Methodist church of Viennese baroque architecture, standing almost opposite the British houses of parliament. At once the Soviet delegate, with the support of the Ukraine, tried to push through an unexpected motion calling for a Norwegian to be appointed secretary-general forthwith and, what is more, appointed by a show of voices rather than formal votes that could be accurately counted. He was eventually appointed, though five years later it was the Soviets who demanded that he step down. The new organisation, while promising so much, was a battlefield.

BEHIND THE IRON CURTAIN

In May 1945 the Soviet armies were visible in most of central and eastern Europe, along with clusters of Soviet bureaucrats and secret police. It was Roosevelt's hope that the individual countries in this large zone would, perhaps under Soviet protection, shape their own national policies, but Stalin preferred to design the policies. He took charge of Poland, many of whose anticommunist leaders had been killed in the battle with the occupying Germans in Warsaw in 1944. In a few of the occupied countries a free election was held. Several governments initially consisted of a mixture of communists and their rivals, but soon the communists took control, sending many of their opponents to lesser posts, prison, or the anonymous grave. For the three small Baltic republics – Latvia, Estonia and Lithuania – which had led independent lives between the two world wars, there was no revival of independence even for a week. In 1945 they became part of the Soviet Union, to whose remote republics were sent, in disgrace, many of their leading citizens.

Czechoslovakia at first seemed likely to retain its independence in the turbulent era. At its free elections held in May 1946 the Communist Party did not win a majority of the votes, and a coalition ministry was formed under the communist, Klement Gottwald. In a familiar pattern the communists began to control the Czech police force, provoking anticommunist ministers to resign in protest in February 1948. A few days later one of the most famous Czech politicians, Jan Masaryk, met his death. He had been the popular Czech ambassador in London for most of the inter-war years and, returning to liberated Prague, had become foreign minister in the Gottwald government. He was still the minister when, on 10 March, he mysteriously fell to his death from his office window.

A fortnight later, when Gottwald rearranged his ministry, only communists were included. A national election was set for 30 May 1948 to approve of his changes, but its result was pre-ordained. No opposition candidate was permitted to stand for any seat. At least the voters were allowed to show their concern by spoiling their ballot paper, but only one in every four voters bothered to carry out the token protest.

Moscow steadily tightened its grip on eastern Europe and its daily life. Serious criticism was usually crushed. The churches, especially the Catholic, were singled out. In 1949 Cardinal Mindszenty in Budapest was sentenced to imprisonment for life, and Archbishop Beran was placed under arrest in Prague and then confined to a place that remained unspecified so that no communication with him could take place. In little Lithuania where three of every people had been Catholic, 1300 priests remained relatively free in the year 1947. In the following three years about 1000 were arrested or deported by the Russian authorities.

Most intellectuals realised that there was no future for independent ideas except in mathematics, physics, agriculture, engineering, and other less-easily politicised professions. Most writers fell into line. Those who remained independent at heart could write to their heart's content in the privacy of their room; but nobody dared publish their work. If a writer hand-printed or painstakingly typed a bundle of copies and handed them around, the readers might find themselves in the police rooms, answering questions. Owners of private businesses of any size had little future: some were declared enemies of the people and were lucky to remain alive. The state factory, mine and shop, the collective farm, a trade union's own holiday resort and other communal ventures took over the economy, though amongst the curious exceptions were the small private farms finally permitted across Poland.

There was a sunnier side to the story. Despite the oppression by the one-party state, daily life in eastern Europe resumed its course. The younger generation had known no other life, and their kindergartens, schools, books, films, newspapers, and young communist leagues insisted at every hour of the day that their life was more purposeful and secure than that lived in capitalist lands. Among the older generation large numbers saw advantages in a communist regime. Once the economy completed its slow steps back to normality, they had an apartment, access to doctors and hospitals, paid holidays, food, beer and tobacco. Eventually the typical parents – especially those in the bottom half of the social ladder – were materially better off than their grandparents had been at the same age.

COLD WAR OR HOT PEACE?

Defeated Germany was an enigma. Notionally it was divided into zones, each under the control of the armed forces of the big four victors. The crippled German economy was initially viewed as a whole; but who would control the whole, the capitalists or the communists? There was no hope of agreement. The United States, under its Marshall Plan, generously financed revival in West Germany – finance that the Russian zone refused to accept – and the West German economy surged ahead. The Russians ripped out machinery and valuable equipment and seized commodities from their zone in East Germany, and as a result its economy suffered. From one zone of Germany people began pouring into another. By 1950 there were virtually two German economies, a vigorous one in the west, and an austere one in the east.

Economic partition went arm in arm with political partition. Soon there were two distinct entities: the Federated Republic of Germany in the west, and the German Democratic Republic in the east. For its defences, one Germany depended on the USA and the new military alliance called the North Atlantic Treaty Organization (NATO), while the smaller eastern Germany depended on the Soviet Union and its defence organisation called the Warsaw Pact. The idea that Germans should not be allowed to rearm was modified. Instead the two Germanys were rearmed by their rival protectors with a limited array of weapons kept under the strictest control. The mass of weapons, and the potent ones, remained only in the hands of Moscow and Washington.

Berlin, the former capital city of the old united Germany, was another enigma. It was a small and isolated territory, encircled by the Soviet zone but controlled by the decisions of the four governing powers. As Berlin depended on outside food and fuel, it was vulnerable to pressure from Moscow. Suddenly, in 1947, Moscow ordered the blocking of the railway lines, roads and canals along which most of Berlin's supplies arrived from West Germany. The British and Americans responded with the urgent and expensive expedient of flying supplies to Berlin in the so-called airlift. A thousand planes arrived a day, many carrying coal. For over a year the airlift continued,

7. IRON CURTAIN, 1948

Finland

Norway

Sweden

• Viborg

• Leningrad

Baltic Sea

• Pskov

Denmark

• Riga

Memel •

Danzig
•

• Vilna   • Minsk

Bremen •

Berlin
•

Poland

• Warsaw

Soviet Union

• Poznan

Germany

• Wroclaw (Breslau)

Pinsk

• Erfurt

• Prague

• Cracow

• Lvov

Nuremberg •

Czechoslovakia

Vienna •

• Budapest

Austria

Hungary

Romania

Trieste •

Belgrade
•

Bucharest •

Yugoslavia

Bulgaria

Italy

*Adriatic
Sea*

• Sofia

Tirana •

Albania

*Aegean
Sea*

Iron Curtain ▬▬▬

Greece

a sign that the west would not give in. There was one solution, short of war. Accordingly the city of Berlin was divided into two opposing zones: a western and a communist zone. Such a partition, in Germany as a whole and in Berlin too, had not been the intention of the victors when the war ended: it had simply emerged.

A phrase was enlisted to describe the political and economic partition running across Europe and even dividing Germany itself. It was said that an 'iron curtain' separated democratic lands from communist lands. Winston Churchill popularised this phrase but it was not his. In 1920, Ethel Snowden, travelling to St Petersburg with a delegation from the British Labour Party, had reported that 'we were behind the iron curtain at last'. After languishing for a quarter of a century, the pithy phrase was revived just before the end of the Second World War by Hitler's colleague Dr Goebbels, writing in the weekly *Das Reich*. He warned German readers that if their nation lost the war, an iron curtain would descend on Germany, cutting it in half. This warning, reported in English newspapers, was probably glimpsed, maybe unconsciously, by that avaricious newspaper-reader, Churchill. On 4 June 1945 'with profound misgivings' he pointed out to President Truman 'the descent of an iron curtain between us and everything to the eastward'. In the following year, in an address to a small American university in Fulton, Missouri, he released the phrase Iron Curtain to the world. It was soon engraved on millions of minds.

It was joined by another phrase, 'the Cold War', which ran alongside like a siamese twin. 'Let us not be deceived,' wrote the American financier Bernard Baruch in 1947, 'we are today in the midst of a cold war.' Only by some stretch of the imagination, however, could the word 'war' fittingly describe the relations persisting between the United States and the Soviet Union. Rather was it a hot, tense peace. The phrase caught on, colouring the mood of a whole era. These twin phrases, Cold War and Iron Curtain, had been launched by men in their seventies, good friends who died long before the rift they vividly described began to disappear.

The position of the Iron Curtain deplored by Churchill was not yet precise. At first some nations straddled the iron curtain but eventually they took a specific place, usually to the east of it. Eventually the curtain extended all the way from the Baltic to the Black Sea with a wide bulge that reached the Adriatic. Two of the Adriatic nations, Yugoslavia and Albania, independently became communist by the process of free elections and together created a common market that turned out to be short-lived. Yugoslavia did not see eye to eye with Stalin and was expelled from the Soviet's league of like-minded nations, the Cominform, in 1948. Albania was to end its friendship with Moscow by becoming the ally of communist China.

DOCTOR SAKHAROV'S BOMB

Russia urgently wanted an atomic bomb of its own. In 1949, with some help from its indefatigable network of spies, it developed one. That was not enough. When Washington devised the more powerful hydrogen bomb, that too had to be imitated.

A young physicist Andrei Sakharov led Russia's nuclear research. A son of the intelligentsia already prominent in the Soviet establishment, Sakharov had studied cosmic rays for his doctorate, and enthusiastically likened the theoretical side of physics to a mysterious and immensely powerful symphony. Posted in 1948 to the secret atomic project, he entered its stiff atmosphere of secrecy with reluctance but found to his pleasure that he was working in 'a genuine theoretician's paradise'. Mastering the theory and the practice of thermonuclear explosions, he became so important to his nation that by the time he was 30 he attended meetings of defence officials presided over by Stalin himself. A keeper of late hours, Stalin would sometimes prolong the meeting after midnight had passed. Sakharov would walk through 7 miles of dim-lit streets to his own house, not realising that he was entitled to an official car.

When Russia completed its hydrogen bomb in 1953, Dr Sakharov was a hero. Much later, becoming disillusioned with the nation whose future he had protected, he spoke out against the prison camps and the lack of liberty for the Tatar people. In 1980 he was hustled away to the city of Gorky where the censor read his mail and the police watched over him, and his radio set was so jammed as to be inaudible.

Meanwhile in their deliberations and debates the United States and the Soviet Union were rarely swayed by each other's propositions and arguments. In their presence the Security Council resembled a game of defensive chess rather than a place of debate. The Soviet's foreign minister and deputy premier, Vyacheslav Molotov, became celebrated for conceding nothing. In the words of one British minister, he was 'smiling granite'. As the Soviet Union developed and tested its own nuclear weapons, the fear of a nuclear war was heightened by the reluctance of the superpowers to compromise.

People who took an intense interest in the health of the world tended to be apprehensive of the nuclear contest. Most well-informed people in the west thought that another major war would break out in their lifetime, and be fought, they expected, with nuclear weapons. The arts reflected the sense that the world was out of control. In plays performed in the early 1950s, Samuel Beckett, Eugene Ionesco and other writers depicted what was called the Theatre of the Absurd. In universities many scientists began to doubt the wisdom of those colleagues who had invented the first atomic bomb. Arnold Toynbee, perhaps the best known historian in the English-speaking lands by virtue of his massive study of civilisations, thought that the future of the world was bleak. Amidst the gloom were optimists who went cheerfully about their work. The Soviet Union had its share of optimists, buoyed up by the Marxist theory of history that promised them an inevitable victory for the forces for Good over the forces for Evil.

Communism's powerful position in the world, a few years after the Second World War, defied its western critics. The Soviet Union had by far the largest military forces; it controlled a mass of land in Europe and Asia; and its ideology was a beacon for revolutionaries in Asian, African and South American countries and colonies. In many prosperous democracies a strong strand of public opinion was loosely sympathetic to communist or socialist ideas, and in France and Italy the communist parties were strong. In the United States, Britain and other democracies the regiments of sympathisers were known as 'the fellow travellers' – in Washington they were to be singled out for attack, and some reputations were smeared unfairly.

The triumphs of communism were far from completed. China was widely foreseen as the arena for its next victory.

THE LONG MARCH OF CHINA

At the start of the century China had the possible ingredients for a political revolution. It was rural, it was poor, it was abjectly governed, and it cut a languid figure in the world even though some of its ancient ways were being undermined by alien ideas. It possessed, after 1910, a widening circle of patriotic critics and would-be politicians. For them it was like a dazzling light when in 1917 the news arrived from St Petersburg of the victory of the Bolsheviks.

One who was dazzled was Mao Zedong. The son of a landowner and his devout Buddhist wife, his family had lived on 4 acres of the fertile rice fields south of the Yangtze River. Mao studied at a local teachers' college before moving in his mid-twenties to the capital city, where he worked as an assistant in the library of Beijing University. He had met few foreigners, and had read little of Marx, but as a young nationalist he thought that revolutionary Russia was pointing the way. When the Chinese Communist Party was created in the port city of Shanghai in 1921, Mao was one of its early members.

The Soviet Union was for many years less interested in the Chinese Communist Party than in the ruling Nationalist Party, the Kuomintang. A moderate party led by Dr Sun Yat-sen, the Kuomintang modelled itself on the Russian Communist Party and operated its own army. For a time China's infant Communist Party and the strong Nationalist Party worked together. The alliance was snapped in 1927. The new leader of the nationalists, the young General Chiang Kai-shek, won financial support from a few of the wealthy in Shanghai, and agreed in exchange to purge the city of the foremost communists and trade-union leaders. In Shanghai on the morning of 12 April 1927, a group of his underlings called the

Green Gang waylaid communists and shot them on sight. In the following weeks, hundreds more were killed.

General Chiang Kai-shek became more and more a military dictator. He did not completely control China – regional war lords remained strong, and the communists remained active. But in 1928 he showed his mettle by capturing Peking and renaming it Peiping, meaning 'northern peace'.

Driven into the hills, the communist leaders, aided by thousands of loyal soldiers and civilians, succeeded in gaining control of six separate territories in the vicinity of the region through which the Yangtze River flowed. Their local popularity depended on confiscating some of the land from rich and middling landowners and giving it to the poor peasants who thereupon became communist supporters. Mao's own zone or soviet, in the mountains near the borders of his native province of Hunan, became the headquarters of the illegal Chinese Communist Party in 1933; and two years later Mao became the national leader. The raggle-taggle armies of these separate communist zones continued to grow, and the 50 000 soldiers of 1930 soon grew tenfold.

General Chiang Kai-shek had no alternative but to attack the communists. His armies, improved by German advisors and instructors, approached the communist zones, forcing the red soldiers to retreat further from the coast. Late in 1935, Mao led his army and his loyal followers in a long, roundabout route-march towards northwest China, near the borders of Inner Mongolia.

In the long history of warfare there have been few bolder ventures. Two separate armies, called First Front and Second Front, had to reach western China before they could veer north. Travelling

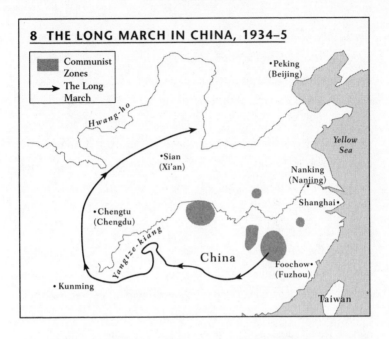

8 THE LONG MARCH IN CHINA, 1934–5

Communist Zones
The Long March

Hwang-ho

•Peking (Beijing)

Yellow Sea

•Sian (Xi'an)

Nanking (Nanjing)

Shanghai•

•Chengtu (Chengdu)

Yangtze-kiang

China

Foochow• (Fuzhou)

• Kunming

Taiwan

on foot for at least 9000 kilometres, they crossed many mountain ranges and at least 20 rivers. At the river crossings the long lines of marchers and stragglers were dangerously exposed to attack; and near the wide Yellow River one communist column was routed by the government's Muslim Cavalry. It was really a long retreat, achieved only through rural help received along the way. But it was to be celebrated in communist folklore as the Long March. Veterans of the Long March were to dominate the party when finally it came to power.

The march saved the communists. In their new remote stronghold in North Shensi they were unassailable. The village of Paoan, decorated with red flags displaying hammer and sickle, was their training ground and thinking ground. Here Mao himself lived in a cave with the luxury of a glass window to admit a little daylight. A sentry guarded the dirt track approaching his dwelling, for Mao was a hunted man with a reward on his head. In his early forties, he was taller than his typical soldier, his thick black hair was long, his face was slightly gaunt, and his prominent chin carried a large mole – so he was vividly described by an adventurous American reporter who arrived at the village in June 1936, to be welcomed with hot pepper-bread and plum compote cooked by Mao's wife. She was later to be supplanted by a politically dedicated, vivacious, city actress, Jiang Qing.

When the Japanese invaded China in 1937, the ruling nationalists and Mao's communists agreed to cooperate against the common enemy. As the nationalists were the government, more was expected of them by the people, but they could rarely deliver it. They did not possess the organising talent of Mao: their officers lacked the dedication of their communist counterparts, and could seem half-hearted in the face of the invading Japanese. Eventually the nationalist government withdrew to the remote western city of Chungking, with the Japanese in control of the eastern half of the country.

Many astute Europeans doubted whether this divided country, supposedly fighting for its life, had a future. In Britain, officials high in the foreign office thought China and its 450 million people were never likely to form a great nation. It was the United States' leaders who had faith in the Chinese. They hoped that China might become a strong western-like nation with a growing Christian presence. Though half of America's people were not even sure where China was – according to a poll of 1942 – they did know that in past decades American congregations had sent thousands of their missionaries to remote Chinese towns as well as to the bustling ports. Chiang Kai-shek himself had been converted to Christianity, his wife, Soong May-ling, being a keen Methodist and – to her credit in Massachusetts' eyes – a graduate of the fashionable Wellesley College near Boston. When she visited wartime United States in 1942, the most publicised of all foreign females, she was feted as a sophisticated symbol of the coming relationship between Washington and China. President Roosevelt, slightly under her spell, sensed that China was on the way to becoming a democracy, a busy capitalist trading partner of the United States, and one of the four policemen of the postwar world.

But in that vast war-shaken country it was the communists who were effectively spreading their message. 'The masts of the New China are rising over the horizon', Mao proclaimed in 1942. He was an exhilarating leader for a nation seeking liberation from foreign influence and from its own past. Possessing vision, he juggled with bold ideas and made sure that high-flown Marxist theories were brought down to the realistic level of the rice fields. A poet, he had a gift for catchy phrases and catch-cries. 'Paper tiger' was one of his own pet terms of abuse: he later said contemptuously that the 'atom bomb is a paper tiger', held aloft by the Americans in order to bully and frighten the poor Chinese. He moderated his view when China developed its own atomic weapon in 1964.

Mao expressed his views like a Churchill. Even after translation into English his imagery comes across vividly, because it is concrete and everyday: 'Every Communist must grasp the truth. Political power grows out of the barrel of a gun', he wrote. He himself was prepared to pull the trigger of that gun. On a visit to Moscow he ruthlessly expressed his willingness, if the political goal was right, 'to sacrifice half mankind'.

At the end of the Second World War the Japanese invaders went home. The nationalists and communists, after an uneasy truce, were left to resume their long-standing war. In October 1949, to the dismay of the Americans, the communists were victorious. Mao at last sat in state in Beijing, the city in which 30 years previously he had been a humble stacker and sorter of books, while his deadly rival, General Chiang Kai-shek, set up his own Chinese republic on the island of Taiwan.

The victory of communism in China provoked shivers of apprehension in various western leaders. A band of communist territory now stretched from the Mediterranean and the Black Sea to the shores of the Pacific Ocean, by way of the Caspian Sea, Siberian steppes, Mongolian desert and those Tibetan mountains that became Mao Zedong's first foreign conquest, after his total victory at home. In this red zone, spanning almost the entire width of Asia and Europe, lived about one-third of the world's population. Would this vast red zone be the springboard for further expansion? That fear – or hope – was widely contemplated in many parts of the world, not least in Korea.

WAR IN KOREA

Korea is rather like Italy, long and slender, with the sea lapping three of the four sides. To the north are mountains, snowy in winter; while along the eastern side runs a rugged range from which swift and short rivers rush to the sea. To the west, facing the Yellow Sea and the coast of China, are harbours with frequent fogs and such a low ebb and high rise of daily tides that boats, tied to the wharves, sit in the mud at low tide. The steamy Korean summers are ideal for growing rice and other crops, but the winters can be harsh.

Korea did not seem a likely site for a world-shaking event. In 1900 its glorious era had been over for centuries. The country's mud-coated and thatched cottages were bleak, little hairy black pigs lolled by the barns, and much of the digging of the soil was carried out with the aid of a kind of spade operated by three men. When shoals of fish were located, the sails of tiny fishing boats converged like a flock of seabirds, but steam vessels were few and mostly were owned by Japanese: in the land was only one railway. By force of arms Japan was increasing its grip on the long peninsula. Soon it became the ruler, downgrading the king into a harmless prince and setting out to exploit the land and subdue the people. Japanese policemen and other officials were more than abundant.

The Koreans were promised their independence by the victorious Allies during the Second World War. The promise was not easily honoured. The Russian forces invaded North Korea in the last days of the war and clung to it after the Japanese surrendered. The assembly of the United Nations eventually resolved that free elections be held throughout the length of Korea and that a united government be elected, but the North Koreans – with Soviet blessings – refused to conduct elections in their realm. So yet another iron curtain was erected, with a democracy in the south of Korea and a heavily armed communist state in the north.

North Korea planned to help itself to a large slice of the richer soils of the south. On 25 June 1950, at dawn, its soldiers and a big contingent of Soviet tanks invaded South Korea, quickly capturing the capital city, Seoul, which stood close to the Iron Curtain. The invaders occupied a large segment of the country before the Americans stationed in Japan could come to the rescue.

Was this the prelude to further communist invasions of vulnerable territories extending from Greece to Hong Kong? In western nations the anxiety aroused by the Korean invasion was intense. In New York the Security Council held an urgent meeting. The Russian delegate had walked out in protest some months ago, and was still absent. So the Soviet Union could not exercise its right of veto against an emphatic resolution aimed at restoring the legitimate government in Seoul. In the course of its life the old League of Nations had conducted no military campaign. Nor had it been envisaged that the United Nations would initiate such a campaign. Now, in the face of the crisis in Korea, the United Nations resolved to endorse military operations in its own name.

The United Nations forces, drawn from 16 nations and led by General Douglas MacArthur, soon commanded the air. A fleet that included 16 aircraft carriers commanded the seas that flanked the narrow Korean peninsula. On land, however, the enemy was strong. The United Nations' armies were outnumbered heavily, especially after Chinese troops poured in to help the North Korean invaders in November 1950. Eventually Chinese troops were fighting on such a massive scale – their casualties reached a total of 900 000 – that the plight of South Korea was desperate. Moreover the Soviet Union sent its new jet fighter, the MiG, to the border of China and Korea in readiness to change the course of the war. Many Soviet airmen, about to fly over Korea, donned Chinese uniforms or flew in plain clothes to disguise the fact that their nation was entering the war.

Until the first American Sabre jets could arrive, the Russian jets briefly commanded the air.

After three years, an armistice was signed. The North Koreans and the South Koreans each controlled their zone. An iron curtain was again drawn across the peninsula. At the end of the century it was still firmly in place.

A TILT OF THE MAP

In the 10 years after the end of the Second World War, several of the world's most significant events occurred in Asia. They included the release of the first atomic bombs, the victory of communism in China, and the fighting in Korea where, for the last time in the century, two great powers – China and the United States – fought on opposing sides. In contrast, during the 19th century perhaps not one political event of clear global significance had occurred in Asia.

That such vital events should take place in East Asia, in the space of a few years, reflected a sharp tilt in political geography. The Pacific Ocean, with Japan and China and the remote part of the Soviet Union on one shore and the United States on the other, was beginning to challenge the Atlantic Ocean as the centre of international power. At the same time, another event mirrored the revival of Asia: India at last was becoming independent. The long reign of western Europe's oceanic empires was hastening to a close.

16

BURNING SPEAR AND
CHANGING WIND

The people of most large European nations were proud to be the possessors of colonies. It gave them prestige, and never more so than at the start of the 20th century. For the first time coloured maps of the world were appearing in schoolrooms, and British children relished the fact that so much of the world was usually coloured with a British red. Germany and Italy, late to join the race for colonies, felt that they had somehow been cheated by not gaining their fair share of foreign lands. On the other hand there had long been statesmen, an eloquent minority, who saw colonies as millstones around the neck rather than diamonds in the hand. The British orator of free trade, Richard Cobden, asked once what would happen 'if France took the whole of Africa'. It would harm nobody, he said, 'save herself'. Certainly many colonies were an economic advantage to their imperial owner, and many were a dead loss. Possibly in the long term nearly all might become busy places for trading and investing, or the site of naval bases, or even a new homeland for migrants.

Some colonies – British India, the Dutch East Indies, French Algeria, the Belgian Congo – were so prized that they shaped the motherland's foreign policy. Other colonies were bargaining counters and cash assets: Russia sold Alaska to the United States in 1867. During the First World War, on both sides, there were secret deals and nods with major powers promising one colony to Italy and another to Japan in return for help in the war.

Within the left wing of European parliaments, and in coffee lounges where revolutionaries met in exile, the view was widespread that the overseas colonies would one day be liberated. Some scholars said Europe, already in decline, could not possibly hold on to so many overseas possessions. Charles H. Pearson, a colonial politician, wrote a far-seeing book which in 1893 predicted that the year would come when powerful Chinese or Indian naval fleets might be seen in European waters, and when the winner of the English Derby might be owned by a rich man from the Zambezi or the Yangtze. Christian missionaries in faraway regions sometimes predicted that the young people they were teaching might one day be rulers of their own land. In like spirit the new League of Nations affirmed that in the newest colonies the governing powers should simply act as trustees for the indigenous peoples. Indeed the colonies transferred from Germany to other imperial powers in 1919 were called 'mandates' or trusts, on whose behalf an annual report had to be submitted.

American commentators went further and argued that the peace of Versailles had dealt another blow to the concept of colonies by

sanctioning the creation of more than a dozen nations out of the ethnic 'colonies' inhabiting Austro-Hungary, Russia and Germany. At
the same time, many European clergymen, politicians and writers
began to think that overseas colonies were a source of shame rather
than pride.

A case could be made that on the eve of the Second World War,
Germany gained militarily from the fact that it held no colonies –
they had been confiscated – whereas Britain and France were
shackled by too many. To be a great colonial power required a large
and expensive navy. The demands of sea power devoured money
that might have gone more wisely into air power. The strategy of
defending colonies on both sides of the equator also led to a disper-
sal of forces: some forces were in Europe when they were needed
elsewhere or were elsewhere when they were needed in Europe.
Britain and France had faced crises in 1940 partly because they
were trying to stretch their military resources over the whole colonial world. Hitler's onslaught proved how perilously they were
stretched.

By 1945 the weight of opinion was beginning to shift against the
very need and justification for overseas empires. Two big victors of
the war, Moscow and Washington, opposed those empires though
not completely. If a colony by becoming independent was likely to
fall into the Soviet sphere of influence, the Americans were not so
keen on supporting its call for independence. The Soviet Union
had a similar viewpoint. At the same time three countries in possession of global empires – Britain, France and Holland – were
exhausted by the war and were incapable of militarily defending
every one of their colonies. Moreover Britain had already promised

India its independence. The thorny questions were: When, and on what terms?

A COMPASS FOR INDIA

Of the colonial men and women who set out to oppose imperialism, Mahatma Gandhi was the most memorable and influential. His India was the most populous land held under European rule. His campaign to liberate it was conducted with a patience and astuteness matched by few other politicians in the century.

A bookish vegetarian reared in a merchant family near Bombay, Gandhi as a young man had gone to London for study. He then practised the law with success in the South African port of Durban and the gold city of Johannesburg. Tugged into the politics of protest, he spent a total of eight months in jail for activities on behalf of his fellow Indians who, treated as second-class citizens, were compelled to carry identity papers in South Africa.

Gandhi's political views were sewn from pieces of ideology chosen from east and west. His almost saintly moderation is often portrayed as the result of eastern spiritualism and mysticism, but it was shaped to some degree by western thinkers. He admired Henry Thoreau, the young New Englander who had lived frugally in a log cabin by a little lake in a forest; John Ruskin, the English art critic and philosopher; and Leo Tolstoy, the Russian novelist.

A child of the British Empire, Gandhi stood for it and against it, though the disapproving mood was to be dominant. Remembered rightly as a man of peace, Gandhi when young had been a campaigner and helper for Britain in its imperial wars. In South Africa he organised fellow Indians in an ambulance corps that served with the British armies fighting against the Boers. In 1906 he organised – under the title of Sergeant Major Gandhi – another team of stretcher-bearers that cared for white soldiers wounded by the Zulus in their rebellion led by the chieftain Bambata. The stretchers would have been more useful for the Zulus because they suffered nearly all the casualties. During the First World War, living in India, Gandhi was again a patriot, offering to become Britain's chief recruiting agent amongst the Indian people. Later he would disown his British war medals.

Britain was willing to grant India a large measure of self-government, but was not willing to withdraw entirely. Gandhi sought to hasten Britain's departure. The Indian National Congress, for long the main forum of protest, hoped to find a compromise with the British rulers. Gandhi did not try. He called for the British to leave India quickly and quietly. His weapon was passive resistance and moral persuasion, which he called 'soul force'. When arrested for peaceful but disruptive activities he went to prison calmly.

His salt march of 1930 was a revealing political and spiritual adventure. He decided to lead a procession of Indians cross-country towards the seashore in order to expose the tax that the government collected from the sale of salt to poor and rich alike. To choose salt as the topic of dispute was shrewd. It struck a cord in Britain where there was no salt tax. Some British newspapers implied that the salt tax, being a tax on a necessity of daily life, was extremely unjust; but such a tax was also collected in other countries. The Chinese government had long collected a tax on salt. Even today an Italian customer – as part of the government's taxing formula – goes to the tobacconist to buy a packet of salt.

As the salt march would last for more than three weeks, Gandhi arranged that each day's walk should take place in the cooler hours of morning and evening. He wanted maximum publicity, and three firms from Bombay filmed his walking and praying. A cleverly organised expedition, it blended the silence of spirituality and the sound of shuffling feet. When at last the procession reached the terminus – the silted, saline shores of the Gulf of Cambay – Gandhi walked onto the beach and, wearing only his loincloth, gathered some sea salt. Auctioning it in open defiance of the law, he announced, 'I am shaking the foundations of the British Empire.'

The salt march, mingling defiance with humility, enthused many Christians who saw it as almost a re-enactment of a scene from the New Testament. In the United States *Time* magazine conferred on 'the little brown man' the title of Man of the Year. Americans remembered that their own ancestors, fighting for independence in the 1770s, had thrown tea overboard in Boston harbour to highlight the heavy British tax on tea; and here was Gandhi pursuing a similar goal with his own march. Above all, his passive resistance and disobedience spurred a host of Indians. Those who spent terms in prison for defying the salt tax numbered 60 000.

As the movie camera became an exciting source of daily news, and as newsreel theatres multiplied in cities in the western world in the 1930s, Gandhi appeared regularly on the screen. Though in India he held no formal office, in cinemas from Durban to Oslo he was easily recognised with his bare head, wistful smile, scholarly spectacles, a white shawl on his bony shoulders, a cloth around his loins, sandals on his feet, and an ever-present retinue of supporters. Competing for news space in European newspapers he often won with ease, for his simple message seemed calming and soothing in a turbulent world. Whatever he did, even if utterly self-effacing, carried the mark of a leader.

Passive resistance is effective only when the governing officials possess a strand of patience and tolerance. Gandhi would have exercised little influence if a distant dictator had ruled India. Stalin and Hitler would have ordered that Gandhi be imprisoned or shot; and then his smiling face, his quiet voice of reason, would have appeared in newsreels and newspapers no more.

The British government was willing to make concessions to India long before it made them to most other colonies. India was so large, and so important, that the future of the British Empire could be threatened if Indians staged, as they had in 1857, a mutiny. In 1917, after the Russian revolutions aroused fears that India too might rebel, Britain began to foster self-governing institutions on Indian soil. Two years later an official Indian delegation actually voted at the peace conference in Paris.

British respect for India was influenced by another factor. India was a home of intellectual talent. Even when only a tiny proportion of its children had an opportunity for education, India produced innovators of world distinction. Two scientists, born in the late 1880s, illustrated that talent. Srinivasa Ramanujan, obsessed by mathematics, worked out for himself, when still a youth, dozens of difficult theories, many of which – unknown to him – had already been discovered in European mathematical circles. In 1914 while a humble clerk at the port of Madras he was invited to England where he was elected to one of science's highest honours, a Fellowship of the Royal Society. Acclaimed as a mathematical genius, he returned to India where he died of tuber-culosis in his thirty-third year.

Venkata Raman, awarded a university degree at the age of 15, was a clerk in Calcutta (his wife Loka his loyal supporter) before becom-ing a professor of physics and a part-time experimenter using the simplest equipment. His main field of study, the scattering of light, was stimulated by Einstein's writings and by his own sense of delight at the first sight of the freakishly blue Mediterranean Sea when he made his first voyage outside India. In 1930 he won the Nobel prize for physics. No scientist outside Europe and the United States had previously won Nobel prizes for science or medicine.

The main British political parties could not agree on how much independence should be granted to India. One vital step in the 1920s was to give India the right to place a tariff on British imports. That proved to be a hard blow for the textile industry in Lancashire. A second step, in 1935, was to divide most of India into 11 self-governing provinces each with its own parliament. Foreign affairs remained largely in Britain's hands, local issues were firmly in Indian hands. This concession, while not enough for most Hindus, was too much for the Muslims who found themselves in a minority in most of the 11 provinces. Increasingly they believed that their future lay not in a united India but in a new nation of Pakistan, made up of those few regions where they formed a majority.

The Second World War gave India and neighbouring Burma a strong bargaining position, for Britain needed their loyalty. In the desperate year of 1940 the British Labour Party affirmed that 'colo-nial peoples everywhere should move forward as speedily as possible towards self-government'. This attitude was reinforced a year later when the United States was drawn into the war. Its hostility towards the very idea of European colonies, of which it originally had been one, increased the likelihood that India would become independent at the end of the war. Roosevelt in private conversations said that he wanted a free India: Churchill disagreed.

THE DIVIDING OF INDIA

The demand of most Indian leaders was for one free nation embracing Hindus, Muslims, Sikhs and Parsees and all other groups. On the other hand Muhammad Ali Jinnah, leader of the Muslims, had long concluded that a united nation would be unworkable. His conclusion was endorsed, in his view, after religious riots broke out. In one week of August 1946, as many as 5000 people were killed and 11 000 injured in fighting and scuffles between Muslims and Hindus in Calcutta. Axes, spears, daggers, bamboo sticks, stones and bricks caused many of the deaths. The violence spread to distant parts of India, threatening to destroy the country. 'Words fail me!', said Gandhi on learning of the violence.

A blind Hindu boy recorded his experiences in the Muslim city of Lahore where the rioting was resumed in 1947. He feared that the women of his parent's household would be assaulted, bashed, raped or murdered, and the house itself would be set on fire by the mobs wandering the streets. 'The shrieks of the mob', wrote the boy, became more frequent and 'vibrated through the sultry night'. Fires could be seen nearby; an exploding bomb was heard. The numerous police in the city were not quick to intervene.

India became independent on 15 August 1947, being split into separate nations. The republic of India, occupying the heart of the subcontinent, held the most people and by far the biggest area. The new Muslim republic of Pakistan was cut into two – the west and the east. At the western end was the vast plain of the Indus River, at the eastern end the flood-prone delta of what later became the nation of Bangladesh. Inevitably, large groups of Muslims were stranded in Hindu India and large groups of Hindus were stranded in Muslim Pakistan.

A fortnight after independence was achieved, the aged Gandhi commenced a fast in the hope of achieving harmony between the two peoples and nations. He had long expressed the wish to live until he was aged 125: the wish had vanished. A year later, he died at the hands of an assassin from an extreme Hindu group. The public tribute to him was delivered majestically and humbly in the parliament in New Delhi by the prime minister of the new India, Jawaharlal Nehru, on 2 February 1948: 'A glory has departed and the sun that warmed and brightened our lives has set, and we shiver in the cold and dark. Yet he would not have us feel this way.' He was 'a man of God', in Nehru's eyes.

In the vast territory covered by the two nations, the intermittent violence went on. In the search for security, at least 12 million people emigrated from one nation to the other. Trains jammed with refugees, even to the rooftops, were attacked by their enemies. Some carriages reached their destination with nearly every passenger dead or injured. At least 300 000 people were killed in these bouts of violence, and yet in some districts there was restraint and patience.

The creation of two separate nations in the old British India was a turning point in Asian history. One effect is little noticed even today. The potential influence of the subcontinent of India was drastically

reduced by the act of partition. If there had been one India embracing both Hindus and Muslims, then by the end of the century its
population would have approached 1.3 billion: larger, even, than
China's.

The new India was to be ruled for 17 years by a politician who
would have felt at home in the House of Commons. Of a learned
family that originated in Kashmir, Jawaharlal Nehru had gone, like
Churchill, to the Harrow School in London and then to Cambridge
University before absorbing himself in Indian politics. As head of
the most populous democracy in the world, he initially tried to walk
in Gandhi's peaceful footsteps, calling for negotiations and conferences. Eventually he marched to a new drumbeat. Accepting that
his nation in the last resort might have to use threats and force, his
army invaded Goa and two other long-held Portuguese possessions
on the west coast in 1961. In the following year India briefly fought
with China along the border they shared. The rivalries that had
bedevilled Europe were becoming conspicuous in Asia.

INDONESIA'S MAGIC MAN

The Dutch flag had flown over the East Indies for three centuries.
As the Indonesian archipelago was rich in oil and rubber it was vital
to Dutch economic life. After the war, the government of Holland
had every intention of regaining it, once the occupying Japanese
departed. Whether Holland was militarily strong enough to defeat
the Indonesians and their growing resistance was doubtful.

The leader of the Indonesians, the dashing President Sukarno,
was resolute. He was magic to those who heard his speeches; and
they listened in their thousands. He had a sense of theatre, like

Gandhi, but there was nothing of the ascetic or the killjoy in him. He enjoyed every available pleasure, but was capable of hard work and of mastering detail when they were important to him. He spoke many languages including at least three from Indonesia – Javanese, Sundanese and Balinese: his mother came from Bali. A graduate in civil engineering he had made his reputation as a political agitator against the Dutch, and for his courage he was sent to prison and to exile in a remote harbour. When the Japanese overran the Dutch East Indies in 1942 he became their right-hand man but not their obedient servant. After their occupation suddenly ended in August 1945, he declared that the new nation of Indonesia now existed. His base was in the celebrated Javanese city of Jogjakarta, near the ancient dark-stone temple of Borobodur, and in the next three years the territory in his control extended across half of the island of Java and most of Sumatra. The clusters of other Dutch islands were outside his direct control.

It was the hope of the Dutch to drive Sukarno out of Java; and several times their army, which eventually numbered 150000, almost succeeded. It even captured Jogjakarta and leaders of the republican cabinet. But at crucial stages, Australia and newly independent India enlisted the United Nations on Sukarno's side. In the end the Americans joined in, advising the Dutch that their era as a major colonial power was over. Indonesia became a nation in December 1949.

The magical, word-spinning Sukarno ruled his 90 million people with early success. Under his spell a quiet sense of patriotism began to unite a nation that consisted of many ethnic groups. He led campaigns to reduce tropical diseases, especially yaws and malaria.

Ruling one of those numerous new nations where more than 80 per cent of the people could neither read nor write, he resolutely set out to increase literacy.

Sukarno called the country's first election in 1955. As four parties, including the communists and Muslims, each polled heavily he realised that democracy would not yield the decisive result his own party demanded. He dispensed with democracy: he knew what the people wanted. When the people, and his corrupt ministers, wanted more money he printed it for them. As a result the price of everything soared, week after week. Within a few years prices had multiplied hundreds of times. He borrowed capital, first from the United States and then from Moscow and finally from Beijing.

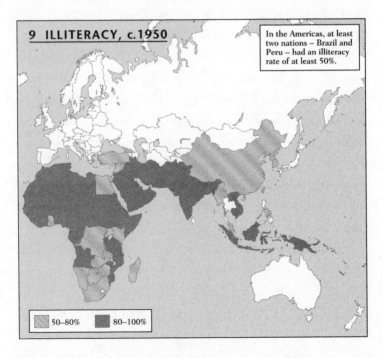

9 ILLITERACY, c.1950

In the Americas, at least two nations – Brazil and Peru – had an illiteracy rate of at least 50%.

50–80%   80–100%

He began to find, overseas, not only friends but also enemies. In the early 1960s his troops briefly skirmished with those of nearby Malaysia, a federation of former British colonies, and his soldiers and bureaucrats took over the west of New Guinea from his old enemy, the Dutch. In Indonesia's capital city, Jakarta, the inner circles began to plot against each other. Six generals were tortured and murdered, and several hundred thousand civilians, many of whom were Chinese, were massacred. Sukarno's glorious reign – he was the founder of what is now the fourth most populous nation – was virtually over. In 1965 it was the army's turn to rule.

KENYATTA OF KENYA

Widely labelled as 'the revolt against the west', the movement to liberate colonies was also a revolt within the west. Towards overseas empires the west itself was sharply divided. Millions of British, Portuguese, French, Spanish and Dutch families, especially those whose relatives and friends had lived in the colonies, wished the colonial empire to continue. The political parties and groups calling for the end of empire were also strong. Their sympathies helped many of the colonial leaders who had earlier travelled as young students to Britain, France, Prague and even Moscow. Some students, when living in the imperial capitals, had been befriended by Christians, Marxists and other groups.

At first mesmerised by Europe, some of these Asians and Africans were ready to rediscover their own land's traditions on returning home. Solomon Bandaranaike of Ceylon studied at Oxford where he showed talent as a debater and player of tennis and billiards in the 1920s. Going home to become a barrister, he decided on reflection that Oxford 'had taught me to love my country better'. As prime minister he elevated the Sinhalese language above English and transferred his faith from Christianity to Buddhism. He was shot by a mad Buddhist monk in 1959, at the height of his power.

'All of the great leaders', wrote John Kenneth Galbraith, 'have had one characteristic in common: it was the willingness to confront unequivocally the major anxiety of their people in their time. This, and not much else, is the essence of leadership.' Africa was speckled with leaders who, in this one quality, were outstanding. Many of these leaders were household names far from their homeland: Gamal Adbel Nasser of Egypt, Jomo Kenyatta of Kenya, Dr Hastings Banda of Nyasaland and Malawi, Patrice Lumumba of the Congo, Kwame Nkrumah of Ghana (which was formerly known as the Gold Coast), and Leopold Senghor, the west African socialist and former seminarian who became the first president of Senegal. Most were so obsessed with gaining independence for their own African territory that little else mattered. What they would do with their nation's independence, if it should arrive, occupied only a fraction of their thinking time.

Kenya gained from a single-minded leader in its fight for independence. The leader came from the Kenyan highlands, and eventually called himself Kenyatta. Educated at a mission school run by the Church of Scotland he became a clerk and a reader of water meters in the big town of Nairobi and a political activist. Indignant that his highlanders had lost so much land to incoming white farmers, he went to Britain in 1929 to campaign. Living with Quakers near Birmingham, he wrote in their testimonial book: 'We, the children of humanity, being brothers and sisters must serve one another in the name of all mankind.' While he disliked the prejudice sometimes shown by British people, he resented the Indians who outnumbered the British by four to one in the colony of Kenya.

Spending two years in Moscow, Kenyatta received military training and lessons in Marxism at a college attended by black revolutionaries. His tutors were absorbed in the clash of classes but he was interested in the clash of races. Back in London he acquired intellectual confidence while studying under the Polish-born anthropologist, Bronislaw Malinowski. In 1938 Kenyatta was the author of a serious book, *Facing Mt Kenya*. On the front of the book his new name, Jomo Kenyatta, first appeared in public – Jomo signified a burning spear. For years he showed little desire to return to Kenya – it was not yet a place where a burning spear was welcomed. In 1946, after 17 years of absence, he returned by ship to Kenya where thousands hailed him as the leader who would guide them back to the land they had lost.

In Kenya the process of liberation was sure to be thorny. It was one of the few African lands – they included Zimbabwe, South Africa and Malawi – where white settlers farmed much of the fertile land, ran the large mines, and provided most of the exports. Being a minority, their future would be endangered when the Africans gained equal voting rights.

They were the minority whom Macmillan, the prime minister of Britain, had in mind when he observed: 'Africans are not the problem in Africa, it is the Europeans.' He knew too that the British who had colonised Kenya and these similar colonies had a legitimate point of view coupled with an affection for the land, which was expressed nostalgically by Sir Edward Grigg, a former governor of Kenya: 'The very thought of Kenya is like sunlight to me, sunlight crisp as mountain air in the high places of the earth.' In Kenya lived thousands of Indian traders whose future, like that of the whites, would be just as threatened if independence arrived. There was no satisfactory solution to this dilemma.

Britain wished to withdraw slowly from Kenya, after providing safeguards for the foreign settlers who would stay on. Kenyatta and other members of his Kikuyu tribe understandably called for a speedy withdrawal. Under the name of the Mau Mau, the tribesmen began to terrorise the countryside, killing and burning. In 1952 the British government, declaring a state of emergency, combated guerrilla warfare with an intensity that still arouses indignation. Kenyatta himself was sentenced in 1953 to a long term of imprisonment. Ten years later, under his leadership, Kenya gained independence. It was one-third of a century after he began his campaign. The new campaign – to govern the nation effectively – would be just as long.

THE WIND OF CHANGE

The territory of South Africa was huge and contentious. It ran 1000 miles from the Atlantic Ocean to the Indian Ocean in the east. It extended 600 miles from the southerly tip at Cape Agulhas to the nearest point of the northern border and the Kalahari Desert, and ran hundreds of miles further north-east to border with Zimbabwe. The country held many climates, both harsh and kind. It held rugged mountains and the Great Escarpment, sweeps of park-like country and grassland, a rich strip of sugar cane in Natal, vineyards and orchards in the shadow of the Table Mount, and rich minerals including the largest goldmines in the world at Johannesburg, the inland city on the high tableland.

South Africa was like Kenya in its mixture of Europeans and Africans, well-off whites and poor blacks, and its noticeable fringe of successful Asian settlers. Its colonial history was longer, being an outcome of much earlier inflows of white settlers, originally from Holland. They had lived so long in South Africa that their language, later called Afrikaans, had deviated from its mother tongue. Later streams of settlers came in small numbers from France and in large numbers from Britain, along with a group of Jews who became powerful in Johannesburg when that city conducted one of the world's busiest stock exchanges. In the last 200 years no country in the whole of the continent received so many European immigrants as South Africa.

Its minority of whites, forming one-fifth of the total population in mid-century, dominated the nation. From Cape Town to Durban they were the drivers of an economy that had long been the most successful on the continent. On the other hand the black Africans and the so-called Cape Coloureds, together forming 80 per cent of the population, served as the miners, farm labourers, road menders, street sweepers, waitresses and domestic servants. They were paid poorly by South African standards but were paid well by the standards of most other African nations.

South Africa's political system took shape when the white people rode high in the world, and the coloured people usually walked behind them. In politics and race relations it had stormy years, but at times a politician from South Africa was a voice for moderation in the world. Jan Smuts, born on a South African farm, was one of the founders of the League of Nations in 1919. A quarter of a century later, as the 74-year-old prime minister of his nation, he reappeared in San Francisco and drafted the preamble to the charter of the new United Nations. In the South African election of 1948 his party of moderation was defeated; and thereafter defeat became its normal experience. The idea of white supremacy, which permeated national politics even during Smuts' terms as leader, was solidified by his successors.

There were already gates separating whites from others. In the Second World War the non-whites, who constituted four of every 10 South African soldiers, performed military duties other than bearing arms. The gates based on colour were augmented by a succession of prime ministers: D.F. Malan, J.G. Strijdom and H.F. Verwoerd. Under new laws, the white people could marry only those who were also white. Only whites could attend the impressive universities such as Witwatersrand, Stellenbosch and Cape Town. In certain towns and suburbs only the whites could own property, run a business and be residents. Most of the skilled trades were open only to white people. Those South Africans who were not white were permitted a meagre role in the parliament which met in Cape Town, and that role shrivelled. The black Africans, who numerically dominated the nation, were permitted to elect three politicians – they had to be white – in the House of Assembly of 159 members. Even that right was available only to literate black men living in Cape Province, and not to those numerous black Africans in the Transvaal and other provinces. Their three seats were abolished in 1959. The more favoured people of mixed ancestry, known as the Cape Coloureds, could elect four politicians, each of whom had to be white. That privilege would be removed in 1968.

Could South Africa withstand the fast rise of black nationalism and tribalism, and the switch of world opinion against the white dominance of black lands? In 1960, Harold Macmillan, on his first visit to that remoter Africa lying south of the equator, delivered to the parliament in Capetown a courteous warning. Surveying the members seated before him, and not a dark face amongst them, he spoke the memorable words: 'The wind of change is blowing through this continent, and, whether we like it or not, this growth of national consciousness is a political fact.' His sentence ranked high on the hit parade of quotable quotations for years to come.

South Africa's leaders applauded him, perhaps without quite understanding the implications of his speech. Their real dilemma was whether to extend their own hard-won independence to the black people who far outnumbered them. But that meant renouncing, one by one, their own political and economic privileges, and endangering the pleasant way of life they themselves lived. They did not select that alternative. Unpalatable alternatives are not easily chosen, irrespective of race, political creed or length of experience. The final decision by most of the white voters was to follow their own road, alone.

Soon after Macmillan sailed in the ocean liner for England, a crowd of black people met in the Transvaal town of Sharpeville and staged a rally against their white government. Police opened fire on the protesters, and 69 were killed and 178 were wounded. Promptly the government declared a state of emergency that, unofficially or officially, was to last for almost three decades. In 1961, after a referendum, South Africa became a republic; it severed its links with the British Commonwealth of Nations; and from the following year it had to defend itself against increasing attacks from the majority of nation-members of the assembly of the United Nations.

Meanwhile the black African National Congress was banned. One of the African leaders, the lawyer Nelson Mandela, responded by calling for sabotage and armed attack. In Johannesburg the secret military arm of his party, 'Spear of the Nation', acquired more armaments. He was arrested, tried, and sentenced in June 1964 to life imprisonment, from which he eventually emerged to become the leader of his nation.

THE EBB OF EMPIRE

France was under persisting pressure to unload its colonies. Britain was prepared for the pressure: France was not. General de Gaulle had no sooner taken office in Paris after four years of wartime exile in London than he had to turn nervously to shaping the future of the French colonies. Spread over two hemispheres, and standing on both sides of the equator, they had been split in their allegiances during the war, some supporting the Vichy government at home, and some supporting the Free French led by de Gaulle.

More than Britain, the new French government was eager to retain colonies. They brought prestige, urgently needed after the gloom of surrender and defeat. In 1945 France owned a necklace of colonies stretching all the way from New Caledonia to Indo-China and from the island of Madagascar to French Guiana in the jungle of South America. The French ruled over a string of elegant cities from Beirut to Saigon. All provided a worldwide stage for the French language – increasingly besieged by the English language – and for French culture, history and commercial products. In the psychological recovery of France, the colonies could play a special role. But first they had to be retained.

Already the Indo-Chinese, having seen enough of the occupying Japanese, tried to seize control of the country. British forces stepped in temporarily, enabling the French to return. The war in Vietnam, in which a French army and then an American army fought for a quarter of a century, stemmed from this initial French determination to remain a master of the possessions scattered across the world. France itself abandoned Indo-China in 1954, after a war in which more officers were killed each year than France's military academies could graduate.

The aggregation of colonies in Africa too was prized by French leaders. The odd-shaped expanse of French territory – stretching from the Mediterranean far into the Sahara and across the equator, and touching the Atlantic shore at many bays and headlands – almost equalled the total area of China. Even empty space was an advantage in the age of the atom. Here, in the desert, the French were to test their first nuclear bomb in 1960. Other parts of this territory were especially valued in Paris because they offered a spacious home for French settlers. Algeria, holding more French-born settlers than any other French colony, stood opposite the southern coast of France. If colonies were explosives as well as jewels, Algeria was a powder magazine at France's back door.

Algeria had long been treated as a special colony, and some French politicians hoped that it might become a permanent part of France itself. In the two big Algerian ports of Algiers and Oran most of the inhabitants were French by ancestry. From the sea the tall minarets of the mosques, the dome of the opera house and the spires of Catholic churches could be seen. The main streets had an elegance reminiscent of the Paris boulevards, and their arcades were invitingly cool on a hot day. According to a writer of the 1920s the newish part of Algiers 'might deceive the traveller into the belief that he is still in Europe, were it not for the throng of swarthy faces he meets'. After the Second World War the people of the colony of Algeria were divided, some wanting to remain with France and some demanding independence.

There was fighting. By 1954 the rebellion was almost out of hand. Soon nearly 500 000 French soldiers were trying to defend this vital French possession and restore civil order. Two years later Tunisia and Morocco, which had been merely classed as French protectorates, were allowed to become independent, but Algeria continued in a state of warfare. The dispute split the French nation, leading to General de Gaulle's recall to power. Clearly the war now was unwinnable. In 1962 the question – whether Algeria should be allowed its independence – was resolved through a referendum held in mother France and all her colonies. By 18 million votes to 2 million, Algeria was freed and farewelled.

France tried to remain a global power by offering its colonies a cosy place in a French federation or community. A variety of colonies accepted the place, combining a degree of autonomy with membership of what was called La Communauté Française. By 1960 the whole French community held almost as many people outside as inside France.

Britain could have nominally held on to much of its empire if it had devised a scheme similar to France's; but it had no such wish. Some colonies it held tenaciously. From some it speedily withdrew as soon as the opportunity arose. In Westminster a succession of governments and ministers came with their own priorities. Some watched the colonial empire slowly die: some helped it to die.

There remained an unusual organisation, the British Common-wealth of Nations, where the heads of the old overseas dominions and the newly independent parts of what was once the British Empire met periodically. That the prime minister of a small African nation could speak at this assembly with the same moral authority as the prime minister of Britain was a sign of how far the world of Churchill had receded. The United Nations reflected the same profound change when in 1961 it selected as its chief executive a Buddhist and former teacher from Burma, the diligent U Thant.

The British Empire had lasted for four centuries. The speed at which it was dissolved was astounding to outsiders, though not fast enough for Africans, Asians, and others who relished the prospect of national independence. In the decline of the British Empire, the seafaring events, on pinpoints of the globe, were often more influential than those on the huge land masses. The loss of the Suez Canal in 1956 was devastating. The decisions in 1971 to withdraw the navy from Singapore and to abandon the bases in the Persian Gulf were far more important than the loss of vast expanses of Africa.

Britain and France retained a few overseas possessions, some of which lay as far away as the Falklands and Hong Kong and Tahiti. The Dutch and Spanish colonies had nearly all gone, and Belgium had lost its only colony. Portugal, alone of the colonial powers, retained nearly all of the overseas possessions that it had held at the start of the century. It clung to Macao, a tiny doorway into southern China; it continued to rule half of Timor, not far from the coast of Australia; and retained vast parts of west and east Africa only through the presence of thousands of fighting troops. A democratic nation was more likely than an authoritarian nation to release its colonies;

and Portugal, at last experiencing a democratic revolution in the mid-1970s, quickly lost its empire.

The breakaway from Europe had formed a stirring chain of events during the 25 years after the Second World War. Several major and many minor international wars, and numerous civil wars, were part of the process. The break gave rise to a deep sense of triumph in the liberated lands but it was often short-lived. Before the century was over, a variety of commentators concluded that many African and some Asian peoples were treated more shabbily by their new rulers than their old.

17

ISRAEL AND EGYPT

In 1896 a Viennese journalist, Theodor Herzl, first promoted the Zionist movement, and the hope of a distinct Jewish homeland. The dream of a separate Jewish nation began to fire the imagination of many who were not Jewish. It kindled a flame in a majority of Jewish hearts, though in the United States and other New-World countries many of those Jews who were prominent in their nation's daily life were, at best, lukewarm to the idea.

It was accepted in many western circles that the Jewish people deserved their own Zion, their place in the sun. The question was, which nation would step forward to offer them a place?

BALFOUR'S GOOD-CONDUCT MEDAL

Arthur James Balfour, a conservative British politician approaching the sunset of his political life, announced the long-awaited plan for the Jews of the world. Of aristocratic background, a student of Eton and Cambridge with a brilliant and speculative mind, he had entered politics when young. As a backbencher he wrote *A Defence of Philosophic Doubt*, not the kind of book which his colleagues rushed to buy. Personal invective did not unsteady him nor did personal danger – he had once held the hazardous post of chief secretary for the troubled domain of Ireland. Prime Minister of Britain from 1902 to 1905, and powerful long after, he had no idea he would be known today primarily for the Balfour Declaration – one of his minor ventures, and perhaps more a result of his philosophic interests, for a Manchester philosopher had indirectly introduced him to what was called 'the Zionist problem'.

His plan was in part an attempt to persuade Russia's Jews, especially those supporting the revolutions of 1917, to do everything to prevent their country withdrawing from the First World War. A permanent Jewish haven in Palestine was a kind of good-conduct medal dangled in front of them. The French likewise supported the idea. Balfour thought it was right that the Jewish people, having such a strong sense of identity, should possess their own land, and develop it in their own way. On 2 November 1917, as Britain's foreign secretary, he sent to Lord Rothschild, a financier of Jewish projects in Palestine, a letter supporting the idea of creating there a 'National Home for the Jewish People'. Admittedly, Britain did not yet own Palestine, but that minor obstacle could be overcome. At that stage of the war the Ottoman Empire faced defeat, after which Palestine would become a possession of Britain or France.

Before the war Palestine had been part of the province of Syria with insanitary towns, struggling farms, backward ports, a few railways and in 1914 just one car. After the war, as Balfour promised, Palestine became a British mandated territory – a new form of colony to be governed primarily in the interests of its inhabitants rather than of the imperial power. Under British rule, the Arabic, English and Hebrew languages received official standing, a police force was set up, and schools were enlarged. As more Jews arrived, Palestine blossomed. There arose a hydro-electric scheme, telephone lines, the new port of Haifa, the new town of Tel Aviv sitting on the sand dunes, and the Hebrew University that was ceremonially opened by Balfour himself.

The experience of many of the new settlers in the 1920s was a mixture of jubilation and disillusionment. Golda Meir, originally emigrating as a Jewish child from Russia to Milwaukee in the United States, was brought up to feel passionate about Israel years before she first saw it and half a century before she became its prime minister. A social democrat, she was more political than religious in her attitude to the Jewish settlements springing up in Palestine. 'I wasn't at all pious myself', she admitted. When finally she set out with her children to live there, she simply wished to work on a Jewish collectivist farm. At last reaching the tiny Tel Aviv railway station, drenched by sun and empty of people, she realised to her dismay that 'no one was coming to meet us'.

Many of the Jews she first met seemed unpredictable, partly because they came from diverse countries and carried a variety of values. But they shared a feeling of ease and relaxation in those parts of Israel that they settled. In Tel Aviv nearly everyone could hurry home from work on Friday evening and share in the Jewish Sabbath, knowing that they were no longer an ethnic minority looking nervously over their shoulders but inhabitants of what they proudly called the only all-Jewish town in the world. Palestine as a whole remained Arab and not Jewish. In 1917 the Jews were outnumbered by more than 10 to one. Even after the first inrush of postwar immigrants British Palestine held only one Jew for every three Muslims.

There was at least one flaw in Balfour's plan. In his declaration of 1917 he conceded that the Islamic and other peoples in Palestine already had 'civil and religious rights' that must be respected. But the right that the Muslims valued was to be dominant in the land they called their own and to shape daily life according to the words of Allah. Another right they claimed was the control of Jerusalem and all its places sacred to Islam, Judaism and Christianity. Most Arabs did not like the new order, and many refused to cooperate.

Arthur Balfour had not seen the full implications of what he proclaimed. He tended to see the Arabs in the Middle East as passive. In suggesting that large numbers of European Jews should emigrate to Arab-dominated Palestine he was assuming that the host culture would accept them. At the same time he was willing to support Arabs elsewhere. After the war the British gave strong support to several Arab rulers. They even sanctioned an all-Arab province in the poor territory on the eastern or Jordan River side of Palestine, known as Trans-Jordan.

The Jews arrived in Palestine in increasing numbers – without a parallel inflow of Arabs – and slowly altered the old way of life. To this many Arabs objected, and took up arms. Moreover the nations surrounding Palestine, being Islamic, did not wish the Palestinians to take second place. At times the British government tried to restrict the Jewish inflow and so maintain a 'balance'. An impartial scholar, writing on Palestine in 1926 for a British encyclopaedia, rightly predicted that this problem 'will tax the powers of British diplomacy and statecraft to its utmost for years to come'.

A homeland for the Jews became a high priority after 1945 when the World Zionist Congress called for 1 million Jews, bewildered and destitute in Europe and elsewhere, to be admitted to Palestine. The idea of Palestine as the Jewish homeland acquired millions of new friends, especially after the sombre details of the holocaust became known. The British who still formally controlled Palestine under its mandate and trusteeship, conferred initially by the League of Nations but now by the new United Nations, began to see Palestine as an insoluble problem. If the United Nations was to prove its worth it had to devise a solution; but a solution was a pipedream.

Many armed Jews went underground, even planning a dramatic attack on a British official who worked in the King David Hotel in Jerusalem. On 22 July 1946 part of the hotel was blown up and 91 people were killed. Of such terrorist tactics many Jews disapproved. At the end of that year Chaim Weizmann, soon to be the first president of the independent state of Israel, warned the Zionist Congress meeting in Switzerland of the perils of Jewish terrorism: 'Terrorism insults our history; it mocks the ideals for which a Jewish society must stand; it contaminates our banner.' Jewish terrorists, many of whom were openly applauded by sympathisers in New York, continued to mock the banner. Explosions, assassinations and raids went on and on. Families arriving in Palestine from central and eastern Europe, in search of a haven, concluded that they had jumped from one frying pan into another.

Close to 90 000 British troops were trying to maintain order. One in every 10 members of the armed forces of the British Empire were risking their lives in this area no larger than Wales, a territory in which Britain had no economic interests. Moreover by the second half of 1947 Britain's economy was in difficulties: the currency was weak, fuel was scarce, and food and clothing were still rationed. The financial burden of empire, and the debts incurred in the Second World War, were too heavy. As Britain in 1947 was withdrawing from India where its links were old and strong, why should it remain in Palestine where its interests were few and the risk to its troops was high?

On the surface, Palestine's warfare seemed to have little connection with the Cold War but the contest between Americans and Russians simmered in the background. Official British circles and several influential American circles thought that communists might seize control of Palestine. After all, social democrats were the strongest group among the Jewish immigrants; the favoured Jewish method of farming – the kibbutz – was collectivist; and Jews were beginning to acquire arms from the Soviet bloc. Moreover the Soviet Union was more and more interested in the oil potential of the Middle East. Even the fear of communism, however, could not persuade Britain to remain the guardian and peacekeeper in Palestine.

In May 1947 the United Nations set up a committee to determine how enough living space could be found for both peoples in the tiny land of Palestine. The members of the vital committee could not agree. The majority report, fair in spirit, recommended the making of two independent states, an Arab and a Jewish, each of which would belong to a common market. In short there would be an economic but not a political or cultural union. The report also recommended that the holy places in Palestine should be set aside as neutral and held in trust by the United Nations. Bethlehem, the birthplace of Christ, would be part of that neutral zone.

The assembly of the United Nations in November 1947 voted on the plan, but the way each member-nation voted was ominous. Approval was given by a total of 35 nations, including the Soviet Union and the United States; but another 32 opposed the plan or abstained from voting. The plan seemed practical but the Arabs disapproved, just as they had rejected a similar plan years previously. Their argument was that they once had held all the land, but now it was proposed to allow them less than half. To this the Jews would reply that at an even more distant time their own ancestors possessed the whole of Palestine.

As the British prepared to leave, their control of Palestine was loosened even further. The Arab village of Deir Yassin lay to the west of Jerusalem. On 9 April 1948 it was attacked by an unofficial band of Jewish soldiers. In all, 240 Arabs were killed: half were women and children. No other event did as much to persuade Arab villagers that they had no future in Palestine.

One month later the republic of Israel was born, its first prime minister being David Ben-Gurion who had emigrated from Poland more than 40 years ago. The British forces sailed or flew away: the mandate was over. An Arab army crossed the border from Trans-Jordan, and Egyptian soldiers advanced from the south. It was widely expected that the Israeli forces would be defeated, once the five surrounding nations fully organised their forces in support of the Palestinian Arabs.

The United Nations sent out a peacemaker, Count Folke Berna-dotte, who imposed a cease-fire for one month. A member of the Swedish royal family, a citizen of a nation noted for its neutrality, a leader who was influential in such international groups as the Red Cross and the Boy Scouts, he possibly possessed the prestige and impartiality necessary to persuade the two opposing sides to behave. Unfairly he was viewed as anti-Jewish. On 17 September 1948 in Jerusalem he was pounced upon by Jewish terrorists of the Irgun group and killed. The sense of outrage circled the world. As the fighting continued, the Jews, with the aid of aircraft and tanks secured from Czechoslovakia and other communist lands, defeated the Egyptians and other Arab forces.

A senior official of the United Nations, Ralph Bunche, an Afro-American when the bureaucracy of that organisation was overwhelmingly white, became the new peacemaker in Palestine. Almost nobody could make peace out of such explosive ingredients. He skilfully negotiated a truce, for which he was awarded the Nobel peace prize in the belief that the truce meant something. It meant little.

In the space of a few months of fighting, Israel had expanded its territory beyond the boundaries recommended by the United Nations. It had no intention of withdrawing its troops. Israel's neigh-bours for their part had no intention of accepting the result of that fighting. Most Palestinian leaders and followers believed that they would – not next year or the year after, but someday – drive the Jews into the sea.

What had been largely an Arab land, measured by population, was speedily becoming Jewish. A stream of Arabs hurried away, driven out by war or fear. In April 1949 some 726 000 Palestinians – they had recently formed a majority of the population of Palestine – were living in refugee camps that lay just outside the new borders of Israel. To fill their places more Jews arrived, mostly with only a few suitcases and bundles, for the new Law of Return gave all Jews, no matter where they lived, the right to settle in Israel. In 1950 alone the immigrants totalled 170 000, including 40 000 Yemeni Jews who came by air from Aden. It would be hard to find any other country in the 20th century where the racial and ethnic composition was so quickly reversed. By 1956 only one in every nine people living in Israel was an Arab. The mayor of the town of Nazareth, and eight of the 120 members of the parliament were Arabs, but the nation was dominated by Jews.

The new Israel was increasingly marvelled at or feared. Its hills and sand dunes, its deserts and irrigated communal farms, and the cities of Tel Aviv and Jaffa were booming in a way inconceivable when the Arabs dominated the land. Israel, while materially more successful than the sleepy lands across the border, was not quite what visitors expected. It was widely assumed that its politics would be more conservative, and yet in the Israel parliament, the Knesset, the socialist and labour parties were usually dominant. It was widely assumed that the new state would be ultra-religious; but it held every shade of Jewish opinion including lukewarm Hebrews and atheists. It was widely assumed that Jews, when the opportunity arose, would prefer the mercantile and professional world; and yet their nation displayed skills in warfare that were unexpected: every young man and woman had to perform some kind of national service. Though dwarfed by the combined population of Arab neighbours,

Israel easily defeated them in irregular and regular warfare. After Russia supplied its latest jet aircraft to Israel's foes, the result of the fighting was not altered.

The Middle East, even if the nation of Israel had not arisen there, was likely to face increasing tension. It was the largest producer of oil at a time when oil was rivalling coal as the world's main fuel. The Middle East was also a seat of growing rivalry between the super-powers. As Israel's main ally and financial friend after 1948 was the United States – the home to more Jews than was any other nation – the rival Islamic countries began to accept the Soviet Union as their own protector. When the Balfour plan had been approved a genera-tion previously, Palestine seemed an appropriate site because much of it was desert and dry riverbed. Now it was a torrent that tumbled and roared.

THE FIGHT FOR SUEZ

For centuries Egypt had been far more strategic than Palestine. It owned that narrow coastal corridor joining Africa and Asia. Egypt was also the site of a man-made waterway that ranked with the mouth of the Baltic, the English Channel, the Strait of Gibraltar, the Dardanelles, the Straits of Malacca and the Panama Canal as one of the world's crucial sea lanes. It was France that had built the Suez Canal, opening the maritime short-cut between Europe and Asia, but it was Britain that guarded the canal. Egypt and its river Nile, a rich producer of cotton as well as food, was also the gateway to the Sudan and populous regions in north-east Africa.

In 1922 Egypt had largely regained its independence from Britain. Its Sultan became king, and a year later a constitution modelled on that of Belgium apportioned most of the power, in theory, to a newly elected parliament. The democratic institutions did not operate smoothly. The nation was like an orchestra controlled periodically by three different conductors: the king, the British government, and Egypt's prime minister. On the eve of the Second World War, it was ruled more by the playboy King Farouk than by elected politicians, and was defended largely by Britain. In 1941, when it was almost invaded by the Italian and German forces rolling across the desert, it relied on British, Australian and New Zealand forces to defend its proclaimed neutrality. Not until February 1945, when the long war was almost over, did Egypt declare war on Germany.

When Israel became a nation in 1948, Egypt was one of its indignant opponents. In potential, it was the most formidable enemy of Israel, because it held the largest population of any nation in the

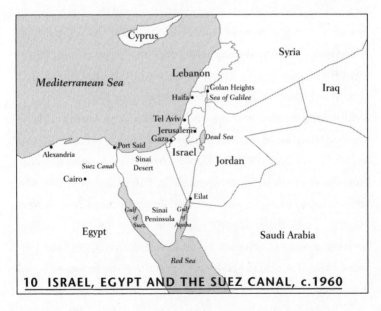

10 ISRAEL, EGYPT AND THE SUEZ CANAL, c.1960

vicinity and a horde of recruits capable of forming an army that would dwarf Israel's. It played a major part, with Jordan and Syria and Iraq, in the first short, unsuccessful war against Israel but it lacked drive until its king was deposed in 1952 by officers in his own army. These nationalist officers, led by Colonel Gamal Abdel Nasser, sent shivers down the spine of Israel's leaders. Aged 34, Nasser had fought against Israel in the recent war and was a more aggressive leader than the stout playboy king.

Like most leaders of simple origin who become the saviour of their country, Nasser was hailed as a son of the ordinary people. Depicted as the peasant product of a sleepy village far from the sea, he was actually the son of a postmaster in a suburb of Alexandria. Big and handsome, with a thin moustache and close-cropped hair, he could be charming and moderate – he refused demands that the deposed king be executed. While some observers predicted that Nasser would promote Islam at every opportunity, he was denounced as too secular by the radical Muslim Brotherhood, which tried to assassinate him in 1954. In foreign policy he fiercely opposed Israel and Britain. As a schoolboy he had carried placards denouncing the British.

Emerging as the most vigorous leader in the Arab world, he asserted his independence of Britain, which finally agreed to evacuate its troops from the Suez Canal. He showed hostility towards Israel by encouraging guerrilla raids by Palestinian refugees who were camped on the Gaza Strip, recently captured from Egypt. Finally, in 1955 he arranged to buy armaments and raw materials from communist Czechoslovakia and in effect from the whole communist bloc. Granting formal recognition to China, he placed Egypt even more firmly on the communist side in the Cold War.

The US and Britain distanced themselves from Nasser. Having promised to finance, at Aswan on the Nile, the first stage of a high dam that would almost satisfy the Egyptian farmers' thirst for irrigated water, they withdrew their promise. Nasser was single-minded: he would not be thwarted. He responded by announcing that he would nationalise the Suez Canal Company which, from its headquarters in France, ran the canal and collected most of the annual profit. As it was one of the two main canals in the world and vital for European commerce, his demand was audacious. In the way he leapt, some observers heard echoes of Hitler, an analogy that was too emphatic.

Promptly, Britain and France carried their complaint to the Security Council of the United Nations and won its support. The Soviet Union exercised its veto: the Cold War now embraced the canal. Britain and France – and Israel too – took military action. On 29 October 1956 Israel's forces invaded Egypt and moved towards the canal. A week later, Britain and France launched attacks on Egyptian airfields and landed near the canal. As the Soviet Union was the quiet backer of Egypt, this was the kind of local war that might explode into nuclear war.

While the eyes of most of the world were fixed on the crisis in Egypt, Moscow used this diversion to strengthen its grip in central Europe. There had been unrest in communist Poland and Hungary – perhaps the most serious Moscow had encountered since the end of the Second World War. While the tension was tightening in Egypt, Moscow resolved to invade rebellious Hungary. On 4 November it sent in tanks and soldiers, quickly winning control.

Turning its attention back to the canal zone, Moscow threatened war if Britain and France did not accept a cease-fire. It warned the

United States, on the eve of its presidential election, not to intervene in Egypt. Momentous events, their outcome impossible to predict, they occurred less than three weeks before the Olympic Games were to be staged – at a time when the contest between athletes from the Soviet Union and the United States was becoming part of the Cold War. Allocated for the first time to the Southern Hemisphere, the games were to begin in Melbourne on 22 November 1956. Nine days before the opening, the Soviet Union received a warning that if it fired 'rockets' near Suez, American rockets would be fired in response. Seven days before the opening, United Nations' peacekeepers landed near the border of Egypt and Israel in readiness to take over from the French and British forces camped near the canal.

The games went on. Hungarian and Soviet teams fought with fists at the water polo, but other athletes from 68 nations competed as if the anxiety and indignation in Cairo, Budapest, New York, Moscow, London, Paris, Jerusalem and both banks of the canal did not exist. Australia's prime minister, R.G. Menzies, who had just returned from futile negotiations in the Middle East, summed up the mood of an Olympics that could easily have been wrecked: 'I have seen nothing more stirring than the opening and closing days at the main stadium.'

Remarkably, the crisis passed. The United States, which would have felt outraged if the Panama Canal standing in its own hemisphere had similarly been endangered, refused to support Britain and France and even applied financial pressure against them. The Soviet Union, in its own domain, suppressed the angry protests and rounded up more and more Hungarian rebels, including the

Premier, Imre Nagy, who was eventually hanged. The last of the Anglo-French invading forces withdrew from the Egyptian harbour of Port Said, at the southern end of the canal, three days before Christmas.

It was a humiliating episode for these two nations which, ruling so much of the colonial world, had built and guarded the Suez Canal. During the two world wars Britain had made numerous sacrifices in sailors and warships in order to control it. Now Sir Anthony Eden, Britain's prime minister, resigned from office, humiliated by defeat. Nasser, in contrast, was in an enviable position, thanks to the Soviet Union's support. Though the wreckage of his air force and his Russian-made tanks littered the desert, he could clap his hands. The canal was his.

18

VESSELS OF VENGEANCE

In 1903 – the year the first aeroplane flew – a Russian teacher named Konstantin Tsiolkovsky completed a far-seeing book entitled *The Exploration of Cosmic Space*. According to his calculations, a rocket burning a liquid fuel could rise high and then orbit the earth. In the 20 years between the two world wars, amateur and professional scientists of various nations launched rockets, many of which could be carried by hand to a launching site. Some exploded before taking off, others failed to rise, but a few soared to exciting heights. That the rocket and its accompanying missile could be a weapon of war was a spur to these experiments, especially in Germany and the Soviet Union.

Hitler encouraged his rocket chief, Walter R. Dornberger, to experiment at Peenemünde, a German seaside village on the shores of the Baltic. Rockets of increasing sizes were built there in the late

1930s. In some experiments a long-range ballistic missile was launched, amidst a cloud of black smoke, from a tall structure rather like the high diving tower erected at outdoor swimming pools of the era. By 1942 the most advanced rocket could travel at 3300 miles an hour, a supersonic speed that made the fastest aircraft seem like a slowcoach. Here was a novel weapon, maybe capable of clinching victory for Hitler at the very time the German army was advancing far into Russia and the Japanese were extending their military empire almost to the Australian coast.

A REGATTA OF ROCKETS

A triumphant day for Germany was 3 October 1942, when a rocket reached a height of 60 miles. After the launching, Dornberger announced that someday an era of 'space travel' would dawn. This confident news, after further tests, he conveyed personally to Hitler who viewed the films of the launching, and the models of rockets.

When the war turned against the Germans, the novel weapon offered hope that they could regain the initiative. After the coastal factory and experimental station at Peenemünde were bombed by the Allies in 1943, a more secure factory was built underground in the beautiful wooded folds of the Hartz Mountains in northern Germany. Eventually 10 000 employees, many of whom were slave workers imported from captive nations, worked on Germany's rocket program on the seashore and in the mountain tunnels.

Named the Vengeance Weapon, and eventually produced in the hundreds, it was carried to launching sites on the North Sea and targeted against Britain. The rockets appeared over southern England at night, just after D-day in 1944. 'I can see them clearly', wrote a spectator in his diary, 'since they are illuminated like little launches at a regatta.' Their loud noise, he thought, was like that of an express train rushing overhead but in the opinion of many others it sounded more like a loud motor mower. This simpler V-1, noisy and visible from the ground, was driven by an engine that cut out when the target was approached.

The larger and revolutionary V-2, propelled by a rocket, was closely directed only in the first phase of its flight, after which it travelled almost like a golf ball, following its own natural trajectory towards a target that could be several hundred kilometres away. About 24 metres long and shaped to a point like an ornate writing-pen, the V-2 carried a warhead weighing almost 1 tonne. Silent and swift, it inflicted damage on London and the south of England, killing several thousand Britons and unnerving countless others, without proving to be decisive. In a parallel invention, the Germans produced an air-to-air guided missile for making lightning attacks against enemy bombers. The war ended before the completion of these projects which seemed almost as epoch-making as the secret atomic weapon being produced on the far side of the Atlantic.

During the first weeks of May 1945 the advancing Soviet army reached the recently abandoned German rocket base on the Baltic Sea. Several of the high testing-towers still stood. Soviet forces were also first to reach the V-2 factory far underground where they found tools, parts of rockets, and plans and drawings. They captured skilled factory workers but only a few rocket specialists.

In contrast, a team of 116 German specialists and their two leaders fell into American hands – it was their wish to be captured by the

Americans and not the Russians. The chief prize, Wernher von Braun, only 33 years old, was the most experienced rocket scientist in the world. Photographed soon after his capture, he was above middle height, slightly baby-faced, with his hair neatly parted in the middle. Though a broken left arm, in plaster, impaired his glamour he conveyed the air of a minor movie star. Indeed he was a star, for his team was viewed by a few American scientists as one of the main trophies of their victory in the Second World War.

In the United States, von Braun resumed his old work for a new employer. The V-2 eventually became the basis of the Redstone missile in the early American space program; but even in the mid-1950s when Eisenhower was president of the United States his space program did not display the former German vigour. It was almost as if the presence of a famous wartime general in the White House was sufficient assurance that the United States would maintain its supremacy. Therefore the shock was unimaginable when it was learned that the Russians might be snatching the lead. However could it have happened?

When von Braun, his team and his secret plans, were captured by the Americans in the last days of the war, it seemed a decisive blow to the Russians' hopes. In their rocket research the Russians were far behind. Admittedly, they had established a reputation in rocketry before the war but Stalin thwarted their experiments. In 1937–38 his massive purge of those military leaders whom he saw as potential traitors included even rocket scientists: some were killed and others deported to Siberia. When Wernher von Braun was riding to triumph on the shores of the Baltic, Russia's leading designer of rockets Sergei P. Korolev, was working as a labourer in the goldmines of

Kolyma in Siberia. Eventually released, Korolev was allowed to rejoin the Russian wartime rocket program, which was active again. Though accompanied by guards on his journeys, he was now directing a rocket program of importance.

The American capture of most of the German rocket scientists gave Stalin a sense of urgency. The dictator whose whims and suspicions had frustrated the prewar program now promoted the Cold-War program. In secrecy, under the redeemed Korolev, the Russians overcame all kinds of technical obstacles and perfected vital engineering skills until at last there emerged a Russian version of the German V-2. By 1949 the Russians were making test flights with a 'crew' of dogs or rabbits, which were filmed as they sat in their cramped capsules.

To shoot a missile or a space vehicle into outer space, beyond the earth's own atmosphere, called for very high speeds, and they now seemed attainable. There remained doubt whether a vehicle so far away could even communicate with the earth. As late as the 1940s it was mistakenly believed that a layer in the upper atmosphere formed a barrier through which the radio waves could not penetrate. Moreover the typical radio set, being so heavy, was an encumbrance in a small space vehicle sent aloft by a rocket. But that obstacle was brushed aside by the new electronics.

On 4 October 1957 a small Russian vessel, without a pilot, appeared more than 500 miles above the earth. Called Sputnik I, it weighed no more than a healthy grown man. Orbiting the earth in 95 minutes, the sounds from its twin transmitters could be detected by amateur radio enthusiasts. The sounds were heard with dismay in Washington.

A more disturbing sound and sight awaited Washington. There had long been speculation whether an animal or human being could enter a space capsule and be rocketed safely into the heavens. The doubts came from the fact that outer space was an unpredictable environment for living creatures. In the space-research headquarters of the Soviet Union it was recommended – not altogether impartially – that animals should resolve the doubts. On 3 November 1957 the much larger Sputnik II, weighing about half a tonne, went into orbit. It carried Laika, a black and white dog of dubious pedigree. Vital information was gathered from this flight but the passenger did not return to earth.

The American program, even with the help of von Braun, had slipped behind. The shock to the whole nation was intense. The world's greatest military power, it was traditionally the dynamo of inventiveness. But Washington now was humiliated at the very time when it was spreading throughout the free world the concept that communism, since it thwarted personal freedom, was incapable of real creativity and inventiveness. In 1958, as compensation, Wernher von Braun helped to launch the first communications satellite, the primitive Explorer I, followed by another. Within a few years the magical power of a satellite to transmit news and pictures was visible on millions of televisions screens. But for a time that was no consolation, for Russians were winning the space race.

Eventually von Braun vanished from the arena in which he had been, under Hitler's umbrella, the pioneer of the wartime rocket. Hollywood kept his name alive, making him the hero of a space saga called *I Aim at the Stars*. A subtitle for the movie was mischievously suggested: 'But Sometimes I Hit London'.

The tension between Moscow and Washington rose and fell. There were pleasing lulls, and then weeks of anxiety when a nuclear war seemed around the corner. The soaring spacecraft were nervously viewed as a search for vantage points from which to wage nuclear warfare. Europeans, Russians and North Americans knew that they themselves would be the first targets for the nuclear weapons but even remote peoples, unlikely to be nuclear targets, shared the tensions. Kwame Nkrumah, leader of the infant nation of Ghana, regretted in 1958 that independent Africa, on the verge of an exciting future, might see that future wrecked by a thermonuclear war between the superpowers. 'The greatest issue of our day', he said, 'is surely to see that there is a tomorrow.'

A vivid warning came from the popular novelist Nevil Shute. Knowledgeable in engineering, he had been a chief of the team that built and travelled in one of those British airships which, it was once expected, would be the long-distance carriers. Believing that a nuclear war could break out, and that much of the hazard would stem from the radioactive dust, he completed a novel on this theme. The film of his book, *On the Beach*, gave a global audience a gloomy view.

JOURNEY INTO SPACE

In the early attempts to reach for the moon the Soviet Union was also the leader. In January 1959 its unmanned vehicle, Luna I, flew close to the moon. Its younger sister, later that year, reached the moon and crashed there. A third of the sisters went around the moon and, from the side that was permanently concealed from earth, took photographs and transmitted them back.

These triumphs were hailed throughout the Soviet Union. Newspapers proclaimed them; radio programs analysed as many of the scientific breakthroughs as could safely be revealed; and teachers in a thousand schoolrooms explained on blackboards some of the scientific laws that had just been tamed in the interests of space research. It all promoted the greater glory of communism. Possessing low levels of literacy when the Bolshevik revolution began in 1917, Russia was so transformed by networks of kindergartens, primary schools, high and technical schools and universities, all scattered across a vast expanse of territory, that it was able – with little outside aid – to prepare the scientific path for these remarkable journeys.

The ambition to send a person into outer space fascinated both the Russians and the Americans. The dangers were all too apparent. If the vehicle or spacecraft failed to achieve tremendous acceleration at the required speed – and failed to achieve 10 times the speed of the future Concorde aircraft – then the earth's gravity would take over, depriving the spacecraft of momentum and allowing its passengers to crash to certain death. Once aloft, the spacecraft faced a new hazard, being sandwiched between extremes of hot and cold. One side was heated by the rays of the sun to 120 degrees Centigrade while the other side was cooled by the chill, sunless space to far below zero.

Even when the astronaut – that word was new – reached a mere 80 kilometres above the globe he could survive only by living in an intricately designed space suit. The risks were high that in flight he would suffer from an aerial version of seasickness, that his heart and muscles would become slightly smaller under the pressure, and that his bones would lose calcium and become brittle. Because of the weightlessness he had to be strapped down so that he could be stable enough to sleep and to eat. Even then the food did not remain on the plate and the drinking liquid did not stay in the cup. Moreover if any crumbs and fragments of food took to the air and floated about the cabin, they were likely – in freak conditions – to infiltrate the delicate instruments. One of many precautions was to prepare all food in small cubes and coat them with gelatin.

Scientists in both nations grappled with hundreds of such quandaries and challenges, but the Soviets remained the more advanced and the more adventurous. Early in 1961 several Soviet astronauts, trained in deep secrecy, were ready to make a single orbit of the earth. The chosen one, Yury Gagarin, aged 27, had been reared on a collective farm, the son of a carpenter. In his space suit and headgear he looked like a deep-sea diver, with a glass-like door enclosing his face. Whether the cheerful smile he gave to the waiting photographer expressed his feelings is not clear, but a smile was necessary for the beginning of an adventure that combined personal heroism with science and show business. His spacecraft, a most complicated vehicle, was lighter in weight than a small delivery van. Called Vostok I, it was launched on 12 April 1961, at 9.07 a.m., Moscow time.

Soviet officials, fearing that the astronaut might suffer from psychological distress while in orbit, nervously watched his spacecraft soar out of sight. All alone, he must have wondered whether he would ever return; but return he did less than two hours later – at 10.55 a.m., to be precise. One of the most startling events in the history of the world, his voyage excited the people of all nations much more than it did the scientists whose mental framework could encompass it. Briefly he was the most famous man in the world. Declared a hero of the Soviet Union, Gagarin also received the Order of Lenin. He died seven years later, not in outer space, but in an aircraft crash.

One month after Gagarin travelled in space, the United States announced that, by the end of the decade, it would send a man safely to the moon and back again. Moscow made no similar promise. It did not have to. It was ahead in the space race and was expected by many neutral observers to be the first to reach the moon, if that was its goal.

The rocket that launched a spaceship could also launch a missile carrying a nuclear warhead. The science of rocketry and the accuracy and speed of the missiles had advanced far since experiments came to an end in Hitler's Germany. By 1960 more and more American missile sites, situated not far from the Soviet Union, were ready – if called upon – to make a nuclear attack. Some sites, on the border of Turkey and the Soviet Union, targeted the big Russian cities. The Soviet Union could not yet send a missile to the distant United States but its targets, its hostages, were Paris, London, Munich and other European capital cities of America's allies.

While Washington and San Francisco were not yet within the range of the Soviet's land-based missiles, they were within reach of missiles launched by submarines. The United States in 1958 showed what a nuclear submarine could achieve. Setting out from Pearl Harbor the submarine travelled to the far north of the Pacific Ocean, sailing between Siberia and Alaska. After diving under the icecap and passing the North Pole it emerged in the open sea near Greenland. The nuclear engine enabled a submarine to travel vast distances, and to hide for days on the sea bottom, before approaching closer to the nation at which it would direct its nuclear missile. Another version of nuclear attack was made possible by the creation of very small bombs that were both powerful and portable. Theodore Taylor, a young physicist without even a PhD, designed at Los Alamos a tiny specimen bomb that could be as devastating as the first bombs dropped on the two Japanese cities.

THE CONTESTS OF THREAT AND ESPIONAGE

The two superpowers were armed empires, conscious that their huge territories were increasingly vulnerable to attack. They spent massively on armaments; they deployed troops in more and more parts of the world; and they organised battalions of spies. They were engaged in a cluster of contests: a nuclear armaments race, a propaganda war seeking to win the minds and emotions of the world's peoples, a tussle to attract the votes of independent nations in the United Nations, and a spectacular contest to win command of outer space.

The emergence of a new leader was enough to transform the contest. The ultimate successor to Stalin, Nikita Khrushchev, was the son of a peasant. He was theatrical as well as stolid. When he walked in the snow, heavily capped and coated, he was like a large bear; and when he met a delegation of foreigners he was capable of giving them a cheerful hug and responding with a belly laugh. In addition to personal warmth he was capable on selected occasions of displaying a new frankness, for eventually he denounced in public the ruthless purges enacted by Stalin in the name of communism. That Khrushchev himself had taken part in several of them, actually ensuring that the killing of Russian political prisoners was efficient, was not yet known.

Unlike Stalin he was willing to step beyond the communist bloc and taste the pleasures and weigh the threats of the outside world. He visited England in 1956 – no Soviet head had travelled so far west – and later he and his wife, Nina Petrovna, visited the United States. In contrast, no leader of a major democracy had visited Moscow in the last 40 years, except when Churchill briefly talked with Stalin in the Kremlin during the Second World War. Indeed no American president was to accept a Soviet invitation to visit Moscow until the 1970s.

Fear of espionage was one of the factors that prevented these high-level visits. After Harold Macmillan, Prime Minister of Britain, set out on an official visit to the Soviet Union in the cold of February 1959 he realised that it was risky to talk frankly to his own ambassador in Moscow. A protective tent was erected inside the British embassy in the hope that his discussions there would at last elude the hidden Russian microphones. When he travelled in official Russian limousines he was warned that they might be bugged. Though he usually kept a private diary he ceased to make notes for fear that they might fall into the hands of his ever-attentive hosts. In this atmosphere of acute mistrust, the boldness of Khrushchev in travelling abroad, whether to China or Albania or Switzerland, was noteworthy.

A new era of spying began when the latest satellites, passing high overhead, could photograph the rival's territory and bases. At the start of the satellite era, the United States still employed a single-seater jet capable of spying at high altitudes. Gary Powers, flying on behalf of the Central Intelligence Agency, secretly set out from Pakistan to make the long flight across the Soviet Union to a friendly airfield in Norway. His jet was flying high over the Urals on 1 May 1960 when it was detected by Russians and shot down. He parachuted safely, and when captured he could hardly deny his part in a secret mission that Washington persisted in pretending was none of its business. He was sentenced to 10 years in prison, but gained early release in exchange for a Soviet agent.

Just after the spy plane was downed, a long-awaited 'summit' between the four big leaders – Khrushchev, Eisenhower, Macmillan and de Gaulle – was about to take place in Paris. As President Eisenhower did not extend the apologies demanded of his country for the spy-flight, Khrushchev announced after arriving in Paris that he would take no part in the summit, which forthwith collapsed. While he was entitled to feel indignant that his country was being spied upon, he was himself employing satellites, presumably for spying. He was reminded privately by President de Gaulle that the latest Russian satellite had flown over France 'eighteen times without my permission'. Indeed the Cold War was a form of theatre as well as a military contest.

BERLIN'S THREATENING WALL

The tension between the superpowers did not ease in the following year, after John F. Kennedy became president of the United States. Much younger than the world's chief leaders and still inexperienced in foreign policy, he began to make his name. He asked his own Congress, several times, to sanction increased spending on armaments at a time when his nation was definitely superior in nuclear weapons. He supported, as we shall see, a half-baked plan to invade communist Cuba. But he was willing to talk with Khrushchev. They met for the first time in Vienna in mid-1961, and at first exchanged friendly handshakes and hearty assurances. They agreed that there must not be a replay of the Second World War in which, they discovered, each had suffered personal losses. Khrushchev had lost a son and Kennedy a brother during the war with Germany.

The Russian mentally and emotionally dominated their discussions. A blunt and experienced debater, he demanded that the Americans and their allies should completely abandon West Berlin. Kennedy left Vienna, feeling slightly overwhelmed by the Russian's determination.

Khrushchev applied more pressure to the United States and its loyal British ally. In Moscow, attending a ballet in the Bolshoi Theatre in which Margot Fonteyn was starring, he summoned the British Ambassador to his private box at the interval and warned that if any reinforcements were sent to West Germany, in expectation of a crisis over West Berlin, the Soviet Union would retaliate. He pointed out that six Soviet hydrogen bombs would destroy Britain and nine would destroy France. Why, he argued, should 200 million inhabitants of western Europe die simply to preserve the independence of 'two million Berliners'?

An oasis surrounded by communist territory, West Berlin was increasingly a goal for discontented East Germans who longed for a higher standard of living, bright lights and individual freedoms and were now arriving at the rate of 10 000 a month. As East Germany had lost 2 million people in one decade, its People's Chamber

(Volkskammer) found a solution. It resolved, and Khrushchev consented, to post guards around the entire circumference of the city of West Berlin. On the night of 12–13 August 1961, without issuing a warning, the communists began to build a thick fence of barbed wire around West Berlin.

It was a formidable undertaking because the wall had to run for 45 kilometres, completely dividing the largest city into two Germanys. The builders also erected a thick wire fence for another 120 kilometres around the other suburbs of West Berlin that bordered East Germany. For more than a decade the city of West Berlin had been an island, reached overland only by canals, roads and railways that had to pass through East German territory, or reached by planes landing at West Berlin's own airports – now it was completely barricaded. The barbed-wire wall was eventually replaced by a high wall of brick and concrete, often topped by wire, with stretches of electrified fence and armed border-posts running right around the edge of West Berlin. It was literally an iron curtain. Those East Germans who tried to cross it, and refused to halt, were shot. Gateways, railway viaducts, canals, roads and other links between the two zones of Berlin were to be heavily guarded for another 28 years.

DANCERS AND WAR HEADS

The Russians, still ahead in the space race, were determined to catch up to the Americans in the nuclear race. They exploded one of their powerful hydrogen bombs in the open air in their Arctic territory. A further test created the largest explosion in the history of the world – except for the eruptions of volcanoes and the noisy impact of landing meteors.

President Kennedy resolved to tell the world for the first time how far his country was ahead in nuclear weapons. Rather than make the threatening-like speech himself he allowed a senior defence official, Roswell Gilpatric, to read it to businessmen at Hot Springs, Virginia, on 21 October 1961. Gilpatric listed the heavy intercontinental bombers capable of carrying nuclear bombs, the land sites that could launch missiles capable of crossing a continent, and the six Polaris submarines now at sea with their 96 missiles. The grand total was 'tens of thousands' of ships, planes and fixed sites, each of which could fire at least one warhead. The most frightening statement of military might ever made, it slightly put in the shade the Soviet's lead in outer space.

The wonderful publicity from the Soviet astronaut's first orbit of the world was also deflated by an episode at the Le Bourget airport in Paris in June that year. Rudolf Nureyev, aged 23, a brilliant ballet dancer, breathtaking in his leaps, was a master of that artform in which Russia probably still led the world. Born in the remote Siberian city of Irkutsk, and partly of Tatar ancestry, he was an individualist. Even as a teenager he did not always obey the strict rules of Soviet society, and as a Russian on overseas tour he certainly did not conform. His ballet company, the Leningrad Kirov, had performed in Paris and was about to board a plane for London where it was to dance at Covent Garden. There must have been suspicions that the young star would try to defect. Soviet officials prepared to foil him, and he learned or guessed at the last moment that he would be escorted home. Seizing his last opportunity to escape he walked across to French policemen at the airport, and sought asylum. The plane flew to London without him, and he promptly recommenced his dancing career in the west.

Nureyev was more bohemian than any communist regime could permit. Noel Coward, writer of songs and plays, entertained Nureyev and Margot Fonteyn at a dinner in Rome, just three years after his defection. In Coward's diary appeared the note: 'He's a curious wild animal, very beguiling and fairly unpredictable. He is given to sudden outbursts of rage and is liable to bite people.' During the same evening he had bitten Coward's finger – so reported the victim, perhaps with a tinge of pleasure.

The defection to the west of the celebrated dancer damaged the prestige of the Soviet Union. Wherever he danced and whenever he was seen on film, he was a reminder of a regime that resented any spirit of independence in its own leading citizens.

19

EXPLOSIVE ISLAND AND
GHOSTLY GALLEON

No other major nation was as secure as the United States. It had long enjoyed the military security provided by the wide Atlantic and Pacific oceans. Moreover it possessed only three near-neighbours of substance, all far smaller in population and economic might: Canada, with which it usually enjoyed harmonious relations; Mexico, with which it occasionally quarrelled; and the fertile sugar island of Cuba, which was so small that it rarely mattered.

Cuba held only 7 million people, of whom the people of Spanish descent were the most numerous. The democratic tradition, not secure, was respected by the nation's leaders only so long as it kept them in power. Fulgencio Batista followed this tradition. Joining the Cuban army as a stenographer, he was a head of the rebellion that won control in 1933. Seven years later – by now he led the armed forces – he was elected president. In the eyes of many he was an able ruler, but he was also capable of filling his own pockets. In due course Batista was rich enough in his forties to retire to Florida where his newly won money was safe. Returning to Cuba in 1952, he became a dictator and again augmented his bank accounts.

It was Fidel Castro, an opponent of General Batista, who performed the unpredicted feat of conveying the Cold War to the Caribbean. The father of Castro was a Spanish immigrant tilling a cane-sugar farm in a rugged part of the island, and living with a wife and sleeping with a mistress, a cook by occupation. Fidel was one of the five illegitimate children of the cook. After attending a Jesuit boarding school and the law school at the university, and after serving a fiery apprenticeship in politics, he retreated to Mexico. Arriving home with a miniature army he used the security of Cuba's forested mountains to harass the forces of the dictator. On New Year's Day 1959, Castro toppled him. Tens of thousands fled across the strait to Florida while they had the opportunity.

In some ways Cuba was a commercial colony of the United States, just as it had once been a province of Spain. Castro set out to confiscate or expel the major American interests. A nationalist more than a Marxist, he drove out the Mafia which had controlled gambling and drugs, he broke up the big landed estates, apportioning much of their land to peasants, and nationalised the big sugar mills, most banks and many American-owned city properties. America retaliated by removing the valuable preferences that allowed Cuban sugar to fill the bowls on many American kitchen tables. Castro replied by giving official recognition to communist China. This was like waving red flags in the face of a bull. Washington, the bull, responded by banning exports to Cuba except medicines and foods. The decision drove Cuba into the economic arms of the Soviet Union. What had been an American sphere of interest was a Soviet sphere at the end of 1960.

Fidel Castro's grip on Cuba was tightened by the spoken word, for he was a mesmerising orator – at least for the first hour. His propaganda, pervading state-owned radio and television, captured a wide audience because Cuba possessed a higher ratio of TV sets than most European nations, and led all Europe in introducing colour television. Though he dressed like a senior motor-mechanic, wearing work clothes and a peaked cap, he conveyed authority and purpose.

THE NARROW CUBAN SEAS

Narrow seaways, vital for navies in earlier centuries, remained vital. The naval battle between Japan and Russia in 1905 was fought in a narrow strait; the landing on Gallipoli in 1915 was part of a battle for the throat of the Black Sea; and the massive naval contest of the First World War, the Battle of Jutland, was fought near the narrow entrance to the Baltic. Again in the Second World War the English Channel, the Strait of Gibraltar, the Straits of Singapore, the Red Sea and other confined waterways were crucial to the outcome of the war. Early in the era of air power it was widely argued that the narrow seas might not be so decisive as in the waning era of sea power; but Cuba's position near the United States remained of decisive importance.

Cuba had flanked the sea route to Mexico during the era of Spanish empire and was astride the newer sea lanes to New Orleans and, above all, the Panama Canal which was opened in 1914. Many of Cuba's harbours, shaped like horseshoes, were safe for ships. Its air bases, if the need arose, could be used to attack the United States nearby.

The United States, through its Central Intelligence Agency, gave 1500 Cuban exiles military training so that they could invade their homeland. The harbour selected in April 1961 for the landing, the Bay of Pigs (Bahia de los Cochinos) was on the south-western coast; and the small army landed soon after camouflaged American planes had bombed the Cuban airforce. It was strange that President Kennedy should have backed such an embarrassingly small army, for its prospect of success was small. Within two days most of the invaders were captured. Their eventual release came only after a large ransom in the form of food and medicine was paid to Castro.

Khrushchev, who possessed no missile base close to American soil, realised what a valuable ally he had found in Cuba. He snatched the initiative. Three years earlier, Washington had angered him by installing Jupiter missiles in Turkey, close to the Russian border. Now he responded by establishing a Cuban base from which he could fire missiles against the United States. Russian missiles, landed secretly in Cuba, were capable of hitting Washington, and destroying Cape Canaveral on the way.

The threat of an attack on their capital city was a rare experience for American leaders. The last effective raid on the heartland of the United States had been a British thrust into Washington in 1814, when the White House was set on fire. A deadlier raid on a dozen southern American cities was now feasible.

An American spy plane detected the hustle at a construction site in Cuba on 10 October 1962. Four days later President Kennedy learned that 10 Soviet missiles, capable of hitting Washington, were

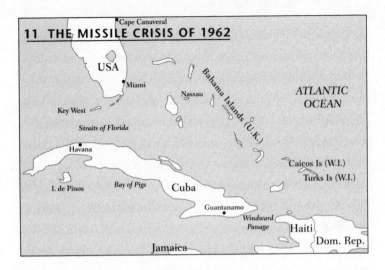

11 THE MISSILE CRISIS OF 1962

USA
Cape Canaveral
Miami
Key West
Straits of Florida
Nassau
Bahama Islands (U.K.)
ATLANTIC OCEAN
Havana
I. de Pinos
Bay of Pigs
Cuba
Caicos Is (W.I.)
Turks Is (W.I.)
Guantanamo
Windward Passage
Haiti
Dom. Rep.
Jamaica

in place. Whether they were equipped with nuclear warheads was impossible to tell. Kennedy now decided to encircle Cuba with a large naval force that could halt and inspect incoming Soviet shipments of war materials. At 7 p.m. on Monday 22 October, speaking on television and radio, Kennedy broke the news to the American people. The Russians, he announced in a short tense speech, were converting Cuba into a launching pad.

Alert journalists thought that the next step might be war. Kennedy saw war as a high possibility. If the two superpowers did fight, they would be tempted to fire missiles carrying nuclear warheads. Of the Soviet shipments of 80 missiles and 40 nuclear warheads, half were already in Cuba and the others were expected daily.

On the evening after Kennedy's speech, 20 Soviet ships were seen approaching the American naval blockade, which had been set up 500 miles from Cuba. One Soviet ship, the *Poltava*, carried nuclear warheads. Two other Soviet ships, protected by a submarine, seemed likely to cross the blockade line, in which event an American warship had firm instructions to force the submarine to the surface. Conferring with colleagues in the cabinet room, Kennedy could see the forbidding implications. Even if the war around Cuba was postponed, he expected that the Soviet Union would attack or blockade West Berlin. Never before had the United States and the Soviet Union been so close to waging war against each other.

Then came reassuring news from the site of the blockade. The Russian ships sailing towards Cuba had turned back – on instructions from Moscow. On 26 October, after days of acute tension, Kennedy offered to end the blockade of Cuba and to give 'assurances against an invasion of Cuba' – if all the Russian missiles were removed from the island. Two days later, Khrushchev promised to remove the missiles. Firm preparations were made for Soviet ships to carry away more than 40 missiles, but Castro refused to allow an inspection of missile sites on his soil. He was adamant that 15 000 Russian scientists, technicians and troops would remain in Cuba.

The relations between the United States and Cuba continued to be tense even after the missiles had been shipped back to Russia. Cuba remained a threat on the doorstep of the United States. Moreover it became a base for exporting revolutionaries and arms to trouble spots in Latin America and to the west coast of Africa, where Cuban troops would later arrive to bolster pro-Russian regimes.

The Cuban crisis was unparalleled. The two confronting powers, in their ability to destroy each other, dwarfed any other pair of nations in history. The venerable historian Arnold Toynbee tried to sum up the continuing peril: 'The human race's prospects of survival were considerably better when we were defenceless against tigers than they are today when we have become defenceless against ourselves.' A nuclear war directed from Moscow or Washington would probably lead not to victory but to mutual destruction.

One year after the end of the Cuban crisis an event in the Texan city of Dallas revived the tension. On 22 November 1963 President Kennedy was shot dead. In Moscow the fear, after the sensational news became known, was that Russia would be blamed for the assassination. In Havana the anxiety was that Castro would be blamed. It was not immediately realised that the assassin, Lee H. Oswald, had deserted the American marines a few years before and had defected to the Soviet Union where he married a Russian. On returning home he had become an ardent supporter of the Fair Play for Cuba Committee. If these facts had been instantly known, all the emotions aroused by the Cuban missile crisis would have been revived, and the full suspicion would have fallen on Moscow and Havana. In fact the Russian and Cuban leaders would not have dared to sanction such an assassination, for they knew the situation would become inflammable.

Khrushchev and his wife, paying more than the respect normally offered to a dead leader, called at the American embassy in Moscow to sign the official book of mourning. Mrs Jacqueline Kennedy responded. On one of her last days in the White House, she sent in her own handwriting a private letter of thanks to Khrushchev. She praised him for possessing the same determination as her dead husband: 'You and he were adversaries, but you were allied in a determination that the world should not be blown up. You respected each other and could deal with each other.' Jacqueline Kennedy requested that her message should be passed on to Mrs Khrushchev, for she heard that the Russian woman 'had tears in her eyes' when she and her husband publicly expressed their sorrow in Moscow.

The threat of a nuclear war persisted. The early fears were that the two superpowers would attack one another, but now Britain and France had also developed nuclear weapons. As more of the secrets of a closely guarded technology were escaping, other nuclear-armed nations might emerge.

On 11 December 1964 the British Cabinet heard Prime Minister Harold Wilson, who had just returned from Washington, delineate the hazards of the world. There was war in the jungles and cities of Vietnam, where the United States hoped in vain that Wilson would become an ally. More importantly, nuclear weapons were *proliferating* – a verb that in the 1960s came to be indelibly associated with such weapons. That China had in 1964 developed its first atomic bomb increased the chances that India would develop its own: the two nations had recently fought one another on their mountain borders. Richard Crossman, writing his diary after returning from the long Cabinet meeting, recorded Wilson's fears of the widening risk of nuclear war. The Indians, said Wilson, 'could become a nuclear power in eighteen months once they had decided to do so'. In due course the Indians did develop nuclear weapons, and then arose the danger that Pakistan would need them, in self-defence. That too came to pass several decades later.

CRISIS ALONG THE CANAL

The narrow seaways, central to the crisis between the United States and Cuba in 1962, intensified another conflict four years later. The

Suez Canal and the Red Sea were at the heart of a dispute that threatened the economic stability of the world.

In the restless peace that returned to the Middle East after the Suez war of 1956, Nasser had strengthened Egypt in arms, secured from the Soviet Union, and in morale. The high dam along the Nile was rising. The daily convoys of cargo ships, oil tankers and passenger liners again passed through the Suez Canal, with the Egyptians collecting the tolls and controlling the pilots. All was well with Nasser's world. He even spoke of that vague entity, 'The Arab Nation', which, should it come to pass, would control half the shores of the entire Mediterranean.

In seeking to widen his influence Nasser gave no sign of the Islamic radicalism that would be bubbling one generation later. A reading of his major speeches in 1958 reveals that they were more secular than religious. Only when he addressed an Arab audience did he conclude with a religious message, which he usually limited to the sentence: 'May God be with us always!' At the same time he continued to oppose Israel, accusing it of 'expansionist ambitions' because of its need to feed and house more and more immigrants. 'The result will be new aggressive actions', Nasser told American broadcasters on 7 April 1958. He hinted that Israel wished to create a promised land running all the way 'from the Nile to the Euphrates'. To the pointed question, 'Did Egypt wish to destroy Israel?', Nasser gave no answer.

During the 10 years after the Suez crisis, the confidence of Nasser and his allies was rising. Syria and Jordan were becoming allies, while the new Palestinian Liberation Organisation was intent on guerrilla activity. On the other hand Israel rearmed itself, acquiring the latest anti-aircraft missiles from the United States. In the Gaza Strip, in sight of Israel's border, more than 3000 United Nations' soldiers tried to keep the peace until May 1967 when Nasser ordered them to leave. He then blocked Israeli ships from entering or leaving Eilat, Israel's only port facing the Red Sea. 'Our basic objective is to destroy Israel', he announced.

Israel, having no wish to be destroyed, replied with one of the most devastating attacks ever made by a small nation. On 5 June 1967, out of a clear sky, its aircraft swooped on Egypt's numerous military airfields. Much of the Egyptian air force was destroyed in a day. The war was virtually over. There had been a military sensation in 1866 when Prussia had defeated Austria in seven weeks – the Seven Weeks' War – but here was a Six-Day War.

In those few days, Israel captured the city of Old Jerusalem and the West Bank from Jordan, took over the Gaza Strip from Egypt, and bulldozed a road up the steep Golan Heights. Captured by Syria in 1948, the Heights were like a stony balcony from which the Syrian soldiers could overlook Israel's Sea of Galilee and Jordan River far below. Along the bulldozed road the Israeli armoured forces fought their way to capture the forts on the Heights. In six days Israel had captured from its enemies a jigsaw of territory that greatly enlarged its own cramped homeland. In the skills of war Israel had been almost too successful. Revenge by its enemies was assured.

Meanwhile, Nasser appealed for help from his friends in Moscow. He was too late. The leaders in Washington and Moscow, having already conferred on the secret telephone channel set up to connect them in times of emergency, decided not to intervene. Here was a comforting sign that the Cold War might be abating.

The short war closed the Suez Canal, littering it with the wrecks of ships. Tankers carrying oil from the Red Sea and the Persian Gulf to Europe and North America, the world's main markets for oil, were therefore diverted to a long, roundabout and expensive route. They had to cross the equator, sail in the strong swell past the Cape of Good Hope, and sail north in the Atlantic Ocean in order to cross the equator again. To cope with this alternative sea route, huge oil tankers were built – too big even to fit into the Suez Canal. When the canal finally was reopened after eight years of idleness, its importance had declined.

MARS AND THE MOON

Khrushchev announced that he would not join in the race to the moon. But his country continued to win many of the prizes along the way. It sent the first woman into space – Valentina Tereshkova. It arranged for one of its astronauts to leave his vessel and walk in space. In both programs the planning was so meticulous, the engineering so precise, that the risks to life were largely eliminated. Only one Russian astronaut lost his life in the first decade of space journeying.

To millions of people the space race was fascinating whenever a familiar landmark in the sky was the destination. Mars was an early destination. One-tenth of the mass of the Earth, Mars was thought likely to hold living organisms. It was Giovanni Schiaparelli, in his observatory near Milan, who had seized the opportunity to examine Mars on 5 September 1877, a day when that planet was close to Earth and the atmosphere above the industrial city was clear. Fixing his telescope on the distant planet he thought he could detect the outline of 41 long channels or canals. If they were canals, he argued, they must be 'the work of intelligent beings'. In the early 1900s the Arizona astronomer Percival Lowell similarly concluded that the dark lines on Mars were evidence of a marvellous civilisation that had dug canals to convey water from the planet's polar ice caps to its plains.

The long-awaited opportunity to inspect the mysterious canals arrived in 1965 when an unmanned American vessel, Mariner 4, flew near Mars. Its instruments could detect no sign of life. Eleven years later the result was confirmed when two robots were landed on Mars. The thousands of photographs and other images transmitted to earth revealed a chill and reddish terrain, strewn with rocks, and swept by rushing winds. It was not until 2004 that two American spacecraft, landing on different sides of Mars, transmitted evidence that long ago the environment might well have been 'hospitable to life'.

Preparations for landing on the moon were pushed forward at prodigious expense. In 1965 a space vehicle took more than 4000 clear photographs of the moon's surface, in an atmosphere that was free from fogs, dust storms, fine volcanic debris, and rain. Later the moon itself was inspected by unmanned spacecraft, both American and Russian. At last, on 16 July 1969 in Florida, a huge rocket, Saturn Five, launched a spaceship and its crew of three Americans. Five days later Neil Armstrong, walking down a flexible ladder – his slow footstep witnessed by hundreds of millions of people on television – stepped onto the surface of the moon. The excitement of those who watched him from afar was intense.

Earlier explorers of distant realms – whether the Americas in 1492 or New Zealand in 1642 – had made their discoveries in relative loneliness, with only a tiny audience as witnesses. Several years passed before news of their adventures finally reached their homeland. But on the surface of the moon in 1969 there was no delay. Neil Armstrong was walking in full view of the world when he repeated the words he had learned by heart: 'That's one small step for a man, one giant leap for mankind.'

After the triumphant walk on the moon there sometimes lingered, down on earth, feelings of regret and even a sense of let-down. Ever since the human race began to flourish, few sights were more soothing, frightening or mysterious than the stars blazing in the dark night sky or the full moon bathing earth and sea with light. The Bible and the Koran hinted at the majesty of such scenes. The Roman poet Virgil watched the evening star 'lighting his late lamps'. Less than a hundred years before the first Sputnik, the priest Gerard Manley Hopkins gazed at 'all the fire-folk sitting in the air', while Alfred Noyes imagined the moon as 'a ghostly galleon tossed upon cloudy seas'. Now, in the course of the long voyages into outer space, the moon and night-sky were tamed by trespassers. Never again would they be quite so mysterious.

20

CLIMBING THE EVERESTS

The 1950s and 1960s were a mix of the exciting and sobering in the western world. Life for millions had returned to normal after two decades of the abnormal: the world depression, an all-out war, and finally in most lands a postwar phase of scarcity and even hunger. Now the recurring fear of a war between the superpowers was offset by a simple sense of wellbeing in the family kitchens and the main streets.

The wellbeing did not come quickly. Many European lands had lost one in every 20 buildings, and Poland and Greece had lost one in every five. Inside European cities that had been bombed and shelled heavily, even the tiniest and most dilapidated apartments were scarce; and newly married couples were delighted if they could find a shared house in which they had one bedroom and the right to share a lavatory and washbasin. In the winters, fuel was scarce, and power stations and gasworks could not produce the power that was needed. In the schools notepaper was a luxury, in the shops clothes were few. Wartime scarcities persisted long after the war was over. In 1950 in some countries, cigarettes and pipe tobacco were not for sale – unless you happened to be an old customer of the tobacconist. A pot of hot tea – so reassuring to the English in an era when they consumed little coffee – could not be brewed too often because tea was rationed until October 1952. Butter, meat and sugar were still rationed in some countries. Meat was scarce in eastern Europe and simply flavoured the soup on many days.

While the United States revelled in abundance, many car-owners in Europe could not buy petrol – unless they had a special coupon as well as the requisite cash. It was difficult to buy a second-hand car, the demand far exceeding the supply. There was one consolation. Most people in 1960 knew that their way of life had improved and would probably continue to improve.

One facet of daily life was totally unexpected. Almost everyone could find work. Whereas jobs were scarce just after the First World War, with many European cities counting their unemployed at 12 or 15 per cent of the workforce, the aftermath of the Second World War provided full employment. Governments, fearful of communism and its apparent attractions, believed their prime task was to provide work; and they did. There had been no period like it for at least 100 years.

On both sides of the North Atlantic and beyond, it was a reassuring era for capitalism and democracy. A system that was humiliated in the early 1930s, and shivering in the shadow of communist Russia, was enormously productive during the first postwar decades.

In the ultimate winning of the Cold War no factor was more important than the sheer drive and inventiveness of the capitalist democracies. At the same time communism, by issuing a challenge and a shock, had played its part. It emphasised that some social security had to be provided by every nation that could afford it; and the western world from the 1940s onwards learned that lesson.

Such were the scarcities of labour after the war that a few European governments sanctioned the arrival of coloured labour. West Indians arrived, shiploads of them, initially to work on London buses and railways. Later came Pakistanis and Indians. Britain's coloured immigrants from its old empire or commonwealth numbered only 10 000 in 1954 but were 14 times as numerous in 1961. Eventually old industrial cities such as Birmingham and Bradford gained large black suburbs; and famous football clubs where a black face was unknown – even in the crowd – began to field teams in which several players, often the stars, were coloured. Mosques and temples arose in neighbourhoods where the Christian chapels had once rung their Sunday bells.

Turks moved into West Germany to work in car factories and other places crying out for labour. Holland acquired a population of immigrants from Indonesia and other colonies. Paris eventually acquired large Muslim populations from North Africa. A slow process, this cross-culture migration began in the era of full employment and went on long after the boom had ended. Nowhere was it more conspicuous than in the United States where the doors were officially opened wide to refugees from communist lands and to migrants from almost everywhere. The Mexicans, meanwhile, were pouring through the back door.

THE URGE TO TRAVEL

In traditional rural life, few people travelled far from home. Even in 1939 probably half the people in the world had not travelled more than 200 kilometres from the place where they were born. Even in Europe, where railways boosted tourism, most adults had not visited a foreign country, and tens of millions had not seen the sea. Many had seen the sea as excursionists for a day. Most European families did not own a car, and even those who did were wary of making long journeys into neighbouring lands.

Aircraft were to promote foreign travel on a massive scale but at first only the well-off could afford a ticket. When Pan American Airways opened the first commercial flight across the Atlantic in June 1939, the four-engined flying boat could carry 22 passengers. Alighting with a splash on the harbour at the Azores to take on fuel, and alighting again on the water at Lisbon where passengers went ashore to sleep, the flying boat resumed its journey to Marseilles the next morning. Flying at night was considered unsafe. It was unimaginable that within one generation, international tourism would become one of the world's major industries.

After the end of the Second World War it was still cheaper to travel to almost every part of the world by ocean liner; and every week the stately mail steamers of the Orient, P & O, Cunard, Lloyd Triestino and other shipping lines would leave Europe for such distant ports as Buenos Aires, Cape Town, Singapore, and Auckland. Most of the colonial officials sent out to administer the empires travelled by sea. Many businessmen crossing the Atlantic favoured the sea voyage, though not by a large margin.

Ten years after the war was over, air travel was booming. The passenger aircraft and their enhanced engines could be heard over London and Paris at all hours of the day; and letters to the editor deplored the commotion. The passenger jets, the first of which was Britain's Comet in 1949, began to expel nearly all large passenger ships from the seas. They were to be reborn as cruise liners.

Tourists who wished in earlier decades to see the hub of Paris, Berlin or Moscow had visited the central railway stations – gigantic temples where the senior staff were dressed like ship's officers, an array of clocks marked the hours of departure for the main trains, and porters eager to carry luggage clamoured for custom. Outside the stations in tall signal boxes were the railways' equivalent of today's flight controllers; and their signalmen, by moving tall vertical levers, decreed which train should have precedence on the railway tracks. In the early postwar years the grand station was challenged by the spacious airport on the city's outskirts. Once a wooden or tin shed, the air terminal became a palace for duty-free shopping; and its waiting crowds had a fashionable look, for initially most people dressed in good clothes for air travel. After Chicago completed its freeway from the inner city to the new O'Hare Airport in the early 1960s, it took pride in operating the busiest airport in the world. One decade later the jumbo jets and the crowds they carried made the wide corridors of the big air terminals as congested as big-city pavements.

Labour-saving devices invaded factories, offices and kitchens in the United States. Cars of new design won admirers in North America and Europe; and the wartime Willys 'Jeep' with its four-wheel drive and the 1948 Willys Station Wagon were marvels. The years 1947 and 1948 were a feast for car-fanciers, even for those who could not afford to buy a new car; and in those two years France produced the cheap Renault 4CV, Sweden produced the two-door Volvo, America the low slung and luxurious Hudson Convertible, and Australia the Holden with its rugged suspension. Italy produced the first Ferrari – called the 166 Spyder Corsa – capable of winning major races, and the German firm that had made the famous Messerschmitt fighter aircraft now made the Messerschmitt 'cabin scooter' for motorists.

CHRISTIAN DIOR AND LOGIE BAIRD

Attractive inventions, fashions and commodities were unveiled in speedy succession in the 15 years after the war. Ideas that could not even be tested in the frugal 1930s and the warring 1940s were suddenly feasible. Rarely if ever in the history of the world had so many innovations or the seeds of innovations appeared.

Everyday life and leisure were shaken and rearranged. The gramophone was transformed by what was called the long-playing record. Magnetic recording, so important to television and the computer, emerged from an earlier Danish invention. The very wide screen, called cinemascope, was installed in many cinemas in the early 1950s. Feature-films in colour, as distinct from black and white, became frequent. A few city newspapers began to illustrate one or two of their news stories with brilliant colour. Hitherto newspapers were simply black and white, except for the red-coloured heading for late news called 'Stop Press'.

Dress shops were reawakened when Christian Dior of Paris, in the chilly February of 1947, introduced his New Look. The frugal, short dresses of wartime – designed to utilise as little cloth as possible – were challenged by his long, flowing, stiff-lined dresses and thin-waist jackets which restored elegance to women's clothing. One bold fashion, displaying bare arms and even bare shoulders, startled the Vatican which responded by decreeing in 1960 that women wearing such clothes should not be allowed to receive the sacrament in church.

The television picture, though its clarity was increasing, had not yet conquered the wide world. Its arrival was slow. Perhaps it owed most to the ingenuity of the German 24-year-old Paul Nipkow, who invented a 'rotating spiral disc' capable of scanning and reproducing images – the essence of television. The British inventor, J. Logie Baird, used a Nipkow disc to produce the ghostly, wriggling images in his early experiments with television – years before public television was first broadcast in London in 1936. Nipkow died in Berlin in 1940, aged 80, just when the art of broadcasting by television was becoming practical.

After the war it was the prosperous United States and its mania for advertising that boosted the demand for television. Whereas its households owned a mere million television sets or receivers in 1949, they owned 50 million in 1959 – more than the rest of the world added together. Most of the sets showed only black and white, and even those images were possible only because of a procession of microwave towers which, roughly 25 miles apart, spanned the entire continent.

Britons fell in love with television. During the coronation of Queen Elizabeth II in June 1953, a godsend to television, it was reported that many British viewers dressed in their best clothes before sitting in front of their set at home. By 1960 two of every three British households watched television. They even adopted the radical idea – defying all the previous rules of family life – of eating their evening meal while watching.

At first vast distances were a barrier to the television picture. There was no way of transmitting it over a wide ocean. A film reel showing street tensions in Berlin had to be carried in a passenger aircraft to New York and rushed to the nearest television studio before it could be transmitted to the American fireside audiences.

A satellite, launched by a rocket, was a potential way of transmitting live broadcasts to the far side of the earth. The first broadcasting satellite had been envisaged as a space station in which the crew took up residence, but an unmanned satellite could also transmit television. A momentous satellite was launched on 10 July 1962. Moving quickly around the globe, it beamed live television across the Atlantic in those brief periods of the day when conditions were favourable. To be sitting by a television set in Paris and watching a spacecraft launched in Florida was a fascinating experience for the generation of viewers who first experienced it.

The satellites were improved and multiplied. The opening ceremony of the Olympic Games in Tokyo in 1964 was transmitted live to Europe and North America. Next year the wonderful satellite called Early Bird sang its first message. Soon it was transmitting pictures of a war in which large American forces were absorbed. The day's episodes of jungle warfare, filmed in South Vietnam and beamed next evening into millions of living rooms in America, boosted the peace movement. In New York one television critic labelled Vietnam 'the living-room war'. The grip and immediacy of television was increased by colour, which the United States and

Japan were the first to embrace. Not until 1967 did the Soviet Union, Germany, France and Britain introduce colour television.

Television immersed whole nations like a tidal wave, except that they ran to greet the wave. It enhanced or tainted most facets of daily life: leisure, sport, music, religion, politics, news, cooking, advertising, morality, children's playtime, and even national pro-nunciation and grammar. An Italian author Enzo Biagi argued that television finally gave to the diverse regions of Italy and Sicily and Sardinia a common language and customs: 'Television has done more for the unification of Italy than Garibaldi and Cavour did.' In symbolism and emphasis the same television aerial pointed in opposite directions, promoting intense nationalism through sport, and fostering internationalism by offering viewers a sympathetic glimpse of life in foreign lands they had barely heard of. While giving enormous pleasure, television could be insidious. As Sir David Frost observed: 'Television is an invention that permits you to be entertained in your living room by people you wouldn't have in your home.'

As soon as television was widely watched in a big city, the sub-urban cinemas began to close, the afternoon newspaper began to decline, and the radio stations lamented the departure of their evening audience. The future of the book was initially said to be endangered, but was not. The big political meeting in the town hall or the street square soon gave way to the debate in a television studio: a nation's political leader grew in importance, and the opin-ions of the second and third ranks of politicians were relegated to the radio or a letter to the newspaper. Television often converted political debate into the half-minute mouthing of rival half-truths. It seemed in retrospect that the Japanese were wise in not allowing – until 1969 – their election contests for the Diet to occupy television space.

This was the decade when the portable radio made its startling conquest of streets, public transport, and summer beaches. Whereas the early radio set was a heavy item of furniture, kept permanently in one room of the house, and listened to by the whole family, the new transistor radios were tiny and cheap. The luckier teenagers could carry their own radio, though the cackle of broadcasts coming from so many hand-held radios was at first disturbing. A solution devised on the Italian island of Capri in 1963 was to ban the transistor radio in public places, but the real answer was the ear-plug speaker.

Nothing did more to spread the pop culture – and its songs directed to the young – than the transistor radio. This individualist product came from Japan, a culture that theoretically did not approve of utensils that diminished the authority and unity of the family. The first tiny radio or 'trannie' – the Sony portable six-transistor model of 1958 – was not much bulkier than a double packet of cigarettes, and could be held close to the ear. At the big sporting stadiums arose the spectacle, strange at first, of people watching the game while listening to a radio commentator telling them what they were seeing. By the 1980s the so-called 'Walkman' and the tiny transistor radio were common. By the year 2000 the tiny hand-held telephone was to be in vogue, and people walking along a busy street could be heard enthusiastically imparting into their mobile phone intimate matters in loud voices.

THE RISE OF THE COMPUTER

In about 1560 an unknown craftsman in Germany made a fascinating wooden toy that today can be inspected in the Deutches Museum in Munich. Called the Preaching Monk it was distinguished by a beard and sandals; and to disguise the simple iron, mechanical, workings installed near its feet it wore a long wide cloak that was almost a male version of the crinoline. Progressing on concealed wheels, the stiff legs moved in rhythm, the arms swung, and the head turned from side to side. As a sequence of controlled steps were programmed inside the toy, it could be called a forerunner of the computer.

That the monk could walk was a revelation. What if it could be persuaded to add and multiply? Almost three centuries later, accountants and bankers often relied on printed tables to calculate wages, prices, rates of interest and the cost of life insurance, and captains of ships relied on printed astronomical tables to help them when navigating. Charles Babbage set out to help them. A gifted and somewhat cantankerous mathematician, he designed a machine that could make calculations with speed. He called his manually operated machine the 'Difference Engine'. Almost half of the 25 000 individual parts that Babbage needed for his engine were made in the early 1830s but he then developed a streamlined engine that required only 4000 parts. Made of gunmetal, steel and cast iron, and weighing about 3 tons, the new calculating engine slightly resembled a big organ-grinder or player-piano. It was not completed. A century and a half later, in 1991, a model of this machine was completed by the Science Museum in London as a gesture to mark the bicentenary of Babbage's birth. He would not have been surprised to know that his machine worked.

As Babbage's machine could imitate human mental skills, it was bound to spur imitators. Just before the Second World War it was taken up by young scientists including a Berlin engineer named Zuse, and a young British mathematician named Turing. Conceived in British India and born in London, Alan Turing was eccentric, untidy in dress, a long-distance runner and persistent in chasing brilliant ideas. At about the age of 25 he published a description of an automatic computing machine which, he hoped, could compute all the numbers 'which could naturally be regarded as computable'. A few years later his talent was harnessed in wartime England where, from 1939, he worked in secrecy for the official Code and Cypher School at Bletchley, on the railway line between Oxford and Cambridge, from which so many of Bletchley's talented staff were recruited.

Bletchley's mission was to crack the secret codes used by Nazi Germany in communicating with its naval and military commanders and its allies. Alan Turing hoped to unravel the German code called Enigma by enlisting mechanisation to sort and classify combinations of its code words. The code-breaking formula had to be programmed in advance, because the time available for unravelling an intercepted radio message was brief, and moreover the Germans varied their code. By the time a secret message was uncoded, a German submarine or warship receiving that message might have completed its mission of destruction. As a vital preliminary to unravelling future German codes, an existing German code had to be captured. One of Germany's armed trawlers was boarded so speedily near Norwegian islands on the Arctic Circle in February 1941 that the captain was shot before he had time to destroy his secret papers.

Alan Turing's colleague, a young mathematician named Max Newman, helped to build in high secrecy an electronic digital computer that was relatively quick in sorting information. Riding on the back of generations of earlier metallurgical and engineering advances, it was the first special-purpose and large-scale computer ever built. Quaint and plodding by today's standards of breathtaking speed, and holding 1500 electronic valves, it was so large that it deserved its name, Colossus. For each new project, it had to be wired afresh. As it was capable of scanning 25 000 characters in the one second, its speed enabled the British to decipher secret German messages, and so learn the whereabouts and plans of attack of the German submarines that dominated the Atlantic Ocean, especially in 1942. This computer was a vital part of a secret code-breaking project that yielded so much knowledge of German plans, on sea and land, that it increased the chances of a British and American victory.

Already the uses of the computer in peacetime were foreseen. At the University of Manchester, Newman and two engineers set out to build a grander postwar machine. Completed in June 1948, it received the ornate name of 'The Manchester Automatic Digital Machine', but the day was near when plain English would win, and the simple word 'computer' would reign. Alan Turing, now in Manchester, marvelled at the cumbersome machine and forgave its inadequacies. In the journal *Mind* in October 1950 he ventured the brave prediction that computers would ultimately 'compete with men in all purely intellectual fields'. He did not live to see it happen, for he swallowed poison at the age of 41.

England was ahead in various facets of computing in 1952, with two rival machines operating at the Manchester and Cambridge universities, and the baking firm of J. Lyons already operating a computer to automate its payroll. In this fast advancing industry the United States was about to snatch the lead. Its first automatic, electronic digital computer had been built at the University of Pennsylvania in 1946 at the request of the United States army which could see the advantage of making quick calculations to guide soldiers in firing artillery. The American machine, dwarfing the earlier one at Bletchley, was blessed with a powerful memory, devised by Johann von Neumann, a Hungarian-born mathematician. The needs of the Cold War, including a capability to intercept enemy weapons in flight, called for infinitely faster computers. Most were built in the United States.

By 1955 in the whole world about 250 massive computers were at work, some occupying an area as large as a suburban living room. Consisting of half a million connections, each soldered by hand, they were also gluttonous for vacuum tubes, of which they required as many as 18 000. The computer was at the stage that the steam engine had reached when Boulton and Watt were busily improving it in the 18th century: cumbersome, expensive, and not used widely. A mammoth, its size had to be reduced. The transistor or semiconductor, first made by the Bell Telephone Laboratory in 1947, was a solution. Like many advances the transistor was spurred by the war, being developed in England to help radar research and then in the United States to guide warfare against submarines. It not only made possible the small portable radio set but also converted the computer into a smaller, faster instrument.

In some ways each computer was like a giant telegraphic network, tightly joined together; but the wiring, instead of being elongated, was coiled and crammed into a confined space. Even in the late 1950s a computer needed a mass of wires that had to be soldered together in a painstaking way at countless joining points. Once it was working it was vulnerable at the joining points, for one fault was sufficient to close down temporarily the entire transistor circuit.

At a company called Texas Instruments, Jack Kilby, a 34-year-old engineer, worked in the laboratory during the summer of 1958, when most of his colleagues were on vacation. Using his temporary freedom he looked for a way of thinning the jungle of wires that supported a computer. By carving the various parts of the complicated circuit on a block or chip of silicon he eliminated the mesh of wires, thus saving space and reducing the need for running repairs. In a sense Kilby was the Marconi of the new electronics industry; and only at the very end of the century was the magnitude of his contribution appreciated: he was awarded a Nobel prize for physics. A chain of other innovations had to be tested before the silicon chip could revolutionise work in home, office and factory, and before the computer, satellite, optical fibre and other devices become, in their ability to reshape work and leisure, the potential successor to the mighty steam engine.

MOUNTAINS AND OCEANS: THE CONQUERORS

The computer fired the imagination, but the climbing of the world's highest mountain also aroused wonder. In the exploration of the earth, pursued over thousands of years, the climb was viewed by some geographers as the last of the spectacular triumphs.

After virtually all the high peaks in Europe and the Americas had been climbed, ambitious mountaineers turned to central Asia.

Straddling the border of Nepal and Tibet, the iced escarpments of the Himalayas were a challenge, especially as the higher altitudes were deficient in oxygen. Mount Everest, at 29035 feet the tallest peak in the world, was the main goal; and in the 1920s and 1930s the teams of climbers – French and Swiss, German and British, Polish and Italian – climbed into its clouds. One of the leading climbers was F. S. Smythe, who had been retrenched as an airman in Egypt partly because of sickness. He led the first Himalayan party to climb more than 25000 feet. Prominent in other attacks on unclimbed peaks were Germans, of whom 16 were killed by an avalanche in 1937.

Mount Everest was now such an obsession, with personal and national pride at stake, that a veteran English mountaineer, Tom Longstaff, who in earlier decades had climbed numerous peaks in Asia, said of Everest, in exasperation: 'For Heaven's sake climb the wretched thing and let's get back to real mountaineering.'

The Second World War pushed the 'wretched thing' out of sight. It also produced for alpine soldiers and high-flying airmen in Europe a cluster of novel items that the mountaineers, eventually returning to the foot of Mount Everest, eagerly adopted. There were oxygen tanks, collapsible stoves, walkie-talkie radios, light and cosy clothing, and even a mortar-like gun capable of dislodging snow and ice. Colonel John Hunt commanded this best-equipped of all British expeditions to tackle Mount Everest. Two of his climbers – Edmund Hillary from New Zealand and an experienced Sherpa guide, Tenzing Norgay – were sent ahead of the team. On 29 May 1953 they stood alone on top of the world. The victory of Hunt's team coincided with the ascent of young Queen Elizabeth II to the throne, making it appear to be the year of the young in a Britain that, according to some critics, was feeling its age.

The ocean too had its conquerors. Shiplovers who gathered at the ocean headlands or at the city wharves, noticed in the late 1950s an unexpected change. Newer ships were changing shape: at the start of the Second World War a big oil tanker was about 15 000 tons deadweight but by 1960 it was 100 000 tons – a long monster of a ship that was far too big to glide through the Suez Canal when carrying oil from the Middle East. Soon ships of 200 000 tons were carrying iron ore or coal across the oceans.

Another newcomer was the container ship, her open deck packed with large boxes. She was the solution to long-standing problems. For generations the task of carrying goods from wharf to ship – and moving them at the end of the voyage from ship to wharf – had absorbed an army of physically strong men. They practised the old methods: lowering the cargo with the aid of a winch into the hold of the ship, and then carrying by hand or on the shoulder the individual cargo boxes, sacks and bags to the chosen spot in the hold and stowing them there, one by one. In many western lands, partly as a result of these ways of work, the waterfront carried the scars of fierce industrial conflicts and a record of crippling accidents and injured backs. Men hated their bosses and the feeling was reciprocated.

There must be easier ways of moving cargoes. Perhaps items could be packed into huge boxes, thereby saving the constant re-handling. The same box or container could be fitted onto semitrailers or railway wagons for the journey from a factory to the nearest port, loaded onto the ship, carried to a far-off port, and then unloaded onto a truck or rail wagon. This idea was tested in the United States in 1960 when a ship of the Matson Line, with 436 large containers in her hold, sailed from San Francisco to Hawaii. By the use of wharf cranes and containers a skilled team could safely load or unload in a few minutes a consignment of cargo that previously might have required five or more hours.

Harry Bridges, head of the waterfront union, persuaded workers in Californian ports to adopt the new method permanently. They agreed to the mechanising of the waterfront at San Francisco and Oakland in return for much higher wages. Three changes were soon visible. The army of men dwindled; industrial relations improved; and the theft of cargoes was reduced because the strong container was normally locked and sealed.

The giant tankers, bulk carriers, and container ships decisively cut the cost of carrying raw materials across the world. Every motorist, every shopper gained from lower prices. The effects on some lands were almost as revolutionary as the transition from sail to steam during the previous century.

THE EMERGENCE OF JAPAN

In Britain old workmen could remember the era when their country dominated the world's seas. In 1900 both its armed navy and merchant navy were the largest in the world, and the British flag waved over ports around every continent. British ships carrying British coal were seen in a hundred ports. Britain was also the world's biggest builder of ships: the huge liner *Titanic* was built in Belfast, and orders for battle cruisers to be built in British shipyards came from navies as far away as Turkey and Australia.

Between the two world wars Britain lost some of its ascendancy in seafaring activities, but as late as 1950 it was building 40 of every 100 tons of shipping in the world. Rapidly its lead was overtaken by Japan which improved the assembly-line processes that had been devised by Americans in wartime to build their astonishing tally of 2600 Liberty ships. In 1956 Japan passed Britain to become the world's largest builder of ships, and 10 years later it was far ahead. Rarely in a major global industry had one nation superseded the long-time leader so quickly.

Other Japanese industries jumped ahead. The Korean War in the early 1950s gave Japan, lying just across the straits, the opportunity to supply many American needs in the war zone. Japan ventured into the new electronics. Wherever there was an overseas market, Japanese salesmen were busy. From 1966 to 1970, Japan's rate of economic growth averaged an annual 12 per cent which, all in all, was probably more impressive than China's dazzling rate of growth at the end of the century.

At one time it seemed unlikely that the Japanese – leaders in the manufacture of trucks – would ever make first-class cars capable of storming the home of the mass-produced automobile, the United States. In the 1920s Japan had exported a few of their own Datsuns, which resembled the Austin Seven, a very small English car that competed with the motor bike and its attached sidecar. When in the 1930s the Japanese house of Nissan began to make a big fast six-cylinder car, its design was largely borrowed from Detroit. The house of Toyota, which originally made textile machinery, branched into cars with an inaugural model that resembled another US car, the Chrysler Airflow. Mr Honda had a contract to make piston rings for Toyota before building the small-engined motorcycle, which by

1960 was the world's most popular. Beginning in humble ways these vehicles were not always taken very seriously outside Japan. Initially imitating the best from overseas, the Japanese were dismissed as copycats. Before long they were showing the way.

The Japanese automobile industry leaped over barriers. The huge car markets of North America and Europe were almost out of bounds, for they were protected by tariffs, by the nationalist preferences of Italians for a Fiat or the French for a Peugeot and Renault, and by the huge production runs of American cars. The Japanese responded. They began to saturate their own market – only a few of the rich had owned a car one generation earlier – and export at competitive prices. Their Honda Civic with its tiny, efficient engine caused a small sensation in the United States in the early 1970s when expensive petrol – and the rise of women car buyers – lifted it into favour. By then Japan was the second biggest maker of cars in the world.

The car in its popular postwar era was moulded by the losing nations of the Second World War. Ferdinand Porsche had been instructed by Hitler to design a simple Volkswagen; and at the Berlin motor show in 1938, Hitler declared that it would eventually become 'the general means of transport for the German people'. It was mass produced for the German market in 1939, not a year in which to launch a new model. Thirty years later the people of many nations, some of which had fought Hitler's Germany, relished this frugal beetle-like car. Meanwhile the Japanese, now the master of automotive electronics, turned their skills to the larger car, and eventually their latest Toyota was to outnumber the latest Ford on America's own freeways.

The economic success of Japan was at first seen as the result of unique causes. But it was the herald of the economic success achieved by South Korea, Taiwan, Hong Kong, Singapore, Malaysia, Thailand and later China and India. Ever since the industrial revolution, manufacturing had been the economic activity in which the peoples of European birth or descent were the specialists. It was a source of their success in warfare, and the employer of the biggest section of their workforce. By 2000 it was as if the Ruhr had moved to China, Birmingham had moved to India, and Pittsburgh to South Korea. Many of the major steelworks, shipyards, car and textile factories, chemical and electronic works now stood on ground that at the start of the century grew mostly rice.

21

THE CHEF AND THE DOCTOR

The sharp rise in foreign travel, spurred by cheap air fares and the longer annual holiday, quickened the appetite for exotic food in the home city. In Bonn, Toronto and 50 other western cities the numbers of fine restaurants grew – in France and Italy they already flourished. The banker and his wife, the lawyer and his family, the headmistress and her husband and all those people of similar social standing who in the 1930s had entered a restaurant only for a wedding breakfast, if at all, now ate out in style, five or even 20 times a year. Business lunches multiplied, and lasted until not a drop of wine remained.

The fashion for eating out was aided by rising prosperity and the advent of smaller families. In the era of many sons and daughters – aided by the presence of several servants in the more prosperous households – the family meal in the evening and the meals at weekends, with each child in a set place, was a pillar of family life. By 1960 the presence of fewer children and the corrosive effects of prime-time television – and its programs that absolutely had to be viewed – undermined the formal evening meal. To dine out occasionally became almost a substitute for that traditional meal at a dining table, set with a white cloth by the domestic servant who, after the war, vanished forever.

The decline of church-going coincided with the rise of the restaurant in the Protestant west: indeed a favoured restaurant became a place to be seen in and a place for exchanging gossip – roles that the church had provided on Sunday. The growth of the restaurant in various western cities and lands was also aided by the decline of the temperance and teetotal movement, which even in the 1930s had been vigorous in the United States, Canada, Scandinavia, Britain, Australia, New Zealand and a few other nations. At the height of the temperance crusade, a host of Protestant churchgoers had been reluctant to enter a restaurant or a hotel that served meals, for on the table sat temptation itself, a wine bottle with a German or French label.

French wine found increasing favour in the British Isles. 'For every Briton who had seen some of the more renowned French vineyards before the First World War there must be a thousand today', wrote the wine critic P. Morton Shand in 1960. The roads winding towards the famous French vineyards were now signposted in minute detail so that motorists on summer holiday could call in for tastings; and Shand depicted fresh amateurs relishing that 'brief enraptured moment: a whiff of the unforgettable scent of the vine in flower coming round the windscreen on a smiling May morning'.

This engulfing fashion for wine led eventually to a torrent of New World reds and whites, outselling French wines in many British and Scandinavian bottle shops.

Julia Child helped one of the world's richer and more puritanical nations to view its menu afresh. A Californian, she worked for US Intelligence in wartime K'un-ming where the American food she ate was 'terrible' and the regional Chinese food was a revelation. When her husband was posted to Paris she studied cooking at the Cordon Bleu school with such zest that, finally making her home in Boston, she gladly launched in 1963 a television series called 'The French Chef'. As more Americans watched her cooking, sipping, and chatting, and enjoyed the multiplying newspaper columns on wine and food, their preferences and palate – especially after their first stint of foreign travel – began to change.

After the cover of *Time* magazine displayed her slightly tomboyish face on 25 November 1966, she was known across the nation. In due course her home kitchen was deemed to be a domestic monument, and it was placed as a permanent exhibit in the National Museum of American History in Washington where spectators can now see her sprawling table, big stove with its six cooking points, utensils arranged on walls in the style of a carpenter's workshop and, still visible, the white napkins that she wore when she ate, drank, and occasionally spilled French wine.

In 1960, when large groups of Americans and Britons showed this growing devotion to exotic meals and fine cooking, the French influence was vital. It was a time of ferment in French cuisine, though daredevil chefs were not yet arranging on their large and half-empty plates their 'nouvelle cuisine'. Curiously France was spreading its refinements at the very time when its own language, for long a desirable accomplishment amongst cultured Europeans of all nationalities, was being shouldered aside by English as the global language.

The typical English-speaking family did not yet eat out – unless they bought fried fish, potato chips or saveloys and consumed them piping-hot in the street or carried them home. To eat in a cafe or restaurant was too expensive. To eat cheaply in a chain of quick-food restaurants was not yet the fashion. Here the United States, where time was precious, would show the way.

By the end of the century a profound change in cooking and eating – and every day life – was far advanced. At the century's start, the kitchen had been the hub of the typical household. Flour and sugar and basic foods were stored in bins and bowls, and from the rafters hung onions, herbs and smoked sides of meat. On a stove kept alight by wood or coal, nearly all the meals were cooked and the water boiled for drinks and clothes-washing. Much of a woman's life was spent in the kitchen, preparing food and doing numberless other tasks. By 2001 this way of life was becoming unusual in Europe, the Americas, much of Asia and all of Australasia. Tinned, canned, packaged and frozen food had taken over the shelves. Gas and electric stove, and microwave oven, had replaced the fuel-burning stove and its nearby coal cellar or stack of firewood. A sleek cluster of specialised machines ranging from hot-water jug to toaster, coffee machine and dish-washer had crammed themselves in spaces so tiny as to be called kitchenettes. As a result the daily time spent in preparing and cooking meals had been cut drastically.

Standing in pride of place in the fireless kitchen was the tall refrigerator. A brainchild of the United States, only 5000 were produced in 1921. But 30 years later, nine of every 10 urban households in that country used a refrigerator. In the final decade of the century an arresting statistic came from Brazil, a country where some regions were very poor. In Brazil, 75 per cent of all households owned a refrigerator: it was more common than a phone.

Across much of the world, in western and eastern hemispheres, the can-making and food-processing factories – and supply lines of road transports, refrigerated ships and cargo aircraft, the supermarkets and fried-chicken shops, and the power lines and gas mains – had served to push aside and remake the old-time kitchen. An extraordinary change in human work and social history, it happened in one lifetime, and already half of the world was experiencing it.

THE BATTLEFIELDS OF MEDICINE

Katherine Mansfield was born by the windy shore of the harbour at Wellington, New Zealand, in 1888. The wooden house of her childhood, two storeys in height, was wedged between the harbour and hills that were almost too steep to be built on. Inside the house can still be seen a photo of Katherine at about the age of 10: eager, attractive, and wearing small spectacles. In London in her twenties, a distinguished writer, she caught tuberculosis and went to Switzerland in search of a cure.

In a chalet in a forest clearing, with a view over the treetops, she described a typical day she spent with her husband in the summer of 1921. Writing, reading and always smoking their cigarettes, the couple worked methodically, she observed, 'like two small timetables'. Eighteen months later she died, at the age of 34, of the disease that was viewed by some as a special enemy of intellectuals. Victims in her own lifetime, and a little later, included the writers Robert Louis Stevenson, Anton Chekhov, Franz Kafka and George Orwell.

The deaths from infectious diseases filled the record books of cemeteries. The United States as late as 1908 attributed more deaths to tuberculosis than to any other cause. Around the world during the previous century this single disease, by its persistent death toll year after year, probably killed more people than all the wars added together in the same period. Other infectious diseases – smallpox, tuberculosis, scarlet fever, rheumatic fever, typhoid, cholera, malaria, measles and whooping cough – could kill tens of millions in a short time. Just after the First World War, the Spanish influenza killed as many people as the war itself.

Katherine Mansfield's brother had died in 1915, on the western front, when she was living in England. When we visit the French war cemeteries of 1914–18 and read his name and millions more on the white headstones or the memorial walls, and when we visit the war cemeteries of 1939–45 and see the headstones near Rangoon, Singapore or Florence, we lament the death of so many, most of whom were young. But if we visit a thousand civilian cemeteries and are shown the scattered graves of the young who died in the same period of simple diseases that are now curable, we might equally be shocked. In the course of the 40 years after the outbreak of the First World War those who died of infectious diseases are likely to have far exceeded those who died violently on the battlefields.

The Second World War gave a sharp stimulus to medical discovery. The urgent and competitive atmosphere of war and its aftermath seemed to stimulate research. The 1940s and the 1950s, in their ability to save human life, were surpassed by no previous decades. The loss of life in the Second World War was sobering, but it was low compared to the lifesaving gains that stemmed from the medical discoveries, many of which were spurred by the war and the emergencies it created.

The ability to combat malaria in the tropics was enhanced by the experience of war. Amongst the Australian and American soldiers fighting in New Guinea and the island of Guadalcanal in 1942, the malaria was often more dislocating than wounds inflicted by the Japanese – until the correct daily dose of atebrin was determined by thorough tests conducted at Cairns in Queensland. In addition, the swamps that bred mosquitoes were tamed by the new Swiss chemical called DDT. One reason for the success of the invasion of Japanese-occupied Burma in the last phase of the war was that troops could at last cope with malaria. The global campaign against malaria after the war was even more a beneficiary.

The discovery of penicillin, like most wartime advances in medicine, owed much to earlier research. There had long been a search for a medicine that would attack a specific disease without attacking the whole body. In 1910 the German Paul Ehrlich, building on his own nation's remarkable discovery that bacteria caused diseases, devised an arsenical potion that could attack syphilis but not weaken the whole body's resistance. Another new substance attacked sleeping sickness, the curse of central Africa. In 1932 the German research laboratories of the giant chemical firm IG Farben developed the first of the sulpha drugs which, in the following 10 years, began to challenge pneumonia and dysentery.

A more important discovery along these lines was made in the Second World War. Howard Florey had travelled as a young scholar from Australia to Oxford where, seeking a way of fighting microbial infection, he experimented with a tantalising bacteria mould that had been observed earlier by a London bacteriologist Alexander Fleming, but not persevered with. Assisted by Dr Ernst Chain, a research chemist who had fled Berlin, Florey achieved exciting results with a resultant drug that he called penicillin. Tests with mice in May 1940 – just when Hitler's army was racing towards the English Channel – indicated that the penicillin had the potential to save lives. After effective clinical trials the new antibiotic, awarded the highest priority, was mass-produced in America.

Flown to battle-front hospitals, it began to work its miracles, specially on patients who had undergone serious surgery or were suffering from venereal disease. Never had a novel and precious drug descended in such a deluge. Previously rare, the penicillin was soon abundant enough to treat nearly all the urgent cases in the American and British armed forces, with some to spare for the Russian hospitals. Penicillin saved tens of millions of lives during its first half century, and its success led to the discovery of drugs that attacked other infectious diseases.

Tuberculosis was so common that it was one of the few diseases to be known by its initials – it was simply called TB. Spread by coughing and spitting, and by the sale of polluted milk, it continued to be the target for medical investigations. France introduced a vaccine – not as effective as was hoped – against the disease in 1921.

Germany imposed a compulsory X-ray on its soldiers recruited in the 1930s, and at Rutgers University near New York in 1944 an Ukrainian-born scientist, whose speciality was soil microbiology, made influential discoveries. Analysing microbes that flourished in soils, Professor Selman Waksman and a research student found an enemy of microbes. It became the basis of the drug, streptomycin. After further Swedish, German and American discoveries during the next 10 years, the campaign against tuberculosis seemed to be on the way to victory. Like many other victories, however, it would depend heavily on improved hygiene and nutrition.

Children's illnesses were curtailed and cured by painstaking research and occasionally by individuals who, having no high degrees to their name, had to shout before their voice was heard. Between the 1930s and the 1950s many children were victims of severe epidemics of poliomyelitis. Enclosed within an 'iron lung' with its strange hissing sound, or lying stiffly on beds with their legs held rigid by splints, the sick children and teenagers were a pitiful sight. A novel way of attacking the disease was advocated by an Australian nursing sister, Elizabeth Kenny. Her pleas that the rigid splints favoured by medical opinion were a hindrance to recovery, and a physical and psychological danger to the sick child, aroused feverish controversy. Public support for her, at a time when polio was often in the headlines, was startling. In 1951 an American poll, enquiring which woman in the world was held in the highest esteem, gave second place to Mrs Eleanor Roosevelt and first place to Sister Kenny.

Some of the controversial methods she practised were eventually accepted, though the lasting attack on polio came from medical research and systematic vaccination. After Jonas Salk of Pittsburgh developed, in 1955, a safe vaccine that could be injected with a needle, polio was in retreat. Rheumatic fever, so often diagnosed in the first half of the century, was also wilting but less rapidly.

Surgeons too were making brave experiments. For a defective heart, which was once an insoluble defect, help was in sight. Those suffering from certain disabilities could be fitted with a device initially called 'a pacemaker for the heart'. It was not yet appropriate to label it as simply a pacemaker, for that word belonged to professional cycling and racing. As the pacemaker was not yet in miniature form, the recipients, once they had been treated by the surgeon, had to carry the necessary electronic equipment in a pocket or handbag. For children suffering from congenital heart disease, which was now close to the largest cause of death in American babies, open-heart surgery was practised cautiously and riskily. Soon the success rate would leap. To the general public one of the stunning events in medical history was the successful transplant of a heart, first performed by Dr Christian Barnard at Cape Town.

Another spearhead of medical research, a tiny object called the gene, aroused only modest excitement in the early 1950s. Like a grain of sand but far smaller, the gene was found to be the humblest item in the building block of life. Unlike sand, the gene could reproduce itself. Transmitted from parent to child the genetic information was encoded on molecules of DNA, which is short for deoxyribonucleic acid.

DNA was unravelled by two researchers who between them did not have wide experience: Francis Crick, an Englishman in his mid-thirties, and James Watson, an American who was younger.

As Watson later suggested, the simplest path to scientific discovery is 'to stay away from subjects that are overpopulated', and that proved an advantage. They had come together in 1951 at Cambridge University, in the laboratory that one generation previously had been the birthplace of the innovative process called X-ray crystallography. Possessing little equipment or money, they were blessed with intuition and an alertness to the clues offered by those in the forefront of X-ray crystallography and chemical theory. One scientist in the forefront was Rosalind Franklin, who was happy to work largely on her own. 'Rosalind was so intelligent that she rarely sought advice', recalled Watson half a century later, but she generously passed on ideas, thus stimulating the tentative theory being developed by Crick and Watson. She was to die of ovarian cancer before the value of her own research was fully appreciated.

The success of Crick and Watson came in 1953, only 18 months after they agreed to become a team. Their theory about DNA, expounded briefly in the journal *Nature*, did not initially cause a profound stir. Half a century later James Watson was asked what public response 'did your discovery get?'. 'Almost total silence', he replied. Not until the 1960s did learned journals vigorously discuss their theory. More research was needed, especially on the riddle of how the genetic code 'was turned into proteins'. A vast amount of investigating and calculating, aided by the computer, was needed before the valid theory could become a practical tool.

In the last 20 years of the century, the study of genes became a key that unlocked doors. It was discovered that a defect in a certain gene caused diabetes, that another gene was linked to mental retardation, and yet another was likely to produce inherited deafness. Genetic screening became the ally of detectives. In criminal courts the samples of semen, skin or hair taken from prisoners were increasingly viewed as the equivalent of a fingerprint. From similar clues a champion female Spanish hurdler was found to be a male in 1985, and disqualified. Huge dividends in the understanding of plants, animals and human beings were coming from the theorising by Crick and Watson and from subsequent research in a thousand places.

Meanwhile in the 1950s, more research scientists queried the safety of traditional pleasures. The smoking of tobacco, usually in a wooden or clay pipe, had been a growing source of pleasure for men in the 19th century; but wages were low and tobacco was expensive, and that restricted smoking. Moreover most workplaces placed a ban on smoking, less for reasons of health than because the frequent refilling and re-lighting of the pipe wasted time. Late in the 19th century the cigarette became popular: it was easily lit with the help of the new safety matches but was more harmful to health.

War and its tension and boredom boosted the smoking of cigarettes. In the First World War the United States recorded a remarkable increase in two habits, the chewing of gum and the smoking of cigarettes. The consumption of tobacco was multiplied by four in the space of six years. In the British army a popular chaplain and hymn-writer, William Studdert Kennedy, was so well known for giving away cigarettes to soldiers at the front that he was given the nickname of a popular brand of cigarettes, 'Woodbine' Willie. Aided by another world war, the army of cigarette smokers was again multiplied. Initially men, young and old, were the eager smokers but women now shared in the craving; and at many dinner parties in private houses in the 1950s nearly everyone was smoking at the table even before the first plates of food were placed before them.

As more people smoked cigarettes, more died from lung cancer. In Germany in the 1930s the causal link between cigarette smoke and the increase of lung cancer was strongly suspected, and as early as 1952 Richard Doll in England confirmed the link; but not until the end of 1963, by which time the evidence was compelling, did the US Surgeon General sound his alarm. In many nations, especially the prosperous, the habit of smoking was to decline during the last quarter of the century whereas in others – the Pacific islands and China for instance – it went on increasing.

Other facets of medical knowledge and surgical skills, now commonplace, had their origin or gained their momentum during this astonishing period of medical vitality. A birth-control pill was devised. Cholesterol began to enter the vocabulary of the well informed, after research (commenced in 1958 in seven different countries by Professor Ancel Keys of Minnesota) warned that too much meat, cream and egg fostered heart disease. The laser, an invention of 1960, began to transform some branches of surgery. There also arrived that surgical boon – a new hip – which was to hearten millions of people in old age.

A British publisher issued a series of books which, in their very titles, proclaimed the high confidence that was permeating so many of the medical fields in the 1950s. One was called the *Conquest of Cancer*, another the *Conquest of Pain*. His optimism was premature but he mirrored the exuberance of an era, the likes of which had not been seen.

22

A SEESAW MOVES

In 1960 the intellectual and emotional mood that would pervade the end of the decade was not yet discernible. That mood was shaped by the enthroning of the teenager, the call for black rights, the birth of the green movement, the roll of a new wave of feminism, and the invention of the pill. The mood was shaped by loud, rebellious music and addictive drugs. It was flavoured sharply by the Vietnam War. It was influenced by such cities as Liverpool, San Francisco, Hanoi, Paris and Congoville, and by the air of western prosperity.

'I HAVE A DREAM'

As more African colonies became independent nations an awkward fact emerged. For these people there seemed more hope of equality than for the Afro-Americans whose ancestors had lived in the United States for generations.

Africans in the United States were freed from slavery in 1865, and five years later their right to vote was embodied in the US constitution. But they took little part in the nation's parliaments. Few blacks gained a university education, and few were lawyers, bankers and doctors. Their contribution to public life was mostly in the southern churches where their oratory could be spellbinding, but few whites sat in the pews and heard their words. Even their distinctive music was heard mainly by their own audiences.

At the start of the century most Afro-Americans were rural labourers working for wages in the old south. After decades on the bottom of the income ladder they were offered a higher rung by the First World War. As migration from Europe to the United States fell away, agents scoured the rural south with offers of train tickets and high wages to black men willing to work at railways, factories, steelworks and hotels in Chicago, Detroit, Pittsburgh, Boston, New York and other northern cities. There were already a few black suburbs in these cities, some prospering with their own shops and newspapers including the forthright *Chicago Defender*, and grand churches in which tall pipe organs were played. When in 1917 the United States entered the war and initially accepted only white recruits in the army, that heightened the scarcity of labour in wartime factories. The Ford factory at River Rouge was one vigorous recruiter of black labour, carefully selecting people with the advice of the local Afro-American pastors. By the 1920s these Afro-Americans enjoyed a standard of living higher than that of any factory workers in Europe.

They did not clamour for a larger role in public life. After Oscar de Priest in 1928 became the first black elected to congress for 30 years, his victory was only a slight step forward. It was the Second

World War and its aftermath that indirectly created another step up the steep ladder. How could Washington, in its global role, espouse political equality across the seas but ignore inequality when it existed only a bus ride from the White House? How could it denounce the lack of civil liberties in the Soviet's southern land of Georgia when its own southern state of Georgia was imperfect? As late as 1948, black and white soldiers were often segregated within the US forces. Segregation on the basis of colour was also practised in most schools in the south, and in 1957 the troops were sent to Little Rock in Arkansas to maintain order after the policy was officially abandoned. Legal opinion was now reluctant to condone what had long been normal in the south – separate classrooms, bus stops, cafeterias and other amenities for blacks and for whites. Washington intervened, strengthening civil rights in 1957 and 1960.

The firm of F. W. Woolworth ran a chain of luncheonettes where customers could sit down to eat, drink and chat. In the north, as the custom was, people of all races sat together in the same luncheonette but in the south they ate separately. On 1 February 1960, at Greensboro in North Carolina, several black students from a local technical college resolved to visit the Woolworth's white-only luncheonette. Sitting neatly dressed on stools at the counter, in defiance of the social custom, they chattered, studied their textbooks and occasionally selected items from the menu such as chicken hot pot, lemon meringues and pepsicola. On the third day so many students joined them that only a few of the 40 stools were vacant. The white luncheonette in effect had become black. The silent protest spread to other bars and cafes, and Woolworth finally announced on 25 July that it would no longer practise segregation.

Year by year, protests, court rulings, and new laws removed or pro-hibited many of the old impediments against Afro-Americans. When the Texan, Lyndon Johnson, won the 1964 presidential election by a massive majority and set out to build what he called 'the great soci-ety', Afro-American people were at the front of his mind.

Understandably, many white Americans who believed in self-help and the work ethic were reluctant to subsidise the lives of people who, it was widely believed, shunned those practical qualities. Understandably black Americans who, along with their grandpar-ents, had long suffered disadvantages did not readily cheer when their conditions were notably improved. In some regions the ten-sions increased as conditions eased. In the summers of 1966 and 1967 came surges of violence in northern cities, and during one month 43 people were killed in Detroit. A new confidence entered black politics, 'Black is Beautiful' becoming a popular slogan. The small revolutionary group, the Black Panther Party for Self-Defense, demanded that all blacks be released from prison and that no blacks be drafted for the army then fighting in Vietnam. In this ferment it was assumed by many that some day the United States would no longer be united, and that a black band of independent states, a black Confederacy, would arise.

The young clergyman who, faithfully pursuing his strategy of peaceful persistence, became the leader of black America was Mar-tin Luther King Jr. A disciple of Gandhi as well as Christ he had become known nationally when he tried in 1955 to boycott buses that segregated blacks and whites in Montgomery, Alabama where he served as a Baptist minister. Eight years later, when he addressed a huge crowd of marchers from the steps of the Lincoln Memorial in

Washington, his words, through television and radio and print, were heard around the globe.

'I have a dream today', he said to the marchers stretching far in front of him:

I have a dream that one day this nation will rise up and live out the true meaning of its creed: 'We hold these truths to be self-evident; that all men are created equal.'

I have a dream that one day on the red hills of Georgia the sons of former slaves and the sons of former slave owners will be able to sit down together at the table of brotherhood.

I have a dream that one day even the state of Mississippi, a desert state sweltering in the heat of injustice and oppression, will be transformed into an oasis of freedom and justice.

I have a dream that my four little children will one day live in a nation where they will not be judged by the color of their skin but by the content of their character.

King was spared only a few more years of life with his wife and four children. In Memphis in Tennessee, on 4 April 1968, he was assassinated.

At that time it was hoped that the Africans both of the United States and of homeland Africa would enter a new era of freedom. Those hopes of freedom in Africa were already dimmed. Many of the new African nations did not elect their own rulers. A change of government was determined more by armed force than by a popular vote; and a new ethnic or rural group or another political alliance seized power. In 1955 the army mutiny in Sudan – Africa's largest country in area – was a foretaste of how power would frequently be snatched and wielded in the liberated continent. In the next quarter of a century the typical African country experienced a coup or two, an uprising, a civil war, or an assassination from which emerged a different type of government. Some African countries experienced every kind of overthrow except the one performed quietly at the ballot box. Martin Luther King's eloquent lament was more appropriately directed to a score of countries in Africa than to his own Alabama and Tennessee.

THE LOUDEST SONGS

Those who heard the Beatles singing with their Merseyside accent could not foresee the changes they heralded. Their first album, in 1964, seemed un-revolutionary though irreverent. They brought people together in a cheerful and seemingly harmless way. Boyish, the four Beatles appealed to mothers as well as their children. In selling more 'records' in a shorter time than any other musicians in history they exerted a slightly radical influence. They helped to popularise rock-and-roll in England; along with the Rolling Stones they shipped black American music back to white Americans. They became politicians as well as entertainers and sang of peace and war, Indian mysticism, hallucinogens and other subversive and fashionable themes. Above all, in the six years from their first coming together to their parting in 1970 they made teenagers feel that they were part of a vast and exciting community to which their parents, and maybe their teachers, did not quite belong.

This was the first generation of teenagers with money to spend. In earlier decades, after children left school, they went straight to work and usually handed over their small weekly wage to their parents, with whom they continued to live. In France and Britain in 1900 the working children contributed much more than the mother to the total income of the family: it was vital that they stayed at home. Now children of the same age put themselves and their needs higher up the list of priorities. They left home early: and second-hand cars, cheaper than ever before, and their own portable radios helped to liberate them. They took less notice, if any, of their parents' opinions. It was a half-declaration of independence. In the mid-1960s only a minority of young Americans made this break-away, but it was a noticeable minority, large enough to flavour the mood of the decade, especially in California.

The Beatles and the Rolling Stones and Bob Dylan's electric guitar set the first scenes on the stage. The note of dissent grew. The hippies appeared. Drugs, including heroin, and alcohol flavoured the atmosphere. The counterculture grew more contrary. America's growing involvement in the war in Vietnam, and its conscripting of young people to fight that war, made many of those young people say 'no'.

The war in Vietnam superficially resembled the war in Korea. Both countries had been split into a communist north and an undemocratic south, and the disciplined north had attacked the south with early success. The Americans and Allies came to the aid of South Vietnam while the Russians and Chinese sent weapons and ammunition – but not soldiers – to help North Vietnam. Unlike the landscape and climate of Korea, that of Vietnam was perplexing for the Americans. It was tropical, so covered with jungle or rice fields that it was suited to guerrilla warfare rather than the massing of a large, heavily mechanised American army. It had a coastline that the American navy quickly controlled but the defending Vietnamese did not use the coastline for their reinforcements.

North Vietnam and its mass of sympathisers and support groups in the south devised a line of supply along hidden tracks meandering through the hilly jungle. America had superiority in the air, but its air power was much more useful for bombing a superhighway or railway line than jungle tracks. So the world's great possessor of military technology could not employ it effectively. Nuclear missiles were out of the question. Those weapons would have invited retaliation from Chinese and Russians and also inflamed world opinion. America increasingly depended on men on the ground – eventually their numbers reached half a million.

To conscript so many servicemen and their replacements from every city and crossroads in the country called for public loyalty; but loyalty slowly dissipated. A war, which at first seemed easily won, became unwinnable. In the late 1960s, the air of protest in the United States grew vociferous. Radical alternatives gained favour. They did not necessarily win over the majority of American people but won a large enough minority to shake the political scales.

The Vietnam War, and the divisions it caused within the United States, mixed various ingredients in the same pot. As more of the young people opposed the war, they also opposed the mainstream values of the American politicians and citizens who supported the war. In opposing the destructive technology of war, the young began to see virtues in Asian peasants and defects in American city dwellers. The jungles and rice fields of Vietnam symbolised a simple and even spiritual way of life, but the bombs that fell on them were denounced as the products of the wasteful, materialistic west.

Likewise, the very idea of the United States waging war for the sake of the personal freedom of the Vietnamese seemed strange when many black Americans had fewer freedoms than white Americans. Such were the kinds of arguments that inspired hundreds of thousands who attended anti-war rallies. They overlooked the fact that the freedom to protest was available in Washington but not in Hanoi.

THE GREEN CRUSADE

Distinctive merits of the old America were now singled out as its faults. The nation that was once praised by nearly all of its citizens for harnessing the environment, for taming the west, and for applying technology to solve multiple problems, was now being scorned by vocal groups because it was polluting the environment. The Vietnam War boosted the infant green movement.

The green movement had deep as well as surface roots. Of the major religions, Hinduism and Islam and Buddhism were possibly the more sympathetic to nature but even Christianity had its green tradition. Saint Francis of Assisi, preaching in medieval Italy, so revered nature that according to tradition he even made peace with the wolves that roamed the steep ranges near the hill town of Assisi. In the 19th century one of the most popular hymns of evangelical Protestants was written by Reginald Heber, the first Anglican bishop in India. Opening with a pictorial sweep, 'From Greenland's icy mountains to India's coral strand', the rousing hymn rejoiced in the tropical lands where 'sunny fountains roll down their golden sand' and the spiced breezes blew. Nature was beautiful: 'only man is vile'.

This Christian tradition was joined in the 1960s by a tougher, secular concern for nature. A few observers began to notice the unseen as well as the visible effects of the new machines and chemicals. The novel pesticides that waged war on the malarial mosquitoes and saved a host of human lives were now suspected to be wide-ranging destroyers, as Rachel Carson argued in her book of 1962, *Silent Spring*. Elsewhere a variety of farmers used too many chemical fertilisers and sprays, loggers destroyed forests at too swift a pace, fishermen and whalers netted the seas too rapidly, and a thousand species, once plentiful, were endangered.

At the same time a small group of scientists began to call for conservation in their special corner of the world, Antarctica. It was little explored. The highest of the continents, for it was underpinned by nine-tenths of the world's ice, it was larger than Australia and Indonesia combined. It had witnessed heroic adventures, especially in the days of Scott and Amundsen and Shackleton, but most of its interior had not been seen or walked upon. From 1 July 1957, in a collaborative effort to mark the International Geophysical Year, a dozen nations set up bases in the Antarctic and studied and measured it as never before. They took the liberty of extending the year for another six months, and justified it by the striking additions they were making to knowledge of the world's climate.

During that extended year a dozen nations set out to devise an Antarctic Treaty, the first important pact in which nations of the Southern Hemisphere – Argentina, Chile, Australia, New Zealand and South Africa – were almost as strongly represented as the Northern. Remarkably, the treaty was finalised during a tense phase of the Cold War, and both the Soviet Union and the United States signed it. They resolved that nuclear wastes must not be dumped in the Antarctic, and nuclear bombs must not be tested there. The nations resolved that the Antarctic and surrounding oceans should be a zone for open rather than secret science, and that each nation could inspect the research results of its rivals. The treaty, a landmark in the history of conservation, came into force on 23 June 1961.

The green movement gathered strength, and widened its perspective. It lamented the soaring population of Asia, Africa and the Americas. Alarmed by the new pressures each additional billion people would impose on plain and alp, shore, river and marsh, it enquired how the world's limited resources could feed all these people, provide them with houses and firewood and electricity, and give them the steel, plastics, aluminium, and oil on which industrial life depended? In 1969 a United Nations' commission revealed that the world's population had increased far more than predicted in 1950: it was doubling not in 85 years but in less than half of that time. The world's supply of food might be inadequate within 20 years. In Stockholm the president of the International Council for Scientific Unions saw a widening gap between rich nations and 'permanently miserable' nations. He warned that the world was heading for famine, nuclear war, and a 'new stone age', a prediction also supported by Professor Paul Ehrlich's book, *The Population Bomb*. These gloomy forecasts somehow ignored the cheerful fact that in the last 20 years the world's harvest of grains had been growing faster than the population.

The warnings of scarcity grew loud. It was widely predicted that soon oil would be too dear for most cars, tractors, trains, ships and aircraft to use. The Club of Rome publicised its gloomy findings in 1973. That unusual year seemed to warrant gloom. In the aftermath of the Yom Kippur War and the Arab boycotts on oil, the price of petrol reached record heights, even prompting a swing towards smaller cars in the United States, the traditional home of the large 'petrol-thirsty' car.

In assessing the future supply of foodstuffs, minerals, fertilisers and fuels, some warnings were overdue and some were timely. Other warnings of global scarcity – of iron ore, copper, coal and a variety of minerals – rested on statistics that appeared to be sound because they were produced by capable scientists, of whom few, alas, had spent time near a mine. In some of these minerals the world's reserves were to increase startlingly during the very years for which a dearth was predicted. Exaggeration tinted the green crusade in its more feverish years.

By questioning science and technology, the greens were confronting the whole way of life that had developed since the industrial revolution. Here was an attack on an individualist society, on its obsession with material progress and new machines, and on its careless trampling on the face of nature. In contrast the simple tribes of the remote past were said to have been contented, healthy and even saintly. Seemingly a simple, ancient way of life displayed all the virtues, and the modern way displayed the defects. This view – worthy but overstated – gained a wide following, especially in primary schools.

The green movement of the 1960s rightly drew attention to the smog and the pollution of air in Los Angeles, one of the world's fastest-growing cities. Its fine climate and clear sunshine had originally attracted the filmmakers to Hollywood, and in the 1920s it boasted that its climate was also attracting a 'great number of invalids'. Increasingly, as cars multiplied, Los Angeles' aridity and unusual layout – a corridor of suburbs tucked between the Pacific Ocean and the rugged mountains – permitted a layer of cold air to sit on the layer of warm polluted air, and prevent the smog from rising. The unclean air impaired the breathing and irritated the eyes, prompting a resolute campaign against air pollution in the 1970s. The battle was almost won and then lost because traffic kept on increasing. In the same decade, dusty and smoky Mexico City, soon to become the second largest in the world, experienced a doubling of acidic and other emissions from vehicles and chimneys. It was one of the many smoggy cities where respiratory illness became common.

Reformers lamented the excessive noise of the latest technology. At the start of 1976 the Anglo-French Concorde was ready to fly passengers at double the speed of sound to remote cities. Many nations, fearing the effects of the supersonic boom, banned the plane from flying over their territory. That the longest flights proposed would be mainly over wilderness, desert or ocean was no longer accepted as a persuasive argument. The wilderness, which traditionally was disdained as lonely and perilous, was now hailed as a haven of majesty, harmony, and concealed ecological diversity. Attempts to preserve wilderness for future generations had an urgency rarely witnessed since the last third of the 19th century when Yellowstone National Park in North America, the summits of three volcanoes in New Zealand, the sandstone country south of Sydney, and the first segment of the Kruger National Park in South Africa were set aside. Now, from the 1970s onwards, the places safeguarded as national parks and wilderness reserves were multiplied in every hemisphere.

Endangered species became the focus of more campaigns. The largest species in ocean and on land – the African elephants hunted for their ivory and the deep sea whales hunted for their oil – were an early concern. The Antarctic seas had abounded in huge whales, and on 14 January 1930 the explorer Douglas Mawson noted about 50 whales along the edge of the pack ice, while on that same day a Norwegian whaling ship reported another 150 nearby. Such numbers, when hunted vigorously, could not last. After attempts failed to restrict the hunt, the whaling nations finally resolved in Stockholm in 1972 to ban the killing of whales for 10 years. Though the ban was not fully effective, a pattern was set. The Antarctic oceans were the scene of several effective campaigns. The elephant seal which was thought to be close to extinction, through over-hunting, was again counted in the hundreds of thousands.

Several new nature groups focussed on the risk of nuclear war; the warning phrase 'a nuclear winter' came into vogue. Greenpeace was founded in Canada in 1971 in the hope of halting the nuclear tests on an island in Alaska. The influential German political party, the Greens, was founded in 1979 partly with the hope of creating in central Europe a zone devoid of nuclear and other armaments. At this stage the Soviet Union and the Third World had faint interest in such concerns.

The green leaders were full of ardour. Forcing the majority to take notice, they began to speak on their behalf. In the 1970s it was not clear what later became transparent: that in the west were two distinct and sometimes clashing kinds of greens. The Dark Greens, vocal but few in number, believed that the world was in a permanent state of ecological crisis, while the Light Greens – the majority of western people – desired economic development coupled with the preserving of rare species and unique places of grandeur and solitude. The Light Greens, less militant, were vital.

Few mental changes of the century were more spectacular than the sense of 'one world' that these groups expressed. What happened in the ozone layer above the Antarctic became the concern of people in Prague; what might happen in a rain forest in Brazil was the concern of people in Hiroshima. These global concerns were aroused by the speed and range of foreign travel, the orbiting satellites that gathered information everywhere, and the computers that made sense of it.

The intricate question of global warming emerged in the 1980s, arousing alarm. That the industrial civilisation is wasteful and polluting is beyond doubt. That ground temperatures were higher at the end than at the start of the 20th century is beyond doubt, several years of the late 1990s being the hottest of all. But Europe's temperature was erratic, with a short period of warming ending in 1942, a slight cooling extending to 1977, and then a strong phase of warming. This fear of climatic change did not persuade China and India to imperil their own industrial revolutions by erecting costly windfarms rather than smoke stacks. It was the European peoples who feared the effects of the fossil fuels on which their industrial might had once relied.

There was one curiosity about the ideas that gathered momentum in the 1960s. Most had been briefly in favour in the 1890s and early 1900s. An early green movement flourished then, and feminism too had surged. There had also been a reaction by a powerful minority of thinkers against the idea of progress and the merits of technology, while at the same time the savage society and the wilderness too had been regarded with favour in certain intellectual circles in western Europe. This tilt of the seesaw of ideas was reversing before the First World War, only to reappear, invigorated, in the 1960s.

WOMEN: 'IS THIS ALL?'

The crusades to elevate the rights of women, of coloured peoples, the young, and even rare plants, birds, insects and animals were subtly linked. All were movements in support of the overlooked. Admittedly the campaign to raise the status of women was different. They already possessed the vote, but something was missing.

Support for a vote by all women, after gaining impetus from New Zealand and Australia, had swept through the western world; and by 1950 Greece and Switzerland were amongst the few democratic countries that did not allow women to vote. But the hope, so fervent at the start of the century, that women would become leaders in parliament, courts and the professions was rarely fulfilled. Most, after their marriage, became absorbed in home and family. When they did remain in the workforce, whether teaching or in factories or post offices, their pay was much lower than that of men doing the same work. The few who won seats in parliament did not attain the highest office. The feminist movement, it was often observed, had run out of steam.

Betty Friedan was a talented graduate of Smith College, who worked as a psychologist before half accepting her new life as the mother of three in Grandsview, New York. In the 1950s she began to realise that the alternatives for her were narrower than for a Soviet woman of her age. An American married woman became primarily a mother and housewife, but if she wished to follow a career she thereby chose 'lifelong celibacy'. Friedan regretted that western society frowned on women who tried to combine marriage and a serious career. She discovered that the harnessing of female talent had actually retreated in the United States after 1920. During the following 35 years the proportion of university doctorates awarded to women went into decline, as did the proportion of women studying as undergraduates.

She observed an emptiness in the daily life of so many college graduates of her generation: 'As she made the beds, shopped for groceries, matched slipcover material, ate peanut butter sandwiches with her children, chauffeured Cub Scouts and Brownies, lay beside her husband at night – she was afraid to ask even of herself the silent question – "Is this all?".' Friedan argued that it was utterly naive 'to give the illusion that dumping the clothes in the washing machines is an act akin to deciphering the genetic code'. The genetic code, incidentally, was not yet a topic of wide discussion. In her eloquent lament, published in 1963 under the title of *The Feminine Mystique*, she called for married women to seek outside work and take their place in the professions. She expressed her dream in the same year as Martin Luther King Jr voiced his. Her book was more in the self-help tradition so strong in the United States than a cry for women to chain themselves to the Golden Gate Bridge and compel the government to help them. She caught a rising mood and accelerated it.

THE PILL: A MEXICAN YAM TRANSFORMED

The invention of the pill did not begin a sexual revolution: it was as much the effect as the cause. The public discussion of sex was already changing. Television, now entering millions of homes, was less cautious in displaying sex than radio, which reflected a more puritanical era. In the opinion of Paul Johnson, the increasing influence of journalists and the declining influence of newspaper owners also did much 'to cut America loose from its traditional moorings'. In the second half of the 1950s, such best-selling books as *Peyton Place*, *Lolita* and the unexpurgated edition of *Lady Chatterley's Lover* were sexually more explicit than best-sellers of the previous decade.

The birth-control pill, as a substitute for rubber condoms and diaphragms, emerged slowly from a variety of experiments. One version was developed in the 1940s by Gregory Pincus, a young biologist, while another pill based on a Mexican yam was patented by Carl Djerassi in 1951. An enthusiast for such experiments was Margaret Sanger, whose New York clinic helped married women to restrict their pregnancies. Worried by the prospect of overpopulation, especially in the Third World, Sanger believed that the future of civilisation in the next quarter century would 'depend on a simple, cheap, safe contraceptive to be used in poverty-stricken slums and jungles, and among the most ignorant people'. On the basis of this argument she attracted help for Pincus's research from a philanthropist in her late seventies, Katherine McCormick, whose husband's family had made a fortune from wheat-harvesting machines.

Pincus had tried his pill successfully on rabbits but a Massachusetts law prevented him from trying his pill on women. The McCormick money enabled his experiments to proceed in Puerto Rico in the mid-1950s. Occupying half a mountainous island, Puerto Rico was densely populated and was also primarily Catholic, though marriage was taken less seriously than the Vatican wished. Not many Puerto Rican women, when invited to join in the experiment, were willing to try the pill for a period of one year. Apparently they did not object on moral or spiritual grounds but rather felt that the taking of the pill was a bother. In all, 123 Puerto Rican women persisted with the pill for the year. Side effects could not be monitored adequately, but the pill served its main purpose.

To publicise such a simple method of preventing pregnancy was viewed as a dangerous incentive to immorality, especially in the young. The pill was initially prescribed for the married, mature woman. A pill first released in 1957 by a Chicago firm had the advertised aim of preventing miscarriages and easing menstrual troubles. Not until 1962 in the United States and Britain were pills licensed to be sold as general contraceptives. Their full debut was cautious, even shy, and in the early years the doctors rarely prescribed them for unmarried women. In 1965 a doctor at Brown University, Rhode Island, was denounced when he recommended the pill to students, even though they were over the age of 21. The pill was powerful: but its power would have been smaller if social attitudes towards marriage, divorce, sexuality and the female role in the workforce were not already altering. These social attitudes, altering at varying paces, tended to lag in the more devout Catholic countries such as Ireland, Italy and Argentina. Not until 1974 did a referendum in Italy legalise divorce.

The combined effects of the pill and the new set of social attitudes will long be debated. The birthrate declined rapidly in Europe and other strongholds of people of European ancestry; but in the United States the decline of the birthrate was offset by the large immigration from Mexico, Asia and other lands outside Europe. The decline of the birthrate had profound consequences. In 1950 Europe held a much larger population than either Africa or the Americas. By the end of the century it was far behind them. Of all Europeans, 20 per cent were aged 60 years and over, whereas only 5 per cent of

Africans had reached that age. Europe had become the continent of the old and middle-aged.

A RULER OF INDIA: THE LANDMARK WOMAN

The white world was inclined to see itself as the leader in nearly all things called progressive. In the women's movements it tended to lead. Thus in the Soviet Union in 1970 an unusually large proportion of doctors were women, and in Sweden one in four of the politicians was a woman. But it was in India that the most coveted prize was won. The prime minister, Lal Shastri, died suddenly in January 1966 and the compromise candidate selected to succeed him was a woman. Hitherto no woman – unless a queen – had presided over a major nation.

Mrs Indira Gandhi was almost born into the position, for her father was Jawaharlal Nehru, the first prime minister of independent India. He had long tutored his only child for high office. At the age of nine she sailed with her family to Europe where she studied in a Swiss school while her mother, ill with tuberculosis, tried to renew her health in nearby mountains. Even then young Indira had dreams of becoming India's Joan of Arc and driving the British from her homeland. After studying in Oxford she went to London and learned to drive an ambulance during Hitler's bombing.

In 1942 Miss Nehru became Mrs Gandhi. That she carried in succession the surnames of India's two celebrated politicians was uncanny. Her husband Feroze Gandhi, not a relative of the great Gandhi, was a member of that tiny and wealthy sect called the Parsees, who were influential in Bombay. Her marriage stirred controversy because neither Parsees nor Hindus normally wished their members to marry outside their own own religion. In her early career she seemed as capable as her father of building bridges between rival cultures and perhaps move effective in tapping empathy within her own culture. Her father had addressed the masses in the Urdū language, with its Muslim religious and Persian literary links, and could only sprinkle his speech with Hindustani words, but Indira could speak in Hindi to a massed audience.

Her father had been inclined to socialism – a visit to the young Soviet Union in the late 1920s had impressed him – and during his terms in prison, on various charges of political disobedience, he had read thousands of pages of Karl Marx in the hope it would illuminate his country's future. His daughter imbibed his attitude. On her first visit to the United States in 1949 she decided that she did not like the extravagance of capitalism: at the Waldorf Astoria Hotel, when she licked an envelope, she found it tasted of peppermint. On her first visit to the Soviet Union she felt more at home. Despite her travels, India and not the world stage was her dominant concern.

Indira Gandhi rose rapidly in her father's last years. President of the ruling Congress Party in 1959, she became minister for information and broadcasting five years later. Some of her father's moral authority was vested in her. In 1966, in her first of 15 years as prime minister, she set the pattern of packing her daily life with duties. Rising at 6 a.m. she read or skimmed six newspapers – the seventh she shunned. At 8.30 she met the clusters of unscheduled callers, while those callers who had made appointments gained her attention later. She neither drank alcohol nor smoked, and usually did not eat until 11 a.m. when she sipped a bowl of soup. Many outsiders such as Henry Kissinger of the United States decided that she was cold-blooded, but her family – her dynasty – and personal staff felt no such chill.

She was to show a toughness that many observers had not expected of a female leader. When India's soaring population outpaced its fragile supply of food, she pinned her faith on the irrigation, new seeds and chemical fertilisers of the green revolution. Centralising power she nationalised India's largest bank, its insurance companies and coalmines. In foreign policy she moved closer to Moscow and further from Washington. Expelled from her party she formed her own. Expelled briefly from parliament, she then returned. She was not enamoured with democracy if it produced an unwanted result.

When East Pakistan, now Bangladesh, rebelled against rule from distant Pakistan, Mrs Gandhi gave the rebels armed support in 1971. Such was India's dominance that it took 100000 prisoners. Mrs Gandhi was therefore the first female leader of a major country – in all the years since Catherine the Great of Russia waged her second war against Turkey in 1787 – to declare war. She contradicted the contemporary hope that if all the nations were led by women, wars would come to an end. In the quarter century after 1957, when Mrs Bandaranaike of Ceylon became the first female prime minister, the three important female leaders – Mrs Golda Meir in Israel, Mrs Margaret Thatcher in Britain and Mrs Indira Gandhi – all accepted the responsibility of leading their nation into war.

Indira Gandhi's ascent was remarkable; but the various wings of feminism that had waited so long for such a daring ascent were silent or uneasy. She did not quite imbibe their spirit. They also regretted that she had won high office more through kinship than talent; they seemed to forget that scores of male politicians in the democracies had family connections that aided their rise to power. It was India's vigorous democracy that had really placed her in power. Alas, violence ended her rule. In October 1984 she was assassinated by her personal Sikh bodyguards, in protest at her army's destruction of the sacred Sikh temple at Amritsar. Among the nations that counted the most, she was entitled, at the time of her death, to be called the world's most experienced national leader.

23

THUNDER AND LIGHTNING IN MOSCOW AND WARSAW

The landing on the moon was a dazzling day for the United States and its new president, Richard Nixon. Few countries in the history of the world had experienced such a triumph. At the same time, Nixon was losing the contest in Vietnam. The Soviet Union and China, increasing military aid to their ally in North Vietnam, maintained communism's supremacy. In 1972 it was firmly in control.

The United States was overextended, rather like the British and French empires when they were assailed by the Japanese in the same region in 1941. It operated bases, barracks and airfields in too many foreign countries. War in Vietnam was costing a huge sum, and in American lives alone the death toll would reach 57 000. America's full range of expensive activities, whether in outer space or Vietnam or the home front, could no longer be adequately carried on. A compromise peace was the only solution.

A deficiency of oil made the United States more vulnerable. Whereas the Soviet Union was self-sufficient in oil the United States was not. It had to rely on long and exposed sea routes, along which more and more oil was carried from the turbulent Middle East. Therefore an interruption to the inflow of oil could pummel its economy and that of the free world too. Between 1969 and 1973 the control of most of the world's oil was passing from big companies, mostly owned by the United States, to independent Islamic producers. Within the space of four years the vital oilfields of Algeria, Libya and Iraq were nationalised.

A shrewd observer of international relations could argue that in the oilfields and in Vietnam the United States was losing the prolonged Cold War. Nixon, however, made the most of his adversity. After China was admitted in 1971 to the United Nations, he resolved to shake its hand, at least tentatively. In February of the following year he visited China. While it seemed an obvious gesture it was not. No president of the United States had even visited Moscow, let alone Beijing. Three months later he visited Moscow too.

Nixon's decision to talk more freely with the two big communist countries was shrewd, for they were becoming bitter rivals and even enemies. The two-sided Cold War was coming to an end. In January 1973 the Americans signed a cease-fire with North Vietnam. They were enabled to retreat from the region where their military prestige had suffered such a dint. In retreating the Americans were liberating themselves.

Vietnam was the last major victory for communists in the course of the prolonged Cold War. That they would experience a resounding defeat in the following decade was not foreseen. That the defeat would be in their own heartland was still beyond the comprehension of the Russian leaders in the Kremlin, the heads of their armed forces, the commanders of nuclear submarines deep beneath the ocean, or the Soviet astronauts still performing feats in outer space. Defeat of communism was almost unimaginable to the ranks of the leaders of the six satellite nations who in Warsaw or Prague, Budapest or Bucharest, East Berlin or Sofia, stood to attention while the rumbling tanks and the marching platoons and overhead jets swept past or above the saluting base on each anniversary of the Bolshevik revolution of 1917.

THE HEYDAY OF PRIVILEGE IN A COMMUNIST LAND

Groups of western tourists were visiting Moscow every day and entering the foreigner-only shops, travelling in the palatial underground railway, watching the traffic flow easily along the wide boulevards, seeing from afar the skyscraper of Moscow University astride the Lenin Hills, and coming to the conclusion that the Russian people, though not as far behind as had been imagined, still lagged markedly in their standard of living and civic amenities. For tens of thousands of high Soviet officials, however, life was easy in the 1970s.

At the very top a few hundred officials sat in cushioned splendour. They expected polished limousines with chauffeurs to wait for them, and at the major intersections foot policemen might halt all other traffic to let the long black car pass by. Their wives no longer knew the meaning of a food queue. Their holiday cottages in the woods were more than cottages. While not always as grand as in a western country, the privileges seemed odd in a land where all people were proclaimed to be equal. A middling party-official some-day might acquire a car whereas the coalminer and kindergarten teacher, factory worker and street sweeper, dentist and librarian, could only dream of it.

There were shops where foreign foods and other luxuries could be bought only by the privileged few. In 1975, Moscow had 15 exclu-sive shops within the Berezka or birch-tree chain of stores. Country houses and seaside hotels on the Black Sea, and special hospitals and medical services, were provided for the higher officials. For their children, opportunities were open, and a stiff-fingered young son could study the piano at one of the higher institutes.

For the average Soviet citizen in the 1970s, living apartments were cramped and crowded. Bread and potatoes formed a large part of the diet, and fruit and vegetables even in summer were not always fresh and not always available. The number of hours a Soviet citizen worked in order to buy the weekly food was much higher than in London and Washington. A big loaf of bread cost four times as many working min-utes in Moscow as in London, a packet of tea cost eight times as many minutes of paid work as in London. On the other hand, the month's supply of beer and beef could be earned by working roughly the same number of working hours in both cities in 1979.

There was an underground economy. In the early 1970s a Russian newspaper complained that one in every three private cars used pet-rol that was 'borrowed' from the state's own petrol tanks and pumps. One in every four nips of vodka drunk in Russia came from the black market – the proportion had been higher in the late 1950s. The scar-city of consumer goods was a reflection of an economy that was working less effectively than in earlier decades. Moreover the military absorbed 10 to 12 per cent of all economic activity – far more than any other western country. In many workplaces the absentee-ism was frequent, lethargy was high, and morale was weak. There was a popular joke about the low wages paid by the Soviet govern-ment: 'you pretend to pay us, we pretend to work'. One of the brightest sectors was the country's rich oil and gas fields, and their pipelines stretched from Siberia to eastern Europe. Despite extremely high prices for oil and gas there was no economic growth in several years of the early 1980s. The official statistics of course painted a rosier picture.

The head of the Soviet Union, Leonid Ilich Brezhnev, did not believe his country was lagging. It still vied with the United States as the most powerful nation in the world; it competed vigorously in the space race; and more or less held its own in the arms race. Brezhnev controlled a vast land empire as well as bases and spheres of influ-ence over the seas.

The western journalists did not take in him the same interest they had taken in Stalin and Khrushchev, whom he succeeded. He was less colourful, though he did resemble a prizefighter with his bushy eyebrows and stern look. A land surveyor and then an engineer, he was a political official in the Soviet army in the war against Hitler, receiving the title of major general. In the mid-1950s he was the head of the farm region of Kazakhstan – a vast inland province spreading beyond the Caspian Sea and into Asia. Heading what was called the Virgin and Idle Lands Campaign he tried to boost the production of grain.

Brezhnev was formidable, and became more so, for his tenure in the Kremlin went on and on. When in 1968 the Czechs under Alex

Dubcek tried to gain more independence from the Soviet Union he pounced on them. Under no circumstances would he tolerate dissent in the lands of his communist satellites. Of the Soviet heads of state, only he and Stalin ever held the supreme military rank – that of marshal. He exercised the second-longest reign of any Soviet leader – some 18 years – and for much of that time could be classed as the most powerful man in the world. His power came partly from longevity. He faced or opposed five different presidents of the United States, and few of them gained even a fraction of the experience he had acquired in brinkmanship.

In Brezhnev's first years in power, the arms race was becoming dangerous for world peace. The two superpowers increased their destructive powers. Submarines driven by nuclear power could hide in deep water and not be found by echo-detectors. They could stay below for several months, if the morale of their crew would allow it, and could travel under the ice in the Arctic regions and even make their way from the Pacific to the Atlantic oceans, undetected. Capable of firing missiles including the flat-trajectory cruise missiles, they could endanger the distant cities of the enemy. Moreover intercontinental missiles, based on land, were capable, year by year, of reaching more distant targets. In the early 1970s they could travel 2000 miles: soon 5000 miles would be their range. Eventually no city in the United States and no city in the Soviet Union, no matter how far inland, could be safe from a sudden attack by missiles carrying thermonuclear warheads.

The sheer cost of the arms race was a strong reason for curbing it. Both sides could see a merit in such curbs; but could the other side be trusted to carry out what it promised?

In 1967 Lyndon Johnson, president of the United States, pro-posed a curb. As his government was spending heavily on the war in Vietnam and on the war against black poverty at home, it would gain if there was a halt to the competition in long-range missiles and nuclear arms. Discussions began with the Russians in mid-1968 but ceased two months later when the Czech rebellion was being crushed. After a long gap the conference table was again set up, and eventually an agreement was in sight. It is rare in a period of peace for an arms race between major powers to be slowed down, but the rare event happened and a treaty was signed on 26 May 1972. It limited each side's missiles, whether launched from land or from submarines. Another agreement to limit the missile race was signed at the port of Vladivostok in November 1974, and another major pact was signed in Vienna in June 1979. By now Brezhnev had negotiated with a succession of four different presi-dents. There was a deep feeling in some circles in Washington that he was the stronger negotiator, that he had especially outwitted Jimmy Carter, who was the fourth in his procession of American opponents, and that the USA was surrendering at the negotiating table some of the military advantages it had gained by strenuous spending and research.

The Soviet Union, while closely watching Washington's world-wide chain of armed bases, seized opportunities to expand. Its navy was huge and could encompass the world. The Persian Gulf and its oil, vital to the world, had long been in America's and Britain's sphere of influence; but in the late 1970s the Soviet Union increased its power around the two vital Middle East outlets: the Red Sea and the Persian Gulf. Ethiopia in 1977 was in Moscow's fold, and in April of that year America's military mission was expelled. The People's Democratic Republic of Yemen was in Moscow's fold, and so too was the crucial port of Aden, commanding the approaches of the Red Sea. On the other side of the Red Sea the French territory of Djibouti became independent in June 1977. Would Moscow intervene, thus guarding both sides of that narrow entrance to the Red Sea? In Saudi Arabia the legitimate fear was that Moscow could close, if it so desired, this seaway leading to the Suez Canal.

With the collapse of the Portuguese empire in Africa in the mid-1970s, a vast area of Angola in south-west Africa was taken over by a Marxist government. Soon in trouble, it was backed by soldiers from distant Cuba. So communism was fighting to gain territory at both ends of Africa.

In central Asia in 1979, Soviet soldiers moved into Afghanistan to support one side in the civil war. Afghanistan had been a place of troubles intermittently for a century – Russia and Britain almost went to war in its valleys in the 1880s – and now it was again on the map of wars. At first the Russians seemed assured of victory. They outweighed, in potential military might, the Afghans even more than the Americans had outweighed the North Vietnamese. Moreover the Russians were fighting close to home. Their prolonged failure to win in Afghanistan was to be one cause of the ultimate disintegration of the Soviet Union; but in the first years of the war a defeat was not foreseen.

Meanwhile, in Brezhnev's last years in office, communism around the world seemed vigorous. The Soviet Union and China were its strongholds, with lesser strongholds extending from Cuba to North Korea, Albania to Romania, and the unstable communist outposts on the shores of the Red Sea. There was one acute embarrassment, Cambodia.

Standing to the west of Vietnam and with a long coastline, Cambodia had been ruled in authoritarian style by Prince Sihanouk until 1975. Then the local communists called the Khmer Rouge began to take control of the capital city. Led by a former schoolteacher, once named Saloth Sar but later known as Pol Pot, and backed by China, the new regime set out to cleanse the nation of those deemed to be undesirables. This category encompassed nearly all those who were formally educated and nearly all who had owned property. As a first step, schools and hospitals and Buddhist monasteries were closed, private property was abolished, and the people of the city were deported to the countryside to take part in the collective activity of rice growing. There vast numbers died through exhaustion, starvation and sickness. Thousands more, including many loyal communists, were interrogated and shot. There are no official statistics but by the time the communists fled, late in 1978, the death toll was close to 2 million people, or 20 per cent of Cambodia's population.

STORMS IN EASTERN EUROPE

Of the communist satellites in eastern Europe, the Polish People's Republic gained the most independence, though to some outside observers it seemed like a dog on a chain. Its heavy industry was owned and directed by the state but its agriculture was in private hands to a surprising degree. Many of Poland's intellectuals paid only lip service to Marxism and some paid none. Though communism assigned no place to churches, Poland's Catholic church remained strong. Its rebellious primate Cardinal Wyszynski had survived three years of detention in the early 1950s before gaining the vital concession that his church could be autonomous and could even teach a little about Christianity in schools so long as it did not undermine the ruling Communist Party. Poland possessed the one dynamic church in eastern Europe, a symbol of Polish patriotism; and most people gave it deep loyalty.

It so happened that in 1978 a cardinal from Poland was in the running for the supreme office of pope. The son of a sergeant in the army, the future Pope John Paul II had been the Archbishop of Krakow for 15 years. It was remarkable that he even had a prospect of being selected for the church's highest office. But his prospects soared when the previous pope, who might well have reigned for 10 years, died after one month in office. Even then it was widely assumed that an Italian would be chosen as the new pope, because only Italians had held that office during the last four and a half centuries. Why, after seven ballots had failed to agree on a successor, was the Polish prelate finally elected? According to one source the College of Cardinals decided that by electing an East European they were parachuting the foot-soldiers of Christ into the heartland of communism, at a crucial phase in its history.

The new pope remained absorbed in the troubles and discontents of his homeland. During his first year in office he returned to Poland on an official visit and, descending the steps from the aircraft, he made his eloquent affirmation: 'I have kissed the ground of Poland on which I grew up; and the land from which, through the inscrutable design of Providence, God called me to the Chair of Peter in Rome; the land to which I am coming today as a pilgrim.' An enormous crowd, estimated to number 2 million, lined his route between the airport and Warsaw. Poland, in allowing such liberties to dissenters, was like no other communist country.

As Poland could sustain a relatively independent church, answerable more to the Vatican than to Moscow, maybe it could also create an independent trade union. Called the Solidarity Movement, it arose in 1980. Its leader was Lech Walesa, a Catholic and an unemployed electrical worker from the Gdansk shipyards, one of the huge communist workplaces that flourished on the southern Baltic coast. The Solidarity Movement recruited millions of members and even claimed the right to strike – a right that did not exist in communist lands. For a short time Solidarity challenged the authority of communism in Warsaw and even in Moscow.

In Moscow, Brezhnev and his colleagues viewed with some alarm the agitation in Poland. Massive popular protests had arisen before, especially in Hungary in 1956 and Czechoslovakia in 1968, but neither country had the personal sympathy of the pope and thereby the silent support of hundreds of millions of Catholics living around the world. The pope, in becoming a vital influence on both sides of the Iron Curtain, became also a political target. In the Vatican in May 1981 an unsuccessful attempt was made on his life as he moved amongst the crowd. The attacker firing the semiautomatic Browning was a Turkish criminal. More significant, he had Bulgarian accomplices, and had himself received elaborate camouflage and money from the communist government of Bulgaria. The suspicion, expressed by historians but impossible to prove, was that the attack had also been endorsed by agencies within the Soviet Union.

In Poland at the end of that year a coordinated campaign was directed against the agitators. On a snowy night, thousands of the

Solidarity leaders and supporters were arrested by the Polish army. Martial law was proclaimed in city and countryside. Printing presses and radio stations were silenced. Dissent in Poland was curbed but not crushed. Lech Walesa was placed under arrest and eventually moved to a place of confinement, comfortable rather than harsh, far from Warsaw.

At this delicate stage a new president of the United States, Ronald Reagan, began to test the relationships between the two superpowers. Son of a shoe salesman in Illinois, he had made his first reputation through his many Hollywood films and the first of his marriages – to Jane Wyman, an actress. It was a surprise to many observers when he became Republican governor of the dynamic state of California in 1966. Fourteen years later he was elected president of the United States, the oldest candidate to win that office. Just as J.F. Kennedy and his charming wife appealed engagingly to Americans by virtue of their youth, Reagan attempted the more difficult task of exploiting his considerable age. As he wittily said in one televised debate: 'I will not make age an issue of this campaign. I am not going to exploit for political purposes my opponent's youth and inexperience.' He brought to Washington his make-up kit and actor's diction.

A Protestant with conservative leanings, Reagan reaffirmed old American values when they were being eroded by the young radicals of the counterculture. His policies combined two ingredients that did not quite mix: he wished to lower taxes and he wished to spend more money on defence.

Disappointed with the disarmament discussions of the late 1970s he decided that they were weakening the United States at a time when it should be boldly confronting communism. He did not think that under the present state of armaments his nation could be safe from a nuclear attack launched from the Soviet Union. Accordingly he proposed to spend heavily on what he called the Strategic Defense Initiative and what others called Star Wars, a title adopted from a movie. Under Reagan's scheme, foreshadowed by his televised speech in March 1983, American weapons, ready on the ground and at sea and in space, would intercept any attacking Russian missiles.

Brezhnev died in November 1982, and a fast-growing Russian city with the largest truck factory in the world was renamed in his honour. In the arena of brute power, his experience and determination were missed. Moreover his immediate successors were short-lived, allowing the initiative and the sense of command to pass some way towards the United States.

THE 'PERESTROIKA' MAN

Mikhail Gorbachev came to power in March 1985 after his three predecessors in the Kremlin had died in quick succession. Only 54, he was younger than most of his colleagues near the top. The son of peasants in a rich farming region north of the great Caucasus mountains he spent there much of his early working life – driving a combine harvester in summer, and returning to the region after he won his law degree in Moscow. As a prominent official in agriculture, he came to the notice of various Soviet leaders who arrived to take the spa cure in his home town of Stavropol. He was noticeable because of his quick mind as well as a red birthmark on his forehead.

He looked fresh-faced and eager but he was a product of the tough politics in the Kremlin. When he was rising to high office he was careful what he said even in his own house. He later recalled how in 1984 his friend and superior Yuri Andropov, who was dying of kidney failure one year after becoming Soviet leader, glanced suspiciously over his shoulder while on his deathbed. Gorbachev observed that 'the suffering induced by the illness was aggravated by another worry: he sensed the intrigue'. At the funeral in the Hall of Columns, the subtle displays of personal loyalty and disloyalty and even the concealed jockeying for office could be glimpsed. While some mourners were in tears, the pleasure in other faces was just visible.

Gorbachev had learned how to disguise his own thoughts while rising to high office. As the rooms in his Moscow apartment and rural dacha might be bugged, he talked politics with his wife, Raisa, while strolling in their private Moscow garden, sometimes in the early hours of the morning: 'one never knew . . .'

Mrs Gorbachev was rather stylish and yet sensitive – qualities rarely observed in the stout and homely wives of the former leaders. She was intellectually inclined – philosophy was her field. Though it was not the custom for Soviet wives to appear on the platform on grand occasions, Mrs Gorbachev broke this taboo, thus arousing critical comment around the nation. Indeed President Reagan, watching the televised funeral of a Soviet leader, gained the impression that Mrs Gorbachev was perhaps religious. She was different, and her husband too.

When Gorbachev became head of the Communist Party and therefore head of the Soviet Union, his concern was the economy. Its rate of innovation and growth was slow, and many senior employees preferred to grasp the spirits bottle rather than the latest insight into their profession or industry. He realised that such a sluggish economy could hardly support the vast military effort – an army fighting hard in Afghanistan, a large army at home, another army watching over eastern Europe, a huge navy and air force, and all the breathtaking costs of trying to match Reagan's Star Wars. After Gorbachev toured his country, denouncing alcoholism and corruption, he announced that the time had come for 'perestroika', a word that meant restructuring.

Gorbachev could see merit in arranging a summit with Reagan, for he was eager to reduce his expenditure on armaments. Such a reduction was vital if he were to provide a higher standard of living for his people. It was not easy, however, to arrange a summit. None had been held for more than six years.

Reagan agreed to attend the summit partly because of the advice from the British prime minister, Margaret Thatcher, whose conservative political instincts he trusted. She had met the Gorbachevs on the very eve of their assumption of power, at an informal lunch she hosted at her official country house, 'Chequers'. Gorbachev thought she was rather like a wedding cake, all firmness beneath the attractive icing, but he respected her. The two had a brief discussion about the nuclear arms race during which he showed her a diagram setting out the main nuclear arsenals, arranged in 1000 squares. 'Each of these squares suffices to eradicate all life on earth', he told her. She was impressed by his earnestness.

So Gorbachev and Reagan met, for the first time, at Geneva on Tuesday 19 November 1985. Reagan came to the meeting believing that Gorbachev had an incentive 'to reduce the burden of defense spending that is stagnating the Soviet economy.' The two men – 20 years apart in age and far apart in ideologies – first had a private discussion. Scheduled for 15 minutes it lasted an hour, during which each leader expressed firm views. Gorbachev thought that Reagan was a political dinosaur – a relic of ages past – while Reagan detected a Russian bear, grinding his jaws. During the day they reached a cautious rapport. In the words of Gorbachev, 'We shook hands like friends'. It was one of the influential meetings in the history of the 20th century.

At a private dinner for the Reagans, Gorbachev delivered a speech that included biblical verses from Ecclesiastes: 'There is a time for everything' – meaning that the time had come for each of the big two nations to look at their relationship afresh. To quote the bible in an official Soviet speech was a rarity, and the official Russian interpreter watched the faces of the listeners. Whether Reagan instantly realised the magnitude of his host's gesture is not clear.

At the end of the summit the two leaders issued a communique proclaiming that 'nuclear war cannot be won and must never be fought'. Gorbachev, contrary to the traditional Soviet practice, held a long press conference at which he argued that today the 'world has become a safer place'. When Reagan flew home, however, he retained his plans to gain a higher level of military ascendancy. He was not yet ready to make strong concessions.

In all they were to hold five summits. An agreement on arms control was not easy, and required gradual concessions from each leader: from Gorbachev because his bargaining position was frayed, and from Reagan because his bargaining position, with his ever-improving, computer-carrying missiles and their thermonuclear warheads, was growing stronger. Together they broke the long deadlock.

At the start of 1989, when Reagan stepped down as president, the

Cold War, though he could not have realised it, was about to end. His part in ending that long conflict will always be debated, but probably it was as vital as that of Gorbachev. More than two powerful leaders, however, were needed to end the Cold War. Equally important were the rush of events and quiet changes extending from Riga to Kabul and from the Vatican to Brussels.

24

THE WALLS ARE TOPPLING

Gorbachev faced acute difficulties with the United States: he faced trouble at home. Both in the space race and the nuclear race, the Soviet Union was exhausting itself. Its city and rural households – in what they could and could not obtain – were paying the price. Moreover the capitalist west's values, material goods, and emphasis on liberty and even on licence, were infiltrating the Soviet way of life. When the Helsinki Accord on Human Rights was signed by the Soviet Union and its European communist allies in 1975 – in return for an acceptance of their national boundaries set in place in 1945 – it seemed to be a small nod towards human rights. But the nod weakened the communists' insistence that they were entitled to do what they wished within their own borders.

In Gorbachev's first years, dissent was heard more often. The religious-like zeal for communism was fading. The people's vision of communism, as a guide to the good life and a blueprint for the whole world's future, was waning. The newer generations were instructed to admire their political creed; but zeal cannot always be imparted by unceasing propaganda. While the propaganda affirmed the principle of equality, many of the leaders did not live by that principle. It was pointless to emphasise the principle of self-sacrifice for the sake of all people when local party leaders were corrupt, and a black market flourished even in state-owned activities.

Many of the eastern European intellectuals who once were enthusiastic Marxists were now cynical or neutral. The Russian cult-poet Yevtushenko argued in 1986 that the Soviet Union was a failure by many measurements. Inside their own country Russians had to carry passports and residence permits – 'shameful rudiments of serfdom'. They were tired, he said, of standing in queues in order to shop. The average Russian family now knows that it 'lives badly, and that there are countries where people live better'. In one essay the poet deplored the intolerance of the Soviet Union in refusing to print and sell copies of the Bible which had been so powerful in Russia's literary tradition. He lamented that the Bible could only be bought on the black market, whereas the Koran was printed by the government and sold freely, especially in its central Asian republics where Muslims prevailed.

With the rise of the green movement in the west, the Soviet Union was criticised by yet another criterion. While it did not multiply the waste of a consumer society, for packaging was frugal, it had its own failings. Nuclear waste was regularly dumped in the Arctic seas, and dumps of toxic waste were allowed to accumulate on land. Chemicals polluted towns; and tall chimneys belched out coal smoke that was thick with solid waste. Oil leaked from pipelines and no repair gangs arrived. Reportedly more oil was spilling in the Russian countryside in a few days than was lost by the huge oil tanker *Exxon Valdez* in the Alaskan disaster of 1989.

In many Soviet cities the drinking water was contaminated by heavy metals. On the inland Aral Sea the fast-retreating water became very salty, and professional fishermen returned home with empty nets. Sturgeon, the fish that produced caviar, almost vanished from stretches of the long Volga River. Lake Baikal, the largest lake of fresh water in the world, was harmed by the pulp and paper mills operating in the forests of Siberia. More than one-fifth of the world's fresh water and nearly one-fifth of its forests lay in the Soviet Union, and the health of these resources was at risk.

The production of nuclear power for the generation of electricity was at first a Soviet triumph and then a tragedy. The Chernobyl power station lay in the Ukraine but was actually closer to Warsaw than to Moscow. In the early hours of 26 April 1986 a sudden surge of energy blew the roof off the nuclear reactor, and fire broke out. A nuclear accident seven years earlier at the power station at Three Mile Island in the United States had been tackled promptly, but the Chernobyl engineers were less prepared. When firemen arrived they breathed the fumes and 'their boots stuck in the melted bitumen on the roof'. From the vicinity 135 000 people were eventually removed but the evacuation began too late, only commencing 37 hours after the accident. In the wider contaminated area lived several million people, and they were slow to receive their doses of protective pills. Moreover for a few days, not far from Chernobyl, people picked wild berries and mushrooms and they fished in a large reservoir, ignorant that the food they gathered might be contaminated with iodine-131.

The official toll of the disaster was cautiously reported as 28 deaths from radiation sickness and three from other causes, and in 1991 the International Atomic Energy Agency based in Vienna published a similarly complacent report. A few critics, however, disagreed, claiming that 10 years after the disaster 38 000 Russians were suffering from skin diseases, difficulties in digesting and breathing, a high incidence of heart attacks, or from thyroid cancer. The dispute about the fatal effects of the fallout is intense.

Meanwhile the Soviet Union's long war in Afghanistan hurt morale at home. A national army that once had fought brilliantly against Hitler was now thwarted in the valleys of a nation that was initially viewed as third rate in military capacity though not in bravery. Young men, especially from ethnic minorities, resented having to serve in the Soviet Army, and to fight for the sake of the principles of Lenin and Marx in a foreign land. The war was to Moscow what the Vietnam War had been to Washington. It was especially galling to Russian generals, for they had enjoyed the reputation of leading the most efficient land forces in the world.

Gorbachev tried to invigorate the Russian economy. On May Day in 1987 a new law allowed people to set up a private business though not to employ others in the business. Curiously private business on a humble scale had long been allowed in the countryside, and in summer the home gardeners had sold rural produce on railway stations and in street stalls. Private ownership of homes became widespread. Absenteeism and unsafe working methods in the factories were tackled partly by limiting the supply of vodka. While possibly lifting efficiency in the workplace, the vodka drought increased indignation.

There was a sudden vogue for what was called 'glasnost' (openness). There must be more debate, Gorbachev insisted, and an airing of problems rather than the usual, official claim that they do not exist. He even talked about the virtues of setting up a secret ballot for elections to the Communist Party. It so happened that one of the propaganda triumphs of the Soviet Union was the succession of national elections in which the official communist candidates always won nearly 100 per cent of the votes. A genuine secret ballot in party and in national elections was obviously too dangerous to contemplate. Frankness, however, was in the air. Disillusionment with communism was let loose. Even Mrs Margaret Thatcher, visiting Moscow in March 1987, was invited to speak on Soviet television. Everywhere the dogs were let off their chains: they did not thank their masters, they barked.

The Soviet Union and its ring of satellite nations were approaching an economic crisis but it is easy to exaggerate the extent of that crisis, as distinct from the crisis in authority. Customers, in what they could buy, were better off then ever before. They could travel more freely than in the past, though capitalist nations were out of bounds to most citizens. Certainly the Soviet Union could not compete, as an economic machine, with the United States, but that had been true for decades. It was still vigorous in the space race, and one Russian cosmonaut Yury Romanenko created an extraordinary record by enduring 237 days of sitting and lying in space. Moreover the United States suffered its own aches. Its economy in the 1970s had suffered the economic malady called stagflation – a mixture of economic stagnation and high inflation. Its pockets of poverty were conspicuous. The United States government, in financing its adventure into Star Wars, was amassing annual deficits that perturbed many economists.

A KETTLE ABOUT TO BOIL

The collapse of communism in Europe was initiated less in Russia than in its satellite nations. In 1987 nationalism, economic discontent and an aching for freedom were visible all the way from Estonia and Poland to Romania and Moldavia.

East Germany relished the highest standard of living in the communist bloc. It was a shoppers' paradise compared to Poland, where meat and meat products were still rationed for the 37 million citizens. East Germany had experienced pleasing economic growth, measured by sluggish Soviet-bloc standards, but its people worked long hours to buy the same basket of goods that could be purchased in West Germany with a few hours' pay. This was a dangerous contrast. There were not two Russias, and not two Polands, but there were two Germanys. The one ethnic group was inhabiting two different material and mental worlds.

The contrast between the two was increasing, thus imposing pressures on the government of East Germany. In 1987 it relaxed some of its harsh rules and allowed working people to apply for a permit enabling them, if they could evince compassionate grounds, to visit relatives in West Germany for 30 days. During the year a host of East Germans made brief visits, returning punctually because they knew that other members of their family were virtually held hostage. Others of course came back because they preferred life in East Germany: it was home. Many were proud of what socialism, in their view, had accomplished compared to Nazi Germany, which many of them could remember.

In East Germany, as in the other communist satellites, the young were becoming sympathetic to western culture. When rock concerts were staged in West Berlin in June 1987 the amplified sound could be heard on the other side of the wall, where crowds of the young gathered to eavesdrop on three successive nights. The police tried to drive them away. It was no longer so easy because their ranks included voices of dissent.

Two years passed. The dissent, aided by Gorbachev's policies and fanned by nationalism, grew in eastern Europe. The prestige of the communist leaders was ebbing fast. Their grip on power was looser. They were forced to experiment a little.

Poland, in economic chaos, permitted its own stunted version of free elections. Solidarity, the defiant trade union, won by massive margins all the seats in which it was allowed to field candidates. In August 1989 it was invited by the ruling communists to form a government. Other governments in eastern Europe could no longer rely, as in the past, on the help of Moscow's iron heel. Gorbachev had made that clear earlier in the years by withdrawing Soviet troops from Czechoslovakia and Hungary: the border between communist lands and Austria was virtually unguarded.

By the autumn of 1989, East Germany was a kettle about to boil. On 18 October its leader, Erich Honecker, aged 77, was pushed from office. Gorbachev's hand was prominent in pushing him, though the reason for the dismissal was disguised at first in the language of a medical bulletin, 'gall bladder surgery' being called for. Honecker was dismissed as a party member seven weeks later.

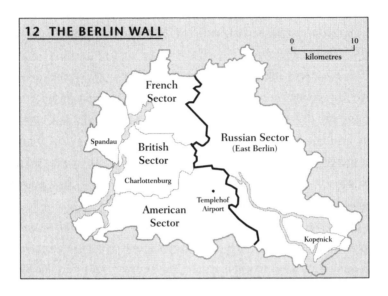

12 THE BERLIN WALL

0   10
kilometres

French
Sector

Spandau

British
Sector

Russian Sector
(East Berlin)

Charlottenburg

Templehof
Airport

American
Sector

Kopenick

East Germans assembled in small and large crowds in the main streets. Even if initially they did not make speeches of protest, their mere act of assembling was an ominous sign for a government that was suspicious of unauthorised gatherings. More and more people were leaving the country, carrying their newly issued visa allowing them 30 days of absence. Lutherans who, like the Catholics in Poland, had remained influential in East Germany, publicly told the discontented how to leave the country without a visa. Public amenities were increasingly disrupted. In East Berlin 3 of every 10 tram drivers had left the country and 5 of every 10 bus drivers too.

Tuesday 7 November had long been a communist day of celebration, marking the anniversary of the Bolshevik revolution of 1917. On the 72nd anniversary, protesters in the capital of the socialist republic of Moldavia clambered onto the Soviet tanks about to take part in the procession. In Moscow, demonstrators assembled on the

Ring Road and marched to the Olympic stadium with banners inscribed '72 YEARS – ON THE ROAD – TO NOWHERE'. In the heart of the city Mikhail Gorbachev, standing on Lenin's mausoleum to review the annual parade of Soviet might, stepped down and, speaking to the television cameras, calmly called for his own policy of slow reform to receive a fair trial.

During that same week Lenin's mausoleum was closed so that the long-embalmed body could be touched up. It was more than the body, however, that was decaying. The whole Soviet society was disintegrating. In Moscow the world's greatest land army and most powerful intelligence agency, the KGB, were at loggerheads. The heads of the army had to be replaced. Gorbachev, at times, was barely in control.

In every big empire, whether healthy or sick, decentralising forces are at work. The leaders in two large Soviet republics, Kazakhstan and the Ukraine, were resisting Gorbachev's reforms. Two more power bases, the cities of Leningrad and Moscow, played tug of war with him. The power of the Soviet Union to intervene in the affairs of other nations within the communist bloc was being weakened by discord at home. Moreover, with the decline of official censorship, the news of protests in one communist country travelled quickly to another, thus spurring more daring acts of dissent.

The rumbles of discord in Moscow on the public holiday of 7 November 1989 were heard in East Berlin where the ruling council of ministers and its 42 members resolved that their government should resign. Such a resignation was unknown in the communist orb. More important, a free democratic election was promised to the citizens. Hitherto, East Germany, though officially called the

German Socialist Democratic Republic, was no more democratic than a political prison.

The turn of events made numerous East Germans shake their heads with disbelief. Were they hearing correctly the news? They rang the official state television station and asked the announcer to repeat the latest official news items, promising them rights of which they had been long deprived.

It was still a crime to leave East Germany without a travel visa, but a host of people thought it sensible to escape rather than dutifully line up at public offices and seek a visa. China's ruthless suppression of demonstrations in Beijing's Tiananmen Square had occurred only two months previously, and many eastern Europeans feared that tanks and machine-guns would appear suddenly in their main streets, squashing their silent revolution against communism. The outflow of people turned into a torrent. It was as if the water, dammed up for so long, found holes in the surrounding walls and poured through, enlarging them. Czechoslovakia was one of these gaping holes that other eastern Europeans exploited.

The Krainers were amongst the restless East Germans eager to join their daughters in West Germany. The parents and one son packed their best clothes and possessions into six suitcases and three carrier bags, and squeezed them into a friend's car. Travelling southwards during the night, in a state of high anxiety, they crossed an unguarded corner of Czechoslovakia, said farewell to their driver, and walked past abandoned bicycles and cars to the welcoming border of West Germany. In less than one week some 50 000 East Germans used this roundabout route to reach the freedom of West Germany. That the Czech government should be sanctioning this mass escape from communism showed how far the solidarity of the red world had fractured.

On Thursday evening, 8 November 1989, the East German government gave in. It announced that people were free to leave, though rules were soon instituted. On the following morning at nine o'clock a bulldozer was heard breaking a hole in the wall that had long prevented East Berliners from entering West Berlin. Crossing points were cut in the wall, as well as at other places in the long fence with which communist East Germany had isolated itself from the west. The following Saturday and Sunday were like a carnival. West German cities near the border attracted East German day-visitors, many of whom returned home that night with perfumes, walkman radios, jeans, lottery tickets and other purchased items that were not freely for sale in East Germany.

At first it was assumed that liberated East Germany would be an independent nation with its own democratic government. Just before Christmas 1989, the heads of West and East Germany held formal discussions in Dresden about the future of their countries; and at a public rally, in the square next to the ruins of the Church of Our Lady, Helmut Kohl, the chancellor of West Germany, expressed the mood of exultation. 'Dear friends,' he said, 'in the coming year you will have free elections.' That evening he offered the hope of unity to nearly 80 million Germans: 'And let me also say – on this square that is rich in tradition – that my goal is, whenever the historical hour allows it, the unity of our nation.' The two Germanys were finally united on 3 October 1990, with the support of all those major powers that had insisted at the end of the Second World War that Germany should never again be united.

The sheer momentum of the events of 1989 and 1990 in eastern Europe was bewildering. Every communist government was either overthrown or forced in self-defence to renounce its past. The long-suppressed nationalism called for secession. The three Baltic states – Lithuania, Latvia and Estonia – were breaking away from the Soviet Union. The loose federation known as Yugoslavia broke up into separate nations.

The Soviet Union, cracking under nationalist pressures, ceased to exist in 1991. In its place stood an independent Russia and a long line of new republics, including Ukraine, Kazakhstan and Georgia. Mikhail Gorbachev, who had played a distinctive part in initiating these astonishing events, had long ceased to control them. By the end of 1991 he was the leader of no nation. The collapse of the Soviet Union and the collapse of czarist Russia had much in common. Their belated efforts to reform themselves were seen as signs of weakness and were pounced upon.

CHINA: STRUGGLING TO LEAP FORWARD

During the spread of communism as a global force, China made its own path. Its communist leaders were suspicious of a Soviet desire to dominate them: their ideologies drew apart. By 1960 the rift was clear. One sign was Albania's hurried retreat from the tutelage of Moscow to that of distant Beijing. Another was the reluctance of the Soviet Union to help China to make its own nuclear weapons.

Mao Zedong in his early years in power made his own experiments and coined his own slogans. While he reduced infectious diseases and illiteracy, his Great Leap Forward in economic policy was a leap backwards. Agriculture slipped, and in the famine of

1959–61 close to 30 million people are said to have died. Mao weakened the incentives of a people who traditionally had been noted for their economic energy and stamina.

To travel by train across China in summertime in the mid-1960s was to revisit scenes that belonged to the economic life of the Old Testament: the legs of thousands of men and women turning treadmills that raised irrigation water to a higher level, crowds of labourers standing in the barnyard with wooden flails and threshing the grain from the stalk, people sowing seed by hand, an old woman spending all day caring for a mere three geese, and camels carrying their loads, their driver walking alongside. China admittedly operated locomotives but they were black, puffing monsters of early design. The Soviet Union was dynamic compared to China.

As if to rejuvenate China, Mao set in motion the turbulence of the Great Proletarian Cultural Revolution in 1966. Beginning with the Mayor of Peking a procession of communist potentates was deposed. Tens of thousands of comrades and cadres further down the line were singled out for denunciation. At public meetings those considered as traitors or ideological deviants, whether in economic theory or western music, were hastily tried and despatched in humiliation to the countryside where they cleaned out the pigpens and drains, or were locked in prisons or shot. Hordes of young people called Red Guards arrived in the big cities, bringing juvenile enthusiasm to the art of persecution. For a time one of the most popular books in the world was 'the little red book' which outlined the thoughts of Mao Zedong.

His thoughts were turning his country upside down. The outer gates of China were almost locked for a year or two. Hardly a foreigner or tourist was to be seen in Beijing and Shanghai and Guangzhou (Canton) where the corridors of the few new Moscow-style hotels fell silent. Relations with the Soviet Union so deteriorated that the 7000 kilometres of border between the two countries became a line of friction. By 1972 the Soviet Union deployed 46 divisions of troops along its Chinese borders – more than it posted in eastern Europe.

After Mao Zedong died in 1976, and was safely embalmed, the leaders engaged in another power struggle. The Gang of Four disappeared, and there emerged another unusual leader, the elderly Deng Xiaoping. A native of the western province of Sichuan, he had studied in France in the early 1920s before returning home to support the rising communists, whom he joined in the Long March. His talents recognised, he rose high several times and then was pulled down. He was too pragmatic for a party that sometimes enthroned theory. One of his favourite sayings was that a cat can be either black or white: who cares so long as it catches the mice?

As leader of China he set out to modernise farms, factories, the defence forces and all workplaces where new technology could be applied. He tried to restore the work ethic, which was conspicuous amongst the overseas Chinese but not in the homeland. He reduced the rate of population growth by ruling that each family should have only one child – a ruling that was not always obeyed in rural areas. Most peasants decided that if they were to rear only one child it would be a boy. Births of boys reportedly exceeded girls by a ratio approaching 119 to 100.

Freedom darted here and there in economic life but not in politics where the communist agenda ruled. Deng briefly lost favour with the outside world when his armed forces trampled on a tiny rebellion that broke out in Tiananmen Square on 4 June 1989. If such an uprising had been dealt with by Chairman Mao 20 years previously, there would have been barely a footnote in the western media. But now Beijing was alive with foreign tourists and cameras, and the news ran around the world.

To enlist foreign capital and machinery is a difficult task for a run-down economy. China enlisted them with ease from the millions of Chinese living overseas. Their ancestors had mostly left their homeland in the 19th century, sailing as gold-diggers to California and Australia and as labourers and small-traders to the nearer countries of the south-east. Most had emigrated from a tiny section of southeast China, from the provinces of Guangdong and Fujian and especially their tropical coastline; and so they easily acclimatised themselves in South-East Asia as agricultural labourers and miners.

From ports in Fujian province came the ancestors of most of the Chinese now living in Malaysia, Singapore and the Philippines. From a small rural area near Guangzhou came most of the Chinese who multiplied in Indonesia, Vietnam, the United States and Australia. These two flows of Chinese emigration were, materially, amongst the most dynamic in the world's recorded history.

So it came to pass that in East Asia the Chinese permeated every economy, except Japan and the two Koreas. In 1990 there were said to be five billionaires in Thailand and Indonesia, and all were of Chinese ancestry. In South-East Asia lived more than 30 million overseas Chinese, and by some estimates they produced more wealth annually than did the billion and more people living in China itself. Even before 1914 they were sometimes called 'the Jews of the east'. Being more numerous than the Jews of the west, their potential to finance the rebuilding of China was startling. From the 1980s, they diverted into their ancestral home much of their ingenuity and wealth, initially surpassing Japanese and Americans as the main investors in Deng's new China.

In ending a long era of intellectual and economic quarantine, Deng repaired links with Europe, the Soviet Union, the United States, India and – less so – with Japan. He even persuaded Margaret Thatcher to surrender Hong Kong, which had long been a wealthy British colony. In 1997, the year of his death, the portrait of Queen Elizabeth II ceased to appear on Hong Kong's postage stamps.

In coastal China, with mesmerising speed, arose skyscrapers and freeways, fast railways, stock exchanges, towering advertising signs, docks jammed with container ships and power-houses shadowed by coal smoke. This new workshop of the world was encircled by the old wall of China. Its communist government was authoritarian. It oppressed Tibet and occasionally threatened the democratic republic of Taiwan, though these acts of bullying were rarely criticised by the democratic nations wishing to take part in China's economic feast. While China gloried in a novel cluster of remarkable achievements, perhaps India overall had attained more, for it had a high level of personal freedom.

In the year 2001 the only nation in the world to remain ardently communist was North Korea. Not a display case for communism. Its people were under-nourished, over-armed, spied upon by their government, and cut off from nearly all outside contacts. North Korea was a gigantic cage rather than part of an entwined globe. Few peoples of the world in modern times had endured such isolation.

A FALSE SUNRISE

The rush of events in the Soviet Union, Germany, eastern Europe and China in the late 1980s and the very early 1990s had no parallel in modern history. During the last thousand years no other formidable empire in a time of comparative peace had been dissolved so quickly, so unexpectedly, as the Soviet Union. That China changed course at the same time added to the sense of profound change. No extended period of tension, in recent centuries, had been eased so unexpectedly.

Out of the collapse of communism came a floodlight of optimism. During the 20th century only one previous event – the end of the First World War – had given rise to optimism on a comparable scale. And yet that earlier outbreak of peace in 1918 cheered only one part of the world. It had little impact on China and Japan, little impact on most of Africa, and little impact on South America. The end of that war was followed by bitter disagreements at the peace conference in Paris. In contrast the ending of the Cold War was almost world-embracing in its optimism.

In the early 1990s arose a belief that the world had changed forever. It was widely believed that democracy and political and economic individualism had achieved a permanent triumph. Global free trade was hailed as imminent, and trade barriers would collapse forever. Such a conclusion was surprising because no triumph in history is likely to be permanent. At the same time the hope arose that global wars were no longer feasible. Mr Tony Blair, elected Prime Minister of Britain on May Day 1997, mirrored this latest sunrise of optimism: 'Mine is the first generation able to contemplate the possibility that we may live our entire lives without going to war or sending our children to war. That is a prize beyond value.'

In this hopeful decade the Internet spread its web around the world, adding to the air of optimism. People living far apart had not previously communicated with such ease. But the optimism was premature. In modern times each major mechanical advance in communicating initially appeared to be a boost to human under-standing. A similar sense of a dawning age of peace had successively arisen from the rise of the international telegraph, the long-distance mail steamer and railway, and later the wireless, the tourist circuit, and the electronic web. That the web could equally serve not only home-loving people but also wandering terrorists was not yet realised.

SLOW MIRACLE IN EUROPE

Russian communism gained power largely because of the First World War. That the communists, 40 years later, were able to com-mand such a strong position in the vast steppes, mountains, desert and tundra stretching all the way from Russian ports on the Baltic and Black seas to Chinese and North Korean ports on the Pacific Ocean, and that the red flag was carried into outer space, was an indirect result of the Second World War.

Another powerful political movement was also born of the two world wars: the dream of a united Europe. It had deep roots. For centuries observers had remarked on the way in which Europe com-bined distinctive unity and unusual disunity, and how the combination of the two made it dynamic. Europe had shaped the world. Most of the remarkable changes since the Renaissance,

Reformation, and the discovery of the New World had arisen from the energy, ingenuity and imagination of Europe. And yet the continent was dangerously divided.

By the 1920s the concept of a united Europe was budding inside the minds of a few compatible statesmen. Knowing the disaster of the First World War and the hatreds that were almost cemented into national life, they hoped for a peace that would be more forgiving. A few of these statesmen were drawn together in 1925, being their nations' foreign ministers. Sir Austen Chamberlain, representing Britain, belonged to a famous political family from the city of Birmingham and wore a ribboned monocle through which he saw Europe with informed and sympathetic eyes. His first ally at the conference table, Aristide Briand, had been 11 times premier of France, and from April 1925 he was to be foreign minister in 14 successive governments: he lent continuity to the turmoil of French politics. Briand was the delight of cartoonists because of his drooping dark moustache, incorrigible wit, and captivating oratory. According to Chamberlain, Briand delivered his speeches in a caressing way, with 'a deep, melodious voice which could sing to a whisper or ring out like a deep-toned bell'. The third foreign minister was Dr Gustav Stresemann of Germany, whose unyielding look and formidable manner concealed a willingness to listen, empathise and negotiate. When he died he was praised by Chamberlain as a 'true friend of peace'.

The three ministers took pleasure from each other's company. They shared an ability to combine patriotism with a sense of responsibility for the state of the wider world. At Locarno in Switzerland in 1925, together with the representatives of Italy and Belgium, the three signed a pact of peace that seemed likely to bring to western Europe more stability than the Treaty of Versailles had offered. If the three had remained in power, the war of 1939 would have probably been averted; but by then they were dead.

It was Briand who in 1930 outlined an idea which, coming from an experienced politician, startled many who heard it. He called for a federal union of Europe. In effect France, Germany and other nations would surrender much of their independence. In Italy at about the same time, Benedetto Croce, writing his history of modern Europe, predicted that its peoples one day would succeed in reconciling a love of their own land with an affection for Europe both as a place and a set of ideals. He felt that the sense of unity was arising, partly as a result of the waste of war. He concluded that the time was coming when 'the French and the Germans and the Italians and all the others will raise themselves into Europeans, and their thoughts will be directed towards Europe and their hearts will beat for her as they once did for their smaller countries, not forgotten now but loved all the better.'

After the Second World War, the destructive effects of the long disunity had to be faced as never before. Europe was divided, perhaps permanently, by an Iron Curtain. The disunity was also a spur to positive action in western Europe, for it was threatened by the Soviet Union.

Winston Churchill, having lost office at the general election of 1945, was free to concentrate on wider problems. In 1946 in Zurich he called for a 'kind of United States of Europe'. Twenty months later in The Hague he chaired a Congress of Europe to which came hundreds of the mighty and influential, all of whom were living west of the Iron Curtain. Other leaders were enthusiastic, including the French politician and brandy-maker, Jean Monnet, who had been deputy head of the bureaucracy in the early League of Nations; Robert Schuman also of France; Paul-Henri Spaak of Belgium; and Alcide de Gasperi of Italy. Significantly three of those four Europeans came from the contentious borderlands – from Belgium which Germany had twice invaded for strategic reasons, from Lorraine where France and Germany had fought, and from the south Tyrol where Italians and Austrians clashed. The four politicians hoped for close economic relations. Schuman even hoped for a united army in Europe.

By 1951 there were three vital pan-European institutions, the most powerful being the North Atlantic Treaty Organization known as NATO, in which the United States, Canada and nine western European nations formed an alliance for their mutual defence. Displaying initially more promise than power were the Council of Europe and the economic body which, four decades later, formally became the European Union. This economic infant embraced the crucial industries of coal and steel in three powerful economies – France, Germany and Italy – and the smaller Belgium, Holland and Luxembourg. The 'common market', soon embracing all commodities, became a free-trade zone with an economic vigour that owed much to West Germany. Such was its economic recovery from the ruins of war that its people in 1965 owned 45 times as many cars as they owned when Churchill made his first call for a new Europe.

In the new west European common market, based in Brussels, some of the former frictions lingered. President General de Gaulle was strong enough to block the entry of Britain, which was late in making up its mind. He and President Adenauer of Germany were also strong enough to help in healing the deep wounds in their countries' relationships, one of the most persistent and dangerous wounds in global politics, and still festering as a result of Hitler's armed occupation of France.

After the death of de Gaulle the momentum was renewed. In 1973, Britain, Ireland and Denmark joined the European common market, increasing the membership to nine. In the following decade, with the entry of the three poorer nations of Greece and Portugal and Spain, more than half of the nations lying on the western side of the Iron Curtain belonged to the common market – known now as the European Economic Community. A powerful trading bloc, its population and home market were larger than those of the United States. Its hallmark was an agricultural policy that, by subsidising local farmers, accumulated hills of surplus butter, mountains of surplus grain, and lakes of surplus wine inside Europe and debarred similar imports from the outside world.

The common market in western Europe looked inwards. Indeed it could not have been created in the decades before the Second World War because so many of its member nations, then looking outwards, believed that their overseas empires offered the economic potential that a uniting Europe has since provided. Surprisingly this European empire was persuaded to include four of France's former colonies, all tiny in territory and all their people entitled to French citizenship: the island of Réunion in the Indian Ocean, the West Indies islands of Martinique and Guadeloupe, and nearby Guiana.

By the end of the century the simple postwar scheme to protect and boost coalmines and steel mills had, by virtue of bold decisions and compromises, become a far wider political and economic union. In its unity it fell short of other long-lasting federations because it did not unite in pursuing a foreign policy and did not control its own defence forces. While it was not 'the kind of United States of Europe' that Churchill and Schuman and others had envisaged, it was a kind of half federation of half of Europe. It had its common market, its own courts, its own busy bureaucracy in Brussels, and its own elected parliament meeting since 1979 at the French river port of Strasbourg. At the end of the century it was almost ready to issue its own banknotes and currency, in place of the lira, franc, deutschmark and other national currencies, and was to admit, in 2004, a cluster of new members from the dismantled communist economic zone in eastern Europe. Indeed, one of the reasons for the collapse of communism in eastern Europe had been the prosperity and freedom of the uniting Europe on the other side of the Iron Curtain.

For Europe the first half of the century had been marred by intense national rivalries breaking out in great wars. The second half was much more peaceful though marked by crises, revolutions and Balkans wars. Towards the end of the century Europe enjoyed a unity not experienced for centuries. It had achieved unity partly through the economic and political union in western Europe. It had achieved a wider unity because communism was collapsing.

Europe, while more united than it had been for centuries, was paying a price for its earlier disunity and its intense traditional rivalries. It had lost the leadership of the world.

25

CITIES, SPORTS AND TONGUES

Experts were not sure what was the population of the world in the year 1900. In many countries and colonies no census had ever been conducted. Moreover the world as an entity was not seen as important: one's own nation or empire was of much more concern. Occasionally overpopulation was discussed but it was usually seen as the dilemma of one country, whether Britain or India. When Sir William Crookes made a celebrated prophecy in 1898 – that a grave shortage of wheat and wholesome bread might appear – he was ruminating only about the fate of European peoples.

Despite the effects of wars and infectious diseases, the world's population grew in nearly every year of the century. In 1927 or thereabouts it reached 2 billion. The milestone was not a major news item, as far as can be ascertained. Then the population began to soar, the pace quickening after the Second World War. The fastest growth of population was in the 1960s when the exploration of outer space was creating excitement: there was even the possibility that someday a fraction of the world's overflowing population might settle on another planet. The total population had reached 3 billion in 1960, and jumped to 4 billion in 1974. The phrase 'population explosion' was widely and nervously employed. In the space of less than half a century the population had doubled. In contrast a previous doubling, completed in 1927, had taken well over a century.

The trend of population was pithily commented upon by Sir Alec Cairncross, born in Scotland in the early 1900s, the son of a village ironmonger. In old age he recalled that in his childhood one in every 10 Scottish children died before their first birthday. That was an enviable record, far superior to most other countries. Such was the improvement in the world's health that towards the end of his life even China and India had a rate of infant deaths far lower than it had been in his childhood Scotland. People who survived infancy were now living longer. When he was born he could expect, by the law of averages, to live to the age of 50 but his grandchildren could expect to live beyond the age of 70. In this same advance China and India were now sharing.

In many large regions of the globe, especially the poorer, the birthrate remained high. But almost everywhere the death rate was falling. Millions of lives, young even more than old, were saved annually by the century's accumulation of medical research, the increasing presence of doctors and trained nurses in the Third World, and the educating of mothers in hygiene. Disasters still occurred. A few old diseases like smallpox were curbed, but new diseases such as AIDS were not. The number of Africans dying of this infection in South

Africa and Botswana and nearby countries was alarming, but in 2000 it was not yet one of the main determinants of the world's death rate. Lives lost annually through heart disease, cancer, and malnutrition far outnumbered those lost through AIDS.

Hunger remained too common. After 1950 a series of famines cost millions of lives: in China around 1960, during the civil war in Nigeria and Biafra a few years later, and in the Sahul drought of the early 1980s. A typical famine in the 20th century, perhaps more than in earlier centuries, was caused by a combination of climatic and political disruption. Nonetheless famines were possibly less disrupting than in the first half of the century, because food relief, if it did come from another country, was aided by quick and cheap transport. Also, far more food was produced globally in the year 2000 than had been anticipated half a century previously, and much of the increase came from India and China where decades earlier many rural experts had predicted increasing scarcity.

Most of the gain in the world's health came in the 40 years after the Second World War. The World Bank reported in 1993 that the health improvements had exceeded those 'during the entire previous span of human history'. Naturally the world's population soared. It reached the milestone of 6 billion in 1999. That milestone aroused less jubilation than the news that in the last three decades the world's population was no longer growing by such a high percentage.

THE KING CITIES

It was the century of the monster city. In 1900, in contrast, the vast majority of the world's peoples had lived close to the soil, in fishing and mining and woodcutting villages, on the farmlands and among the herds and flocks on the plains and hills. Most people had never seen a large town, let alone a city. As the slow mechanising of farming and mining meant that their labour was no longer needed at home, they moved from village to city. Never before had such huge cities arisen. By the end of the century almost half of the people of the world lived in cities.

The giant city in 1900 had been London: the heart of the largest empire and the financial hub of the globe. Most tourists who watched the horse-drawn traffic hurry around Piccadilly Circus on a misty morning, who surveyed the red-coated regiments marching through the wood-paved streets, who heard Big Ben strike or bells chime 'oranges and lemons' before morning service at St Clement's, or who sat in Covent Garden Theatre and heard Melba and Caruso sing, thought that they were in the heart of civilisation. A journalist from the Southern Hemisphere who climbed the gallery of St Paul's Cathedral and saw, all the way to the smoky horizon, almost nothing but housetops, was spellbound: 'There is nothing to compare it with. It is tremendous.' Not again will the world's most populous city, wherever it may be, convey such a feeling of power and mystique, for the big cities of the 21st century will probably arise in poorer nations with no empire at their call.

London was surpassed in the 1920s by New York which became the world's financial centre as well as the most populous city. New York was almost another London, but without the empire, the long history, and the prestige of being a capital city. And yet New York sparkled when discerning Europeans visited it – and not many did. They were delighted by the ornate and clean railway stations, the grand hotels and department stores, the multitude of stylish cars even in the suburban streets, and above all the graceful skyscrapers of a height, variety and majesty unknown in Europe. When the Parisian architect Charles Jeanneret who called himself Le Corbusier made his first visit to the New World in 1935, and his ship sailed up the harbour towards Manhattan, he saw his long-awaited 'mystic city of the new world'. To his surprise the skyscrapers displayed more stone than glass. To him they were incredible towers, like white cathedrals. He observed that 'they carry up a thousand feet in the sky, a completely new and prodigious architectural event; with one stroke Europe is thrust aside'. New York, pushed into second place in the world in the 1950s, remained in that ranking for a long period, while still growing in width and height. By 2001, the year of the sensational toppling of its World Trade Center, it had fallen to fourth place in population.

As the largest city in the world New York gave way to Tokyo. When the Japanese city assumed the title it was neither the home of an empire nor a global centre of finance. Its ascent was remarkable. It had survived a series of setbacks including the earthquake of 1923, and the heavy bombings of 1944 and 1945 which drove so many from city to countryside that by the end of the war Tokyo had lost about half of its prewar population of 7.5 million. Its recovery from war was also extraordinary. Reclaiming land from the big expanse of Tokyo Bay for new suburbs and the international airport, and building its elevated express freeways in time for the Olympic Games of 1964, it cleared room for itself. High skyscrapers were too dangerous for a city in a seismic zone, and land was scarce for horizontal expansion, and therefore Tokyo's skill was to squeeze people contentedly into cramped spaces. That it was already crowded did not deter rural newcomers who adapted easily to the art of living. One reason why postwar Japan exported far more than it imported, thus building up financial credits, was that its citizens could not fit many objects in their own home. What could you store in such tiny apartments?

The first city to reach 20 million, Tokyo increased its lead over rivals by reaching the outskirts of, and then swallowing, three adjacent cities. It absorbed the famous port city of Yokohama and made more bites and gulps. Its business centre coped with the two daily rush hours. The daily sight of skilled railway officials prodding the passengers, so that every inch in a carriage was filled, was a sight unknown to New York and London.

The western cities that were most influential and innovative were no longer the giants. In the last third of the century perhaps the most dynamic urban place was a small urban-rural region extending south of San Francisco Bay. In 1965 it was mainly orchards producing apricots and prunes: the orchards provided more income than the rising electronics firms. Later called Silicon Valley, its proximity to sophisticated defence industries and Stanford University was an asset. The university taught a stream of talent and also did research in fields vital to the expanding electronics firms, helping to make the valley a home of innovation. It was here in 1994, soon after the creation of the World Wide Web, that two Stanford students in their spare time set up the web search engine called Yahoo. By the end of the century the public companies in the valley were valued on the stock exchanges at a far higher price than the combined total of Hollywood's entertainment firms and Detroit's automobile industry.

In the last 30 years of the century the Third World began to produce its own metropolises. Fast-rising Mexico City and São Paulo passed New York though they could not overtake Tokyo as the king of cities. By 2000, of the top 10 cities of the world, four were in the subcontinent of India where Bombay (Mumbai) and Calcutta (Kolkata) were the largest. In all, six of the world's top 10 cities stood in Asia, two in the United States and two in Latin America. Curiously the city expected to leap quickly towards the first or second place in the new century was a tropical metropolis sitting in perpetual danger of floods, Dacca (Dhaka) in Bangladesh.

Europe had lost the eminence that it held for so long. Its slide down the ladder of large cities was dramatic. At the end of the century, no European city sat in the top 15. While Paris, Moscow and London formed the top trio, each was smaller than such Asian cities as Jakarta and Delhi, and the African boom cities.

In 1901, when London had no equal, Lagos was a sleepy port in West Africa. Lying in a belt of high rainfall close to the equator, it shipped away palm oil and palm kernels and other tropical items to Hamburg and Liverpool. Lagos was the capacious port on its stretch of Nigeria's coast; but until a sandbar was dredged, the overseas steamships anchored in the open sea and were loaded from native craft.

The original town sat at one end of a low-lying island, partly sand and partly swamps which were drained by a long canal. An iron bridge carried the railway and road over the lagoon to the African mainland whose shore consisted of sandy ridges and malarial creeks. The island port then held 40 000 people, a racecourse, bungalows for the governor and the British officials, and barracks for their soldiers.

Lagos blossomed in a way that no British official could have predicted. Its population passed 1 million in 1960, by which time it was the capital of the newly independent Nigeria. After another two decades of growth, it was approaching 5 million people. Surely its crazy growth could be checked when it ceased to be both the federal and state capital of Nigeria? The capitals were moved elsewhere: Lagos grew and grew. If a young man from a distant village found work in the ever-stretching metropolis, his extended family began to arrive to share in his good fortune.

Most newcomers relished the excitement and bustle of Lagos, and accepted the frequent failures of electricity, the inadequacies of drinking water, the garbage rarely collected. Shanty suburbs sprang up. In older suburbs the rooming houses catered for newcomers, and one district held more than 4000 such houses, mostly sleeping 60 to 80 in each. Naturally residents tended to spend their spare time in the streets, the few parks and unbuilt spaces. Much of the commerce was transacted from stalls erected in front of houses along the main roads, most stalls displaying a tiny stock of bottled, tinned and other foods. As the traffic became congested – freeways were out of the question – the buses and trucks and even bikes moved so slowly that passengers could jump out, buy and jump back. They nicknamed the wayside shops the 'go-slow market'.

After causeways and bridges and many ferries linked the island city to the mainland, suburbs with their churches and mosques were able to spill along the flat coastline where a second port, Apapa, was carved out. At the start of the new century Lagos, with a total of 10 million people on the islands and coastal mainland, was rivalling Cairo as the largest city in Africa.

These mushroom cities of Africa resembled the expansive European cities of a century previously. Backward in distributing fresh water and disposing of sewage, they were high in infant mortality. But their populations soared as newcomers poured in.

'THE PLOUGHMAN, OUR TEACHER'

The growth of cities in the Third World contrasted with the unchanging ways of the countryside. J.K. Galbraith, after serving as US ambassador to India, described the rulers of its cities as busily designing atomic power plants and drawing up five-year plans. In such plans, he admitted in 1974, 'Village India' had no place. A quarter of a century later there were still two Indias. Conspicuous were the baby skyscrapers with their plate-glass windows and their push-button lavatories, while out of sight were the tens of thousands of rural villages, medieval in their amenities, and crouched at the end of the dirt roads. There a swarm of people operated simple implements in sun-dried fields, while high overhead the jets roared on their way to Holland or Japan.

In the 1990s maybe one-quarter of the workers of the world worked in much the same way as their ancestors had, generation after generation. The seeds they sowed were slightly larger but the tasks were the same: yoking up the beasts of burden, ploughing the ground, planting the seed by hand, and later taking off the crop by hand. The wellbeing of India and China still partly depended on the faithful way these familiar tasks were performed.

The messages of all the world's major religions had been first expressed when these rural tasks were everyone's. Just as Christianity likened God to a shepherd – 'The Lord is my shepherd' – so in

Indian temples the Sikhs chanted verses of the 16th century proclaiming that God, with His firm hands and unswerving sense of purpose, was like a bullock driver:

As a team of oxen are we driven
By the ploughman, our teacher.

Fifteen million carts – nearly all drawn by a pair of oxen – carried most of the grain and firewood produced in India in the mid-1990s. Nearly every Indian farmer knew how to yoke a young ox in readiness for its first day of hard work, which began just after it showed its first pair of big teeth. Sometimes called bullocks and sometimes oxen, they pulled the carts, crushed the sugar cane, and dragged along the cut logs. Whereas observers in mechanised cities now see beasts of burden as backward, in India they actually represented progress, providing a more efficient form of transport than their predecessor, the human carrier.

In Madhya Pradesh, a state embracing one-seventh of the Indian republic and nearly 70 million of its people, one district did not even possess carts. In 1995 the heavy or awkward loads were carried from village to village on the shoulders of men and women. In a corner of Orissa the chickens were carried to market in homemade bamboo coops, heavy loads of rice and vegetables went in bamboo baskets, and fish in bamboo bags. In Bihar a reporter from *The Times of India* marvelled at the loads of firewood balanced on the heads of women who themselves did not weigh as much as their load. Resolving to experience their day's tasks, he set out soon after sunrise on the walk to the places where light timber could be found. He saw them collect the wood and carry it all the way to a village market, walking a total of 40 kilometres during the hot day. If they were very thirsty, he observed, they made a long detour to find a drink. Their firewood was in high demand because no electricity lines reached the district. No woman in the home village, he guessed, was over the age of 50: women died young, under the strain of constant, heavy labour.

Most children did not attend school. Their labour was needed in the fields and, moreover, their parents – in debt to the moneylender – could not afford pencils, slates and notebooks. Similar scenes and dilemmas could be seen in a thousand rural districts in Africa.

In rural India as in many other lands the longstanding way of life, for better or worse, was receding. Most rural tasks required fewer people. One day the electric light will reach the land of the female carriers of wood, and the plastic or cardboard box will throw out of work those who make the bamboo baskets. And the tractor will arrive, replacing the oxen and the walking ploughman, 'our teacher'.

THE RISE OF GLOBAL LANGUAGES

Living languages were influenced by the move from countryside to city. Languages that were spoken in one rural region, and by only thousands of speakers, were endangered when many speakers moved to a city. The same regional languages suffered when the culture of the city – through the new media – reached the countryside. They were also at risk if the invading global language, for example English or Russian, offered more hope of a job, of further education, and access to entertainment.

Away from Europe, hundreds of native languages that were alive and vigorous in 1900 were spoken now by only a few thousand people. When a language so declined, most of the more fluent speakers used it for only part of the day and even then could not exploit its full richness and complexity because their listeners, especially the young, knew the language imperfectly. Of the world's 6000 languages, most possessed relatively few speakers at the century's end. They were in peril, for the radio and television, the newspaper and book, threw their weight behind those languages embracing the most speakers.

Yiddish has barely one-third of the speakers it possessed in 1900, when it was spoken across central and eastern Europe. Ingrian and two other languages spoken near the Baltic Sea each possessed, by the 1970s, only a few hundred speakers. In Denmark and the German-speaking regions of Switzerland in 1900 were distinct district dialects that puzzled those speaking the popular core language, but the dialects died as the old speakers died. Most Italians in 1861 had spoken regional languages with their own grammar, vocabulary and pronunciation; but now the Tuscan dialect is dominant. Several European languages died out completely. The Dalmatian language spoken on the eastern shores of the Adriatic Sea died in 1898. The Manx language spoken on the Isle of Man in the Irish Sea died in 1974.

In Australia many distinct languages died within living memory. One scholar in the last 30 years had been studying five living Aboriginal languages, all in tropical Queensland, but in 1992 he reported sadly that three were extinct, one was in the custody of 10 speakers, while another was kept alive in the mind of just one lonely speaker. These were not simple languages that died through lack of flexibility and vocabulary. Most had a complicated grammar and an impressive working vocabulary of about 10 000 words. Around the world, of the multitude of languages in danger, most would not survive.

In 1900 French was, by a narrow margin, the language preferred for international discourse. It was the accepted language of diplomacy, and the language favoured by polite society in a dozen lands including Russia. Within secondary schools of the English-speaking world it competed with Latin as the most popular foreign language. According to the 1920s edition of the fine English encyclopaedia, Chambers's, French was the most 'uniformly readable of all literature'. There was hardly a branch of learning and culture for which the French language was not suited: 'In France more than in any other country mental power is accompanied by the literary faculty', announced the encyclopaedia. The French language seemed to dance hand in hand with the best of civilisation. But it could not compete with English as the language of commerce – London and New York by 1900 were the commercial capitals of the globe and the pound sterling was the prince of currencies – and so business people of most nationalities, from Swedes to Japanese, learned English rather than French.

Many people hoped for a completely new universal language, and 53 such languages were invented or outlined in the years 1880 to 1907. Esperanto and Volapük, artificial languages, had many learned friends but not enough. The idea was common that a universal language would promote friendship across boundaries and prevent wars, but people preferred their own, especially in wartime. After the First World War the speakers of Esperanto hoped that their neutral language would begin to reign. The members of the League of Nations had to make the hard decision on which language to prefer, and they settled for English and French, resolving to print all documents in both languages.

The military defeat of France in 1940 was a blow to the standing of the eloquent French language, but not in its own colonies. French financial aid to Africa was on the most generous scale, and Africans were happy to say 'merci' and to use French when composing their submissions for further subsidies. The advance of communism was another blow to the popularity of the French language. The Russian language outflanked French by becoming the most favoured second language in China, Mongolia, and the communist lands of eastern Europe.

The English language was now far ahead, thanks partly to the influence of the United States. English also remained a vital language in India because of the conflicts between speakers of Hindi and other tongues. In the 1940s, English was also surpassing German as the language of science and engineering, and a decade later it became the language of the air-traffic controllers. In the emerging world of pop, Elvis Presley, the Beatles and most of the stars sang in English. What more could a language wish for?

In the last third of the century no rival of English gained ground. The liberation of eastern Europe and the disintegration of the Soviet Union ended Russia's brief phase as a potential global language. By then the French and Russian languages each possessed fewer native speakers than Spanish which gained from the rapid growth of population in Latin America. Admittedly Chinese possessed more than a billion speakers and was a vital lubricant of commerce in East Asia, but it was English and not Chinese that became the language of the

Internet. In the year 2000, English was more influential than any other language in the recorded history of the world.

HEROES AND SPORT

England was the birthplace of most of the worldwide sports, and the early English amateurs proclaimed the cult of fairness. The contest itself was said to be more important than victory, the spirit of the game more important than the final score. Some of today's best known English soccer clubs originated as Sunday school teams, and were nourished by the ideology of 'muscular Christianity'. In cricket the cult of fairness gave birth in the 1860s to the popular sporting admonition: 'It's not cricket!' The phrase spread around the English-speaking world. When a footballer's behaviour on the playing field was considered unfair, the accusation would be trumpeted in the following day's newspaper, 'It's not cricket.' Sport and fair play were almost synonymous. If champion players of 1900 could witness big sporting contests a century later, they would be slightly disappointed by the heightened emphasis on victory.

At the start of the century few games attracted a crowd of spectators. Popular sports such as horse racing, bullfighting, cricket and baseball, football and boxing rarely attracted foreign competitors and spectators. Even the main tennis tournament held each summer at Wimbledon was largely for British players. A stir was caused when an American woman, May Sutton, arrived: rather indelicately she played with her forearms bare, earning her the nickname of 'the washerwoman'. In this era of stay-at-home sports, an unusual international tour was staged for the 'New Zealand Native Team', most of whom were Maoris. Crossing the world to the British Isles, they played 74 matches of rugby football in the winter of 1888–89.

International sporting occasions became more frequent in the two decades before the First World War. The all-amateur Olympic Games, reborn in Athens in 1896, were somewhat starved of excellence when restaged in Paris in 1900 and St Louis in 1904 because most of the world's finest athletes could not afford the fare to the venue or, being professionals, were not allowed to attend. Soccer, invented in Britain and now the most popular game in the world, had little claim to be international as late as 1900. Cricket was blessed with international 'tests', some attracting large crowds day after day in the 1870s, but the only teams competing regularly were Australia and England. Professional sculling (individual rowing) and boxing were international sports – the oarsmen drew probably the largest sporting crowds in the world – but few countries competed. The Tour de France was first staged in 1903, though the cyclists were mostly French. The Davis Cup was first awarded in 1900, but only the English tennis team visited Boston to compete.

Children fell under the spell of spectator sport, absorbing it as if it were magic. Neville Cardus, aged 12, setting out from a humble house in Manchester in 1902 to see his first cricket match, took a wrong turn and found himself running along the banks of a canal, across which he could find no bridge. Fearful that he was missing the cricket, he ran so quickly that workmen in a grubby coal barge began to cheer. At last reaching the Lancashire ground he paid his sixpence to join the spectators, and in his own words 'crawled through a hole in the multitude'. At the end of that radiant day, he walked home, 'tired, hungry and thirsty, with a full and contented heart'. As the decades passed, visits by children and their parents to sporting fixtures often took on the emotional character of a pilgrimage.

Few could predict that spectator sports would become such a dazzling part of the entertainment industry. Eventually, electric lights and roofed stadiums allowed games to be played night and day; and even the Sunday games, which once were taboo in English-speaking countries, drew high attendances. Radio and television multiplied the audiences. What the electronic media could do for a sport was glimpsed in Jersey City in 1921 when Jack Dempsey, called the Manassa Mauler, boxed against Georges Carpentier of France. Some 80 000 people paid a staggeringly large sum to witness the fight, and thousands more heard it over the new radio. It was possibly the first major sporting event to be simultaneously experienced by an audience that was present and another that was absent.

Spectator sport slowly broke down barriers of race, sex and class. Initially most sports were played only by men; and in 1900 the Olympics in Paris set aside only two events for women – lawn tennis and golf. Almost 30 years went by before a few track and field events, and one gymnastics contest, were designated for women. Black people were welcome to play some sports but not others. In the world championships for heavyweight boxing the Afro-American boxers were reluctantly admitted, and a sensation was caused in 1908 when black Jack Johnson defeated white Tommy Burns. In the United States for decades, black women were not allowed to compete for the championships in lawn tennis.

In sports the small nations began to display their skills to the world. In the 1920s the new republic of Finland had astonishing success in the Olympics, rivalling the United States in the track and field. In the 1948 Olympics it was Holland that produced perhaps the most versatile female Olympian so far seen, the sprinter and hurdler Fanny Blankers-Koen. Later, East Germany and Australia, though small in population, had remarkable victories. Some of the muscular East Germans of the 1970s, it was observed, were fortunate that drug-tests were not yet applied seriously.

Athletes from the Third World – rarely seen at grand sporting occasions in the earlier years – began to win gold medals. Male sprinters and middle-distance runners from the Caribbean islands of Jamaica, Trinidad and Cuba won six gold medals between 1948 and 1984. The highlands of East Africa first reared Olympic champions in the 1960s, with Ethiopians winning the marathon three times in a row, and Kenyans winning other endurance races.

The highest sporting officials tried to uphold the tradition that sport obeyed its own rules and spirit and was not to be defiled and contaminated by international politics; but even the Olympic Games obeyed political orders. The Germans, as the main enemy in the First World War, and the Russians too were not allowed to compete in the 1920 Olympics. Hitler gained his revenge in Berlin in 1936 by turning the Olympics into a torch of German nationalism. The attempt by many nations to tame the republic of South Africa in the 1970s included sporting as well as economic boycotts. In the Cold War the Olympic Games tended to become a show of strength between the United States and the Soviet Union. In the 1980s, successive Games at Moscow and Los Angeles were marred by politics: at Moscow 60 nations refused to compete, and at Los Angeles the Russians refused to compete.

Sport was a showcase of a world becoming smaller. It was the form of international contact and rivalry that most people relished. More than art, architecture and science, it was the favoured vehicle of nationalism. Curiously, in commerce the globalising process was often resented by the public, but in sport it was accepted. People were happy to play foreign games so long as they could wear their national colours. These sporting fixtures expressed and intensified a nationalism that would not be put down.

The rise of the huge city, the growing mania for spectator sport, the spread of foreign travel, the dissemination of English as the global language, the shipping of food to famine-stricken lands, and even the status of a pair of jeans in the universal language of dress, all were chapters in the shrinking of the world.

26

ISLAM'S MOON SHINES AGAIN

The moon, after decades of darkness, shone again on Muslim lands. By the 1960s, newly independent nations flying flags depicting the crescent moon and the Islamic shade of green were multiplying. Early triumphs were Pakistan, home for most of India's Muslims, and the Indonesian republic, which held the largest Muslim population in the world. Nasser of Egypt and Sukarno of Indonesia represented the new confidence visible in some Islamic countries. Only a quarter of a century previously nearly all Islamic lands had been governed by Christian Europe.

For the first time in 500 years, Islamic nations held a bargaining position in important regions. They had never been diligent explorers for minerals, but by chance the countries that converted to Islam more than a thousand years ago owned many of the known oilfields. Westerners found the oil, and the Islamic nations rejoiced, taking over a large share of the revenue. The Middle East and North Africa, Nigeria and Indonesia, between them now owned more than half of the world's reserves of oil. At the same time the rapid decline of oil reserves in the United States, which once was the top oil nation, accentuated the dominance of Islamic lands. Another change filled the coffers of Islamic lands. By the 1960s, oil was becoming more important than coal as the world's main source of energy.

In 1973 the main oil producers, led by Arabs, raised dramatically the price of oil. They also banned the shipment of oil to nations that were supporters of Israel. The temporary ban on the shipping of oil to the United States created a tumult. At one time the United States might have intervened militarily to renew the flow of precious oil on which the commercial world depended. But the Soviet Union was the protector of many oil nations. Intervention could have brought the superpowers close to war.

With oil commanding record prices, revenue poured into the Middle East. Arabian oil magnates became the owners of some of the English mansions once inhabited by their old rulers. Muslims took their place in the lists of the wealthiest families in the world. Islam had embraced the world's poorer lands but now, for the first time in centuries, it held some of the richest.

MUSLIMS AND CHRISTIANS DIVERGE

The way of thinking of Islam and Christianity drew apart. Their thinking had been alike in 1900. Then Christian nations upheld the family as an institution; they were more wary of excessive use of alcohol; and they honoured Sunday as a holy day. Their attitude to women was closer to Islam's than it is today. Serious crime was viewed more harshly and was often punished by the sentence of death. Sunday in Iowa and Friday in Cairo had much in common.

In the following hundred years, Christian nations became more secular. The American way of life advertised alcohol and drugs and tolerated sexual adventures and rebellious youth. The more devout Muslims reject the commercialism, consumerism and easy morals paraded by the west through television, Hollywood films, and the lives of global pop stars. Islam deplored the pace of change in the west, and the west deplored the slowness of change in Islam. The west deplored the deficiency of personal freedom in Islam, and Islam deplored what the west did with its freedom.

In political views too, the west had stood closer to Islam at the start of the century. In most parts of the world democracy was then a baby. But 70 years later, democracy was as much a hallmark of western lands as autocracy was a hallmark of Islamic lands. Religious and political authorities held sway in most Islamic lands. Strong Muslim monarchs reigned in Iran, Jordan, Saudi Arabia, Morocco and the Emirates, while elsewhere a cluster of Muslim rulers wielded unusual powers. In the eyes of most Muslims, a democratic law or verdict held no merit if it was theologically wrong.

In the latter decades of the century Islam flourished. Able to retain its adherents, it sought more. Sons and daughters of Islam clung to their parents' religion. Muslims tended to produce larger families, and that increased their share of the global population. In 1893 maybe 12 per cent of the world's population had been Muslim, but exactly a century later it had risen to 18 per cent. The world's second-largest faith, it was now almost as large as the Hindu and

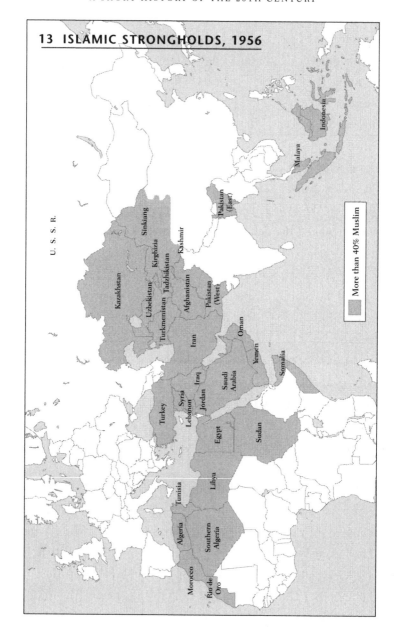

13 ISLAMIC STRONGHOLDS, 1956

More than 40% Muslim

U. S. S. R.

Sinkiang

Kazakhstan

Kirghizia

Uzbekistan

Turkmenistan

Tadzhikistan

Kashmir

Afghanistan

Pakistan (West)

Pakistan (East)

Iran

Oman

Yemen

Somalia

Iraq

Saudi Arabia

Syria

Lebanon

Jordan

Turkey

Egypt

Sudan

Libya

Tunisia

Algeria

Southern Algeria

Morocco

Rio de Oro

Malaya

Indonesia

Buddhist combined. Christianity was still far ahead, with one-third of the world's population, but its lead was diminishing.

Islam's tenacity in its traditional lands was matched by a foothold gained in other lands. Muslims spread their faith by migrating. Back in 1900 a traveller could visit the dynamic cities of the world – whether Paris and Chicago or such southern cities as Buenos Aires and Dunedin – and find prominent synagogues and no visible mosque. In the United States, Muslims had been rare, but by the end of the century they were multiplying faster than the Jews. At the same time in various English cities the mosque attracted as many worshippers as the combined medley of Christian churches. In Paris the mosques were crowded: the Catholic churches were quiet. Muslims, more than Christians, were the energetic builders of 'cathedrals' of a size that astonished tourists. Casablanca in the early 1990s completed the tallest minaret in the world, from which a laser beam pointed straight to Mecca.

The overwhelming majority of Muslims lived the good life. They tried to live by the words of the Prophet, and usually they lived peacefully side by side with other religious creeds. But in some corners of Islam, religious zeal, flowing over, was channelled into militant politics. Iran was such a channel. Millions of its Muslims rejected their own Shah and longed for his downfall. His ardent opponent, preaching in the 1960s from the safety of Iraq and in the late 1970s from the safety of France, was the long-bearded Ruhollah Khomeini, known as the ayatollah, meaning 'sign of god'. After the Shah lost control in January 1979 and went into exile, the elderly ayatollah returned from his exile. He set out to create a God-fearing republic in which the death penalty was widely enforced on many kinds of religious and political dissenters as well as on common criminals.

With his fervour and oratory he roused great crowds massed in the open air. He denounced the United States as 'the great satan'. Responding to their ayatollah, Iranian zealots seized 66 American residents, holding most of them hostage for more than a year. In the course of the disturbances in Iran, Saddam Hussein next door in Iraq seized the opportunity to attack: his huge army invaded Iran. This war between the two Islamic powers, one Sunni and the other ruled by Shi'ites, proved to be one of the five deadliest wars in history.

FERVOUR AND OIL IN THE DESERT

In Arabia the Saud family had long been the protector of Wahhabism, a puritanical Islamic creed. The reviver of its fortunes in the 20th century was King Ibn Saud, the virtual founder of the new Saudi Arabia. One of the kingdom's tallest men, a proven warrior, he moved with a slow dignity and his words compelled attention. Under a liberal interpretation of the Koran he kept four wives, four favourite concubines and four 'favoured slave girls'. A form of slavery continued with his blessing, and one slave became his finance minister. Religious fervour and discipline, as preached by the Wahhabi, also had his blessing.

A wide expanse of sand of many colours, Saudi Arabia was long dismissed as of small economic value. After the discovery of oil in 1938 its wealth slowly and then swiftly increased. Its possession of the largest oil reserves in the world accentuated those human temptations which the Wahhabi branch of Islam had diligently warned against. Even in old age, the king tried to halt the tides of western laxity. Until 1951 he banned football. He refused to permit foreigners to buy alcohol while living in his country. After his death in 1953 and his burial in an unmarked grave – his religion so decreed – several of his successors and thousands of his relatives let their hair down. Palaces multiplied. Visits to the fleshpots of Europe increased, though the upright relatives outnumbered those who ran wild. In mid-century the kingdom's way of life was a contrast between desert-like simplicity and urban jewelled luxury. Its rulers felt the clashing pressures arising from increased wealth on one side and reviving spiritual fervour on the other.

Of the Arab nations, Saudi Arabia was the only long-term ally of Washington. The two nations worked harmoniously, the one supplying oil and the other offering armed protection. As the United States produced less and less of the oil it consumed, it depended more on Saudi Arabia. There American residents had to conform outwardly to the puritanical brand of Islam. By the 1980s, few if any Jews were amongst the American residents of Saudi Arabia; mixed bathing was banned in the swimming pools of the local hotels; and members of the American armed forces agreed not to celebrate Christmas with a formal religious service at their Saudi base. These concessions did not go far enough in the eyes of the more fervent Muslims, ever-conscious that they were guardian of the holy places in Mecca and Medina. Some of the most fervent even disapproved of their own government. They were to sponsor breathtaking acts of terrorism.

THE TERRORISTS MULTIPLY

From the 1970s international terrorism increased. Each successful act seemed to inspire another. In 1982 a little-noticed conference on terrorism, held in Philadelphia, heard that in the previous 10 years a variety of terrorists had seized 50 embassies and consulates, taken as hostage the oil ministers of 11 nations, assassinated president Sadat of Egypt, and attempted to kill the pope and the president of France. In one list of political assassinations compiled over the previous dozen years, Argentina led with 78, followed by Italy with 67, Guatemala with 37, and Spain with 34. In numerous countries extending from Northern Ireland to Spain, and Sri Lanka to Peru, terrorists used their opportunities.

Terrorism was a favoured weapon of the underdogs who lacked military strength. They took advantage of the complacency, the sense of security, found in strong prosperous countries. There the liberal institutions sometimes protected the terrorists' freedom of action. The media unknowingly became the terrorists' friends by giving them the publicity they craved: without heavy publicity, the terror cannot spread quickly.

Terrorism had been dramatically used by Jewish extremists in their fight for control of Palestine in the late 1940s. Two decades further on, Palestinian extremists began to organise acts of terrorism. In Rome on 22 July 1968 three armed Palestinians boarded an Israeli passenger aircraft. When it was halfway to Tel Aviv they threatened to blow it up. The 'news value' of the drama was astonishing. About 110 such episodes occurred in the following 20 years, of which half were initiated by Palestinians and a quarter by Iranians and Sikhs. Another tactic, the concealing of bombs in the luggage of passengers, caused the crashing of at least 15 aircraft. As the cargo detectors at airports became more effective, the terrorists became more ingenious. A bomb hidden in an American airliner that departed from Heathrow just before Christmas 1988 exploded over Lockerbie in Scotland, killing all passengers and crew.

Islamic radicals, like the anarchists of a century ago, were fearless in sacrificing their own lives. Iranian teenagers, not even soldiers, were persuaded to walk as human mine-detectors into a war zone where landmines had been concealed by Iraq. Militant Muslim teachers and preachers were recruiters. In the 1980s their recruits found their way to Afghanistan in the hope of helping their fellow Muslims drive out the atheistic Soviet invaders. When the Afghan war was over they focussed their hatred on the Americans who displayed their western brand of evil: they were Christians, supporters of Israel, and dispensers of a materialist culture that ensnared young Muslims.

A militant recruit was Osama Bin Ladin, a citizen of Saudi Arabia – until his passport was withdrawn. One of the 57 children of a wealthy Saudi family busy in the booming construction industry, he resented his country's long-lasting links to the United States. A religious opponent of the royal family of Saudi, he thought that they were not strict enough and therefore unfit to hold the keys to Mecca. With his sense of mission he was active in fighting the Soviet troops in Afghanistan. He resided for five years in Islamic Sudan, which was another revivalist nation, before returning in 1996 to Afghanistan, now in the hands of the Taliban, where he helped to train young Muslims, both citizens and foreigners, in religion and terrorism. The lives of innocent people meant nothing to him. He combined boldness and ingenuity. His corps of terrorists were victorious in the late 1990s, killing 19 American soldiers in Saudi Arabia, bombing two United States' embassies in East Africa and causing

260 deaths, and killing sailors aboard the warship USS *Cole* near Yemen.

NEW YORK: SEPTEMBER THE ELEVENTH

On the morning of 11 September 2001, 19 unusual passengers prepared to board various domestic aircraft about to depart from the east coast of the United States. All were men, of whom none would have looked out of place in the Middle East. Nearly all carried business or first class tickets, the possession of which possibly assisted them when they were questioned or examined by security guards and other officials at Boston, Washington Dulles, and Newark airports. One man, when interrogated, had no idea what the questions meant, so sparse was his knowledge of English. Though he was behaving oddly and carried inadequate means of identification he was finally allowed to join the boarding passengers.

The four airliners were scheduled to fly to California and so were full of aviation fuel when, from their various airports, they soared into the sky. The last aircraft took off at 8.42 a.m., nearly three-quarters of an hour after the first. Early in each flight, the groups of foreign passengers left their seats and quickly made their moves. Stabbing or hitting any of the crew who intervened, they stormed the cockpits where those who had experience as pilots forcibly took over the controls. Their muscular comrades, with the aid of pepper or another irritant, herded the passengers away from the front of the aircraft. The whole exercise, planned to the final detail, was carried out with briskness and determination.

As the hijackers were outnumbered they could not supervise every action of the passengers and stewards, some of whom secretly

14 FLIGHT PATHS: 11 SEPTEMBER 2001

American Airlines Flight 11
Boston to Los Angeles
Departed 7.59 a.m.

United Airlines Flight 175
Boston to Los Angeles
Departed 8.14 a.m.

began to send messages by mobile phone or the plane's own air-phone to announce that their lives were in danger. The aviation authorities soon knew that a serious incident was under way, but the information was coming to them in bits and pieces and was so incredible that they were slow to piece together the plot.

Meanwhile one of the Boston aircraft, approaching the heart of New York, headed towards the twin towers of the World Trade Center and smashed into the upper storeys of the North Tower, setting them aflame. Everyone on board was killed. The event was so astonishing that the initial reports were confused or downplayed. In Florida, President George W. Bush was about to make an official visit to an elementary school when he received a message from Condoleezza Rice, his security adviser, reporting that the skyscraper had been hit. This early report to the President mistakenly identified the plane as small and twin-engined.

In New York the news-teams were photographing the burning 110-storey tower when at 9.03 a.m. they filmed an airliner butting into the second tower. It too had been hijacked soon after leaving Boston. As at least 16 000 people were working in or visiting the twin towers at the time of impact, the loss of life was likely to be heavy. The news was passed on to the President who was now in the schoolroom actually reading a story to small children. Soon he was on his way to an airport for his urgent flight back to Washington. By now that city itself was in danger, being the target for an aircraft that had left Washington and then changed direction. At 9.37 a.m. this third aircraft, after flying close to the White House, crashed into the Pentagon building.

A fourth airliner was still on its way towards Washington by a circuitous route. Its target was either the White House or the Capitol. A group of its passengers bravely decided to storm the cockpit and snatch the controls from the hijackers. As only four instead of the planned five hijackers were commanding the airliner, the captive passengers almost succeeded. In the face of their counterattack the foreign pilot either lost command or acted precipitously. As the plane rolled onto its back and plummeted towards an empty field in Pennsylvania, the shouts of one hijacker were recorded: 'Allah is the greatest! Allah is the greatest!'

In less than one hour, three airliners had crashed into symbolic buildings in Washington and New York. As their cargo of jet fuel served as an incendiary explosive, the destruction was immense. In the North Tower of the World Trade Center, hundreds of people above the ninety-second floor were killed instantly, and hundreds more were trapped because the lifts and the stairs were blocked.

Black smoke rolled slowly into the sky, for the building was afire on various floors. The South Tower, the second to be hit, was more at risk. It collapsed at 9.59 a.m., killing all civilians and rescuers who were inside the building and even people on neighbouring streets. The North Tower, more and more ablaze, survived for another half-hour, finally collapsing at 10.28 p.m. For a long period the death toll could only be guessed. It was finally determined that 2973 people died as a result of the coordinated attacks.

The 19 air-assassins who were among the dead came from the Middle East, mainly from Saudi Arabia which had long been an ally of the United States. They believed that they were the servants of Islam. The nation they were attacking was labelled by their leader as 'the head of the snake'. The snake, after their attack, was fully aroused.

In modern history no major nation had ever been attacked so dev-astatingly on its home soil in a time of relative peace. The United States had not previously lost so many people through a hostile attack on its own soil. The sheer theatricality of the episode made the American landing on the moon, one generation earlier, seem almost sedate by contrast. The fact that the attack on the second tower in New York was seen instantly on live television in places as far apart as Sweden and New Zealand added to the shock and bewil-derment. The question of whether the 19 air-assassins, in attacking the most powerful nation in the history of the earth, had received deliberate support from an outside nation added to the puzzle.

In the same year the militants carried out a further attack, against an Asian enemy. That enemy was inert and ancient. Outside the small city of Bamian, to the west of the Afghan capital of Kabul, stood a steep escarpment from which two huge statues, over many years, had been slowly carved in solid rock. Images of Buddha, they were impassively tall, one statue being about as high as a 15-storey building. At a distant time the faces of the Buddha had been coated with plaster and decorated with precious and pretty stones brought from afar, so converting the chiselled cliff-face, already majestic, into one of the wonders of that land. Standing alongside an old trade route that crossed the snow-capped Hindu Kush and linked India and central Asia, the Buddhas carved from the stone gave comfort and inspiration, century after century, to an endless procession of travellers, long after the region had been occupied and fortified by Muslims. In 2001, members of the Taliban decided that the statues were sacrilege, an insult to Islam. They destroyed their faces and other features with the aid of artillery and rockets.

So in the same year the twin Buddhas on an ancient highway and the twin towers in the world's financial capital were struck by the restless hands of those who wished to be redeemed. But all that they could offer, in redeeming themselves, was anger and hatred.

27

RETROSPECT

It was a century cut in two, and the contrasts between the two halves were extraordinary.

The century began with unusual optimism. The first decades deflated that optimism. There arrived two world wars and an economic depression of a magnitude not seen before or since. In the well-off countries the standard of living increased little during 50 years. In the poor countries were few signs of improvement.

The brave idea of a League of Nations, which might prevent international wars, was a failure. Democracy, which between 1900 and the mid-1920s, spread widely amongst the European peoples, did not gain the success expected. On the contrary it enabled Mussolini, Hitler and other dictators to take their first steps towards power: they received almost a free rein from the elected parliaments. The major democracies, because most of their voters waxed hot and cold on foreign affairs, failed to prevent Hitler's Germany from rearming. In 1940 France became the first major democracy ever to collapse in the face of an enemy, and it collapsed unexpectedly.

There remained reasons for optimism in the first half of the century. The communist experiment, thickly veiled by Russian censorship, was viewed by hundreds of millions of outsiders as exciting, or tantalising. The Soviet Union proceeded to show impressive resilience in the Second World War, suffering far heavier losses than any other nation and playing a vital part in driving back the German army all the way to Berlin. There was another spring of optimism. In the first half of the 20th century, inventiveness yielded a variety of fruit: the aircraft, the mass-produced car, the radio, cinema, television and the household refrigerator. These were the foundations of the consumer society that flourished in the second half of the century.

Some institutions advanced, and others – including the monarchy – retreated in the course of the century. Democracy was far more successful in the second than the first half, for it did not face such severe tests as in the 1920s and 1930s. Yet in 1901 democracy was a rarity; only a handful of nations gave all men the right to vote, and not one nation gave women both the right to vote and to stand for parliament. Even in 2001 full-blooded democracy remained a brave experiment, the history of ancient Athens notwithstanding. It would be unwise to assume that its victory across the globe is inevitable, for it is not always an easy mode of governing and seems to require an accumulation of experience in politicians and voters.

Economic and political individualism, and the prestige of the capitalist democracies, fell far during the first half of the century and later revived briskly. Communism, following the opposite route, finally reached a precipice. The green movement, barely discernible in 1930, was highly influential half a century later. The consciousness that the world was shrinking and that the people of every continent breathed the same air was spreading wide. Messages crossed the world like lightning: in 1901 the fastest message crossed the world inside wires and cables and in 2001 the fastest leaped over the globe by satellite. In the second half of the century a mass of people, whose great-grandparents had lived and died in the same village, was able to make long journeys to see mountains, deserts, holy places, foreign cities, art galleries and sports spectacles. For the first time in history most people in many of the nations lived in cities rather than in the countryside, worked neither in fields nor factories, and were not physically exhausted by each day's work.

The century began with Europe dominant and ended with it in second place. The vast overseas empires that were governed from western Europe either vanished completely or retained only a few far-off islands as curiosities and imperial trinkets. From these fading empires emerged a host of independent nations, especially in Africa and Asia, but many did not know what do with their independence. The century started with the United States cautiously tip-toeing out of its long isolation and ended with it reigning as the only superpower. The century opened with Asia exercising little power, but by mid-century its rising importance was mirrored in a procession of big events – from the descent of the atom bombs on Japan to the independence of India and the communist victory in China. It was in South Asia that women for the first time were elected as prime ministers.

China and India with their huge populations were increasingly viewed as potential leaders of the world; but the tangled events of the past century had not yet clarified the crucial question of whether a huge population and a large homeland were a natural passport to global dominance. The islands of Britain had presided over an enormous empire; Germany and Japan with a fraction of the world's population had defeated or defied the forces of the combined nations of the world for several years; and encircled Israel – only a handkerchief on the map – had kept the whole Middle East guessing.

The second half of the century achieved in outer space the boldest exploration since Columbus and Vasco da Gama crossed the oceans nearly five centuries earlier. Never before has an era of such medical advances occurred. People lived longer and suffered less pain. Never before had so many people had the chance to be free from material wants. In the world an ability to read and write was the exception in 1901 and becoming normal in 2001. While the world had many failings they were fewer than at the start of the century. Admittedly, thoughtful observers were perturbed by the risks of overpopulation and the pollution of land, sea and air and the wide regions of poverty; but the very identification of these problems was a sign of a global sense that did not even exist in 1901. By strict standards the second part of the 20th century proved to be, unexpectedly, one of the most fortunate half centuries in the long history of the world.

In mood it was a tempestuous century, though the tempest eased. The mood was permeated by war and fear of war. The momentous, far-reaching events of the first half were the decisons to go to war – in 1914 and 1917, and in 1939 and 1941. The momentous decisions of the second half of the century were not to go to war.

After the end of the Korean War in 1953, there arose not even one general war – being a war involving most of the major powers. Though wars between nations were being fought almost everywhere after 1950 – there were many more nations than ever before – not one of those wars remotely resembled a world war. It is the many-sided, global war that – modern history tells us – is the calamitous war, physically and culturally. The second half of the century had its crises, in which some nervous people stayed up all night waiting for the worst. The breathtaking event was the secret installing of Soviet missiles on the island of Cuba in 1962. The two superpowers were on the brink of fighting a nuclear war, until the decision was reached by Kennedy and Khrushchev to find a compromise and avoid a war. Just as remarkable was the decision of Reagan and Gorbachev in the 1980s, after many meetings, to understand one another. The first half of the century fought two great and immensely destructive wars. The second half miraculously avoided them.

Did the invention of such terrible weapons in 1945, and the fear of a terrifying revenge if they were actually used, do more than anything to maintain the long peace between the mighty nuclear powers? We cannot yet be certain of the answer. Whether the nuclear peace will continue is the towering question of the 21st century, and alongside it all other questions and problems may well pale.

On 3 August 1914, on the outbreak of the First World War, Britain's foreign secretary Sir Edward Grey solemnly observed: 'The lamps are going out all over Europe; we shall not see them lit again in our lifetime.' But in the fullness of time, the lamps came on again, in Europe and throughout the world. The lamps were more powerful than ever. That was the marvel, and the danger.

15 BIG CITIES OF THE WORLD, 2001

ICELAND
NORWAY
SWEDEN
FINLAND
North Sea
IRELAND
U.K.
GERMANY
POLAND
UKRAINE
FRANCE
ROMANIA
Black Sea
ITALY
BULGARIA
Caspian Sea
SPAIN
GREECE
TURKEY
Mediterranean Sea
SYRIA
IRAQ
IRAN
Cairo *
ALGERIA
LIBYA
EGYPT
SAUDI ARABIA
OMAN
Red Sea
YEMEN
MAURITANIA
NIGER
CHAD
SUDAN
Arabian Sea
NIGERIA
ETHIOPIA
Lagos *
CAMEROON
KENYA
GABON
ZAIRE
TANZANIA
ZAMBIA
NAMIBIA
MADAGASCAR
SOUTH AFRICA

RUSSIA
KAZAKHSTAN
MONGOLIA
KYRGYZSTAN
CHINA
Beijing *
KOREA
* Shanghai
PAKISTAN
Delhi *
Karachi *
BANGLADESH
INDIA
* Dhaka
Calcutta *
Mumbai *
THAILAND
VIETNAM
Phili
SRI LANKA
MALAYSIA
SINGAPORE
Bay of Bengal
INDONES
Jakarta
INDIAN OCEAN
Timor Sea
AUST

*Cities with more than 10 million people

SELECTED SOURCES

These notes are not exhaustive. They rarely indicate the source for well-known sequences of events, whether battles or political events, which can be found in numerous works of reference. Some of the detail – now called trivia but really the lifeblood of history – I have collected over the last 55 years as an historian; and now, alas, have no idea where it came from. As far as possible I have tried to check it for authenticity.

Occasionally I repeat familiar quotations, whether from Rudyard Kipling, Robert Louis Stevenson or Winston Churchill. If the quotation is to be found in *The Oxford Dictionary of Quotations*, *The Times Book of Quotations*, *The Penguin Dictionary of Twentieth Century Quotations* or a few other well-known authorities, I usually do not include it in these reference notes. The subtitles of some of the books and articles cited below are not always set out in full.

Two primary sources on the early history of 20th century are the little-known supplements to the *Encyclopaedia Britannica*, each of three volumes. They were published in 1922 as the 12th edition and in 1926 as the 13th edition. Mainly devoted to contemporary events and trends, they gained from their wide variety of fluent, specialist authors. They vividly reflect the hopes and fears for the future. Relevant articles are cited below.

1 A FLAMING SUNRISE

10 Slang words emigrating from USA: Henry Bradley, 'Slang', *Encyclopaedia Britannica*, 11th edn, vol. 25, 1910–11, p. 209.

11 London underground railways: Peter Mathias, *The First Industrial Nation: An Economic History of Britain 1700–1914*, New York, 1969, p. 417.

11 Enlarged US navy: Paul Kennedy, *The Rise and Fall of the Great Powers*, New York, 1989, p. 247.

12 Funeral of Queen Victoria, *The Annual Register 1901*, London, 1902, pp. 16–20.

13 Gossip on Russian, Portuguese and other kings featured in daily newspapers across the world: several of these episodes come from *The Barrier Miner*, Broken Hill, Australia, 7 & 12 January, 1905.

14 Royal duel in Paris: *The Annual Register 1897*, London, chronicle, p. 48.

15 Anarchists as assassins: this list, no doubt incomplete, was compiled from various sources but mainly *The Annual Register*. The attempts on the life of Persia's shah and the future Edward VII of Britain are usually absent from similar lists.

17 Charismatic day in Kansas: Jon Butler & Grant Wacker (eds), *Religion in American Life: A Short History*, New York, 2000, pp. 333 ff.

18 Alfred Garvie on immortality: *Encyclopaedia Britannica*, 11th edn, vol. 14, 1910–11, pp. 336–9.

19 W.E. Gladstone on the loss of religious faith: A.N. Wilson, *God's Funeral*, London, 1999, p. 289. Gladstone spoke while defending Bradlaugh's right to sit as an atheist in parliament.

21 Babies and children of 1900–01: the section was compiled after listing influential names of the first 75 years of the century, and then consulting works of biography to see where they lived in 1900. Comment on 'Bertie' comes from Robert Rhodes James, *A Spirit Undaunted: The Political Role of George VI*, London, 1998, pp. 90–1.

22–3 Childhood rituals in New Guinea: A. Chowning, 'Child Rearing and Socialization' in Peter Ryan ed., *Encyclopaedia of Papua and New Guinea*, Melbourne, vol. 1, 1972, pp. 156–64.

23–4 Child-labour: Hugh Cunningham, 'The Decline of Child Labour . . . in Europe and North America since 1830', *Economic History Review*, vol. 53, 2000, pp. 409–28. For truancy cases in English courts, see p. 417.

24 Child-brides in central Asia: R.A. Pierce, ed., *Mission to Turkestan: Being the Memoirs of Count K. K. Pahlen, 1908–1909*, London, 1964, pp. 78–9.

25 Hitler's bookshelves: John Toland, *Adolf Hitler*, New York, 1976, p. 317.

25–6 Winnie the Pooh and nuclear fission: display in Museum of American History, Smithsonian, Washington D.C., January 2004.

26 Burmese boy named Kim: personal knowledge.

2 RYE-BEER AND PERFUME

28 Old Munich festivals: Karl Baedeker, *Southern Germany*, Leipzig, 1895; for beer see p. 138, for butchers p. 142.

29 *Messiah* at Sheffield: H.J. Wood in *The Dictionary of National Biography 1941–1950*, London, 1959, p. 969; *The Annual Register 1901*, op. cit., chronicle, p. 96.

30 Face-washing in Rome train: G.G. Coulton, *Fourscore Years: An Autobiography*, London, 1945, p. 248.

30 Goose and swan quills: J.R. McCulloch, *A Dictionary of Commerce and Commercial Navigation*, London, 1854, p. 1088.

31 Typewriters in British train: *Encyclopaedia Britannica*, 13th edn, vol. 32, 1926, p. 226.

32–3 Rise of Woolworth: Daniel J. Boorstin, *The Americans: The Democratic Experience*, New York, 1974, esp. pp. 113–15.

33 Russian harvesters: Leo Tolstoy, *Anna Karenin* [sic], Penguin edn, Baltimore, 1954, esp. pp. 268–9, 826–7.

33 Salt carriers: C.P. FitzGerald, *Why China? Recollections of China 1923–1950*, Melbourne, 1985, pp. 134–5.

34 Horses: weight of leaning horse in George E. Evans, *The Horse in the Furrow*, London, 1960, p. 194; horses and mules in Boer War, *The Annual Register 1901*, op. cit., p. 208; Roosevelt's love of cavalry, ibid., p. 417.

35 Cats outnumber dogs in USA by 1980s: Constance Urdang, 'Cats', *1992 International Year Book*, New York, 1992, p. 55.

36–7 Italian peasants: Vera Zamagni, *The Economic History of Italy 1860–1990*, Oxford, 1993, pp. 199–200; Maria Bianca Viviani Della Robbia, *Farm in Chianti*, Firenze, 1990, p. 48; p. 61 for long engagements preceding a marriage, p. 27 for baking bread.

37 Tibetan peasants: Percival Landon, *Lhasa*, London, vol. 2, 1905, pp. 346–50.

38 Zanzibar slaves: A 'Correspondence . . . Legal Status of Slavery in Zanzibar and Pemba', *British Parliamentary Papers*, July 1898, esp. reports by A. Hardinge on 26 February 1895 and Commissioner J.P. Farler on 31 January 1898.

38 Ethiopian slaves: Judith Olmstead, *Woman Between Two Worlds: Portrait of an Ethiopian Rural Leader*, Urbana, USA, 1997, pp. 33–7.

3   A TEMPEST OF CHANGE

46 Counting of stars: Agnes Mary Clerke, 'Astronomy', *Encyclopaedia Britannica*, 11th edn, vol. 2, 1910–11, pp. 816–7.

46 Shackleton's camera: *The Annual Register 1897*, pp. 65–6.

49 Abolition of passports in European nations: Stephen Kern, *The Culture of Time and Space 1880–1918*, London, 1983, pp. 194–5.

49 First travellers' cheque: Boorstin, *The Americans*, op. cit., pp. 519–20.

51 Prediction that modern wars will tend to be short: Geoffrey Blainey, *The Causes of War*, London, 1973, ch. 14.

53 G.B. Shaw's New York lady: Diarmuid Russell, ed., *Bernard Shaw, Selected Prose*, London, 1953, pp. 714–5. It was an essay of 1889.

54 Fatalities during strikes: Martin Gilbert, *A History of the Twentieth Century 1900–1933*, London, 1997, vol. 1., pp. 63–4, 267.

54–5 USA's 'equality of manners': Henry Phelps Brown, *Egalitarianism and the Generation of Inequality*, Oxford, 1988, p. 245.

55 Socialists' success in European elections: Oron J. Hale, *The Great Illusion 1900–1914*, New York, 1971, pp. 213–15.

55–6 'New Zealand is better suited': James Bonar, 'Socialism', *Encyclopaedia Britannica*, 11th edn, vol. 25, 1910–11, pp. 307–8. Bonar, who was master of the Canadian Royal Mint, thought that Australia was less likely to become the world's first socialist experiment because political power there was not concentrated. Instead power was divided between the six states and the federal government which itself spent less income than the combined states.

56–7 Democracies' flaws: James Bryce, *Modern Democracies*, New York, vol. 2, 1921, pp. 457–9.

57–8 China's first election. John K. Fairbank, *The United States and China*, 4th edn, Harvard, 1980, pp. 217–22.

58 Tolstoy and the Russian peasants: *The Annual Register 1901*, pp. 297–9; J.H.L. Keep, 'Russia' in David Thomson, ed., *New Cambridge Modern History*, vol. 11, London, 1960, p. 369.

59–60 Feminism: Richard J. Evans, *The Feminists*, Beckenham, UK, 1979, pp. 116–8, 139 ff.

60 Vida Goldstein casts her vote: Geoffrey Blainey, 'The Cabbage Patch That Grew' in The Age, *Reflections*, Sydney, 2004, pp. 23–4.

60–1 Ethel Smyth's musical career: *The Dictionary of National Biography 1941–50*, op. cit., pp. 804–5; Stanley Sadie, ed., *The New Grove Dictionary of Music and Musicians*, vol. 17, London, 1980, pp. 425–6.

61 Russian students in Switzerland and at home: Fredric S. Zuckerman, *The Tsarist Secret Police in Russian Society, 1880–1917*, Basingstoke, 1996, passim.

62 Korean and Japanese marriages: Linda G. Martin, 'Changing Intergenerational Family Relations in East Asia', in *The Annals of the American Academy of Political and Social Science*, vol. 510, July 1990, pp. 102 ff.

63 Polish children's catechism: *The Annual Register 1901*, pp. 278–9.

64 Assassins in Sarajevo: Misha Glenny, *The Balkans 1804–1999: Nationalism, War and the Great Powers*, London, 1999, esp. pp. 250–1, 294–5, 302–4.

4 THE WAR OF WARS

69 Finance likely to shorten length of war: Geoffrey Blainey, *The Causes of War*, London, 1973, pp. 214–17.

71 Jewish-Russian patriot: cited by Sir Paul Vinogradoff, 'Russia', *Encyclopaedia Britannica*, 12th edn, vol. 32, 1922, p. 315.

72 Politicians retreat to Bordeaux: George J. Adam (London *Times* correspondent in Paris), 'France', *Encyclopaedia Britannica*, 12th edn, vol. 31, 1922, pp. 136–7.

73 Compulsory military training: Hale, *The Great Illusion*, op. cit., p. 21.

73 National spending on war: J.J. Spengler in Marcelle Kooy, ed., *Essays in Honour of H.M. Robertson*, London, 1972, pp. 135–8.

75 Warship *Goeben*: C.F. Aspinall-Oglander, *Official History of the Great War: Military Operations Gallipoli*, London, 1929, vol. 1, p. 6.

77 Coal scarcity at Petrograd: Alexander F. Kerensky, *The Catastrophe*, New York, 1927, p. 84.

77–8 Naval attack on Gallipoli: Les Carlyon, *Gallipoli*, Sydney, 2001, chs 5–6.

78 Invading fleet spied on at Mudros harbour: Aspinall-Oglander, *Official History of the Great War,* op. cit., vol. 1, pp. 139–40.

78 Landings on Gallipoli: Robert Rhodes James, *Gallipoli*, London, 1999, ch. 5.

79 Armenian massacres: Rouben P. Adalian in Samuel Totten, William S. Parsons & Israel W. Charney (eds), *Century of Genocide*, New York, 2004, ch. 2.

81 Battle of Somme: John Keegan, *The Face of Battle*, Harmondsworth, UK, 1986, ch. 4.

83 Dysentery at Gallipoli: A.F. Hurst on 'Medicine and Surgery', *Encyclopaedia Britannica*, 12th edn, vol. 31, 1922, p. 905.

84 Blood transfusions: William H. Schneider, 'Blood Transfusion in Peace and War, 1900–1918', *Social History of Medicine*, April 1997, vol. 10, pp. 105 ff.

85–6 War's effects on neutral nation: William Coolidge, 'Switzerland', *Encyclopaedia Britannica*, op. cit., vol. 32, pp. 637–48.

5   REVOLT IN PETROGRAD: PEACE IN PARIS

88 Soldiers close to mutiny: John Keegan, *The Mask of Command*, London, 1988, pp. 334–6.

89 Inflation in Russia: Zuckerman, *The Tsarist Secret Police*, op. cit., p. 235.

89 Police reports: ibid., pp. 237–9.

90 Secret-police help Lenin: ibid., pp. 210–12.

91 Kerensky and frontline soldiers: Alexander F. Kerensky, *The Catastrophe*, New York, 1927, pp. 316–17.

93 'We must . . .', orders Lenin on 24 October 1917 (Russian calendar): M.C. Morgan, *Lenin*, London, 1971, p. 131.

93 Overnight takeover of Petrograd: Isaac Deutscher, 'The Russian Revolution', in *New Cambridge Modern History*, op.cit., vol. 12, p. 411.

94–5 Wilson's personaltity: Kenneth S. Lynn, 'The Hidden Agony of Woodrow Wilson' in *The Wilson Quarterly*, Washington D.C., Winter 2004, pp. 61–5, 79–80.

96 Vital military role of USA in 1918: Correlli Barnett, 'The New Military Balance', in Alan Bullock intro., *History of the 20th Century*, New York, 1976, pp. 101–2.

98 T. S. Eliot on Wilson's welcome: Valerie Eliot, ed., *The Letters of T.S. Eliot*, London, 1988, vol. 1, p. 264.

98–9 Wilson in Paris: Kenneth S. Lynn, op. cit, pp. 80–83.

100 Eating roots, grass and acorns: Sir William Goode, 'Economic Conditions in Central Europe, 1920', in Shepard B. Clough, Thomas Moodie and Carol Moodie (eds), *Economic History of Europe: Twentieth Century*, New York, 1968, p. 100.

101 Wilson tries to persuade American people: Thomas J. Knock, *To End All Wars: Woodrow Wilson and the Quest for a New World Order*, New York, 1992, pp. 26, 252.

103–4 Deaths in war: Niall Ferguson, *The Pity of War*, New York, 1999, p. 298.

104 War weakens Europe and therefore the world: Robert Skidelsky, *John Maynard Keynes*, London, 1983, vol. 1, ch.16.

106   Nehru on communist Russia: cited in Caroline F. Ware et al. (eds), *History of Mankind: The Twentieth Century*, New York, 1966, vol. 6, p. 53.

6   UTOPIA AND NIGHTMARE

109   Dislocated Russian railways: Arthur Ransome, 'Russia', *Encyclopaedia Britannica*, 13th edn, vol. 3, 1926, p. 420.

110   'We are exterminating the bourgeoisie': Zuckerman, *The Tsarist Secret Police*, op. cit., p. 250.

110–11   Russian 'nightmare': Bertrand Russell, *The Autobiography of Bertrand Russell, 1914–1944*, Boston, 1968, pp. 141–2.

113–14   Repressing Orthodox church: Anatole G. Mazour, *Russia: Tsarist and Communist*, Princeton, 1962, pp. 600–2.

114   Lenin's new economic policy: documents reprinted in Clough & Moodie, *Economic History of Europe*, op. cit., pp. 179–206.

115–16   Russian artists in exile: Orlando Figes, *Natasha's Dance: A Cultural History of Russia*, London, 2002. For Rachmaninov, see pp. 542–5; Stravinsky pp. 282, 564–5; and Gorki pp. 473–4, 572.

117   The embalming of Lenin: Morgan, *Lenin*, op. cit., p. 215.

120–2   Russia's industrial advance after 1928: S. Pollard, *Peaceful Conquest: The Industrialization of Europe 1760–1970*, Oxford, 1981, pp. 298–9.

122–3   Stalin's greed for praise: Roy A. Medvedev, *Let History Judge: The Origins and Consequences of Stalinism*, London, 1972, pp. 12, 508.

7   OLD SULTAN AND YOUNG TURK

127–8   Kemal's early career: Andrew Mango, *Atatürk*, London, 1999, pp. 26–33; Donald Quataert, *The Ottoman Empire, 1700–1922*, Cambridge, 2000, passim.

129   Lloyd George and the Gallipoli crisis of 1922: Gilbert, *A History of the Twentieth Century*, op. cit., vol. 1, p. 639.

129   British reinforce Dardanelles in 1922: Paul R. Bartrop, *Bolt from the Blue*, Sydney, 2002, p. 28.

129   'A defeat or a humiliating exodus . . . ': British cabinet discussions reprinted in Bartrop, op. cit., p. 43.

130–1   Last sultan dies in Italy: The *Times*, London, 17–20 May, 1926.

131 Turkish leaflets rain on Indian soldiers: Henry W. Nevinson, *The Dardanelles Campaign*, London, 1918, pp. 187–8.

133–4 Prohibition of the fez and other customs: Mango, *Atatürk*, op. cit., pp. 434–7, 560–1.

134–5 Atatürk's personality: Arnold J. Toynbee, *Acquaintances*, London, 1967. For Atatürk's drinking, see p. 235; for his frown, see p. 249.

8 FASTER AND FASTER

141 US army radio station near Bordeaux: John A. Fleming, 'Wireless Telegraphy and Telephony', *Encyclopaedia Britannica*, 12th edn, vol. 32, 1922, p. 1028.

143 Peephole pictures: Ware et al, *History of Mankind*, op. cit., p. 966.

143 David Wark Griffith, filmmaker: Peter Watson, *A Terrible Beauty*, London, 2000, pp. 87–9.

144 Open-air cinemas: K.G. Hall, *Directed by Ken Hall: Autobiography of an Australian Film Maker*, Melbourne, 1977, pp. 16–18.

145–6 Pop singers: Sadie, *The New Grove Dictionary of Music*, op. cit. For crooning, see vol. 5, p. 60; for popular singing, see vol. 17, p. 346.

147 Woodrow Wilson denounces car: L.J.K. Setright, *Drive On! A Social History of the Car*, London, 2003, p. 32.

150 Motels and other innovations: ibid., p. 394.

152 Cobham flies through South-East Asian monsoon: Sir Alan Cobham, *Australia and Back*, London 1927, ch. 5.

152–3 Polar airship: The *Times*, London, 17–19 May 1926.

155 Baku's oil: Daniel Yergin, *The Prize: The Epic Quest for Oil, Money, and Power*, New York, 1991, pp. 57–61.

156–7 Holmes and Arabian oil: David Holden & Richard Johns, *The House of Saud*, London, 1982, pp. 81–2, 213.

157 Invention of X-ray a bonus for research: Oron J. Hale, *The Great Illusion 1900–1914*, New York, 1971, pp. 174–189.

158 Boltzmann and Bohr: Jacob Bronowski, *The Ascent of Man*, London, 1973, ch. 10.

158–60 Einstein's creativity: Arthur Koestler, *The Act of Creation*, London, 1964, pp. 171–3; Jacques Barzun, *Science: The Glorious Entertainment*, London, 1964, p. 92.

9 AN ITALIAN DRUMMER

161 Italian illiteracy: Zamagni, *The Economic History of Italy*, op. cit., p. 195.

163 Food shortages in war: ibid., pp. 214, 217.

165 Florence bloodshed in 1921: Luigi Villari, 'Italy' in *Encyclopaedia Britannica*, 12th edn, vol. 31, 1922, p. 637.

166 March (so-called) on Rome: Nicholas Farrell, *Mussolini: a New Life*, London, 2003, pp. 116–26.

168–9 Toscanini and fascism: Edward R. Tannenbaum, *The Fascist Experience: Italian Society and Culture 1922–1945*, New York, 1972, p. 280.

170 Motorway and cars: Setright, *Drive On!*, op. cit., pp. 70, 83.

170–1 Vatican and Mussolini: Sir Robert Ensor in *New Cambridge Modern History*, op. cit., vol. 12, p. 95.

171 Italy's triumphs in 1933–4: Farrell, *Mussolini*, op. cit., pp. 230–1.

10 A WORLD DEPRESSION

173–4 Background to Wall Street crash: John Kenneth Galbraith, *The Age of Uncertainty*, London, 1977, pp. 207–13; Sidney Pollard, *Peaceful Conquest*, Oxford, 1981, pp. 209–306.

174 Germany and reparations: Harold James, *The German Slump: Politics and Economics 1924–1936*, Oxford, 1986, ch. 1.

175–7 Panic on Wall Street: *New York Times*, economic news, stock market and trade reports, 24–30 October 1929.

177 France's harmful monetary policy of hoarding gold and liquidating holdings of foreign exchange: Jonathan Hughes, *Industrialization and Economic History: Theses and Conjectures*, New York, 1970, pp. 261–2.

177–9 Isolation of Latin America: John H. Coatsworth & Alan M. Taylor (eds), *Latin America and the World Economy Since 1800*, Harvard, 1998, passim.

180–1 Heinrich Hauser motors by unemployed Germans: an article of March 1933 reprinted in Clough & Moodie, *Economic History of Europe*, op. cit., pp. 247 ff.

181 Rural camping grounds: Kylie Tennant, *Tiburon*, Sydney, 1972, ch. 1.

181 Scavenging coal in Britain in Depression: George Orwell, *The Road* *to Wigan Pier*, Penguin reprint, London, 1966, pp. 90–1. For social role of new products, see pp. 80–1.

182   Depression in China: John K. Fairbank & Denis Twitchett (eds), *Cambridge History of China*, Cambridge, 1986, vol. 13, part 2, esp. ch. 1.

182   Japanese textiles: Nazli Choucri, Robert C. North & Susumu Yamakage, *The Challenge of Japan before World War II and After*, London, 1992, p. 137. Japan in 1936 exported more steel than it imported.

184–5   Political upheavals of early 1930s: culled from Neville Williams, *Chronology of the Modern World:1763 to the Present Time*, London, 1966, pp. 524–41.

185–6   White Sea–Baltic Canal: Martin Gilbert, *A History of the Twentieth Century 1900–1933*, London, 1997, vol. 1, pp. 843–4.

186   Shaw praising Russia: Bernard Shaw, *Everybody's Political What's What?* London, 1945, pp. 19, 21.

186   Thomas Mann, cited in Denis de Rougemont, *The Idea of Europe*, trans. by Norbert Guterman, Cleveland, 1968, pp. 347–8.

11   THE RISE OF HITLER

190   Rathenau's speech of hope: F. Simon, 'Rathenau', *Encyclopaedia Britannica*,13th edn, vol. 3, 1926, pp. 299–300.

191–2   Flag crisis of 1926: Fritz Stern, *The Failure of Illiberalism: Essays on the Political Culture of Modern Germany*, Chicago, 1971, pp. 162–70. For role of German mayors see p. 162 n.

192–3   Hitler as battlefields' courier: Keegan, *The Mask of Command*, op. cit., pp. 240–3.

193   Hitler's name not known to Mussolini in 1922: Toland, *Adolf Hitler*, op. cit., p. 119.

194   Hitler's oratory: ibid., pp. 130, 218, 221.

196   Nazis supported by small rather than big business: Richard J. Evans, *The Coming of the Third Reich*, London, 2003, pp. 203, 204–6.

198   German army's tests within Soviet Union: Rohan Butler, 'The Peace Settlement of Versailles', in *New Cambridge Modern History*, op. cit., vol. 12, pp. 468–70.

199   Weakening of socialist wing of Nazi party: Evans, *The Coming of the Third Reich*, op.cit., p. 244.

200   Pact of 1935 revives German navy: William L. Shirer, *The Collapse of the Third Republic*, London, 1970, p. 230.

201   Failure to help France in 1936: A.J.P. Taylor, *The Origins of the Second World War*, Penguin edn, London, 1964, pp. 131–3.

202   Baldwin, pacifists and British voters: Thomas Jones, 'Baldwin', in *The Dictionary of National Biography 1941–1950*, op. cit., p. 47; Paul Johnson, *The Offshore Islanders: A History of the English People*, London, 1995, pp. 385–6.

203   Singapore synagogue: visited by author in 1988.

203   Jews in Germany: Peter Phillips, *The Tragedy of Nazi Germany*, London, 1969, pp. 104–8; Tobias Jersak, 'A Matter of Foreign Policy', *German History*, vol. 21, 2003, pp. 370, 377, 384.

204   Jews in German media and football: Konrad Löw, 'History, National Identity and Guilt . . . Lessons From Germany', *Quadrant*, Sydney, September 2004, p. 13.

205   Victimising of Germans by Poland: Richard Blanke, *Orphans of Versailles: the Germans in Western Poland 1918–1939*, Lexington, Kentucky, 1993, p. 212.

205   Mussolini and Jews: Tannenbaum, *The Fascist Experience*, op. cit., pp. 78–9, 242–3, 280.

205–6   Gypsies: Sybil Milton, in Samuel Totten, William S. Parsons & Israel W. Charney (eds), *Century of Genocide: Critical Essays & Eyewitness Accounts*, New York, 2004, ch. 5.

12   A SECOND WORLD WAR

207   German stockpiles: 'The Effects of Strategic Bombing on the German War Economy 1945', reprinted in Clough & Moodie, *Economic History of Europe*, op. cit., pp. 318–19.

210   France's military failure: Keegan, *The Mask of Command*, op. cit., 1988, pp. 260–2.

211   Civilians desert Paris: Shirer, *The Collapse of the Third Republic*, op. cit., pp. 5, 7, 752–4.

211   Churchill and imminent fall of France: Robert Rhodes James, *A Spirit Undaunted*, London, 1998, pp. 194–205; E.T. Williams, 'Churchill', in *The Dictionary of National Biography 1961–1970*, London, 1981, pp. 204–6.

215   American reporter in deserted Paris: Shirer, op. cit., pp. 4–5.

217   Petain takes office: David Thomson, ed., *France: Empire and Republic, 1850–1940: Historical Documents*, London, 1968, pp. 18–20, 357.

220   Churchill at work: John Colville, *The Fringes of Power: Downing Street Diaries 1939–1955*, London, 1985, pp. 10, 172.

221   Churchill's 'great days': cited in William Safire, ed., *Lend Me Your Ears: Great Speeches in History*, rev. edn, New York, 1992, p. 229.

221   Mrs Churchill walks out of divine service: Colville, *The Fringes of Power*, op. cit., p. 135; her nephew as potential hostage, ibid., p. 468 n.

224   Hitler's view of Britain, USA and Russia before 1941 invasion: Henri Michel, *The Second World War*, trans. from French, London, 1975, p. 213.

225   Stalin's expectations in 1941: Evan Mawdsley, 'Crossing the Rubicon: Soviet Plans for Offensive War in 1940–41', *International History Review*, vol. 25, December 2003, pp. 855–6.

227–9   Japan's dilemma late in 1941: Geoffrey Blainey, *The Causes of War*, 3rd edn, South Melbourne, 1988, pp. 256–9.

13   FROM PEARL HARBOR TO THE FALL OF BERLIN

232   Japanese air attacks on Philippines: Louis Morton, 'The Fall of the Philippines', *United States Army in World War II: The War in the Pacific*, Washington D.C., 1953, pp. 75, 85.

232   Five of seven US radar sets not working: ibid., p. 44.

234   US convoy diverted to Brisbane: ibid., pp. 144–8.

235–8   Japanese aircraft sink two British warships: S. Woodburn Kirby, *The War Against Japan*, London, vol. 1, 1957, pp. 194 ff.

238   Percival, 'bad for morale': Peter Elphick, *Singapore; The Pregnable Fortress: A Study in Deception, Discord and Desertion*, London, 1995, p. 161.

239   Rescue of MacArthur from Philippines: Morton, op. cit., pp. 353–9.

240–1   Geography of battles of Coral Sea and Midway: Peter Young, *Atlas of the Second World War*, New York, 1974, pp. 136–9.

244   Red sky over Berlin: *The Berlin Diaries 1940–1945 of Marie 'Missie' Vassiltchikov*, London, 1985, pp. 87, 105.

245   Germany's scarcity of raw materials: 'The Effects of Strategic Bombing on the German War Economy, 1945', reprinted in Clough & Moodie, op. cit., pp. 315 ff.

248   Churchill's gloom in Moscow in 1942: Christopher Thorne, *Allies of a Kind: The United States, Britain, and the War against Japan, 1941–1945*, London, 1978, p. 184.

249   Roosevelt on Stalin: John W. Wheeler-Bennett & Anthony Nicholls, *The Semblance of Peace: The Political Settlement after the Second World War*, London, 1972, pp. 297–8.

249–50   Shostakovich's symphony: Boris Schwartz in Sadie, *The New Grove Dictionary of Music*, op. cit., vol. 17, p. 265.

250   New Zealand sergeant observes troops' Soviet sympathies: Keith Sinclair, *Halfway Round the Harbour*, Auckland, 1993, p. 82.

14   A MOST SECRET WEAPON

256–8   Einstein's letter, Fermi's reactor, and chianti bottle: all displayed in Museum of American History at Smithsonian, Washington D.C., January 2004.

259   The bomb's doubters – Leahy and Marshall: Wheeler-Bennett & Nicholls, *The Semblance of Peace*, op. cit., p. 374.

259   Witnesses of first atomic test: Ferenc Morton Szasz, *The Day The Sun Rose Twice*, Albuquerque, 1984, pp. 85, 107.

260   Truman and the bomb: Wheeler-Bennett & Nicholls, *The Semblance of Peace*, op. cit., pp. 371–3.

260–2   Bombs on Hiroshima and Nagasaki: Wesley F. Craven & James C. Cato (eds), *The Army Air Forces in World War II*, Chicago, vol. 5, 1953, pp. 715–22.

265   Acton's burial place in Bavaria: John N. Figgis in *The Dictionary of National Biography 1901–11*, London, 1912, p. 11. For Acton's vast library, see p. 12.

15   A CURTAIN FALLS

270–2   Birth of United Nations: H. Stuart Hughes, *Contemporary Europe: A History*, Englewood Cliffs, New Jersey, 1976, pp. 451–5.

272–4   Moscow grips eastern Europe: Norman Davies, *Europe:*

A History, London, 1997, pp. 1061–2, 1067; Hugh Thomas, *Armed Truce: The Beginnings of the Cold War, 1945–46*, London, 1986, passim; Michel, *The Second World War*, op. cit., pp. 680–97, 815–18.

277–8   Origin of phrase 'Iron Curtain': *The Shorter Oxford English Dictionary On Historical Principles*, vol. 2, Oxford, 1956, p. 2496.

277–8   Origin of phrase 'Cold War': Bernard M. Baruch, *Baruch: The Public Years*, New York, 1962, p. 367. Baruch, borrowing the phrase, first used it in addressing the North Carolina legislature in April 1947.

278–9   Sakharov and Soviet bombs: Richard Lourie, *Sakharov: A Biography*, Brandeis University Press, New England, 2002, ch. 7.

281–2   The Kuomintang and Shanghai in 1927: Lloyd E. Eastman in John K. Fairbank & Denis Twitchett (eds), *Cambridge History of China*, Cambridge, 1986, vol. 13, part 2, pp. 116, 132–3.

282–3   The communist zones in China and the long march: Jerome Ch'en, in *Cambridge History of China*, op. cit., ch. 4, esp. pp. 184, 209–16.

283–4   Mao Zedong in his remote cave-house: Edgar Snow, *Red China Today*, London, 1970, pp. 141–2.

284   Chinese defending against Japanese: Thorne, *Allies of a Kind*, op. cit., p. 185.

284–5   1942 poll of Americans on China's geographical position: ibid., p. 173.

285   Roosevelt's faith in middle-road China: ibid., p. 174.

285   Mao's dismissal of atom bomb as 'paper tiger': Mao interviewed by Edgar Snow, 1965, in Christopher Silvester, ed., *The Penguin Book of Interviews*, London, 1993, pp. 494–5. When questioned, Mao could not recall saying that 'a few hundred million' Chinese could survive a big bomb dropped on China but admitted he might well have said so.

285   Mao's pithy quotations: examples in J.M & M.J. Cohen, *The Penguin Dictionary of Twentieth-Century Quotations*, London, 1993, p. 250.

288–9   First battle between jet fighters in history of warfare, Korea, November 1950: Robert O'Neill, *Australia in the Korean War 1950–53*, Canberra, vol. 2, 1985, pp. 57, 324.

16 BURNING SPEAR AND CHANGING WIND

291   Cobden on colonies: cited in Asa Briggs, *The Age of Improvement*, London, 1959, p. 390.

292   Prophet of Europe's decline: C.H. Pearson, *National Life and Character: A Forecast*, London, 1893, pp. 83–5.

295   Sergeant Gandhi and Zulus: Frank Welsh, *A History of South Africa*, London, 1998, pp. 362–3.

295   Gandhi and his contradictory strands: Richard Grenier, *Capturing the Culture*, Washington, 1991, ch. 6.

295   Gandhi's anti-western phase: Dennis Dalton, *Mahatma Gandhi: Nonviolent Power in Action*, New York, 1993, p. 20.

295–6   Salt march: Dalton, op. cit., pp. 105–115.

296   *Time* magazine on Gandhi: ibid., p. 108.

297–8   Biographies of Raman and Ramanujan: H.W. Thompson, 'Raman', in *Dictionary of National Biography 1961–1970*, London, 1981, pp. 864–6; *Encyclopaedia Britannica*, 14th edn, vol. 18, 1962, pp. 962–3.

298   British Labour Party's views on India in 1940: Thorne, *Allies of a Kind*, op. cit., pp. 57–8. For US views on colonialism, see p. 121.

299   Mob violence in Lahore: Ved Mehta, *Face to Face: An Autobiography*, London, 1967, pp. 144–5.

299–300   Partition of India: Barbara D. & Thomas R. Metcalf, *A Concise History of India*, Cambridge, 2002, pp. 214–19.

300   Nehru on Gandhi: Safire, op. cit., pp. 209–10.

300   Violence in Calcutta during partition; Sucheta Mahajan, *Independence and Partition: The Erosion of Colonial Power in India*, New Delhi, 2000, pp. 226–7; Dalton, *Mahatma Gandhi*, op. cit., pp. 146–7.

302   Indonesians' struggle against Dutch: David Lee, 'Indonesia's Independence' in David Goldsworthy, ed., *Facing North*, Melbourne, 2001, ch. 4.

304–5   Bandanaraike of Ceylon: F.C. Rowan in *The Dictionary of National Biography 1951–1960*, London, 1971, pp. 58–9.

305   Essence of leadership: Galbraith, *The Age of Uncertainty*, op. cit., p. 330.

305–6   Career of Kenyatta: Jeremy Murray-Brown, *Kenyatta*, London, 1972. For Moscow, see p. 168; burning spear, p. 196; and Malinowski, pp. 198–9.

306–7 Grigg on Kenya: cited in Kenneth Rose on E.W. Grigg in *The Dictionary of National Biography 1951–1960*, op. cit., p. 441.

310 Macmillan and 'winds of change': Alistair Horne, *Macmillan 1957–1986*, London, 1989, p. 195.

313 Algiers 'throng' of faces: *The Illustrated Chambers's Encyclopaedia*, vol. 1, London, 1924, p. 161.

314–15 Portuguese empire's last years: Bill Freund, *The Making of Contemporary Africa*, London, 1984, pp. 274–5.

315 Failures of African independence: Niall Ferguson in *Weekly Telegraph*, London, 9–15 February 2005; Thomas Sowell, *Conquests and Cultures*, New York, 1998, pp. 119–20, 132.

17 ISRAEL AND EGYPT

317–18 Balfour's attitude to Jews: Jason Tomes: *Balfour and Foreign Policy*, Cambridge, 1997, ch. 8, esp. pp. 210–11.

319 Golda Meir's first impressions of Israel: *My Life*, London, 1975, pp. 56–61.

319–20 Tel Aviv in 1925: Donald C. Stanley, 'Parallels in the Histories of the Modern Nations of Israel and Australia', PhD thesis, University of Melbourne, 2003, p. 96.

321 Impartial scholar: E.W.G. Masterman, writing in *Chambers's Encyclopaedia*, op. cit., vol. 7, p. 717.

321 Weizmann denounces Jewish terrorism: Michael Ignatieff, *Isaiah Berlin: A Life*, London, 2000, p. 177. Berlin penned the sentence cited.

322 British financial burdens in 1947: William Roger Louis, *The British Empire in the Middle East 1945–1951*, Oxford, 1984, esp. pp. 467, 474–6.

322 Fear of communists taking over Israel: ibid., pp. 43–4.

328 Egypt buys Czech armaments: *The Annual Register 1955*, p. 272.

329–31 War at Suez: Yergin, *The Prize*, op. cit., ch. 24; Geoffrey Warner, 'The Suez Crisis', in Alan Bullock intro., *History of the 20th Century*, op. cit., pp. 410–16.

330 Menzies on 1956 Olympics: cited in Harry Gordon, *An Eyewitness History of Australia*, Adelaide, 1976, p. 396.

18 VESSELS OF VENGEANCE

334 Dornberger predicts era of space travel: Frank H. Winter, *Rockets and Space*, Harvard, 1990, pp. 50–1.

334–5 Sighting the V-1 'regatta': Harold Nicolson, *Diaries and Letters 1939–1945*, London, 1967, p. 380.

336 Photo of captive von Braun: display in Science Museum, London, July 2003.

336–7 Stalin purges Korolev: Winter, op. cit., p. 41.

339 Nkrumah's fears: speech reprinted in Jussi Hanhimäkim & Odd Westad (eds), *The Cold War: A History in Documents*, Oxford, 2003, p. 355.

339 Shute's nuclear fears: Nevil Shute Norway in *The Dictionary of National Biography 1951–1960*, op. cit., pp. 772–3.

340 Hazards of early space travel: Galleries 114 & 210, National Air and Space Museum, Washington, January 2004; Science Museum, London, 2003.

341 Fears for Gargarin: expressed by Khrushchev, and cited in Michael R. Beschloss, *The Crisis Years: Kennedy and Khrushchev, 1960–1963*, New York, 1991, p. 197.

344 Macmillan in Moscow: Horne, *Macmillan*, op. cit., pp. 116–25.

346 Khrushchev issues warning at Bolshoi: Beschloss, *The Crisis Years*, op. cit., p. 244.

348 Gilpatric's warning speech: ibid., p. 330.

348–9 Nureyev escapes: Hanhimäkim & Westad, *The Cold War*, op. cit., p. 431.

349 Nureyev as 'wild animal': Graham Payn & Sheridan Morley (eds), *The Noel Coward Diaries*, London, 1982, p. 570.

19 EXPLOSIVE ISLAND AND GHOSTLY GALLEON

352 Rise of Castro: Hugh Thomas, *An Unfinished History of the World*, London, 1979, p. 536.

353 Cuba and television: *The Annual Register 1960*, p. 451.

353 Narrow seas: examples of this strategic fact, selected from modern European and Asian history, could be multiplied.

353 Cuba athwart Spanish trade routes: J.H. Parry, *The Age of Reconaissance*, London, 1963, pp. 185, 189.

354   Bay of Pigs: Beschloss, *The Crisis Years*, op. cit., pp. 113–5.

356   Soviet ships retreat: ibid., pp. 495–9.

356   Kennedy and Krushchev quickly agree: Victor A. Kremenyuk, 'Controlling International Crises', in Ramesh Thakur, ed., *International Conflict Resolution*, Boulder, USA, 1988, p. 138; Beschloss, op. cit., pp. 534–42.

357–8   Mrs Kennedy's letter to Moscow: ibid., pp. 688–9.

358   Harold Wilson's assessment of world's perils: Anthony Howard, ed., *The Crossman Diaries*, London, 1979, p. 54.

359   Nasser's speeches: *President Gamal Abdel Nasser's Speeches & Press Interviews*, 1958, official Egyptian publication, Cairo, n.d., pp. 384–5.

361–2   Schiaparelli depicts Mars: Patrick Moore, *Patrick Moore on Mars*, London, 1998, pp. 51–4.

362   Lowell depicts Mars: ibid., p. 9.

20   CLIMBING THE EVERESTS

367   Black migration to Britain: Andrew Roberts, 'Black Immigration into Postwar Britain', in Leonie Kramer, ed., *The Multicultural Experiment*, Sydney, 2003, pp. 143–6.

368   1939 flying boat: Boorstin, *The Americans*, op. cit., p. 517.

369–70   Postwar cars unveiled: Albert L. Lewis & Walter A. Musciano, *Automobiles of the World*, New York, 1977, pp. 447–54.

371   Coronation and TV: Setright, *Drive On!*, op. cit., p. 109 n.

372   Televised war: Michael J. Arlen, *Living-Room War*, New York, 1969, pp. 6–8, 81–3.

375   Preaching monk: displayed in Deutches Museum, Munich, 1998.

375   Babbage model: displayed in Science Museum, London.

376   Alan Turing: *The Dictionary of National Biography 1951–60*, op. cit., p. 998; Jack Copeland & Diane Proudfoot, 'Enigma Variations' in *Times Literary Supplement*, 3 July 1998, p. 6.

376   German trawler off Norway: Andrew Hodges, *Alan Turing: the Enigma*, London, 1985, pp. 189–90.

377   Newman machine at Bletchley: ibid., pp. 267–8.

378   Deciphering Germany's submarine code: Noel Annan, *Changing Enemies: The Defeat and Regeneration of Germany*, London, 1995, p. 12.

380   Longstaff and Mt Everest: Eric Shipton, 'Longstaff', *The Dictionary of National Biography 1961–1970*, London, 1981, p. 676.

381–2   Shipping-containers: exhibition in National Museum of American History, Washington, January 1904.

383   Japanese shipyards overtake Britain's: Geoffrey Owen, *From Empire to Europe; The Decline and Revival of British Industry since the Second World War*, London, 1999, p. 102.

383   Japan's fast growth in 1960s: Choucri, North & Yamakage, *The Challenge of Japan*, op. cit., p. 238.

383–4   Nissan and Honda: Setright, *Drive On!*, op. cit., passim.

21   THE CHEF AND THE DOCTOR

388   French vineyards attract English: P. Morton Shand in Cyril Ray, ed., *A Book of French Wines*, London, 1964, pp. 13, 17.

391–2   Mansfield's house and archives, Wellington, NZ: visited in February 2004.

392   Spanish influenza: F.M. Burnet, *Viruses and Man*, Melbourne, 1953, p. 113.

393   Malaria in war: Frank Fenner, 'Neil Fairley', in *Australian Dictionary of Biography*, Melbourne, vol. 14, 1996; Watson, *A Terrible Beauty*, op. cit., p. 367; Robert J.T. Joy, 'Malaria in American Troops . . .', *Medical History*, April 1999, vol. 43, pp. 192–201.

394   Eclipse of pneumonia, Roy Porter, *The Greatest Benefit to Mankind; A Medical History of Humanity*, London, 1997, p. 457. For revival of malaria, see pp. 472, 488.

394   Mass production of penicillin: Caroline F. Ware, K.M. Panikkar & J.M. Romein, *History of Mankind: Cultural and Scientific Development*, New York, vol. 6, 1966, pp. 481–3.

395–6   Kenny and polio: A. Fryberg, 'Kenny', *The Dictionary of National Biography 1951–1960*, London, 1971, pp. 575–6.

396   Salk vaccine: *The Annual Register 1955*, pp. 416–17. Canada achieved 1 million safe injections of the vaccine.

396   'Pacemaker for the heart' in Birmingham: *The Annual Register 1960*, p. 405.

397   DNA: interview with Watson by Michael D. Lemonick, *Time*,

17 February 2003, p. 46. See also Watson, *A Terrible Beauty*, op. cit., pp. 478–81.

397–8 Gene for inherited deafness etc: Encyclopaedia Britannica, *Medical & Health Annual*, Cambridge, 1993, p. 306.

399 Smoking: Stephen S. Hecht, 'Tobacco Use and Cancer', in Malcolm R. Alison, ed., *The Cancer Handbook*, London, 2002, vol. 1, pp. 399–401.

22 A SEESAW MOVES

403 Greensboro luncheonette: now located in National Museum of American History, Washington, visited in January 2004.

405 'I have a dream': Martin Luther King Jr in Safire, *Lend Me Your Ears*, op. cit., p. 535.

406 The Beatles: James Morris, 'The Beatle Generation', in Richard C. Lukas, ed., *From Metternich to the Beatles: Readings in Modern European History*, New York, 1973, p. 219.

407 Tragedies of drugs and alcohol: Alice Echols, *Scars of Sweet Paradise: The Life and times of Janis Joplin*, New York, 1999, p. 305.

407 More explosives aimed by US bombers on Vietnam than on all war zones in Second World War: Paul Johnson, *A History of the American People*, New York, 1998, p. 877.

409 Rise of counter-culture and green movement: Geoffrey Blainey, *The Great Seesaw: A New View of the Western World, 1750–2000*, Melbourne, 1988, chs 11, 14.

411 Intense gloom of Ehrlich and Club of Rome: ibid., ch. 13.

412–13 Pollution in Los Angeles, New Mexico: Mattei Dogan & John D. Kasarda (eds), *The Metropolis Era*, Newbury Park, California, vol. 2, 1988, pp. 24, 74–8.

413–14 Antarctic whales: Fred & Eleanor Jacka (eds), *Mawson's Antarctic Diaries*, Sydney, 1988, pp. 312–17.

415 Global warming: John W. Zillman et al. (eds), *Uncertainty and Climate Change*, Canberra, 2005, pp. 3–24; Fred Pearce, 'Act Now Before It's Too Late', *New Scientist*, 12 February 2005; William Kininmonth, *Climate Change: A Natural Hazard*, Brentwood, UK, 2004, p. 16.

415 Seesaw of ideas: How faith in technology sits at one end of the see-saw and faith in nature sits at the other, and why the seesaw occasionally tilts to a new angle, are described in Blainey, *The Great Seesaw*, op. cit., esp. pp. 311–14.

416–17 'Is this all?': Betty Friedan, *The Feminine Mystique*, New York, 1963, p. 15.

417 Loss of 'traditional moorings': Johnson, *A History of the American People*, op. cit., pp. 846–7.

418 Birth-control pill and Sanger: Linda Grant, *Sexing the Millennium: A Political History of the Sexual Revolution*, London, 1993, p. 47.

421 Routine and habits of Mrs Gandhi: Krishan Bhatia, *Indira: A Biography of Prime Minister Gandhi*, London, 1974, esp. pp. 271–80.

23 THUNDER AND LIGHTNING IN MOSCOW AND WARSAW

427–8 Privilege in Soviet Union: Keep, *The Last of the Empires*, op. cit. For price of petrol and food, see pp. 212–16, 219, 230–1; for joke about work and 'pay', see p. 243.

431–2 Moscow's hands at the throat of the Red Sea: Holden & Johns, *The House of Saud*, op. cit., pp. 272, 467–8, 473, 477.

433 Cambodian massacres: David P. Chandler, 'Cambodia', in *Britannica Book of The Year*, 1994, pp. 524–5.

435 Dissent in Poland: Davies, *Europe: A History*, op. cit., pp. 1108, 1122–3.

435 Attempt to assassinate pope: Nigel West, *The Third Secret*, London, 2000, pp. 10–16.

438 Andropov's funeral: Mikhail Gorbachev, *Memoirs*, New York, 1996, pp. 152–3.

439 Gorbachev meets Thatcher: ibid., p. 161.

439–40 Summit at Geneva: Edmund Morris, *Dutch: A Memoir of Ronald Reagan*, New York, 1999, pp. 544–57.

24 THE WALLS ARE TOPPLING

444 Russians 'live badly': Yevgeny Yevtushenko, *Fatal Half Measures*, Boston, 1991, pp. 96–100. For ban on Bible sales, see pp. 152–6.

444–5 Soviet neglect of environment: Keep, *The Last of the Empires*, op. cit., pp. 257–62.

445 River and oil pollution: *EU Enlargement and Environmental Quality: Central & Eastern Europe and Beyond*: Woodrow Wilson International Center, Washington D.C., August 2002, pp. 60–1.

445–6 Illness at Chernobyl, David R. Marples, 'Chernobyl: Ten Years after the Catastrophe', Encyclopaedia Britannica, *Medical and Health Annual*, 1996, Chicago, p. 32.

447 Glasnost: Davies, *Europe: A History*, op. cit., p. 1121.

448 East European crisis in 1987: Martin McCauley, 'Perestroika and Glasnost – A Progress Report', *Britannica Book of The Year*, 1988, pp. 474–5.

450 Lutheran church and emigration: Mary Fulbrook, *Interpretations of the Two Germanies*, 2nd edn, Houndmills, UK, 2000, pp. 70–1.

452 Krainers flee East Germany: *Times*, London, 9 November 1989, p. 9.

453 Kohl's speech at Dresden ruins, 1989: Richard A. Leiby, *The Unification of Germany, 1989–1990*, Westport, USA, 1999, pp. 149–52.

455 Sleepy China in mid-1960s: Geoffrey Blainey, *Across A Red World*, Melbourne, 1968, pp. 47–52.

456 Soviet troops massed at Chinese border, 1972: Kennedy, *The Rise and Fall of the Great Powers*, op. cit., p. 399.

456 Chinese (1990) census counts more boys: Richard Critchfield, *The Villagers*, New York, 1994, p. 201.

457–8 Wealth of overseas Chinese: Thomas Sowell, 'The Overseas Chinese', in *Migrations and Cultures: A World View*, New York, 1996, ch. 5; Sterling Redgrave, *Lords of the Rim*, London, 1995, passim.

459–60 Tony Blair predicts peace: Martin Gilbert, *Challenge to Civilization: A History of the Twentieth Century 1952–1999*, London, 1999, vol. 3, p. 832.

461–2 The Locarno trio: Austen Chamberlain, *Down the Years*, London, 1935, pp. 178, 185, 188.

462 Benedetto Croce's vision of Europe: Croce, 'History of Europe in the Nineteenth Century' (1933), cited in de Rougemont, *The Idea of Europe*, op. cit., p. 391.

462–3 Churchill and early European Union: Davies, *Europe: A History*, op. cit., p. 1065.

25 CITIES, SPORTS AND TONGUES

467 Crookes' prediction: Geoffrey Blainey, *The Great Seesaw*, op. cit., pp. 88–9.

468 Scots and longevity: Sir Alec Cairncross, *Living with the Century*, Fife, Scotland, 1998, esp. p. 297.

470 View of London's housetops: J.H.M. Abbott, *An Outlander in England*, London, 1905, p. 49.

470–1 Marvellous New York: Witold Rybczynski, *City Life*, New York, 1995, pp. 152–5. For Corbusier, see p. 156.

471–2 Tokyo's expansion: Hachiro Nakamura & James White in Dogan & Kasarda, *The Metropolis Era*, op. cit., vol. 2, ch. 4, esp. p. 180.

472 Silicon Valley: Chong-Moon Lee, W.F. Miller, M.G. Hancock & H.S. Rowen (eds), *The Silicon Valley Edge*, Stanford, 2000, esp. pp. 43–8, 81.

473 World's big cities: *The Times Comprehensive Atlas of the World*, 11th edn, London, 2003, pp. 42–3. For rise of world population in 20th century, see p. 40.

473–4 Lagos: *Encyclopaedia Britannica*, 11th edn, vol. 16, 1910–11, pp. 73–5; Michael L McNulty & Isaac A. Adalemo in *The Metropolis Era*, op. cit., vol. 2, ch. 7.

475 Village India: John K. Galbraith, *A View from the Stands*, Boston, 1986, p. 262.

476 Sikh ploughman and oxen: Critchfield, *The Villagers*, op. cit., p. 270.

476–7 Rural India at work: P. Sainath, *Everybody Loves a Good Drought: Stories from India's Poorest Districts*, New Delhi, 1996. For bullock carts see pp. 163–8; bamboo goods pp. 99–101, human carriers pp. 169–74.

478–9 Dying Queensland languages: Robert Dixon, 'Australian Aboriginal Languages', in Gerhard Schulz, ed., *The Languages of Australia*, Canberra, 1993, pp. 73–5.

479 Delights of French language: F.F. Roget in *Illustrated Chambers's Encyclopaedia*, op. cit., vol. 4, p. 822.

480 Decline of French and rise of universal language: Albert C. Baugh, *A History of the English Language*, 2nd edn, London, 1959, pp. 7–8.

481 The phrase 'it's not cricket' was used as early as 1867: Eric Partridge, *A Dictionary of Slang and Unconventional English*, 7th edn, London, 1982, p. 191.

481–2 History of tennis, boxing and other international sports: John Arlott, ed., *The Oxford Companion to Sports & Games*, London, 1975; Claudio Veliz, *The New World of the Gothic Fox: Culture and Economy in English and Spanish America*, Berkeley, California, 1994, pp. 134–9, 142.

482 Neville Cardus at cricket: Neville Cardus, *Autobiography*, London, 1948, pp. 35–6.

484 Olympic victors from Third World: *Encyclopaedia Britannica*, 15th edn, vol. 8, 1988, pp. 926 ff, for list of gold medallists, 1896–1984.

26 ISLAM'S MOON SHINES AGAIN

487–8 Discovering oil: Holden & Johns, *The House of Saud*, op. cit., pp. 81–2, 113.

488–9 Divergence of Islam and Christianity: it is usual to argue that Islam has changed course since, say, 1900. In fact it is the west and Christianity that have changed more.

489–91 Global population of Muslims and Christians: *Britannica Book of The Year*, Chicago, 1995, p. 275.

492 Slave as finance minister: Holden & Johns, *The House of Saud*, op. cit., p. 240.

493 Saudi ban on football: ibid., p. 169.

493 Jews and US women in Saudi Arabia: commentary by Daniel Pipes, *National Interest*, Winter 2002–03.

494 Bomb attempt by Palestinian trio: Bruce Hoffman in Paul Wilkinson & Brian M. Jenkins (eds), *Aviation, Terrorism and Security*, London, 1999, pp. 55–6.

494–5 Increased terrorism in aircraft: ibid., esp. pp. 31–2, 38–9, 48, 138.

495 Iranian teenage terrorists: Gilles Keppel, 'The Origins and Development of the Jihadist Movement: From Anti-Communism to Terrorism', *Asian Affairs*, vol. 34, no. 2, July 2003, p. 105.

496–9 Terrorism at World Trade Center, 2001: The 9/11 Commission, *Final Report of the National Commission on Terrorist Attacks upon the United States*, New York, 2004, pp. 1–46.

INDEX